The
Tories

Adam Wordsworth

Springlands

Published in Great Britain in 2014 by
Springlands Press,
10 Broad Birches, Ellesmere Port, Cheshire, CH65 3AB

Copyright © Adam Wordsworth 2014
The right of Adam Wordsworth to be Published in Great
Britain in 2014 by
Springlands Press,
10 Broad Birches, Ellesmere Port, Cheshire, CH65 3AB
www.springlandspublishing.co.uk

A CIP catalogue record for this book is available from the
British Library.

ISBN 978-0-9929733-5-3

Cover design © Graham D. Lock

To my girls
Victoria, Isabel & Grace

With all my heart

Dear Graham,

Merry Christmas & all
the best for 2015.

Adam W

By the same author:

The End of Discrimination: What if UK Family Law Was
Fairer?
Collected Political Musings: The Coalition Years

You can follow Adam Wordsworth's Political Musings as
they happen here:

www.adamwordsworth.blog.com

Adam Wordsworth was born and raised in Cheshire and has spent most of his career in public service. He has been commentating on politics since 2009 and his love of the subject is second only to his love of his family. He currently lives near Chester with his partner and two daughters. This is his third book.

Contents

To ry
Origin:
1640–50; < Irish *tóraighe* outlaw, bandit

The Tories

Preface

The idea to write a history of the Tories first came to me several years ago, while I was still very young and, really, had little idea what the history of the Party included. Nor, for that matter, did I at that time appreciate what was involved in writing a book. It was one of those ideas that seem quite interesting but that one never actually acts upon. Then, around three or four years ago something made me recall that idea and I decided to write a list of the leaders of the Party before, again, burying the project, to be revisited at another time. Eventually this turned into the volume that you are reading today.

I have a passion for politics and a passion for history that made this an obvious subject for me to explore. There are plenty of political parties that I could have looked at but a study of Labour would mean a study of the twentieth century. A study of the Whigs/Liberals would mean ignoring the real power-circles from the end of the First World War onwards. The Tories, conversely, have been both present and one of the largest two political parties since the Glorious Revolution.

What is consistent throughout the history of the Tories is that they generally wanted to maintain what was positive about Britain's institutions but they have also consistently benefitted from any changes. I can't comment more on this without giving too much away.

When I set out on my research I genuinely hoped that I would find something special in one of the lesser-known leaders. So many people, when asked about their political idols, will name Churchill or Gladstone, maybe even the occasional Thatcher. I don't know why but I had a sort of romantic determination that I would find an individual that nobody ever really thought of who was, in fact, greater than the rest. Having studied them all I do now have my favourites but have since discovered that it is unfair to compare the lesser-known leaders with their more famous counterparts. The longer an individual spends in office the more issues they face that can define them. If someone is not particularly well known there is probably a good reason for it.

What I have done, throughout my time on this project, is learn. That, above all else, is what I hope this book can give to others. In fact, had some of these leaders learned their history they may have been more successful than they were. Who knows, perhaps politicians of the future may read a copy of this book and learn enough about the past to avoid some of the pitfalls that their forbears stumbled upon. History, they say, repeats itself and this is all too common in the history of the Tories. On that note I am indebted to the scores of historians that have come before me, whose research I have drawn heavily upon to discover what I have now put into print. Most of the books in the bibliography at the end are well worth a read for any student of history, and some would be of interest even to the most casual of readers.

This last year, while I have been writing this book, has without a doubt been the most torturous year of my life. Whenever I finish a project I feel elated and tell myself that now is the time to relax. Invariably, though, I get restless and throw myself into something else without really considering just how much effort is required to get through it.

In the acknowledgments section of one of my other books, *The End of Discrimination*, I included an apology to my partner, Victoria, for neglecting her during the time that I had been writing. This was accompanied by a verbal promise that it wouldn't happen again. But here we are, just over a year later, and it has happened again. So I once again apologise but this time I won't accompany it with any promises.

There are many people worthy of thanks for helping me get to the end of this book. Even people who have not helped directly may have influenced me in some way that has had a positive effect. More specifically I have a tendency to become very excited when I write, the result being a sentence that lasts for a paragraph. There are people who have helped to rein me in, in that respect. Keeping it brief I would like to thank my parents. My mum first encouraged my love of books when I was a child (to the point where even today if I see somebody marking a book I have a reaction similar to that of Priam witnessing the sack of Troy). My dad encouraged my academic side and has helped with editing some of the chapters herein (as well as the inclusion of a word that I had never before heard. It only occurs once, find it if you can). Thanks also to John and Anne for their efforts in revising some of this work. Finally, thanks to Victoria, Isabel and Grace for their love and support.

Preface

Adam Wordsworth, October 2014

Introduction
The Original Tories

WHETHER YOU LOVE or hate them, it is difficult to argue that the modern Conservative Party is not the most successful political party in history. Today's Conservatives can trace their roots back to the Tory Party which ceased to exist as a formal body in the mid-nineteenth century. The Party has thus adapted and changed over time so it cannot reasonably be said that there are such things as 'Conservative principles' (not with a capital 'C' anyway). Non-interference from the state and libertarianism, which underpin the values of the modern Conservative Party, were in fact the positions of the old Liberal Party, which the Conservatives so opposed for centuries. The trade unions – so fiercely represented by Labour and so aggressively anti-Tory today – were given their first official endorsements by a Conservative Prime Minister – Benjamin Disraeli – who legalised peaceful picketing in 1875.

In any given epoch a leader should lead, and the Tories have had no shortage of strong leaders: Pitt the Younger served for over two decades as Prime Minister, beginning at the age of 24; Peel had to create a whole new party, which began the transition from Tory to Conservative, in order to gain a following; Churchill was derided as an eccentric for decades for speaking his mind only to become a national hero when vindicated. That said, the Conservatives' history, taken altogether, can be seen to tell the story of a Party that follows public opinion, not just leads it. This can be evidenced in the transformations that they have undergone over the centuries. From pro-Europe to anti-Europe, from pro-protectionism to pro-free trade, or anti-universal suffrage to the main beneficiaries of enfranchisement, the Tories and Conservatives have altered their positions to suit the public mood. As Geoffrey Wheatcroft put it:

> A party calling itself Tory had existed for more than 300 years. From the early nineteenth century its members had been alternatively known as Conservatives, and for a time at the end of that century and in the early decades of the next as Unionists, but the name Tory

> survived throughout…they had a cannibalistic
> tendency to absorb parties which strayed too
> close, so that Peelites, Liberal Unionists,
> Coalition Liberals and National Liberals were
> first co-opted, then faded from view, and at
> last disappeared even as names[1]

This adaptability has undoubtedly been the main ingredient to
their success (when compared with the Whigs-cum-Liberals
who did not transform themselves in the same way and went
from the height of power in the seventeenth-, eighteenth- and
nineteenth centuries into obscurity during the twentieth
century). However, this adaptable approach is not without its
criticisms, leaving the Party open to accusations of seeking
populism over principle. In fact, this accusation is not new.
Daniel Defoe wrote *A Dialogue Betwixt Whig and Tory* as a
fictional conversation between a member of the Whig Party
and a member of the Tory Party in 1692, just a few short years
after both parties' inception. In it the Whig accused the Tory of
having no principles, of supporting the line of succession of
kings including faithful support of King James II then, when
William of Orange replaced King James in the Glorious
Revolution, the Tory happily supported the new monarch. Just
before the following quote the Whig had suggested that the
Tory could learn some lessons from Jesus, who died for what
he believed in. The Tory then argues:

> Come don't tell us stories of our great
> Grandfathers who troubled themselves about
> Trifles: There is a Fashion in Government (as
> well as in Clothes) which must be comply'd
> with, according to the Humour of the present
> Age; and you may as well pretend to shape all
> Gowns by Queen Elizabeth's Fardingale, as to
> shape our Court's Counsels according to the
> sentiments of that or other times, which were
> as different too from one another, as we are
> different from them.[2]

Even 300 years ago the Tories were prepared to amend their
principles to stay in favour, justifying it on the basis that the
world is not the same from one generation to the next and so
values cannot remain stagnant. The Whig retorted that 'the

Principle of Liberty and Property have always been in fashion amongst Men of Sense and Estates in England, and ever will be'.

The party's evolution will be discussed throughout this book, but to begin with it is important to establish where exactly they came from. The Tories started not as a party as we would understand the term in the twenty-first century but rather as a loosely grouped faction of individuals who shared similar beliefs and therefore worked together in Parliament more than they worked with others. The actual origins of the Tories as a faction can be traced back to three separate yet inextricably linked mid-seventeenth century events, namely The War of the Three Kingdoms, The Restoration and The Glorious Revolution.

The War of the Three Kingdoms is known by most people for the first stage of it – The English Civil War – which occurred from 1642-1649, ending with the execution of King Charles I and immediately followed by ten years of republican rule by Oliver Cromwell and his son Richard Cromwell. However, King Charles I of England was also King of Scotland and King of Ireland and these latter two kingdoms did not accept Cromwell's Commonwealth as readily as the English did. Skirmishes occurred in all three kingdoms throughout the 1640s and 1650s and so, taken together, the term 'War of the Three Kingdoms' is more appropriate than 'English Civil War' because conflict did not cease with the death of Charles and was not confined to England.

Generally speaking supporters of the Long Parliament who had fought against King Charles had been more commonly found in towns and cities, whereas royalist supporters were predominantly country-folk. This rule applied into Scotland and Ireland which, being far more rural in constitution than England meant that these nations were largely royalist. When Cromwell established his New Model Army in the 1650s to quash unrest and take firm control of the Three Kingdoms, rebellion more often took the form of guerrilla tactics rather than direct battle. In Ireland groups of rebels would ambush army regiments as they passed through the countryside. These outlaws were known in Irish as *'Toraighes'*. And so the origin of 'Tory' was born.

At around the same time there were also strong pro-republican groups including an aggregation of Scottish Presbyterians known as the Whiggamores – hence the derivative of the Whig Party.

Eventually though, powerful land owners determined that Cromwell's Protectorate did not suit their needs. They had replaced an uncompromising King with an uncompromising army and once Cromwell died they conspired to have King Charles' son, Prince Charles, restored to the throne subject to his meeting certain caveats including that all past misdeeds were forgiven. His accession to the throne was known as The Restoration.

Charles II endeavoured to be more visible and therefore seem less remote than his father had been. He was tolerant of people of all Christian denominations. However, he was unable to produce an heir to his throne and the line of succession meant in this instance that his brother, James, Duke of York, would become king.

England faced a very troubling dilemma at this time. On the one hand, Episcopalians who had been persecuted under Cromwell were now promoted as a national institution with the Church of England being integral to national life with the monarch at its head. The Church had committed itself in this vein to the notion of the divine right of kings (kings were chosen by God and should be accepted regardless). However, James, Duke of York, had converted to Roman Catholicism as a young man and upon the death of Charles II, England saw a Roman Catholic ascend to the throne and, by default, head of the Church of England.

Nobody desired another civil war and the bad taste left in the mouths of the great landowners over the last one only seemed to strengthen James' position on the throne. James II went on to become the most libertarian monarch for several centuries, accepting people of all faiths into any position in society. He gave Catholics commissions in the army, promoted Catholic MPs, indeed his use of positive discrimination would be right at home in the politics of the twenty-first century. These actions, though, only amplified the distrust of him felt by those around him, who believed, rightly or wrongly, that James would undermine the established Church and return the Kingdoms to Roman Catholicism.

It is a great tragedy of Stuart history that intolerance of other institutions would lead to the Civil War and to the execution of one of their number, yet tolerance of all Christians would lead to their demise as a ruling family.

In 1688 a group of English lords invited William of Orange to come to England and remove James II from power. Due to their intention to remove a King who was seen as legitimately on the throne, their opponents derided these lords with insults – saying things such as that they were little better than the Whiggamores. This was a scathing attack as even amongst republicans the Whiggamores were viewed as eccentrics. The insult was shortened to 'Whigs' and eventually they learned to wear it as a badge of honour.

In response the Whigs attacked their opponents as blindly supporting a monarch regardless of his abilities or what is best for the country, just like those mindless Toraighes in Ireland, pronounced 'Tory' and thus spelt as such in English.

William accepted the invitation and due to the nature of the prevailing winds was able to land in Torbay unopposed; James' fleet was unable to escape the Thames. William marched on London but found no resistance from the landowners he passed en route and actually gained followers on his way. Meanwhile James tried to garner support in the capital and it was at this time that he realised just how unpopular he had become. He fled the city but was subsequently caught by two fishermen who returned him to London. However, the idea of humbly taking over a throne which had been voluntarily vacated by the previous monarch was far more appealing to William than taking it by force or being accused of executing the rightful King, which would have been treason in the eyes of anyone who cared enough to press the issue. So James was allowed to escape again, which he did to France, and William III jointly ruled with his wife, James' daughter, Mary.

This was the Glorious Revolution and from it the factions of supporters and opponents of the divine right of Kings can be seen to evolve into Tory and Whig respectively. It was the Whigs who had invited William to England and although the Tories had not opposed William's accession in practice, they had in principle.

However, it was the Tories who found themselves in favour in William's governments. Some historians attribute this to William wanting to keep his enemies closer, as the saying goes. Others credit William's political skill even further and claim that although the Whigs had supported him personally over James, the Tories supported the right of Kings in general and so William was more able to execute his powers with them around him than with the Whigs. Indeed the Whigs were generally made up of the powerful nobility at this time and so limiting the authority of the monarch would benefit them immensely. But once in power William saw no reason to indulge them in these wishes. The ministers he appointed had been branded as Tories and they were more than happy to allow a King autonomy over taxation and foreign policy,

The Whig in Defoe's dialogue accused The Tory of having no principles, not least because The Tory had supported King James but now seemed more than happy accepting the favour bestowed on him by King William and swearing allegiance to him. The Tory, for his part, will have felt his conscience was clean mainly because of that one act of political genius that William had undertaken upon being informed that James had been captured by fishermen: he let him go. James then fled. Consequently the Tories could convince themselves that James had abdicated so they were not supporting the removal of the rightful King, but installing a King onto a vacant throne.

William III died in 1702 and the throne passed to his late wife's younger sister, Anne. Throughout Anne's reign the Whigs steered through some important legislative achievements, including the Act of Union which united the Scottish and English Parliaments. However, as with William, it was the Tories who found favour with Anne as supporters of the divine right of the monarch.

In 1714 Anne died childless which forced another crisis of principle for the Tories over the issue of succession. James II had died and his son, James Stuart (a.k.a. 'The Old Pretender') was being raised in France at a palace of Louis XIV. Surely if supporting the line of succession, James Stuart should be brought back to Great Britain to rule. However, given who his father had been and given that he had been brought up by King Louis the Whigs could not trust him as he was a Catholic and probably pro-French and so they invited George Hanover to succeed Anne. Once George was on the throne, though, the Tories had to abide by their royalist creed.

It was not difficult for the Whigs to convince King George I that all Tories were Jacobites in disguise (a Jacobite being a supporter of the return of James II and his descendants to the throne) and so the Tories were immediately out of favour. Attempts by the Old Pretender and his son Charles (The Young Pretender) to take the throne only solidified the Hanoverians' anti-Tory sentiments.

It would be nearly half a century before the Tories truly found favour again during which time the office of Prime Minister would first be used in an official capacity in 1721. The 'favour' they found half a century after George I's accession was that the Tory Earl of Bute was appointed as Prime Minister by his friend and former pupil King George III in 1762, but he was leading a government made up largely of Whigs and within a year the King had decided that he no longer had much time for the Earl. The Tories were then out of power for another twenty years and even when they did return it was under the leadership of a man whose father had been a Whig Prime Minister and who himself claimed to be a Whig, although his policies and following were decidedly Tory. That leader was William Pitt the Younger, and he is the one person that most contemporary historians trace the inception of the modern Conservative Party back to.

William Pitt the Younger
(1783 – 1801)

The country calls aloud to me that I should defend this castle, and I
am determined therefore that I will defend it

William Pitt, February 1784

Let me ask you in what Age or Time it was, that Men of Service, or
Men of Honour, did prefer Will and Pleasure to Laws, or Slavery to
Freedom?

Daniel Defoe's *Whig*, 1692

IT WAS SUGGESTED at the end of the last chapter that
William Pitt the Younger was a Tory, though he may have
defined himself as a Whig, at least initially. Before discussing
his career it is necessary to bring some clarity on this apparent
ambiguity, because it, as a possibility, resonates little with what
we understand of politics in the twenty-first century.
Eighteenth century politics differed from modern politics in
many ways, but the important contrast that helps to explain this
intriguing point was alluded to in the last chapter. Elections and
the chambers within Parliament at this time were not contested
by organised political parties as they are today. In fact, during
this time of Whig dominance the main opposition was formed
from various factions referring to themselves as Whigs, rather
than Tories. The term 'Tory' was extremely derisive, still being
linked strongly to Jacobite sympathisers, so even the strongest
opponents of the government were likely to refer to themselves
as Whigs, notwithstanding that their policies may have been
clearly Tory. A second explanation for Pitt's disinterest in
adopting the label of 'Tory' may have been down to his father
who had been idolised by the public because of his detachment
from party politics. Hence his son, Pitt the Younger (a term used
to distinguish him from his father, Pitt the Elder, Earl of
Chatham) referred to himself as an 'independent Whig', with
emphasis on the 'independent' part, and only using the term
'Whig' because 'Tory' was so taboo. The Elder Pitt had been a

Whig rebel, happy to oppose the Whigs in government but not happy to be called a Tory because of these same reasons.[1]

The younger Pitt was something of a child prodigy, attending Cambridge University at the age of fourteen.[2] He grew up idolising his father and seemingly having no ambition other than to follow him into politics. In the years leading up to his election to Parliament, Pitt watched his father give a succession of speeches condemning government policy in the American colonies and in which the former Prime Minister was able to predict with prophetic accuracy the series of events which would transpire, ultimately ending with British defeat in the Revolutionary War.[3] The public at large blamed the government for the humiliation that the world's greatest military force had suffered. Parliamentarians overall felt that perhaps an imbalance in the distribution of seats, meaning that the people were not nearly fairly represented, had meant that the voice of the masses had been silenced. More scrupulous observers, William Pitt the Younger among them, would have seen that Lord North had been a weak Prime Minister easily controlled by a domineering King George III.[4] This should never have been allowed to happen and the fact that it did only served to highlight the flaws in the settlement which Parliament had achieved during the Glorious Revolution, with perhaps too much power remaining with the monarchy.

So it was that in 1780, at the age of twenty-one, William Pitt the Younger, son of the both celebrated and ridiculed late former Prime Minister the Earl of Chatham, became a Member of Parliament. Keeping himself at arm's length from a perception of corruption was therefore always at the back of his mind with political reform at his mind's fore as he embarked on his political journey.

At the end of 1781, when it became apparent that the war in America was all but lost, Lord North's government was never going to survive the coming attacks. Pitt was vocal in his criticism from the opposition benches. He often launched scathing diatribes in such an eloquent fashion that, despite his age and relative lack of parliamentary experience, marked him out already as one of the great political orators of his day.

It was on 20 March 1782 that Lord North announced his resignation and when Parliament reconvened on 8 April, Lord Rockingham was Prime Minister and a twenty-two year old

William Pitt found himself sitting on the government benches, albeit not in a ministerial post. He had been offered the position of Vice-Treasurer of Ireland but declined it in favour of being a backbencher.[5] It may have been the case that he foresaw that the Rockingham administration would be as fractious and, ultimately, short-lived as it turned out to be and therefore felt his career would be better served at a distance from it. On the other hand it may have been that he was simply arrogant (or justifiably confident) enough to believe, in spite of having next-to-no political experience, that such a modest government position was beneath him. What is now known is that by keeping himself at a distance from the government, Pitt was free to pursue his own agenda, including pressing (in vain) for parliamentary reform and his name was not tarnished by the infighting that would cut short the careers of others more closely involved. In particular Charles James Fox and Lord Shelburne, both of whom would play a significant part in the rest of Pitt's life, were at loggerheads with each other in the government.[6]

On 1 July 1782, three months after forming a government, Lord Rockingham died and almost immediately the rival personalities which had made up his Cabinet dissolved into conflict. King George offered the premiership to Lord Shelburne, much to the anguish of Fox, who subsequently resigned from office, unable to bear the thought of working under his Cabinet rival. Pitt, however, was brought into government for the first time, by mid-July, being named as the new Chancellor of the Exchequer. Although they had previously been on amicable terms, the stage was now set for one of the greatest political rivalries in British history: The Pitt/Fox contest would last for the rest of their careers and was high profile enough to compete with Gladstone/Disraeli the following century, or Heath/Wilson the century after that.

It began on 9 July 1782 when Fox spoke in the House of Commons justifying his resignation by criticising Shelburne (and, thereby, attacking the new government). Pitt, as a government minister, felt compelled to retort and in doing so he alleged that contrary to Fox's resignation being a matter of principle – an honourable gesture to prevent further schisms within the government – it was actually more to do with Fox sulking about his being passed over in consideration of the leadership. In future, no love would be lost between these two men, and their enmity would affect Pitt's entire premiership.

In February 1783 Shelburne's government was preparing to announce to the Houses of Parliament the results of the peace negotiations that Great Britain had been undertaking with France, Spain and the Netherlands following those nations' involvement in the American Revolutionary War. Pitt is believed, during this time, to have approached Fox with an offer of a return to government[7] following the resignation of several leading ministers including Lord Keppel, Lord Richmond and Lord Rutland due to their differences with the leadership over the peace negotiations. Fox refused to serve under Shelburne and, instead, approached Lord North to form an alliance whose sole purpose seems to have been to bring down a government which both men despised. Between them they had a following of nearly half of the House of Commons. This unlikely alliance achieved its initial aims – it outvoted the government twice in succession and forced Shelburne to resign. However, if Fox and North hoped directly to obtain the highest office as a consequence of their conniving they would be sorely disappointed. As much as King George enjoyed having North as his First Lord due to the influence he could exert on him, allowing Fox (who had publicly denounced the King in the past) into the top job was intolerable. That said, even without office the pair would still end up with power.

In order to thwart this coalition King George invited William Pitt, as the only plausible alternative, to form a government of his own. Pitt mulled the decision over for three days before declining, apparently being dissuaded by his belief that Parliament would never ratify the decision. He wanted to be Prime Minister, but would not give anybody an excuse to hold conditions over him. He had to have the full authority of the office or nothing at all. So King George was forced to negotiate with the Fox-North coalition. With North unwilling to become Prime Minister due to his past experience, and Fox not an option as far as the King was concerned, the solution decided upon was that the pair serve under an independent minister. The Duke of Portland was settled upon as premier *de jure* but, as it happened, he was easily controlled by both men, making them *de facto* joint first ministers.

Fox and North, though, would in a very short period of time fall victim to the very constitutional component which Pitt had already identified as in need of reform; the influence of the monarchy. King George was never able to accept the government that had been forced upon him[8] and his desperation to remove them from office would prove toxic to his ministers.

In November 1783 Fox presented to Parliament a Bill which proposed wide ranging reforms of the way India was managed, including changes to the constitution of the East India Company. Pitt heavily criticised the Bill as giving Fox personally unrivalled power, allowing him to nominate commissioners to manage the colony who would undoubtedly be his own supporters. Despite Pitt's impassioned opposition the Bill passed through the House of Commons. However, news of Pitt's arguments reached King George before the Bill was heard in the House of Lords. Believing that Fox was not only increasing his own power as Pitt had stated, but that he was doing so at the expense of the influence of the monarchy, George felt that the government had finally pushed its luck too far. He soon hatched a plot to see the Bill defeated and then dismiss the government as unable to function, using this parliamentary defeat as evidence of their shortcomings.

The King therefore let it be known to all Lords that whoever voted for the India Bill would become his enemy. Sure enough the Bill was defeated there and a furious Charles James Fox responded by demanding that influence on the King by anybody other than an appointed minister should be outlawed. Pitt, still eager to distance himself from controversy and maintain his apparent independence, denied any knowledge of or involvement in the affair. The former was probably a lie, the latter was likely true.

On 18 December 1783 Pitt met with King George to discuss forming a new government and later that day Fox, North and Portland resigned. William Pitt, at the age of twenty-four, was now the youngest Prime Minister in history; a title he holds to this day.[9] However, he faced an unenviable struggle. Fox and North commanded a majority in the House of Commons between them. Adding to that other Whigs who were not naturally aligned with Pitt meant he was incredibly isolated. In fact, if the opposition had wished to force a vote of no confidence on the first meeting of Parliament after Pitt's ascension, he would almost certainly have lost.[10]

So upon entering office Pitt faced the choice of asking the King to dissolve Parliament and call a general election, which would cause a great deal of uncertainty, or else find a majority in the existing House of Commons. He decided on this second course of action, safe in the knowledge that he could fall back on the first if things went awry.

Knowing his situation was dire, the new Prime Minister worked tirelessly over the Christmas period to transform the numbers in his favour. He offered peerages to relatives of MPs in order to woo them to his support,[11] King George being more than happy to bestow honours upon people in order to see his plan succeed. At this point it seems that the King was even aware that Pitt was in favour of curbing his monarchical powers, but was prepared to accept this in order to keep Fox out of office. Pitt would be naïve to believe that he was the only person building alliances, as Fox, still aggrieved at the treacherous way in which he had been deposed, was whipping up support of his own. When Parliament reconvened in January Fox did his best to keep up the pressure on Pitt by accusing him of deliberate sabotage of the previous government. Pitt, for his part, used his perceived integrity and independence to his advantage – denying all knowledge of wrongdoing, knowing that people would find it difficult to believe it of him.

For weeks in early 1784 Fox and his supporters outvoted Pitt's government in any Bill it attempted to pass through the House of Commons. Pitt came under increasing pressure to call an election; something he was loath to do because it was unlikely to change the balance of the House in any significant way, and in that event he would have no options left. He also seems to have taken confidence from the support of King George himself who ordered the Prime Minister to muddle through. The King, in turn, appears to have been inspired by an overwhelming volume of letters he received from members of the public supporting his action in removing the Fox-North coalition.[12] The people had little patience with the scheming nature of politicians and this William Pitt, who came across as so different and somewhat independent from the rest of them, made a refreshing change. So Pitt may have been facing an insurmountable opposition in the Commons, but he still had the backing of the public and the King.

As the tide of public opinion flowed constantly stronger in Pitt's direction, so too did his support in Parliament as Member after Member found it increasingly difficult to justify their opposition. By March 1784 the House of Commons was probably evenly balanced but, with government support among the populace incredibly high, Pitt started to feel that perhaps a general election may not be such an unpredictable event after all. Perhaps he could finally obtain the parliamentary majority that he so coveted. It must be remembered that unlike today, up until this time elections were not fought along party political lines. Though clear factionalism did exist, and some voters may have been swayed by the personal loyalties of a Member or a candidate, that is all they were – loyalties. The official forming of political parties had not yet commenced.

The election of 1784 may have been the start of all that.[13] In previous elections voters would be presented with a list of candidates (who then may or may not canvass in the constituency) and would pick the one who best represented them (or else who bribed them the most). These candidates would then go on to Parliament and join like-minded people thereby forming factions. In contrast this election can be seen as a contest between those who were for Pitt and those who were for Fox. These two sides would eventually evolve into discernible political 'parties' and between them these parties would, in various guises, dominate elections for the next 140 years. As a principle the two party government/opposition system still dominates elections today.

The result of the 1784 election was a crushing defeat for Fox. Dozens of his allies in the House of Commons would never again return and William Pitt not only found himself with a majority for the first time, but a substantial one at that. Some reports estimate that his support was at least 100 members in excess of Fox's.[14] Now there was no disputing Pitt's authority and it was an authority which would influence politics for the next two decades.

Pitt's first year in office was dedicated largely to economic reform: he had not lost sight of his previously discussed concerns about the need for parliamentary reform (that injustices of the disproportionate representation of different regions could not be allowed to stand). But he also saw problems with the economy which could not be solved simply by conventional means and required some relatively innovative thinking. For example he reduced import duties to deter smuggling which, in the long term actually increased the revenue to the Treasury;[15] he introduced progressive tax systems and he improved the cost of living for the less well off.

He tackled the 'Irish problem' head on: whereas many of his predecessors had passed legislation choking off any growing industries in Ireland so as to favour their English competitors, Pitt was possibly the first Prime Minister to embrace the idea of free market economics. He was heavily influenced by Adam Smith and had come to the conclusion that a liberal economic policy and free trade between countries improves the wealth of all involved nations. Pitt believed that by removing the trade barriers with Ireland he would create the dual effect of political stability in an increasingly aggrieved Ireland on the one hand, and cheaper prices for the English consumer due to competition on the other.

Once the question of Ireland was settled Pitt planned to turn his attention to domestic parliamentary reform. However, his Irish proposals were far from home and dry. When he presented them to Parliament in early 1785 he found an opposition which he had never anticipated. In much the same way that organised protectionist labour unions would dog governments in the mid-late twentieth century, less formally organised but equally protectionist business interests would seek to quash Pitt's proposals which, they felt, may harm the competitiveness of domestic industries, regardless of the good they would achieve elsewhere.

Pitt made various concessions to keep his proposals alive but in the end the opposition was too great. Through 1785 the Prime Minister then embarked upon pushing through his parliamentary reform but once again found he could not command enough of a following to convince MPs of the need to change their own profession. He was defeated in a Commons vote by a comfortable majority.[16] By mid-1785, with eighteen months in office, Pitt's only real achievement had been economic reform, with his ambitious programs in Ireland and parliamentary elections effectively dead.

Come 1786 Pitt had regrouped and set his sights on more achievable aims. He felt that by turning the national debt (now sixteen times greater than the annual income of the state[17]) into a surplus he could hold his head high and feel as though he had done something worthwhile during his time in office.

This would be a continuation of his successes in the area of economic reform. Over the next year he simplified the tax system, reducing the number of levies so that monitoring and administering revenues was less costly for the Treasury, less open to corruption and more easily understood by those who were obligated to pay taxes. He also allowed sinecures (offices of the state with a salary but no responsibilities, typically held for life as a reward for one thing or another) to be left vacant once the holder passed away or forfeited them by other means. This saved the Treasury money but required no political risk because he wasn't sacking people from these offices, simply abstaining from appointing anybody new.

So Pitt's premiership continued on a principle of fiscal responsibility, with little else in the way of significant events and, consequently, he remained popular. Coasting along with few challenges is not, however, typical for the leader of a nation, and in 1788 years of relative tranquillity would come to be seen as the calm before the greatest constitutional storm to occur before or since. In this year it would become apparent for the first time that King George III was going mad.[18] At times he was so delirious that there was no possibility of him executing his constitutional responsibilities. This threw up several unprecedented challenges: firstly, the King was still alive so surely he had to fulfil his own duties, but what of when he was unable? The obvious answer was to install some form of Regent, but then how much power should a Regent have? What of when the King was clearly lucid, who would govern then? What if opinion was divided on whether or not he was delirious?

There were also personal problems for Pitt brought about by the deterioration of the King's mental state, not least that the obvious candidate for Regency was George, Prince of Wales, already heir to the throne and (annoyingly for Pitt) close friend of Charles James Fox. Surely within minutes of becoming Regent, Prince George would dissolve the government and invite his friends to form a new one.

Fox and the Whigs pushed for a Regent in the form of the Prince of Wales, assuming that this would inevitably mean power for themselves. In December 1788, unable to stall for time any longer by using such tactics as bringing in his own doctors for a second opinion after the King's practitioner had declared his condition permanent, Pitt wrote to Prince George with his proposals for a Regency. In effect, in Pitt's vision, the Prince would be Regent in title only, with no real power.[19] Although he could appoint his own government, the actual authority would still lie with the King, the logic being that King

George could always reverse anything undertaken by the Prince Regent, including reappointing Pitt as Prime Minister, should his condition improve.

The Prince rejected the offer, claiming it would paralyse the government. However, Pitt still had the advantage of popularity with the public, support in Parliament and that King George was personally extremely popular. The Prince and the Whigs came across simply as disloyal, scheming to take the throne from a bedridden monarch. Pitt therefore presented his proposals for a restricted Regency to Parliament in the new year, unaltered in spite of the Prince's protestations. In February 1789 Pitt introduced his Regency Bill to the House of Commons – the Bill that effectively contained his own resignation – having delayed the issue for four months. It passed through the Lower House comfortably but, as it was being debated in the Lords, news broke of the King having recovered from his madness, forcing the peers to suspend their debate.[20] Recovering to find that his enemies had tried to seize power but also that Pitt had so loyally defended his interests (the King could not stand the Prince of Wales) only crystallised his despise of the former and appreciation of the latter.

Pitt then took the time to allow the dust to settle on what had been a passionately fought campaign on both sides. In the event he enjoyed eighteen months of stability before requesting that the King dissolve Parliament in June 1790, more than six years into the then-seven year maximum parliamentary term. Pitt's personal popularity, still high, saw him through the general election with an overall gain in the number of seats held by his supporters.[21] He was now already one of the most successful leaders in history. The year ending with his election victory was a successful one for Pitt in more ways than one. Aside from seeing off the Regency crisis and increasing the number of his followers in Parliament, Pitt had found himself transformed from leader of a small island that had just been humiliated in the American Revolutionary War to leader of the most powerful nation in Europe.

France, crippled financially from her commitment to fighting in the American Revolutionary War, was now undergoing a revolution of its own. Small scale discontent would lead to riots which would progress to the overthrowing of the monarchy, a new constitution and a far less ambitious foreign policy. Spain relied on French support to be involved in any military campaigns and so now both nations were far less significant on the world stage than Britain. Consequently, when a conflict of interests arose between Britain and Spain over control of certain Pacific islands in 1789-90,[22] the latter quickly deferred to the former upon realising that France could no longer be relied upon to go to war with them.

       The French Revolution would have further positive consequences for Pitt in domestic politics. Edmund Burke, seen by many contemporary historians as the father of modern conservatism, was at this time a leading Whig and was vehemently opposed to the Revolution. Charles James Fox, on the other hand, was in support of it. This difference of opinion would eventually tear the men apart and cause an irreversible split in the opposition. According to Horace Walpole both Fox and Burke stood during a debate on Canada in 1791 at the height of their disagreements, each announced that they were no longer friends with the other and each burst into tears.[23]

       Pitt, for his part, was more than prepared to exploit the rift and publicly sided with Burke. It cannot be understated how significant events in France had become for the direction of policy in Britain by the late eighteenth century. *La Revolution*, aside from allowing Britain to pursue a more aggressive foreign policy and creating schisms in His Majesty's Most Loyal Opposition, also affected public opinion in such a way as to change the direction of policy – often against Pitt, most notably on the issue of the abolition of slavery.

       Pitt was a lifelong friend of William Wilberforce (an MP who history would remember as a prominent anti-slave trade campaigner). Pitt even encouraged Wilberforce to pursue his anti-slavery ideals, himself also being opposed to the industry. In 1789 Wilberforce had introduced motions to the House of Commons limiting the practices of the trade and as expected his motions had come up against vested interests, not least from within the government, but had found support from members of the opposition, including Fox. However, the French Revolution would make legislating in favour of banning the trade even more difficult. Firstly, abolitionists were by nature reformists, and just 22 miles south of the British mainland, reform had meant revolution, the fear of which created resistance to change back home. Secondly, in many French slave colonies the slaves, taking their inspiration from events within France itself where revolutionaries had risen up against the aristocracy, had risen up against their slave masters, leading to violence and death.[24] This lost slaves many would-be-sympathisers in Great Britain.

As events unfolded the vested interests couldn't win the moral argument – slavery was clearly wrong. But the consequences of abolition were too unpredictable for passage of an abolition Bill to go smoothly; that is, few people could stomach the thought of causing a repeat of the events in the French colony of Saint Domingue, where slave uprisings had led to the deaths of many French colonists. The result was a compromise: an outright abolition proposal was defeated in the Commons but one passed which promised the gradual abolition of the trade over an unspecified number of years.

All around him Pitt would feel the effects of the French Revolution, and every aspect of his premiership would be influenced by it from its beginning until his death. The real consequences of *La Revolution* were devastating and would be felt in every corner of Europe. Twenty years' worth of wars were to scourge the continent in what are now known as the French Revolutionary Wars (1793 – 1802) and the Napoleonic Wars (1803 – 1815). Pitt did all in his power to avoid armed conflict not least because the expensive nature of mobilisation could ruin his nine years of fiscal stability. He seems to have accepted war as an option only when there were no alternatives remaining.[25] But in 1793 France ended up at war with most of Europe and so acting in a behaviour that would become typical of its people over the coming centuries, Britain entered a war to rescue a continent that its citizens cared little for.

One perverse benefit of the war was that it brought Pitt much support from amongst conservative Whigs. Those who had been horrified by the French Revolution supported Pitt's motions through Parliament to take up arms against France. Into 1794 and Pitt seized the opportunity to split the Whigs forever. He approached the Duke of Portland, a leading conservative Whig and the Prime Minister under which the Fox-North coalition had operated, with an offer of Cabinet positions for himself and four of his followers if they joined him in government. This they duly did, much to Fox's chagrin as he now found himself marginalised in Westminster. Pitt, on the other hand, seemed to have solved his 'Regency problem' from five years earlier; he was now too powerful to be removed even by a hostile monarch.

In the meantime he addressed the threat of a revolution in Britain – feared due to stronger communication links and growing discontent fuelled by poor harvests – by suspending habeas corpus. Fox was horrified.[26] This was a fine example of how a person must be judged according to the age in which they live. In the twenty-first century such an affront to civil liberties is unthinkable, but for a few extremists, and one cannot help but feel sympathetic to Fox's opposition to it. In the eighteenth century, though, Pitt's support was insurmountable and it was Fox who looked increasingly like the extremist.

On the continent France was at war with Prussia, Spain, Holland and Austria. Yet it was the French who maintained the upper hand for much of the early years. In January 1795 Holland surrendered, giving the French morale, momentum, territory, money and, of course, all the Dutch weapons and war ships.

In the March Prussia signed a peace agreement with France and Spain negotiated a truce in the July. Russia, who had been expected to join the war against the Revolutionaries, never did. Pitt became concerned that the war would no longer be supported within Britain due to this isolation, notwithstanding his unprecedented Commons majority. He sent envoys to France to begin negotiations for peace but these were swiftly rebuffed. Meanwhile, in order to quell discontent on the domestic front the Prime Minister introduced a Seditious Meetings Bill to Parliament, a further infringement on civil liberties which was comfortably carried. All of these actions – suspending the right to a trial, attempting (and failing) to negotiate a way out of war, banning public meetings if they are likely to be against the government in spirit – are the actions of a character who has lost control. They are acts of panic and oppression and suggest that Pitt no longer carried the mood of the nation.

However, in 1796 the Prime Minister called a general election which saw him return to Parliament with another unassailable majority. In fact, if the Portland Whigs can be included in the figures then the government had over four times as many MPs as the opposition.[27] This fact suggests that he did actually understand the zeitgeist. The logical conclusion of these two apparently opposing sets of circumstances, therefore, is that Pitt's more panicked actions were the result of a *belief* that popular opinion was against him, when in fact it wasn't. In an age without opinion polls it must have been difficult to gauge. Pitt's popularity was high, as was the popularity of his policies, only his self-confidence suffered.

The war with France was bound to affect him in this way as little seemed to go as planned. All his years of paying down the national debt were reversed within a couple of years of war, all of Britain's allies surrendered or negotiated a peace with France and by autumn 1796 Spain had even agreed a military alliance with the French meaning that they now re-entered the war but this time *against* Britain.[28]

December 1796 saw a French fleet set sail for an invasion of the British Isles at the same time as Pitt had sent yet another doomed peace envoy to Paris. It was only snow and wind that drove the enemy ships away. One month later in January 1797 the first efforts of the Spanish entry to the war took effect as they sent a naval armada from their Mediterranean coastline out into the Atlantic heading for Britain. They were intercepted in the February by a British fleet half the size just off the south-west coast of Portugal and were comfortably beaten. Britannia did indeed rule the waves in this age.

The problem was that much of the war in Europe was fought on land. From West to East France was dominating, now having allies in Spain and Holland and with the skilled French General Napoleon Bonaparte tearing through northern Italy, Britain's only remaining ally, Austria, looked on the brink of surrender. In April 1797 Pitt made a final bid for peace. He sent an envoy to Vienna to convince the Austrians to stay in the war long enough to allow Britain to negotiate a peace with France on behalf of both nations, surely a stronger position than them retiring one at a time. However, by the time the representative arrived Austria had already capitulated, ceding much of her territories to France[29] who now had no reason to negotiate anything with the only remaining European nation who opposed her – especially not when that one nation was just a remote island to the north. Britain was well and truly isolated.

Pitt pressed on with his peace negotiations but from a much weaker position. Lord Malmesbury was despatched in June to discuss terms with the French, which continued through the summer. But a *coup d'état* in Paris that September resulted in a more hard-line leadership in France and demands changed from difficult-but-possible (recognising French conquests, for example) to outright humiliating (Britain forsaking all of its own conquests).[30] Once again peace talks came to nothing.

This result seems to have changed Pitt in both his outlook and his behaviour in war. Once desperate for peace and all the more reserved for it, he now accepted that it was all or nothing and committed himself entirely to defeating his enemy on the battlefield. It would not be the last time that a British leader would learn the lesson that when faced with despotism, negotiation and appeasement seldom work. He introduced graduated taxes across most industries to help finance the conflict, finding once again that the public were on his side as he wrote into his tax plan the option for voluntary contributions by the people which, incredibly, saw revenues increase by £2 million.[31] He saw over 100,000 extra men volunteer for military service in 1798. During the early months of that year intelligence was received once again that the French were planning to invade the British Isles via Ireland. Prudence suggested that the naval fleet should stay close ready to intercept any such offensive. However, the Prime Minister was long past playing it safe and, keen to draw Austria back into the war, he sent a fleet into the Mediterranean Sea in April 1798 in order to attack the French head on right in front of the other major European nations.

By coincidence (because as it happened Pitt's intelligence was flawed and the French were not heading for Britain) in the May Napoleon and his army had taken to sea in a fleet of over 300 ships in the Mediterranean. With Napoleon's destination being unknown this information only added fuel to the fears that invasion was imminent. For over two months the British fleet, led by Rear Admiral Horatio Nelson, searched the sea for the elusive French ships to no avail. Napoleon was wise to his pursuers and successfully enforced a secrecy as to his whereabouts at all times. He captured the island of Malta completely undetected, thereby increasing the range of French territory whilst British ships sailed idly about. It seems incredible that such a large fleet could sail around such a relatively small sea for months without being detected, but such was the fear that Napoleon could instil in anybody considering talking. In the July of 1798 the French army landed in Egypt, capturing Alexandria and later Cairo. It was at this time, with French ships anchored in the Nile ready to transport the victorious army to its next destination that Nelson finally caught up with his quarry. The Battle of the Nile was about to begin.

Nelson's victory in this battle was absolute – the French fleet was annihilated and the British triumph would be a milestone of the conflict. Even in the short term it meant that the French army was stranded on a separate continent with no means of returning home. In the longer term French actions in the Mediterranean would eventually bring Russia into the war against them. It would be well over a year before Napoleon was able to return to France but when he did he would install himself as First Consul almost immediately. With their greatest general as their national leader, France would be more dangerous than ever.

During all of this Pitt was able to reflect on what could have been. Had Napoleon attacked the British Isles, could he have conquered them? Any invasion attempt would undoubtedly have started in Ireland, where their reception would be far less hostile and they would more than likely pick up a number of sympathisers from Ireland's substantial anti-Royalist populace. Security in the homeland, therefore, meant securing Ireland. Pitt consequently spent much of 1799 planning for an Act of Union between Great Britain and Ireland. His thinking was that uniting the two as one country, rather than having one subjugated by the other, would bring about a dignity to the people who otherwise felt discontented. Pitt's vision was not just a union between the two countries but an equality amongst all their citizens, meaning Catholic emancipation. This ideal was not dear to the hearts of many of his Westminster colleagues, nor indeed to King George. The arguments in favour of emancipation were clear enough at the time – fewer reasons for unrest on the Emerald Isle – but to Pitt, who genuinely appears to have favoured equal treatment of all persons (hence his anti-slavery position), and was by no means a religious zealot of any persuasion (albeit he was Anglican in the sense that all Englishmen were) it was a matter of principle, a matter of fairness.

In 1800 his Act of Union would pass through both the Irish and English Parliaments, but without any guarantee for equal treatment of Catholics. At the time it was hailed as a great victory and it certainly was an incredible feat; it created a Union that would last for 120 years. However, from the benefit of hindsight we know that it was doomed to failure. English unwillingness to allow equal treatment for their Popish countrymen created a resentment that would eventually tear the Union apart. Even once emancipation was established, it was all too little, too late.

Although the Act of Union did not give any specific guarantees for the rights of Catholics, it did not strictly rule out emancipation either. Pitt had deliberately been vague on the issue, knowing that the Bill would not pass with it but assuming that he could force it through separately once Great Britain and Ireland were united. He intended to revisit the issue when the new Parliament, complete with 100 new Irish MPs, reconvened in January 1801. There was no way that he could have foreseen that this issue would be his downfall. In that January Pitt took soundings from his Cabinet on the likelihood of emancipation being passed into law. It seems that the majority were in favour[32] but a minority were resolute in their opposition. When the King got wind of the government's plotting he was alleged to have had a public explosion of anger, which Pitt found deeply embarrassing.[33] He corresponded with the King over the issue but the sovereign was steadfast. Pitt tendered his resignation and the King accepted. It all came about extremely suddenly for someone who had led the country for seventeen years.

At this time Pitt suggested that the Speaker of the House of Commons, his lifelong friend, Henry Addington, succeed him as Prime Minister, which the King was agreeable to, as was Addington. Pitt saw through the government's budget in February and prepared to return his Seals of Office. Many of his Cabinet decided to leave with him, including Henry Dundas and William Grenville, who had been directing the war with France. However, with perfect timing the King succumbed to another bout of madness and was therefore unable to accept the Seals from his ministers. Having resigned, the government was forced to continue governing![34]

Pitt met the Prince of Wales and asserted to him that any Regency would be acceptable only on the terms which the Prime Minister himself had demanded during the previous Regency Crisis thirteen years earlier. With the opposition in no position to cause trouble for the government the Prince had little option but to accept.[35] However, the issue became academic as, during the first week in March, King George recovered and Pitt was released from office.

During his seventeen years in power William Pitt had transformed British politics. The Prime Minister is the person who is able to command a majority of supporters in Parliament but up until Pitt's tenure it was whoever had the most support from one group known as the Whigs. From his tenure onwards we can see for the first time two discernible political parties emerge. Although Pitt would never have used the term 'Tory' to refer to himself, his supporters – the 'Pittites' – would adopt this name and evolve into the party we now know as the Conservative Party.

Pitt embarked on a great deal of honourable policy pursuits during his time in office. If success is a measure of the extent to which one achieves ones pursuits, then Pitt would go down in history as a failure as he, like so many before and since, was unable to see through most of his long term initiatives. He set out to achieve parliamentary reform, but had to abandon it due to the strength of opposition to it. He attempted to abolish the slave trade, but this necessarily had to be delayed due again to opposition in Parliament. He tried to get the country's finances in order but the war with France led to greater borrowing than at any time in the nation's history. He took Britain into a war with France but this was still ongoing at the time of his resignation. Finally he attempted to gain equal rights for Catholics, which led to his losing office.

However, there are other ways in which to measure success. William Pitt had been First Lord of the Treasury for seventeen years at this point, a longer tenure than anybody since the first office holder – Robert Walpole. He had during this time commanded an unprecedented majority. He united Great Britain with Ireland and although many of his major policy initiatives were incomplete at the time of his resignation, he put these ideas onto the agenda so that they could be pursued more readily in the future. He did what he felt was right even if it meant defeat for him politically or, ultimately, the loss of the office he held dear.

Eventually the slave trade would be abolished, Britain would defeat Napoleon and bring peace to Europe and Catholics would be given equal rights to Protestants. Occasionally history needs somebody to bring these issues to the fore so that even if the task is impossible for them, future generations can see them through. At the turn of the nineteenth century, William Pitt the Younger was that somebody.

Henry Addington
(1801 – 1804)

I used to think all the sufferings of war lost in its glory, now I
consider all its glory lost in its sufferings

Henry Addington

If you were so instrumental as you say in setting up this
Government, why are you so out of Humour with what you have
made?

Daniel Defoe's *Tory*, 1692

THE CIRCUMSTANCES in which Henry Addington
ascended to the premiership should have made for a positive
atmosphere. He had the full support of the King; he inherited a
huge parliamentary majority; and the previous Prime Minister
had resigned on a matter of principle but had pointed to
Addington as his successor. Further to this, Pitt tried to
convince many of his old allies to take up posts in Addington's
ministry[1] in order to make life easier for the incoming Prime
Minister. Of course, when a change in leadership comes about
there will always be those high ranking ministers who feel that
their time to step down has also come and this instance was no
exception.
　　However, Addington found that coming to power in
such circumstances was less than smooth and keeping the Party
together would not be easy. Firstly there were those Pittites who
felt that Addington had been too heavily favoured by the King
at a time when their leader had suddenly fallen from preference.
For this there could be only one explanation and that was
skulduggery on the part of Addington in order to oust Pitt and
form his own ministry. There is little evidence to support this
and Pitt himself was convinced that it was untrue, but those of
his supporters who believed it, such as Grenville and George
Canning, outright refused to work for the new Prime Minister.[2]
Grenville even went so far as to sit on the opposition benches
during Addington's tenure and though he would one day

become Prime Minister himself, history would remember him as a Whig, rather than a Tory.

Indeed keeping the Party together would be difficult. Addington's next trouble was with people accepting him personally because he had a clear problem in that 'he was not an aristocrat, he was not an orator and he was not William Pitt.'[3] He had huge boots to fill but his evident political mediocrity meant that he never could fill them. Few thought him up to the challenge and still more damaging, even though Pitt had given Addington his blessing, he would become a thorn in his side within a relatively short space of time.

Upon taking office, Addington saw his primary mission as bringing about a peace with France. There were plenty of reasons for this. Firstly, the war had brought Britain to the point of financial collapse; the strain placed upon the people was becoming unbearable and a peace settlement widely regarded as necessary. The public wanted it in order that they may be freed from Pitt's income tax and the opposition Whigs had been against the war from the beginning so would support renewed negotiations for peace. Secondly, Pitt's Cabinet had been largely against negotiation with the French, believing that an out-and-out military victory was the only acceptable end to the war. However, most of Pitt's Cabinet had resigned and many believed that although Catholic emancipation was ostensibly the reason given, there was more to it than that. Pitt himself believed that negotiations needed to be made with France but that he could not do it personally because of the strength of opposition within his own Cabinet. By resigning, he knew that others would follow and a fresh approach could be made.[4] This is unlikely to have been the primary cause of Pitt's departure from office, however the issue of emancipation also seems not to have been close enough to his heart to force him to leave the only position he ever coveted. The logical conclusion, therefore, is that both played a part. So Addington's ministry may have been seen to come about as a necessary instrument for concluding the war. We know now that Pitt supported Addington's premiership at the outset and that Addington closely consulted Pitt on all policy decisions in the early days. Pitt gave his blessing for Addington to enter into peace negotiations and so the third reason for seeking peace becomes apparent: the policy had the support of the one man who could direct the votes of the majority of the House of Commons. Addington's premiership can be divided into three distinct sections. Firstly from the beginning up until peace had been settled with France, he was incredibly popular in spite of himself, due to the backing he had from the King and William Pitt. This did necessitate, though, a dependence on Pitt and a constant need for his approval on all decisions. The second stage 'from the election to the renewal of war, saw the storm clouds gather'[5]. The final stage saw Addington desperately trying to find an honourable way to end a doomed premiership.

The first phase was, effectively, a twelve month period in which all efforts were directed towards bringing the war to a conclusion. Pitt's support in this policy must have been a great boost for Addington who could use the wartime leader as a shield against attacks from those who would otherwise denounce him as a coward. For this first year Pitt and Addington were still as close friends as they had been throughout their adult lives. By making some small conciliatory gestures towards the French in the spring of 1801 Addington was able to open up formal peace negotiations throughout the summer and autumn in London, led by Robert Jenkinson (then known as Lord Hawkesbury) on the British side and Monsieur Otto for the French. The British negotiating position was strengthened by a series of military victories in the early spring (including the famous naval victory over the Danish fleet in which Horatio Nelson ignored the signal to retreat by claiming that his only having one eye gave him the right to be blind when it suited him, going on into battle unsanctioned and devastating the enemy).

That notwithstanding the government was prepared to give away much more than other Tories may have felt comfortable with due to their conviction that peace was necessary, whatever the cost. By the end of September Hawkesbury and Otto had agreed a preliminary peace, in which Britain agreed to restore all French colonies taken during the conflict and evacuate Malta. The French, it seemed, were required to surrender very little. Some saw this as an embarrassment for Britain, but peace was generally heralded as a positive move amongst the public. It was supported by the government, by the Whigs and, equally as important, by William Pitt. In the meantime, final negotiations continued in France between Lord Cornwallis, now representing Britain and Joseph Bonaparte, brother of Napoleon. Peace would not be concluded until March 1802 and up until early that same year Pitt and Addington looked as close as ever. However, in the February, the seeds of separation were beginning to be sown and, although both men would convince themselves and others both publicly and privately afterwards that they were still united, doubts must have lingered in the backs of their minds.

During this period Pitt had been suffering from one of his many bouts of illnesses and had been absent from Parliament since his resignation as Prime Minister. On 8 February 1802 George Tierney, who had once challenged and fought William Pitt in a duel, rose in the House of Commons and praised some of the newer government Ministers that had been appointed since the Christmas recess. This was unusual in itself because up until that point he had been in staunch opposition to the government. However, Tierney was playing an underhanded game because his speech praised ministers by contrasting them with the irresponsibility of their predecessors, not least William Pitt.

By all accounts Addington rose to dismiss some of Tierney's arguments but Pitt's understanding of the situation, which may have come from one of Addington's despisers in the form of Rose or Canning, was that the Prime Minister hadn't gone nearly far enough in defending someone who was supposed to be his friend. Pitt wrote to Addington complaining that his character had been attacked and his friend had not been as supportive as he should have been. Addington replied that Pitt must have misunderstood and that he was as loyal to him as he ever had been. Pitt decided to speak to other witnesses before deciding on how to deal with the situation and once he had finalised his investigation he informed Addington that he had concluded that the Prime Minister could be excused from not being particularly staunch in his defence of him on the basis that others had already sufficiently done so before Addington had spoken (probably referring to Dundas). Both men moved on and appeared to put the incident behind them. However, as stated, doubts must have lingered, particularly in the mind of Addington when considering how quick his friend was to assume the worst of him and turn against him.

In the meantime peace negotiations between Britain and France were dragging on. What had been agreed in London in the September for some reason needed to be renegotiated over and over for the following six months. This may have been due to delaying tactics by the French who felt that the longer negotiations continued, the more nervous the British would get and therefore there may be more to gain. Eventually Cornwallis was instructed to put an ultimatum to France which was effectively a copy of the last draft that the French had found acceptable before changing their minds. If they didn't accept and sign the agreement he was to leave France. This seemed to do the trick and the Treaty of Amiens was signed by Cornwallis and Joseph Bonaparte on 25 March 1802.

The Treaty was discussed in Parliament shortly afterwards and was approved in both Houses by comfortable majorities, as was expected. However, although peace was approved because it was so desirable, the terms were not thought of as particularly attractive. Since the preliminary peace agreement six months earlier Napoleon had taken over most of Northern Italy, in violation of the Treaty of Lunéville signed between France and Austria in 1801, which suggested that Napoleon could not be trusted to keep to his agreements. Some felt that this would have justified Britain pushing for more favourable terms.[6] However, the motion was carried and Addington could now revel in achieving his ultimate goal.

With the peace agreement now behind him, Addington could take to pursuing whatever domestic policies he felt were necessary with the support of a huge majority in Parliament and without the concerns of having to fund an expensive conflict. With this in mind he introduced his first peacetime budget in June 1802 in which he scrapped Pitt's income tax which had been both unpopular and less effective than it had been assumed it would be. Shortly afterwards, Parliament was dissolved on 29 June 1802 for a general election to be held – the first general election for the United Kingdom of Great Britain and Ireland. Addington had every right to feel confident going into the election: Pitt was onside, peace had been signed with France and taxes were now less of a burden for the people. He wasn't to be disappointed as his followers would come away with over 380 seats.

Even though Pitt had supported the government and the King had used all his influence in their cause (he was still determined that a Whig victory which may lead to any position of prominence for Charles James Fox must be fought against with every sinew), the scale of the victory was still impressive for Addington and could conceivably have changed the way he felt about his leadership. Firstly, he won the election in spite of opposition from both the Whigs, who felt he were too closely aligned with Pitt, and the war-Tories who would rather have had Pitt back. Secondly, the new Parliament was now his own, one formed after a general election that he had fought as leader of the Tories and therefore he should now feel less indebted to his predecessor.

It is very difficult to determine exactly what happened during the following year or so to change so substantially the relationship between Addington and Pitt which would ultimately result in the downfall of the former, the restoration of the latter and the deterioration of their friendship for ever. Those historians biased towards Pitt argue that he was heavily influenced by friends, ambition and, most importantly, his fervent belief that Addington was incapable in office, and even more so to lead the country in war.[7] He therefore felt duty bound to supplant him. On the other hand Addingtonian historians suggest that his success at the general election and apparent popularity with the populace led to him becoming less dependent on Pitt for advice and support, which in turn created a resentment[8] that would only be satisfied by Pitt's removing him from office. The chronology of events follows.

In May 1802, just before the general election, Canning organised a celebration in honour of Pitt's birthday, to be held in the Merchant Taylors Hall. Canning, as well as being the most fervent of Pittites, was also known as a master of verse and had several times written poems aimed at causing embarrassment to Addington and his government (often being reprimanded by Pitt and made to apologise). At the party that he had organised around one thousand people were present, including Addington, but not Pitt. Towards the end of the evening the guests were serenaded with a song written by Canning in dedication to Pitt and entitled *The Pilot That Weathered The Storm*. It painted a picture of Pitt as a grand hero at the helm of the ship Britannia, bravely sailing through the tempest of war. Now that the storm has ended, Canning claimed, the nation's gratitude to the pilot should not die with it. The song ended with an explicit call for Pitt's return, should war be renewed:

And O! if again the rude whirlwind should
rise,

The dawning of peace should fresh darkness
deform,
The regrets of the good and the fears of the
wise
Shall turn to the pilot that weathered the
storm[9]

This would no doubt have festered in the mind of the current Prime Minister. Yes, Canning was zealously loyal to Pitt. Yes, he was a trouble-maker for the government. But if the peace with France did not hold out, how many other people would be asking for the return of William Pitt?

In August 1802 Dundas was elevated to the Lords as Lord Melville. Pitt had convinced Dundas to work for the new government but had believed him still to be loyal to the old regime. In fact he was, but to Pitt it appeared as though Addington was starting to bribe Pittites to keep them onside in the event that their leader may turn, and it seemed to him to have worked in this case. It was around this same time that the first suggestions that the peace may not hold began to surface. By this point Addington was convinced that his very survival in office depended on the staving off of war. Any renewal of conflict would undoubtedly result in calls for the return of The Pilot That Weathered The Storm.

The difficulties began with Napoleon ostensibly complaining about the way he was portrayed in the British press. Even at the turn of the nineteenth century freedom of the press was a cornerstone of British democracy and nobody was free from criticism; from the Prime Minister to the King to the First Consul of France. Desperate to keep his peace, though, Addington used whatever influence he had to rein in the guilty editors, to little avail. Many felt that insinuations from ministers that recalcitrant editors could be removed from government protection were as abhorrent as any threat they could envisage receiving. The issue was quietly dropped.

In the October Napoleon took control of Switzerland: an invasion is the way it would be described by any impartial bystander although the First Consul himself would claim he was invited to take control. The Treat of Amiens did not address Switzerland specifically and was therefore not breached, but many in Britain felt horrified by Napoleon's continued expansionism on the continent. For Addington this was not worth going to war over but he did promise money to support the Swiss if they wished to fight. With no other European nation assisting them, however, this was never going to be an option.

Addington was in a hopeless position. The war-Tories accused him of being weak in the face of oppression, whereas the Whigs were shocked by what they saw as a Prime Minister being far too casual about how far he could provoke the French, who they still saw as victims, rather than aggressors. However, Fox and his supporters, although quick to criticise the government, refused to strike any knock-out blows, knowing full well that removing the Prime Minister from office would more than likely result in the reinstating of the one man even more insufferable than him.

Come the autumn and Pitt was telling his friends that he would take no further part in assisting the government with their foreign policy, apparently because he disapproved of the direction in which it was headed. He let ministers down gently by informing them that he could not advise them simply because he did not have all the facts to hand as they did. However, in spite of his growing frustration with the administration of the day, Pitt refused to go into out-and-out opposition, apparently still feeling bound by his promise of nearly two years previously to support Addington.

For his part the Prime Minister wrote to Pitt urging him to leave Bath, where he was making use of the spa waters to try to ease his illness and gout, and visit London where all information at the hands of the government would be made available to him and his advice readily accepted. Pitt decided to accept, but when the Grenvilles and Canning got wind they began once again to give their own advice, decidedly anti-Addingtonian, imploring Pitt to distrust anything said to him by the Prime Minister.[10]

Addington and Pitt met three times in January 1803 from which Addington seems to have come away with the impression that Pitt would continue to support his government. Pitt, however, did make it clear that he did not approve of Addington's most recent budget, in which wartime spending was maintained in spite of the ongoing peace and that he felt Addington should withdraw the budget or else Pitt would denounce it. At some point Addington suggested to Pitt the idea of them forming a joint ministry. We now know that this never would have been acceptable to Pitt. In 1803, much like in 1783, he would not accept power on anybody's terms but his own. The idea of leading a government doomed to failure or with conditions imposed upon him by a sovereign had been unattractive enough to decline office in 1783, the idea of serving with or under Addington or anybody else for that matter was enough for him to avoid accepting in 1803. For Pitt, it was all or nothing.

When Addington put the proposal of a coalition government to Pitt it seems he may have given a noncommittal reply. In the months that followed Pitt would assure his supporters that he made it quite clear that he would never serve under Addington, but Addington seems to have been left with the impression that Pitt had shown a keen interest to join with him, perhaps with another person as head of the government, much like the Fox-North coalition twenty years earlier. It is rather telling of Addington's character that at this point in time he would have been well aware that he had the support of the King, he had the support of the electorate and he had the support of a majority in Parliament, albeit not of the major names such as Grenville, Fox, Canning or Rose. But in spite of this he could not face the thought of continuing without the support of Pitt. His desperate search for a coalition when in fact he had a strong outright majority is one of the factors that have led historians to consider him a weak leader.[11]

Lord Melville was despatched by the Prime Minister to see Pitt to try to sell the idea of both men serving under a third party, suggesting Pitt's brother, Lord Chatham. All this served to do was to crystallise Pitt's suspicion that Melville had sold himself to Addington for a peerage, and so the bitterness increased. Pitt now admitted for the first time that he was being driven to opposition.

Finally Addington made what seemed like the offer Pitt had been waiting for. Pitt could become Prime Minister, Addington would convince the King of the necessity of this action, and the only condition was that the ministers who had served under Addington should not be removed from office and any new appointments should not include the Grenvilles. Even this, though, was too restrictive for the man who wanted complete independence to govern as he pleased. Shortly after receiving the offer Pitt was visited by Grenville and discussed the matter with him. Grenville strongly advised Pitt to resist, stating that it was not Addington's place to offer him anything, let alone place restrictions on what he should do with a ministry. That privilege remained with the King. Clearly, Grenville had a stake in this as Pitt's accepting these terms necessarily ruled him out of government. Addington and Pitt met a few days after the proposal had been made and during the meeting Pitt laid out his demands: office without restrictions. Addington rejected the ultimatum on the advice of his Cabinet and now the schism between the two men was irreparable.

At the end of January Napoleon made demands that the British evacuate Malta, as they had pledged to do in the Treaty of Amiens. However, due to Napoleon's actions on the continent, including his invasion of Switzerland, Addington did not feel comfortable withdrawing British forces from the Mediterranean in case war broke out again. From Napoleon's point of view Switzerland had not been addressed in the Treaty and was therefore fair game. He made it clear that if Britain did not surrender Malta then the only option left was war. It seems he anticipated a refusal here but thought that by another round of protracted negotiations he may gain some ground elsewhere. By this point, though, Addington had had enough. He told the British Ambassador in Paris to demand French withdrawal from Switzerland immediately and, if refused, to come home because the country would no longer be safe for a Briton. Of course the French couldn't agree to such audacious terms and so, on 18 May 1803, Addington's government declared war on France. They knew that doing so meant that their crowning achievement had failed and more than likely spelled the end of Addington's premiership. During the debates in the House of Commons the following week it was Pitt who enraptured MPs by condemning the French and arguing with conviction the justness of the British position.

The government would never really recover. On 3 June a resolution was put forward in the House of Commons to censure the administration for failing to steer the country safely away from war by negotiating properly with the French. The motion was eventually defeated but the issue damaged the government on three fronts. Firstly the whole episode exposed the weakness of the administration – a stronger government would never have even had to have debated the issue. Secondly, Pitt abstained, refusing to vote against the government to whom he had pledged his support but, significantly, unable to bring himself to vote in their favour. This symbolised to the world that the breach between the two men was now irreconcilable. Finally, the margin by which Addington won was so great that the opposition leaders had to consider that should the status quo remain, the government would be able to carry any motion it pleased. For the first time Fox and Grenville decided to enter into discussions about joining forces to create an opposition worthy of facing such an administration.[12]

Addington did his best to amble through in spite of his own inferiority complex when it came to standing against Pitt. He knew that war required finance and so he reinstated the income tax that he had received so much credit for scrapping only two years earlier. This may be one thing, albeit not a particularly exciting one, that a modern student of history can attribute to Henry Addington as having done well with. If Pitt takes credit for creating the income tax, Addington can receive the glory for increasing its efficiency and moulding it into the system we know today, albeit a far more primitive version. He implemented the principle of taxation at source, meaning individuals received their income with the tax deducted. Pitt's version relied on people to calculate their own taxes (and do so honestly). The improvements were such that a lower level of taxation now produced a similar yield for the Treasury.[13]

While the country prepared for war the only battles that appeared to take place were in Westminster between the Addingtonians and the Pittites. Addington's strategy for the war was to sit and wait. Before the conclusion of hostilities in 1802 it was clear that France could not overcome Britain's naval supremacy but that no single nation could match Napoleon's army in a land war. The only way for Britain to break the deadlock in her favour would be to recruit continental allies to fight alongside her. However, Addington believed that Austria, Prussia and Russia would need more time before they were able to re-enter a war owing to the fact that financially, militarily and in terms of morale they were all fragile. One certain way to lose the war would be to allow the French army to land on British shores and therefore it made sense to keep the navy close, guarding the channel and keeping French ships in port. So although war had been declared, it seemed pointless to him actually to begin fighting. Many of his contemporaries, however, saw his procrastination as weakness.[14] Where were

the great military victories of Copenhagen and the Nile that
they had witnessed under Pitt?

Further criticisms were levelled at the government
sporadically throughout the summer and autumn of 1803 and it
seems that by this point Addington had accepted the
inevitability of his being supplanted by Pitt. He still had his
majority in Parliament, he still had the support of the King and
the country but he could never stand up to his predecessor. 'The
government was sick, a sickness not based on real weakness but
psychosomatic, almost imaginary. It would not be too much to
say that if the Government had not clearly been about to die, no
one would have suspected that they were ill at all.'[15]

Now an alliance of parliamentary leaders came forth
from clandestine negotiations into outright opposition.
Grenville and his supporters, vehement believers in the need
for war with France and that the government was too weak to
wage it, allied with Fox and his followers, zealous champions
of the need for peace and convinced that the government
consisted of war-mongers that never really attempted to
negotiate with Napoleon. The only thing that they had in
common was that they both wanted Addington out of office.
Rarely has the view that 'in politics, shared hatreds are almost
always the basis of friendships'[16] been more apparent.

Pitt now had to choose his actions carefully. He knew
that the government was doomed long before this new alliance
but he must now have realised that this development would
accelerate the administration's demise. To defend the
government may allow Grenville and Fox to claim victory but
to join in their attacks would tarnish him with their brush, and
he still wanted to appear as the opponent of Fox, particularly to
the King who still had the authority to choose his First Lord of
the Treasury and who hated Fox.

On 15 March 1804 Pitt introduced a motion on the state
of the navy. The idea was to embarrass the government by
exposing its lack of preparedness for war, whilst allowing Fox
and Grenville to conduct most of the impassioned attacks. The
government defeated the Pittites, Grenvillites and Whigs by a
majority of seventy one. However, previous government
majorities had been much higher. The decline had begun.

On 16 April the House voted on the Irish Militia Bill.
The government carried it with a majority of twenty one. On 25
April the Army Reserve Act was carried by thirty seven votes.
Addington felt rejected and, on 29 April, informed his Cabinet

that he would be stepping down. Once King George found out he was said to be deeply troubled. He now associated Pitt with Fox as they had both opposed his Prime Minister. When he sent for Pitt to discuss a potential new administration, Pitt suggested a broad ministry including all the best talents, meaning Grenville but also Fox. The King found this idea abhorrent and insisted that he would never accept any ministry including Charles James Fox, even if it meant finding a new Prime Minister altogether. In the event Pitt could accept keeping Fox out, but Grenville couldn't. He felt that if a ministry couldn't be formed including all the most talented people, then he could not be part of it.

Addington's premiership has been viewed by history as a failure. In terms of policies pursued, unlike Pitt, Addington saw through most of what he wanted. He brought about a peace with France and it was only the belligerence of the other side that made it unworkable. Upon re-entering the war he held off hostilities in the hope that he could buy time to bring more allies on board. He scrapped Pitt's unpopular income tax. He had the support of the King and was widely liked. His failure was a human one, an inability to carry people where he wanted to take them and an inferiority complex that made him want to roll over instead of stand and fight. Due to his popularity in the country he would have stood a chance had he challenged Pitt outright; the Whigs would possibly have supported him against Pitt in Parliament and with the backing of the King he could have won another election. He didn't have the stomach to fight, though. In the end every time somebody deserted him – be it the Whig supporters who wanted Pitt out initially but then sided with Fox later on; be it Grenville; be it the Tories who joined Pitt when he decided no longer to support the government – his defeatist mind worked against him, making these relatively small defectors seem a much greater force against him than his swathes of supporters were a force for him.

For all his human failings, though, often forgotten are his human strengths, which served the country well during his tenure and afterwards. He was a competent Chancellor of the Exchequer (then an office also held by the Prime Minister); his income tax is still utilised by the Treasury today, he did not preside over any great national disaster, or any great disturbances. Nobody felt the need to protest or rise up against his government.

That said, his feeling of inferiority next to the leading statesmen of the day showed. Whether because of his birth, his oratorical style or that he was not William Pitt, Addington could not convince any of his contemporaries (or indeed himself) that he was their equal, and as such he failed to lead them.

William Pitt the Younger
(1804 − 1806)

I have received a broad hint to retire…broad as the hint may be, it is
not broad enough for me to take it

William Pitt, 18 June 1804

If you run a man down, he will support himself at any rate; for Men
are but Men

Daniel Defoe's *Tory*, 1692

SO IT WAS THAT IN MAY 1804 William Pitt retook the office
that he and many other Britons felt was rightfully his. It is a
curious thing that 20 years after his becoming Prime Minister
for the first time he took office again as a much more
experienced and respected statesman – internationally as well
as domestically – with a Cabinet made up of political giants
rather than a gang of his young friends, and yet his tenure would
be viewed by history as a much less authoritative premiership
than his first had been. His new Cabinet included Portland,
whose defection from the Whigs had so helped to increase
Pitt's majority in Parliament ten years previously. Experience
and respectability came with this man – he had himself been
Pitt's immediate predecessor as Prime Minister first time
around and would again be one of his successors. Lord
Hawkesbury was also present as Home Secretary; he was
extremely capable and would himself be a future Tory Prime
Minister under the title he would inherit from his father, the
Earl of Liverpool.

Pitt's difficulty in 1804 was simply one of numbers.
Yes he had some strong and able characters in his Cabinet but
so did the opposition, not least with Fox and Grenville. Pitt's
main issue here was that one half of this alliance had been on
his side only a few years before and whereas his Cabinet was
all made up of his supporters, Fox and Grenville had small
armies of their own followers that made up a strong opposition.
The final factor was entirely his own doing; the rift he had
created with Henry Addington. Addington by this time had a

loyal following of his own[1] and although he was not allied in any sense to Grenville or Fox – both of whom Addington felt had treated him heinously – he was certainly in opposition to Pitt.

In three short years the entire landscape of Parliament had changed. Pitt would find that he could no longer pass through any legislation he wished to unchallenged. It would take every bit of his sharp mind and political instinct just to survive and many of his old difficulties still existed: within the first two months of his taking office the controversial issue of the abolition of the slave trade reared its head. In 1789 his attempt to end this inhumane trade was filibustered with a piece of legislation which satisfied nobody; it contained a pledge to end the trade at some point without specifying a time limit. Now William Wilberforce, possibly sensing a more sympathetic ear to his cause with the return of Pitt, decided to force the issue back onto the agenda. The Prime Minister spoke passionately in favour of outright abolition but once again the House of Lords defeated the motion.

That same summer he would have to fight just to keep his Cabinet together after his long term friend, George Canning, stirred trouble by making a speech in the Commons during a debate on the government's Additional Force Bill. Canning, who had caused so much trouble for the Addington administration in his obsessed loyalty to Pitt, decided to take some time on the floor of the House to criticise the previous ministry as severely as he could get away with. The problem was that six of Addington's ministers had stayed on to work for Pitt[2] and so this attack was as much a criticism of current ministers as it was of the outgoing ones. Canning had no doubt been incredibly upset at not having been awarded a position in the government himself, in spite of his unwavering loyalty to Pitt. His speech caused Hawkesbury to tender his resignation in disgust, knowing how close Canning was to the Prime Minister, and Pitt had to work hard to convince him that this was not the right course of action.[3] In itself this was not a huge issue but it added to a burdensome workload which would mount over the coming months and years and would eventually lead to the death of the Prime Minister.

Just to add to the strain Pitt was once again managing the country at a time of war and with no allies yet established. He was, as back in the 1790s, convinced of the need for a coalition to defeat his foreign enemy, and so his finite energies were further sapped by negotiations with Austria, Prussia and Russia. Meanwhile, the coalition against Britain was about to expand. Napoleon was receiving financial assistance from Spain for his war efforts. British intelligence concluded that the Spanish were importing gold bullion onto the continent for payment to the French and that it was probable that upon receiving the next import, they may offer direct military assistance rather than paying such heavy subsidies. Regardless of which course of action the Spanish took, France was going to benefit either with an ally in their war efforts or with a huge amount of gold to finance their military. Pitt decided that this was unacceptable and, in spite of not being at war with Spain, he sent a fleet out into the Atlantic to intercept the Spanish convoy carrying the bullion in September 1804. The opposition in Parliament was relentless in its criticisms but Pitt felt that there was nothing to defend – allowing the money into France was not an option. However, the incident gave Spain the excuse they needed to join the conflict, declaring war on Britain on 14 December.

Pitt's final years in office would be marked by failed attempts at coalition building, both domestically and internationally. Whilst negotiations drew out in Europe, at home he tried to bring Grenville and Fox into his government, apparently accepting that with the status quo the opposition was too strong. It was an unrealistic aim to bring about 'a coalition of all the bitterest enemies of the previous quarter of a century'[4]. The fact was that in spite of Pitt's naïve optimism the King would still not allow Fox to work in his ministry and the exclusion of Fox meant that Grenville would stay away on principle. The only option left for the Prime Minister was to approach Addington for support, however unabashed that may require him to be. The former Prime Minister's following may have been as many as sixty MPs, which would certainly have tipped the balance. The pair met on Christmas Eve, 1804, with Lord Hawkesbury brokering the negotiations. Pitt was prepared to offer Addington and his followers positions in the Cabinet but he insisted that this be accompanied with the condition that Addington accept a peerage. Ultimately Pitt could not countenance the thought of his friend-turned-rival remaining in the Commons next to him. Addington was resistive to this particular issue but Pitt was adamant. Looking back some have argued that 'it is hard to see why Pitt was so bent on forcing Addington into the House of Lords'[5] rather than accepting a much-needed alliance on any terms. Others claim it is obvious that Pitt would want 'to build a ceiling on Addington's career' in order to remove 'one rival from the Commons'.[6] However difficult or otherwise it is to understand, the fact was that Pitt was unmovable and Addington possessed too much respect for his former friend to stand fast against him.

In January 1805 Henry Addington became The Viscount Sidmouth and was named as President of the Council within the government. For now Pitt had his majority in Parliament, although it would be short lived. He had created a government which would surely permit him to pass through whatever legislation he needed to at home, allowing him to focus his attention on building his alliances on the continent. However, fate had other ideas and unforeseen domestic challenges would break Pitt's majority in a very short space of time. Meanwhile, the stresses of all these pressures, still burdening himself with more work than he necessarily had to, would take such a toll on his health that time was not on his side. Rebuilding his majority following the final breakdown with Addington was not something he would live to see.

His troubles for 1805 started with a report from the Commission of Naval Inquiry which had uncovered some financial irregularities from the 1790s. It seemed that one employee of the Admiralty had been using public money for his personal use and that Lord Melville, then Henry Dundas, who had been Treasurer of the Navy at the time, had turned a blind eye. On 8 April 1805 a motion was presented to the House of Commons criticising Melville for his behaviour at the time. This motion would eventually destroy Pitt's coalition. The problem was that Melville was a personal friend of the Prime Minister, had been for decades and Pitt took loyalty very seriously indeed. However, Melville did have enemies in the opposition which meant that the motion could easily succeed and embarrass the government. This would be troublesome but not devastating. What made it so was that Melville also had enemies within the government itself.[7] Many of Addington's followers could not forgive him for his voicing his opinion during their time in power that Pitt's return was desirable. Would government ministers vote against their leader? Or would Pitt, to save face, distance himself from his friend and throw him to the wolves? This latter course of action would be consistent with his view that corruption was abhorrent but his loyalty to his friend was too strong.

Pitt argued strongly in defence of Melville, suggesting that rather than the House condemning him an independent committee should be set up because the report so far could not be trusted. During the debate William Wilberforce, good friends with both Pitt and Melville, stood to declare his support for the motion. Wilberforce, unlike Pitt, always put his own beliefs ahead of his friends.

In the event the result was tied at 216-216. The Speaker then voted for the motion, defeating the government.[8] Pitt had been voted against by enemies from every corner of the House – not just by the opposition but even Addingtonians within his own government. How many other politicians, over the centuries, would find that however talented they were, every vote that isolates just a small number of people means that after a long period in office the numbers would start to work against them?

Pitt was devastated but more to the point, this issue had divided the government and the strong feelings on both sides looked set to fracture the Cabinet further along a Pitt-Sidmouth line. Melville was forced to resign his post of First Lord of the Admiralty which opened up this position in the Cabinet. Pitt had previously promised Sidmouth that more of his supporters could be brought into the ministry as and when vacancies arose but he now felt loath to give anything to the Addingtonians[9] who had caused him so much grief by their disloyalty on this issue. He refused to appoint an Addingtonian to Melville's vacant role and Addington threatened to resign in protest. Pitt convinced him to stay with vague promises of further positions for his supporters in future, but by this point even he seemed unconvinced that their relationship had any longevity. It was simply a matter of surviving for as long as possible.

Not content with Melville's resignation, the opposition put forward further motions for his impeachment and removal from the Privy Council. Pitt fought these initially but, on 6 May and on the advice of Melville himself,[10] he proposed striking his name from the list of Privy Counsellors. The position of defending Melville was unwinnable, so keeping the government afloat was far more practical. He could justify this to himself on the basis that impeachment was preferable to prosecution, which was the only realistic alternative.

The opposition became relentless now, determined to see Pitt either crushingly defeated or slowly eroded by the amount of pressure that was being applied to him. On 13 May Fox and Grenville introduced a motion to the House of Commons in favour of Catholic emancipation, hoping to force him into a corner: the majority of the House were against it but they knew that Pitt was for it, indeed he had resigned over the issue once. On this occasion it was not to be; Pitt stated candidly that although he was personally in favour of emancipation but that it was not the right time for it to be passed into law and so the motion was defeated.

By July it became clear to Addington that Pitt was never going to see through his promises of Cabinet positions for his followers, but for Pitt the last straw had been during the debates about impeaching Melville: Addingtonians had overwhelmingly been in support, not just of impeachment, but of a criminal prosecution, which Pitt viewed as nothing short of vindictive. On 4 July 1805 Sidmouth resigned from the government. Pitt's hopes of a large majority in Parliament were ended once and for all. There was nobody who could replace him for the time being but his government would be a minority one for the foreseeable future.[11]

During the summer it became apparent that Napoleon had stationed forces along the north coast of France ready for an invasion that would never come. A combination of the wrong winds, British naval defences of the Channel and an uncoordinated French naval strategy meant that his army would be prepared but never utilised for this. From the British point of view there was no scenario more desirable: forces waiting to mobilise without actually being deployed were likely to suffer from low morale. In September 1805 Napoleon finally gave up on this plan in favour of moving his armies eastwards. Austria and Russia had signed an alliance with Britain that month and so the First Consul wanted to see them defeated as soon as possible. At around the same time Admiral Nelson visited Pitt in Downing Street where he was instructed to sail to the Mediterranean and destroy the Spanish and French ships which were stationed at Cadiz. An absolute victory, the sort that only Nelson could produce, was needed for the morale of the country and for assuring British domination of the seas for the long-term future. They had evidently planned for a spectacle but they could have no idea that they had just organised the most famous naval engagement in history. The real tragedy is that whilst both men would live to know that Britain won at Trafalgar, neither would be alive for much longer than three months after this, their last meeting.

The war for the next few months consisted of great highs and terrible lows, but could not be described as uninteresting. It followed the same formula that it had before hostilities had ceased in 1802, with Britain dominating the seas and France seemingly unbeatable on land. On 19 October, only a month after declaring war on France, Austria had suffered a terrible defeat at Ulm and it seemed that Napoleon's army would continue on to Vienna. The Austrians had been taken completely by surprise by the speed of Napoleon's land forces and had been outclassed at every turn on the battlefield.

Two days later, on 21 October, a battle raged at sea off the south-west coast of Spain, near Cape Trafalgar. Twenty-seven British ships fought against a combined French and Spanish fleet of thirty-three ships. The French and Spanish had twenty-two of their ships destroyed whilst Britain didn't lose a single vessel. Leading his sailors into battle with the signal 'England expects that every man will do his duty' Nelson's victory was decisive and made all the more famous for the fact that he died seeing it through.[12]

Due to the nature of communications in the early nineteenth century it was several weeks before news of Trafalgar reached Pitt, and this a fair while after news of Ulm had broken in Britain. That autumn would see Pitt desperately negotiating with Prussia for their entry into the war, because Austria had been so heavily weakened. He felt that Britain's fortunes against the French depended now on securing Prussian support. However, news from then on would only get worse. On 2 December Austrian and Russian armies were destroyed at the Battle of Austerlitz by the French. Within three months of learning that Austria and Russia had entered the war, Napoleon had successfully driven them out of it. Now there was no grand coalition of nations opposing him and, therefore, Prussia saw no reason to get involved.

At the beginning of December 1805 Pitt had travelled to Bath to try to restore his health, which had deteriorated rapidly over the preceding months, by bathing in the waters there. He was there when he received the news that Austria and Russia had been beaten out of the war, that Prussia would no longer get involved and that his plans for a continental coalition were shattered. He is said to have taken the news badly, and many of his contemporaries as well as modern historians believed that this accelerated the decline in his health.[13] Whether or not this is true, Pitt would now never again grace the House of Commons with his presence, or indeed make another public speech.

On 9 January 1806 he left Bath still extremely poorly, returning to London in time for the opening of Parliament, due on 21 January. His friends became aware sometime around the 14th or 15th that he was probably dying and they were aware, too, that without Pitt, the Tories could not survive in government. They were barely able to function with him. He had been ordered to rest by his doctor but couldn't keep himself away from the affairs of state, taking regular updates from whatever visitors he had. The difficulty with having been intertwined so heavily with politics for so long was that all of Pitt's friends were also his colleagues and advisors.

Parliament was opened without Pitt on 21 January, as by this point he was completely bedridden. On Wednesday 22 January he lived out his last day. Accounts from those with him claim that he became delusional into the night, crying out 'Hear Hear!' as though he were on the benches in the House of Commons. At about half past two on the morning of Thursday 23 January 1806 he is alleged to have exclaimed 'Oh, my country! how I leave my country!'[14] and then passed away.

The events that occurred after his death almost serve to demonstrate the story of Pitt's life. His Cabinet colleagues realised that they could not continue in office and subsequently resigned. King George realised that he could no longer prevent the formation of a ministry without Fox, so he appointed Grenville as Prime Minister with Fox as Foreign Secretary. This was Pitt's legacy: keeping Whigs such as Fox out of government. His second term in office was less successful than the first and again left many things incomplete: the war with France was ongoing at the time of his death; he had given up completely on achieving Catholic emancipation; slavery was not yet abolished. But the second term, much like the first, meant that those who would conciliate with France and turn a blind eye to her oppression rather than stand up to Napoleon would not get a chance to govern. As long as Pitt lived, Fox could not be a minister, and that was his real achievement.

There were positives to be taken away from this second term in office. The British people were no longer living with the threat of invasion thanks to Nelson's obliteration of both the Spanish and French fleets at Trafalgar. In fact, Britain would dominate naval warfare for well over a hundred years following Pitt's death. Yes, the war with France was going badly, the coalition had crumbled and Napoleon looked unstoppable on the continent, but if Britain walked away from the war the day after Trafalgar at least the people could live without the worry of being attacked by the greatest army the planet had ever witnessed. This security was something that could not have been guaranteed just a few months before Pitt's demise.

Ultimately, though, Pitt's commitment to politics killed him, and in many ways he knew it would. He was a bachelor for his entire life, unwilling to dedicate himself to anything that was not service to his country. He was overworked, stressed, drank too much alcohol on the advice of his physicians and this was a deadly combination. The Greek hero, Achilles, was once presented by his mother with two options for how his life would unfold. He claimed she told him that if 'I play my part in the siege of Troy, there is no home-coming for me, though I shall win undying fame. But if I go home to my own country, my good name will be lost, though I shall have a long life, and shall be spared an early death'[15]. This seems appropriate for Pitt. Had he never entered politics and instead served as a lawyer, which he was qualified to do, he may have lived a lot longer, although would eventually have faded into obscurity. Instead he worked for his country, died at the age of 46, unmarried and with no descendants. No family surrounded his bedside or mourned his passing but his name is known two centuries later even by those who are most ignorant of political history.

Spencer Perceval
(1806 – 1812)

I have nothing to say to the nothing that has been said

Spencer Perceval, May 1809

Prey thee Whig, grow wise, and do not torment thy self with State-Affairs; let Princes take care of themselves, and the People of themselves

Daniel Defoe's *Tory*, 1692

UPON THE DEATH OF THEIR LEADER the Tories fell into disarray and to some degree this is understandable. Party politics was not then as structured as it is today and there was neither a clear line of succession nor a single individual well respected enough to command a majority in Parliament. Resigning and handing power over to their enemies was probably the right thing to do. This is exactly what they did, leaving the King with no choice but to accept a Whig ministry. Grenville came to power with what would be known as 'The Ministry of All The Talents',[1] bringing in all the most capable people including himself and Fox.

Historians are divided on which of 'Pitt's Friends' became leader of the Tories from this point onwards as the major names all seem to have gone back to leading their own core factions. Many claim that it was surely the Duke of Portland[2] for he would be the first to become Prime Minister once the Ministry of All The Talents burnt itself out a year after forming. However, Portland always maintained that he was a Whig and only went into coalition with Pitt as a matter of convenience and influence for his supporters. Also, his becoming Prime Minister was a means for Pitt's Friends to regain power whilst bringing Portland's own supporters into the new government, rather than leaving them on the opposition benches. The real influence lay with the Chancellor of the Exchequer (Pitt had been both Prime Minister and Chancellor of the Exchequer during his own time), who in this instance was Spencer Perceval.

Some historians claim that the real leader of the Tories was Lord Hawkesbury[3] who, once he inherited the title of Lord Liverpool would go on to be Prime Minister for fifteen years. When Pitt died King George offered Hawkesbury the chance to form a ministry but with Addington having deserted them due to the fallout with Pitt, Hawkesbury saw no way to form a government able to survive. This made Addington's next moves all the more unforgivable in the eyes of the Tories: Grenville wanted to form a ministry with all the brightest and most capable people serving. Pitt's most loyal supporters refused to join but Addington, feeling that having a chance to influence the government[4] rather than letting the Whigs run away with themselves, accepted. George Canning and even Spencer Perceval saw this as a complete betrayal,[5] particularly when Hawkesbury could have formed a Tory government of his own had Addington made himself available. However, as influential as Hawkesbury was, his day was to come later on, once Perceval had died. In the meantime the latter pulled more strings.

Then there was George Canning and Lord Castlereagh, both of whom commanded a sizeable number of votes in the Commons. Canning, Pitt's staunchest supporter, and Castlereagh who himself had also always been steadfast for Pitt, were opposed on many areas of policy and shared a personal enmity[6] surpassed only by that of Pitt and Fox. Canning would go on to be Prime Minister one day and both men would be highly influential in every government for the next fifteen (Castlereagh) to twenty (Canning) years. However, it was their feud with each other that most affected the ministries they were involved in, rather than any personal following or genuine influence that they held. Therefore, neither could ever really be considered the leader of the Tories at this point in time.

It was Spencer Perceval, a hard-working and dedicated man, who took the reins; lawyer by trade and evangelical Christian by religion, which guided his decision-making on any issue which could be considered one of morality. This in itself, though, occasionally led to questionable judgments. For example, he was opposed to the slave trade as a matter of principle but also opposed to Catholic emancipation as he felt it represented a threat to the British establishment. Perceval appears to have felt obligated to try to keep the disparate factions of Tories united in some semblance of opposition, weak in number but strong in character,[7] much like Fox and Charles Grey had done with the Whigs in the 1790s.

When the Ministry of All The Talents took office in February 1806 Perceval found that there was not a great deal to oppose. The ministry was divided over the war with France with Grenville being in favour of war but his Whig allies all being in favour of peace. Consequently nothing was settled upon and the conflict half-heartedly dragged on. The Ministry's crowning achievement would be passing legislation abolishing the slave trade. Again this was largely supported by Perceval personally and by the opposition benches generally, with the body of the legislature on this occasion not having a 'Saint Domingue' to terrify them into opposing abolition.

Perceval hadn't foregone practising law whilst serving as either an MP or minister and this continued through to the opposition years. For him, the easy job that the Ministry of All The Talents gave the opposition by keeping their legislative agenda as benevolent as they did gave him more time to practice law and bring in a decent salary doing so. In this field, though, he would encounter far more controversy, which could quite easily spill over into his political career. During the first half of 1806 he took on two high-profile civil cases, notable because in both instances the Prince of Wales had a vested interest in the outcome and in both instances Perceval was on the opposing side to his future King. Both cases ran at the same time. In the first case one Mrs Fitzherbert, the Prince of Wales' mistress (or first wife, depending on your point of view) with whom he was very much in love had been the adoptive mother of an orphan named Minney Seymour. However, the guardians named in Minney's father's will had, after some time, decided that they were unhappy with this arrangement, not least because Mrs Fitzherbert was a Catholic. They decided to challenge the custody arrangement through the courts, eventually going through the Court of Appeal and House of Lords. Perceval acted as counsel for the guardians and, of course, the Prince of Wales stood by Mrs Fitzherbert. Eventually, due in no small part to some arm-twisting of Law Lords by the Prince, the decision went in Mrs Fitzherbert's favour in June 1806.

Simultaneously the Prince of Wales' wife, Caroline, whom he despised, had been accused of illegitimately mothering a child which, if true, would give the Prince grounds for a divorce, which he desperately coveted. An inquiry was set up which established that she had acted improperly in the company of others but that there was no evidence of any illegitimate children borne of her. This occurred in the July of 1806, just one month after the Seymour episode. King George still decided on the back of this that Caroline was no longer welcome in his household, until Perceval got involved. Acting on behalf of Princess Caroline he wrote to the King stressing that she had done no wrong and so should not be ill-treated. Eventually the relationship between the monarch and his daughter-in-law was smoothed over, much to the chagrin of the Prince of Wales. Clearly upsetting the future King in such a personal manner twice within the space of a month was not the most sensible thing for an aspiring politician to do, but the situation does demonstrate the extent to which Perceval was driven by justness (or at least his perception of it) above his own ambition.

In September 1806 Charles James Fox died. He had been ill for a while but more than one historian has suggested that following Pitt's demise Fox simply lost his *raison d'être*. There is little doubt that he will have died disappointed. During his brief return to power as Foreign Secretary he tried to achieve his long term ambition of achieving peace with France, in spite of Grenville's opposition to it. It was only now, at the very end of his life, that he began to understand Napoleon's intransigence. Perhaps this man was in fact a dictator and not just the tragic victim of a tyrannical monarchy as the Whigs had believed for so long.[8]

Fox's death threatened to throw the government into disarray. This government referred to itself as a Ministry of All The Talents but it was far less comprehensive than its name suggests: Perceval had been offered a position but had declined; Hawkesbury did not feel able to serve; Wilberforce enjoyed his time as an independent campaigning for the issues he was passionate about such as abolition of the slave trade. In fact Charles Grey, Lord Grenville, Lord Sidmouth and Charles James Fox had really been a quadrumvirate of talent within a mediocre ministry. Now Fox had died and Sidmouth was looking increasingly isolated as he differed with his colleagues over the issue of Catholic emancipation, leaving the government looking weak. On 23 October Parliament was dissolved and an election called. The result was that the number of Addingtonians in the Commons fell,[9] which put Sidmouth in even more of a difficult position during the disputes that were to come.

The trouble had been building for a while. Unrest had been growing in Ireland over the rights of the citizens there not being recognised as they had been led to believe that they would be following the Act of Union. In order to appease the disaffected masses, the government settled on making a concession in the form of allowing Catholics to hold military office up to the rank of Colonel (but no higher) in England, Scotland or Wales (they already could in Ireland). However, to Sidmouth this was unacceptable. He felt that such a concession would be the thin end of the emancipation wedge, against which he was resolutely opposed. He clashed with his Cabinet colleagues over the issue, his position being weakened by his dwindling support following the election but a thorn in Grenville's side nonetheless. A big problem form Grenville was that Sidmouth was still a favourite of the King, whose support would be essential for the passage of any legislation giving away rights to Catholics.

Eventually Sidmouth was convinced that giving the Irish in the United Kingdom the same rights that they enjoyed in Ireland was a natural consequence of Union and he was despatched to convince the King of the same. However, it seems that the government were not entirely sure what had been settled upon and, when communicating with the Lord Lieutenant of Ireland who was to pass on the proposals to Irish leaders, the ministry suggested that all military offices would be open to Catholics throughout the UK, not just those up to the rank of Colonel.

Once the King found out about these communications he made his rage clear to his ministers. He would not give Catholics rights beyond those already applicable to them in Ireland and that was the end of the matter.[10] In March 1807 ministers made it clear that they would defer to the monarch but publicly stated that they believed him to be wrong. Now their days were numbered. The King turned his attention from Grenville and Grey to Hawkesbury, Portland and Perceval. This would mark the end of Perceval's legal career as the responsibilities of public office consumed too much of his time to allow him to continue.

On 31 March the Duke of Portland was invited to form a government, mainly because he was a high profile figure who could unite the Tories, but the reality of the situation was that he was beyond being fit for the responsibilities of high office. He was now two weeks away from his 69th birthday and his health was poor. Perceval was appointed as Chancellor of the Exchequer which gave him the bulk of power within the government (Pitt and Addington had held the office of Chancellor as well as that of Prime Minister when in power. Grenville had ended the practice which worked out well for Portland who would not have been up to the challenge had he been required to hold both). As well as being *de facto* leader of the government Perceval would be *de jure* leader in the House of Commons.

There is no doubt that Perceval had contributed heavily to the downfall of the Talents. He had risen to speak, as he saw it, in defence of the Protestant Church and had written into newspapers staunchly opposing emancipation as a dangerous proposition. The Talents' crowning achievement had certainly been the passing of legislation which would allow for the abolition of slavery. Perceval was in favour of this and managed to secure support from Wilberforce and his followers for the Portland administration on the basis that the final passage of this legislation would not be opposed.[11]

Other familiar names returned to the Cabinet with Perceval and Portland, including Canning as Foreign Secretary (which, in turn meant that there could be no place for Sidmouth due to the enmity between the two men harking back to *The Pilot That Weathered The Storm*) and Castlereagh as Secretary of State for War. Almost as soon as they took office the new government decided to go to the King to dissolve Parliament for the second time in seven months. The idea was to increase their majority and the resurfacing of the issue of emancipation gave them the platform on which to do it: the Tories intended to play on the fears of the electorate over emancipation by pushing a No Popery theme which they claimed was a defence for their position of ardent establishmentarianism.

Once the election was completed and the Tories returned to power with a comfortable majority,[12] the main issue facing the government was the ongoing war with France (the spectre of emancipation need not be raised again, and the anti-slavery legislation would pass through with little work necessary). In 1807 Canning became aware of intelligence that Napoleon intended to capture the Danish naval fleet to utilise against the Royal Navy. In a decisive move Canning ordered that the Royal Navy should seize the Danish fleet first so as not to allow the French to increase its military strength. British ships approached Copenhagen and presented a naïve proposal that the Danes should surrender their ships to Britain for safeguarding against the French, on the proviso that they would be returned at the end of hostilities. Of course this was rejected and so the navy bombarded the city of Copenhagen with artillery until they agreed to forfeit their entire fleet, which were then incorporated into the Royal Navy.

Supporters of the government congratulated Canning on taking a strong stance in difficult circumstances. Opponents suggested (and given what we know about Canning's ruthlessness and hot-headedness it is not difficult to understand why they would think this of him) that Canning had maliciously attacked a neutral nation, which was a friend of Britain, to achieve a cheap and easy improvement to the size of the navy.[13]

The war developed further in 1808 when Britain once again committed ground troops to the continent, this time on the Iberian Peninsula. 'The Peninsula Campaign' is where the tactical and leadership abilities of Sir Arthur Wellesley, who would become honoured later as the Duke of Wellington, came to light.

Portland's health continued to deteriorate and, more and more his able ministers such as Canning and Perceval came to make the decisions that affected the country whether abroad (Canning) or at home (Perceval). During the last few months of Portland's premiership tensions within the Cabinet rose with the long-standing feud between Canning and Castlereagh coming to a head. In March 1809 Canning wrote to Portland stressing his determined belief that Castlereagh must be removed from the government (he was currently serving as Minister of War). Portland ended up agreeing with Canning, probably owing to a growing need for him to shy away from confrontation due to his weakening health. Perceval found out about the plan at some time in the spring of 1809, Castlereagh still being completely ignorant of the discussions, and told Portland in no uncertain terms that with the various military expeditions that the government had planned imminently, now was not the time to remove the Minister of War. Both Portland

and the King deferred to Perceval on the issue of Castlereagh's removal.

What we now know to be the Walcheren Campaign was a military push by British troops in the Netherlands which commenced in the summer of 1809. It went terribly badly, which Castlereagh, understandably, took the blame for. When Parliament reconvened in the September Canning used this new turn of events to push once again for Castlereagh's removal from the Cabinet but Portland was clearly in no position even to fulfil the most basic of his constitutional duties. His health was failing him and it became clear to his supporters that they would need to find a successor sooner rather than later. Of all the ambitions collecting within the government, outsiders saw Portland's potential successor as being one of two people: Perceval, who maintained that he was not interested but seemed to have a large amount of support from his ministerial colleagues; and Canning who desperately wanted it but what little support he did have he would squander away in the immediate future.

Castlereagh discovered Canning's renewed push for his removal and, along with it, the whole saga which had gone on behind his back over the spring with Portland, King George and Canning all plotting his demise. He was infuriated and resigned from the Cabinet immediately. However, he still required satisfaction from Canning for his deceitful actions and so he challenged him to a duel. Perceval desperately tried to prevent this, telling Castlereagh that in spite of what had happened Canning had wanted to be open with him throughout about his views. His sway was not enough and, on 21 September, two members of the government met for a duel on Putney Heath. In the event Castlereagh wounded Canning in the upper thigh. He had achieved his satisfaction and, possibly more gratifying, the whole affair had damaged Canning to such an extent that he was no longer considered a serious contender for the role of Prime Minister.

Portland offered his resignation to the King at the end of September, staying on for a week or so to ensure that Perceval was officially named as his successor. Perceval took over on 4 October 1809 and Portland died less than four weeks later. Canning, in a characteristically self-destructive move motivated more by emotion than reason, refused to serve in the new ministry.

Perceval's government would be under extreme pressure from the off. The Peninsula Campaign was still raging on and the entire balance of the war seemed to rest on British success or failure there. Perceval's credentials in leading the campaign were strengthened by the addition to his ministry of Richard Wellesley, General Arthur Wellesley's elder brother, as Foreign Secretary. Meanwhile the government took heavy criticism from the opposition for the Walcheren debacle[14] (British forces had planned to attack the French station in Antwerp but, upon capturing the island of Walcheren to use as a base, thousands of soldiers contracted Malaria and died. The expedition was doomed from that point on), and the first year or so would see them being attacked by most sections of the media. This latest problem was over an issue not created by ministers but for which they came down on the wrong side and were berated accordingly.

The media difficulties started in February 1810 when ministers were being examined by a Committee of Inquiry into the Walcheren expedition. Charles Yorke, then not a government minister but a man certainly aspiring to be (he would be brought into the Cabinet in May 1810 as First Lord of the Admiralty) enforced a standing order requiring the removal of all strangers from the House during the Inquiry. He probably felt that he was doing ministers a favour by sparing them the glare of the public eye during this embarrassing examination. Supporters of the freedom of the press launched a protest by placing placards around Westminster, demanding their right to watch and report on proceedings within. Yorke responded by summonsing John Gale Jones, one of the instigators of the protestors to the House to justify his actions. The result was that Gale Jones was sent to prison. When Sir Francis Burdett MP spoke out in favour of the rights of the press the House voted for him to be sent to the Tower of London, which Perceval supported.[14] The government had not initiated the argument, but when forced to choose they had come down on the side of oppression. Rioting shortly ensued and only when Gale Jones was released did it abate. Burdett was released two months later during the summer recess but the whole saga had stained the government.

The end of the riots was a far cry from being the end of Perceval's problems. The Regency crisis that had once plagued

William Pitt and led to arguably the most difficult predicament of his two decades in power was about to rear its ugly head once again. In October 1810 King George started to suffer with bouts of the madness that had attacked him so many times in the past and by December it became clear that a Regent was needed. The Cabinet settled on a Regency based on the proposals put forward by William Pitt in 1788 with all the same limitations on power.

The Prince was unhappy with this; he already despised Perceval following their clashes during the legal cases of Mrs Fitzherbert and Princess Caroline and now his enemy was attempting to restrict his power. When Perceval introduced his Regency Bill into Parliament Prince George ensured that all of his Whig allies opposed it[15] with passionate speeches in the House, but it was not enough. Perceval had a majority in Parliament and he was able to steer the legislation through restricting the powers of the Regent for a period of twelve months. This is not to say that the legislation as approved by Perceval was not without its risks. The fact was that restricted or not, the Prince was still the Regent and he had the power to install and remove the Prime Minister. This meant that Perceval's position was far from secure and certainly the Whigs felt that their time to return to power had come. However, the Prince refrained from making any sweeping changes to government. It seems that he was held back by a combination of fear that his father would make a recovery and reprimand him; the fact that Charles James Fox was now dead and so the Prince was not as strongly affiliated with the Whigs as he once was, and certainly not on a personal level; and the fact that regardless of how sycophantic the Whigs were towards him, this new generation's views diverged from his own on a number of key issues, not least the war with France (of which the Prince was a vehement supporter) and Catholic emancipation (which he was against, notwithstanding the religion of his beloved mistress).

In February 1811 the Prince of Wales was sworn in as Regent for his father, George III and, for now, Perceval was to remain as Prime Minister. However, the problems he faced deepened. Britain entered a difficult economic period, which was always a basis for discontent. The problems were that the war with France cost money and the French had disturbed overseas trade as a tactic to win the war (which the British responded to by taking the same course of action and intercepting any cargo ships bound for or leaving France). The industrial revolution had begun which, although would technically increase competitiveness and improve trade for those areas that embraced it, meant that machines were starting to be used to do the jobs of people. The first industries that saw this were the textiles industries, where knitting machines were used to produce goods at a faster rate than their human counterparts. Skilled knitters in the East Midlands responded to what they saw as a threat to their livelihoods by smashing machines. They became known as 'Luddites' and their methods soon spread across the country. Perceval tried to combat this by introducing legislation specifically criminalising the destruction of machinery.

The Orders in Council which directed the navy to search and seize any cargo ship believed to be trading with France had caused the US Congress to pass the Embargo Act 1807 and the Non Intercourse Act 1809, both of which placed an embargo on trade with the United Kingdom and with France due to their annoyance at their ships being intercepted by both navies. Trade with the US was affected, the fact that the Royal Navy was stopping ships from neutral countries trading with France meant that the French navy could not stop doing the same for nations trading with Britain, meaning that trade with almost everywhere was affected. The people of the country blamed the Orders in Council for causing the depression and the government came under heavy pressure to repeal them. Perceval was reluctant, arguing defiantly that France had started the trade war, France would not relent and so the government had a duty to force British interests overseas rather than rolling over and accepting Napoleon's behaviour. However, as pressure built up throughout the year the government agreed in April 1812 to establish a committee to consider the issue.

On Thursday 7 May 1812 Henry Brougham MP suggested that the committee meet that coming Saturday, which Perceval objected to. Brougham then proposed the following Monday at 4.30 p.m., which Perceval accepted. Objecting to the Saturday in favour of the Monday was probably one of the more trivial decisions that Perceval ever had to make as Prime Minister, yet its consequences would be unprecedentedly tragic.

On Monday 11 May, at a little after 4.30p.m., in the Palace of Westminster, Brougham voiced his annoyance that Perceval had not bothered to show up on time. The committee carried on in his absence. At around 5.15p.m., forty five minutes after he was due to arrive, Spencer Perceval walked into the lobby of the Palace of Westminster and was approached by a man named John Bellingham, who he had never met before in his life. Bellingham withdrew a pistol from his jacket and shot Perceval in the chest from point blank range. Perceval shouted 'I am murdered!'[16] and collapsed, dying shortly afterwards.

Bellingham had been imprisoned in Russia some years earlier following a dispute with some locals over money. He had pleaded with authority figures within the government such as Lord Granville Leveson Gower, the British Ambassador in St Petersburg, to intervene to have him freed, but they hadn't. Since then he had held a grudge which had festered. On 11 May 1812 he had entered Westminster intending to kill somebody high up in the government. It didn't have to be Perceval. But Bellingham had entered the palace at 5p.m. and Perceval was the first minister who had entered the lobby while he was there. Had Perceval been on time for his meeting, someone else may have been Bellingham's victim that day.

Perceval is the only Prime Minister in history to have been assassinated. However, apart from his spectacular death he had a very un-spectacular ministerial career, ascending to the highest office in the land *faute de mieux*, given that Pitt, Fox and Portland were dead; Grenville had fallen out with the King; Canning had been shot by another minister for his skulduggery and Hawkesbury (since elevated to the Lord as the Earl of Liverpool) didn't feel ready. During his short tenure in office he did not introduce any radical legislation but acted as a transitional character – he aided the transition from the long Pitt-dominated years to the long Liverpool-dominated years that were to come. He regrouped the Tories following the death of their leader and kept the war with France going. However, whereas his predecessors as Prime Minister passed the Act of Union and abolished slavery and his successors defeated Napoleon, gave relief to Catholics and passed the Reform Act, it is not difficult to see why history has all but forgotten Spencer Perceval. His most famous act was, and remains, the way he died.

Robert Jenkinson, 2nd Earl of Liverpool
(1806 – 1827)

To concede every thing and propose nothing was a course of
Administration neither creditable for the government, nor safe for
the Country

Lord Liverpool, November 1822

I undertake that all the Tories in England…shall take the Oaths of
the King, and serve him heartily, provided he will do one
thing…Utterly discard you Whigs, and give us the Penal Laws again
upon the Fanaticks

Daniel Defoe's *Tory*, 1692

BECAUSE SPENCER PERCEVAL is, to date, the only Prime
Minister to have been assassinated, there was no precedent for
how the government should have reacted. In the days where
political parties were still in their infantile stages, with chains
of command and lines of succession blurry at best, non-existent
at worst, it was almost impossible for the government to know
how to go on. Three years previously, Perceval had been
selected to lead the country not on the basis that he was an
incredible leader, but simply that nobody else was and he was
probably the most tolerable. There had been no new additions
to the top posts in government since then and, given the fact that
there had been no general election there was no change in the
composition of members in the House of Commons. So who to
lead a new government out of those who were passed over last
time? Could the government even continue or would they have
to resign?

In another move indicative of his evolving political
loyalties, the Prince of Wales made it clear that he wanted the
Tories to remain in power, at least for the time being, under
whichever leader they saw fit. When the Cabinet met to discuss
this they were hopelessly divided on what they could
realistically achieve, or even how they should go about trying.[1]

Four months earlier, in the February of 1812, Richard Wellesley
had resigned from Perceval's government over the issue of
Catholic emancipation, for which he was strongly in favour. He
was now making overtures towards leading the group in a new
administration. The Cabinet were all agreed that they could not
work under Wellesley and that instead, one of their number
should become the new leader. However, there was no
consensus on whether they could survive without any further
additions to their group and those who were convinced that they
needed further support could not agree on who to approach.[2]
Suggested names were Wellesley, Canning, Grenville and
Grey. Many still couldn't stomach the thought of working with
Grenville or Grey, whereas others felt that without their support
a new government would be doomed. Castlereagh and Canning
were still unlikely to be able to work together (although both
asserted that the other's presence would not be an obstacle).
　　　Perceval was buried on 16 May and it appears that on
this day the Cabinet had accepted that they should continue on
with Robert Jenkinson, Lord Liverpool (previously Lord
Hawkesbury until his father's death in December 1808) as their
leader. On 17 May Liverpool approached both Canning and
Wellesley with offers to join his government. The following
day, both declined. At the next meeting of Parliament, on 21
May, the new administration presented itself although it was
generally assumed that they were acting in their roles
temporarily as the Prince Regent had the authority to appoint
his ministers and he had not yet made any official decision. At
this session an opposition motion asking the Regent to appoint
'a strong and efficient administration' was carried, the
implication being that the interim administration was neither
strong nor efficient.[3] It was 8 June before the Prince Regent
named Liverpool as his Prime Minister, ending both the
speculation and ambition of his political enemies.
　　　Liverpool was an astute politician, reasoned and
realistic about the limitations of his abilities in the face of
public opinion and the opposition. He was well aware that the
reason he was politically not as strong as he might be at that
point in 1812 was because of the issue of Catholic
emancipation: Wellesley chose to define himself on the matter
and consequently refused to join the government; Canning was
not a single-issue politician but in this instance was willing to

make a stand; Grenville and Grey were opposed to the government on many fundamental issues but none were as close to their hearts as this. So within twenty four hours of being officially appointed Prime Minister by the Prince Regent, Liverpool told his Cabinet that the government would not issue any pro-Catholic legislation but would not formally oppose any introduced by the opposition or independent members.[4] Instead all ministers would be free to vote with their consciences. The intended, and somewhat successful, outcome was that the opposition could no longer criticise or indeed unite against the government for their Catholic position, because they did not formally have one. On the other hand the vested interests including the Crown could not criticise them for being Popish, because that was not their position either. What seems remarkable by twenty first century standards is that what was effectively 'bottling' the issue worked. For once the Cabinet could be united with no major difference of conscience between them.

Lord Sidmouth was appointed as Home Secretary, bringing the Addingtonians back under the umbrella of the government, and Nicolas Vansittart as Chancellor of the Exchequer, where he would stay for eleven years. Now Liverpool could set to making the changes that the country wanted to see, mainly getting the United States of America to lift their trade embargo so that British businesses could improve their revenue streams. With this objective in mind, on 24 June, the Orders in Council were rescinded meaning that the United Kingdom would no longer seize ships from independent countries. However, it was already too late because, on 19 June, the U.S. had declared war.[5] Now the pressures started to mount on the new government as at around the same time Liverpool's Catholic strategy was put to the test through an unexpected loophole. Canning and Wellesley put forward motions in each House (Canning in the Commons, Wellesley in the Lords) that the government should take Catholic claims into consideration after the summer recess. This meant that the new ministry would have to go against its own rule that it would not actively introduce pro-Catholic legislation. The motion was carried in the Commons but, thankfully for Liverpool, defeated by one vote in the Lords.[6]

Once the summer recess was over the government asked the Prince Regent to dissolve Parliament and call an election, which was held in the autumn. Ministers improved their standing in the House of Commons following this election by around thirty seats. The good news was set to continue. Wellesley had had remarkable successes on the Iberian Peninsula during the summer and fears of a strong French resistance were relieved that autumn as Napoleon invaded Russia, which meant that his remaining troops would be heading in the opposite direction from their British enemies. In the December the French army were defeated in battle by the Russians at Smolensk, which may well have marked the turning point of the war.

     A successful leader requires many attributes but one of them is undoubtedly luck. There is no questioning that Liverpool was made Prime Minister out of circumstance, rather than direct ambition, but he had been in the right place at the right time with little in the way of alternatives. Once there, circumstances again seemed to turn favourably for him time and again. He had not organised for Napoleon to turn east, yet he had. This pattern would continue into 1813, during which time the first of many benevolent turns came in the first couple of months when George Canning decided to give up on formal opposition. He had evidently become dismayed at how little influence he had. Although he commanded a decent and loyal following, relative to his hero Pitt, who had influenced scores of MPs with every word he had uttered, his own speeches – which often came across more like tirades – seemed to have relatively little effect. He hoped to be embraced by the government as a new member and asset, but the Addingtonians had longer memories than he would have liked and they refused to have him back.[7]

     British success in Spain and Russian successes in the east convinced Prussia and Sweden to join the war against France in the spring of 1813 and by the autumn the question had not become who would win, rather *when* France would surrender. At this point Liverpool was overtly considering what terms he would impose on the French in the event of their surrender, apparently resolving himself not to place too great a strain on them and not even to try to impose the restoration of the monarchy. His rather modest position was that France should be reduced to its pre-war size, Napoleon could stay on as leader if he so wished and Spain and Holland should be independent, which was essential for British security. The reason for his not pushing for more was that he didn't want the French to feel aggrieved, giving them an excuse to return to their expansionist ways in the future.

The allies soon invaded France from all sides and captured Paris, Napoleon hearing the news whilst en route back from his failed Russian campaign. He ordered his generals to march on the capital and, when they refused, he knew that he had finally lost the war. In April 1814 he abdicated, which meant that the Bourbon dynasty could reclaim the French throne with the accession of King Louis XVIII. The allies exiled Napoleon to the island of Elba, just off the Italian coast, while allowing him to keep around six hundred men as a personal guard.

Wellesley, who had since been created as the Marquess of Wellington, returned to Britain to be made a Duke as the hero of the Napoleonic Wars. At this point it was widely believed that a lasting peace in Europe would be enjoyed. The summer went well for the government as a euphoria swept the country due to the end of hostilities. Canning left the country having been appointed Special Embassy to Lisbon and his followers subsequently re-joined government benches in both Houses of Parliament.[8] The end of 1814, then, marked the occasion that more original Pittites (including followers of the Duke of Portland, Viscount Sidmouth and George Canning) were united than at any other time since Pitt's first tenure in office ended, twelve years earlier. With the exception of Grenville and his supporters all of the various defected factions were now reunited with each other.

With the war in Europe seemingly settled and his popularity at a high, Liverpool could turn his attention to trying to end the war with America. Britain had never wanted to be involved in conflict with the United States and Liverpool was not determined to press for any unreasonable demands to end it now. Throughout the conflict, the U.S. had tried on several occasions to invade Canada, being met with honourable resistance by the locals who were determined to stay loyal to the Commonwealth. For Liverpool, a *status quo ante bellum* would be a more than acceptable conclusion to the fighting. However, negotiations with America protracted, as did negotiations in Europe over a post-Napoleonic-war settlement. In this latter consultation Liverpool dreamed of drawing a new treaty for Europe in which all nations were assigned roles, all were allies of each other and all could be governed by collectively agreed legislation, enforced by the various member states.[9] This was much a similar vision to that which William Pitt had envisaged when desperately searching for a peace with France during the Revolutionary Wars in the 1790s. It is a similar ethos to that of the modern European Union drawn up nearly a century and a half after Liverpool's tenure in office.

All of the allied nations sent envoys to meet in Vienna to discuss how Europe would be divided (Castlereagh, as Foreign Secretary, attended to represent the United Kingdom). Liverpool was determined that the Netherlands should be safeguarded as a key neighbour to Britain, assisting with both domestic trade and security. He was also adamant that the Iberian states should be independent. However, there were other questions which needed settling, such as the fate of Poland. Both Austria and Russia saw themselves as rightful owners of this part of the continent. Consequently negotiations dragged on and as they did the dreaded prospect if yet another war in Europe grew more realistic by the day.

By Christmas 1814 all hope of a peaceful settlement seemed lost. Castlereagh was instructed to return to Britain to be replaced at Vienna by the Duke of Wellington. Once the Foreign Secretary returned, the Cabinet would be able to face Parliament together. However, during this same period news reached Liverpool that Castlereagh had signed a defensive military agreement with France and Austria on behalf of Britain. It seems that Prussia was willing to accept Russian annexation of Poland if, in exchange for their own loss of land there, Russia would support Prussian control of Saxony, to which Austria also had a claim. The agreement between Britain, France and Austria was to act militarily should Prussia attempt to take control of Saxony. This had not explicitly been sanctioned by Liverpool but once he found out about it he stood by his Foreign Secretary[10] and sold the agreement as a government position.

Early into the 1815 parliamentary session Liverpool began to feel vindicated in bringing Castlereagh home. The government lacked oratorical strength in the House of Commons, with Liverpool and Melville holding the fort in the Lords. Castlereagh was a competent debater – though not as eloquent as Pitt, nor as emotive as Fox, not as calm and reasoned as Liverpool nor aggressive as Canning – he had his own style and although he would probably be outperformed by any of those four men, thankfully none of them were standing against him in 1815.

Meanwhile one domestic issue which seemed to be a short-term one in 1815, but would actually play a significant part in nineteenth century politics, was the price of corn. The consequences of this matter would dominate economic theory right up until the present day. This had nearly halved over the previous decade[11] and although this meant cheaper prices for the masses, the international competition, now opened more widely due to the abolition of various embargoes, meant that prices would be driven down further causing difficulty for farmers. During the war although prices had fallen British farmers had enjoyed a steady revenue stream from the fact that the public could not readily access imports. Now that they were in competition with cheaper alternatives their trade was neither as lucrative nor as secure.

Liverpool was instinctively a free market economist, a votary of Adam Smith. However, there is no doubt that he felt the pressure from vested interests building up during 1815 and he started to waver. Firstly, there was clearly a majority in Parliament who wanted to see British farmers protected;[12] secondly agriculture was Britain's largest industry at this time and exposing it to any form of risk was bold beyond a man of Liverpool's disposition; thirdly Britain had just come away from two decades of war and no Prime Minister had ever steered the country through such a difficult transition. Going through something so unprecedented would be enough to rattle anybody's nerves. In the event a combination of all these factors led Liverpool to introduce the Importation Bill (better known as the Corn Laws) into Parliament, defending it as a temporary measure to aid British agriculture in the transition from a wartime economy to a peacetime one. After all, free market principles were only effective if the whole world embraced them, which, presently, they did not. The new law made grain imports unlawful unless the domestic price reached a certain minimum level, in effect keeping the price artificially high. Riots followed the passing of this legislation as the public realised that it was suddenly going to cost them more to feed themselves and their families.

Castlereagh arrived back in London at the beginning of March, probably believing that he had just helped establish a New World Order. However, within days news reached Britain that Napoleon had escaped Elba on 26 February. He made his way to France and was intercepted on the mainland by a regiment of the French army on 7 March. Rather than killing or capturing him, though, the regiment deferred to him and marched with him to Paris. In an incredible turn of events Louis XVIII fled and, on 13 March, Britain was back at war with France under the rule of Napoleon Bonaparte. Russia, Austria and Prussia all allied against the French. Liverpool acted immediately and committed ground troops to oust the Emperor before he could take a strong hold. A substantial British army contingent was already in the Netherlands, as was the Duke of Wellington having conveniently stopped over there once he had concluded his business in Vienna. Napoleon, for his part, decided to go on the offensive, eliminating his enemies from the war as soon as it was declared as he had done so many times before. The stage was now set for one of the most famous land battles in history.

On 18 June 1815 French forces led by Napoleon met with British troops led by Wellington at Waterloo in the Netherlands. The British withstood repeated attacks by the French cavalry which gave the Russian army time to join and attack Napoleon's flanks. In the end the Allies won the day, Napoleon fled back to Paris to find that the politicians and the populace had turned against him. He was taken prisoner and this time the UK took no chances by allowing their continental allies to decide his fate as they had done with Elba. *L'Empereur* was transported to the remote Atlantic island of St. Helena where he was imprisoned, guarded by British troops. He would die there. The Napoleonic Wars were now, truly, at an end.

Now came the task of settling a new peace treaty, which was negotiated amongst senior ministers from the UK, France, Austria, Prussia and Russia meeting in Paris. Castlereagh once again represented Britain. It was decided that France would not be punished in terms of ceding land to the victors, as was favoured by Prussia and Austria, in case this led to a new revolutionary zeal as the French came to resent their European neighbours. Nor would any individual be made an example of for realigning themselves with Napoleon once he had returned, as was favoured by Russia, in case this led to a resentment of the Bourbons that would make their return impossible.

So 1815 ended 'with Britain militarily and diplomatically more powerful in Europe than at any time since the reign of Anne'[13] one hundred years earlier. Yet Liverpool's problems would continue as the country struggled through a recession, with high unemployment and break-outs of Luddite sabotages throughout the UK. The bleak economic outlook had only been exacerbated by the Corn Laws, which, though protecting the income of farmers, drove up prices to such an extent that wages necessarily went up as well in order that people could afford bread. This, in turn, meant that industrialists could not afford to pay the wages of as many workers thereby keeping unemployment high. Riots became commonplace as people aired their discontent and, as 1816 played out, Sidmouth, the Home Secretary, started to push for legislation providing the government with unprecedented powers to deal with civil unrest.

The one stroke of fortune that the government was afforded – though it probably didn't seem so to Liverpool at the time, and certainly never did to many of his supporters – was the death of Lord Buckinghamshire in February 1816. The Addingtonian Buckinghamshire had been President of the Board of Control managing India since 1812. His death gave Liverpool the opportunity to bring Canning back to the Commons and strengthen his administration in the Lower House. Sidmouth and Castlereagh, though still not keen on Canning, were themselves struggling with the burden of carrying the government and grateful for any further assistance.

Concurrently discontent in the country grew and once again Liverpool's political instincts were challenged as his naturally libertarian disposition was consistently bombarded with evidence to support Sidmouth's push for greater oppressive powers to deal with unrest. Committees from both Houses found examples of societies formed throughout the country to discuss and debate government policy,[14] leading ministers to fear the possibility of a revolt. The underlying objectives of these societies were generally to seek parliamentary reform as MPs were viewed as corrupt, but this was easily misconstrued as revolutionary principles. Several pieces of legislation were passed which substantially restricted civil liberties including the suspension of habeas corpus for persons arrested on suspicion of treason and strengthened laws against seditious societies outlawed during Pitt's time when concerns over the French Revolution spreading were rife.

These laws were the 'stick' in the government's attempt to cure the country's social ills, but there were sizeable concessions which made up the 'carrot' as well. Liverpool convinced the Prince of Wales on the need for economies to be made in all areas of public spending, including the Prince's personal allowance granted him by Parliament. The government also abolished all of their sinecures in order to deal with what was a genuine gripe of the masses that the political classes looked after their own by giving them handsomely paid jobs with no responsibility when the people were unable to feed themselves.

Such was the mood going into the general election in the summer of 1818. By the beginning of August, when the election result was known, the government was returned to a different House of Commons as was known previously. Almost 25 per cent of MPs were newly elected,[15] the government had lost several seats but still controlled more than the Whigs who, possibly for the first time, were now largely united behind one leader – Lord Grey – Lord Grenville having retired in 1817 and the small band of followers that didn't follow Grey would sit independently, rather than as Whigs.

One positive for Liverpool during 1818 was that the Duke of Wellington agreed to join his government. The hype over his military victories in the Peninsula Campaign and Waterloo had long since been subdued by the depressed economy but he was still a highly respected and revered figure. He was duly appointed Master-General of the Ordnance, thereby creating a formidable front-bench in the Upper House.

The new House of Commons was just as unforgiving as the old and the government suffered several defeats during the first few months back. Ministers had been unable to keep the income tax once the war had ended in 1815 due to the strength of opposition to it, the result being that massive deficits were being incurred every year, which had to be financed by borrowing, causing inflation, adding to the burden on the poor. Gradually, the new Parliament wore the government down and, finally, Liverpool decided to make a stand. In June 1819 he proposed £3 million of new taxes, on the back of months of opposition victories, with the clear declaration that the confidence of the government rested on the measures. In effect he was saying that in the event of defeat, the ministry would have no option but to resign. Somehow this did the trick and his budget was carried by a huge majority, something he had never been able to do even in the immediate aftermath of Waterloo. However, any feeling that the storm had abated was short-lived. 1819 had seen several gatherings of discontented societies which culminated, just over two months after the government's glorious budget victory that June, in a meeting of somewhere between 60,000 – 80,000 people[16] in St Peter's Field, Manchester, on 16 August 1819. What history has come to know as the Peterloo Massacre soon followed.

The rally, organised by the Manchester Patriotic Union, who forcefully advocated parliamentary reform including representation for the working classes, was intended to demonstrate to the national government the strength of feeling amongst the populace that change was needed. In response local magistrates requested that the military attend to arrest a leading individual named Henry Hunt, a power that they could lawfully execute thanks to Sidmouth's measures enacted against seditious societies. The cavalry charged in and in the ensuing mêlée at least eleven people were killed[17] and hundreds more injured. Sidmouth was quick to express his support for the efficient manner in which the magistrates had organised the dispersal of an unruly crowd, which understandably outraged anybody who didn't share his view of the danger of organised gatherings. So convinced was he of the justness of his position that, rather than lamenting the loss of life at Peterloo, Sidmouth saw it as a reason to propose further legislation against seditious societies and increase recruitment to the army to deal with further such gatherings.

Liverpool procrastinated but the opposition seemed to force his hand. The Whigs decided that what had happened at St Peter's Field was scandalous, and several of their leading members met with various radicals throughout the country to consult on what action should be taken in protest. Lord Fitzwilliam, a leading Whig and then Lord Lieutenant, proposed an enquiry into the matter, an action that the government felt they could not accept. Fitzwilliam was removed from his post as Lord Lieutenant but this only served to harden the position of the Whigs. Now they were united and determined to act against the government.

Liverpool recalled Parliament in November so as to pass through what has now become known as the Six Acts to deal with civil unrest (normally at this time Parliament would be in recess from the summer through until the new year, with no autumn session). In spite of forceful opposition to the legislation from the Whigs, all six Bills passed into law, four before Christmas and two in the new year. The Acts were the Unlawful Drilling Act (no military training may be provided by anybody except the State); the Seizure of Arms Act (local magistrates were given the power to search property or persons for weapons, seize the same and arrest anybody in their possession); the Seditious Meetings Prevention Act (local law enforcement must give permission for gatherings of more than 50 people if the subject of that meeting concerned the church or state); the Blasphemous and Seditious Libels Act (toughened sentences against any writing which contradicted existing laws in this area); and the Newspaper and Stamp Duties Act (taxed publications expressing opinions rather than news).

From the vantage point of posterity we can see that these Acts were generally an affront to civil liberties. However, the ease with which they passed through Parliament show the extent to which many people shared the concerns of the government over the possibility of revolution. It has been seen so many times throughout history that fear of the mob has led to oppression and tyranny, even where the leaders involved are not necessarily oppressive or tyrannical by nature.

Parliament was then suspended until February but Liverpool was to be given no rest during the break. On 29 January 1820 King George III died, meaning that the Prince Regent would be crowned as King George IV. However, this meant that much business which Liverpool had delayed in relation to the Prince of Wales had to be addressed now that he was the King. For example, Prince George had been angling for a divorce from the bane of his existence, his wife Princess Caroline. The Cabinet had been agreed that this must be avoided as it would cause a scandal that they could ill-afford to combat whilst fighting a war followed by economic recession followed by civil unrest. Now that he was King, divorcing the apparent Queen was absolutely out of the question. But the Cabinet still needed the support of their sovereign and so handling this matter, for which the Prince Regent had been pushing harder and harder over the previous years, would need all the diplomacy they could collectively muster. On top of this they needed to settle Caroline's official status, where she would officially reside (she had not been in Britain for several years having taken her leave when King George III had stopped accepting her at his court, but would still need a recognised residence given her new role), and in what capacity she should be acknowledged (the new King was adamant that she should not be mentioned in prayers said for the Royal Family).

The Cabinet in the end advised the new King that he should abandon his hopes for a divorce, that they would formally remove her of her titles and that she could only be entitled to her financial allowances as long as she stayed abroad,[18] thereby sparing him the embarrassment of her returning to stand by her husband's side. King George IV was determined, though, and upon receipt of the Cabinet's proposals in early February he rejected them, informing his ministers that if they would not support his divorce then he would disband the government and find ministers that would. He had several stormy meetings with Liverpool who held firm, initially believing that he was imminently to be removed. However, as the days wore on it became clear that the King was bluffing and, by mid-February, George agreed to the Cabinet's proposals and to keep them in office.

Now that their position was a little more secure the Cabinet requested a further general election due to the change in monarchy, which was called in May and caused little difference to the constitution of the Lower House. However, the King's persistence in attempting to secure a divorce did not abate. Events in this area were to dominate the year for Liverpool as both sides made life increasingly difficult for him. At the end of May Caroline, still completely ignorant of the agreement made between the King and his ministers as to her future, contacted Liverpool announcing that she was near to Calais. She asked for a permanent residence in the UK and transport across the Channel. The Prime Minister despatched Henry Brougham[19] – the Queen's attorney-general – to meet her and advise her that should she return to Britain then parliamentary proceedings would begin against her that would inevitably result in divorce and no financial settlement. All offers and threats fell on deaf ears and in the first week of June Queen Caroline crossed the Channel to England. Liverpool's threats of parliamentary proceedings and tempting offers of titles and an income should she remain on the continent had been designed to keep Caroline away, now that she was present he had to see through his promises.

Negotiations were entered into between the King's advisors and the Queen's but these did not amount to anything (and nor were they expected to). In July Liverpool presented to the House of Lords a Bill proposing the dissolution of the marriage between the King and Queen, with a hearing set for mid-August. The saga unfolded with the result that the Queen was successful, albeit morally defeated. Throughout August prosecution witnesses were heard by the House of Lords, who painted a picture of the Queen as a socialite adulteress whose character was abhorrent and whose infidelity meant that the grounds for divorce were surely unquestionable. It was October before the defence began its case which attacked the character and questioned the faithfulness of the King. When the Bill came to be debated in November the House of Lords could not support the divorce clause in spite of widespread conviction that the Queen had acted unfaithfully. Bishops and religious Lords could not bring themselves to back such a measure. In the end the government withdrew the Bill rather than pushing for it through the Commons with the removal of the divorce clause.

Meanwhile Canning, who had managed to stir trouble for every administration, friendly or otherwise, that century, created difficulties for the Prime Minister once again. A known admirer of Queen Caroline (with rumours abound that they had had an affair two decades earlier) Canning had disagreed with his Cabinet colleagues over their handling of her return to England several times during the course of the year. He had offered to resign on at least two previous occasions[20] but had been convinced to stay by Liverpool on the basis that it would have been humiliating for the government had he done it whilst the issue was unfolding. Finally, in December 1820, it became clear that their differences were irreconcilable and Canning left the Cabinet. This, on the back of economic depression, frequent rioting, Peterloo and the question of the royal divorce, led Liverpool to feel extremely depressed by the end of the year, and understandably so.

Come 1821 Liverpool was ageing, faster than some of his peers because of the job he had held for nine years. The pressures kept mounting, relentlessly, but he kept himself going out of a sense of duty. He had accepted the premiership in 1812 due to a lack of viable alternatives from within his own party, now that he had led his friends through almost a decade of political turmoil and things were not going as well as they might, it was not in his nature to abandon those around him. Also at this time the list of plausible alternatives was as sketchy as it had been at the time of his accession.

In April 1821 the issue of Catholic emancipation was on the political table once again when the House of Commons passed a Bill supporting the enfranchisement of Roman Catholics in the electoral system. Liverpool's position that there should be no strict government policy on the issue was still the line that was being taken but he personally opposed the Bill when it came to the Upper House. The issue was defeated in the Lords but only by a small majority[21] and all this in spite of opposition from the leading ministers in that House and indeed the Duke of York. Liverpool's personal position seems intolerable viewed from the present day. However, if nothing else, that the government was able to face this issue without tearing itself apart was a real testament to Liverpool's strategy, when considered against the backdrop of three previous Prime Ministers who all lost Cabinet members or indeed their own position as a result of this one toxic matter.

Liverpool was well aware of the need to strengthen his government from attack by the opposition, the press and the public, particularly in the House of Commons where they were weak on debating power. Shortly after the emancipation saga he discussed with his inner circle the possibility of bringing Canning back into the government. The logic was that Canning had resigned on a point of principle regarding Queen Caroline, but that issue had now been put to bed. Furthermore Canning was a man of ambition and if he was offered a more lucrative position in the government then perhaps he would agree to return. Sidmouth was coming to the end of a long career so the Home Office may well have been an option. However, the King, incensed by what he saw as Canning's flagrant and unashamed support for the Queen, would not hear of having him back. At this point Liverpool started to consider that King George may well be keeping the government deliberately weak so as to reserve the option to dismiss them at any time he should wish to.[22] After trying in vain to convince the King to change his mind regarding bringing Canning back, Liverpool got his final negative reply on the evening of 11 June 1821. In the early hours of the following morning his wife, Louisa, died. She had been ill for some time but her inevitable demise understandably drove Liverpool to despair. He withdrew from affairs of state for the following weeks whilst he came to terms with his loss.

In the meantime, whether out of guilt over Louisa's death coming so soon after their latest falling-out or out of the persuasive abilities of those who took over communications in Liverpool's absence (such as Wellington and Sidmouth), the King agreed not to veto Canning indefinitely, on the proviso that no decision was made during the present parliamentary session. Then, in August, Queen Caroline also died, which came as a great relief to the King who now no longer had to continue obsessing over the possibility of divorce.

Liverpool gave up on bringing Canning back into the Cabinet, believing instead that the only future for him was in India as Governor-General[23] as soon as that position opened up. Instead, at the end of 1821 it was decided that Sir Robert Peel would succeed Sidmouth as Home Secretary at the beginning of the new session of Parliament in January 1822. Further strengthening his position, Liverpool entered into negotiations with Lord Grenville (long since retired from frontline politics but still commanding great respect in both Houses of Parliament) to bring some of his old followers into the government. These discussions were also completed at the end of 1821 and resulted in the Grenvillite Charles Wynn being drafted into the Cabinet and the majority of the remaining Grenvillite faction now officially endorsing the government. Liverpool's motivation for striving for this alliance had been to strengthen his position in the House of Commons and to ensure that the King had fewer options in terms of replacements if he decided that he was going to remove the government in future, since this would now also mean removing the Grenvillites. Admittedly the King and Prime Minister had been on better terms since the death of both their wives, but the monarch was still unpredictable so this move was certainly an advisable one. It also represented the reunification of the last outstanding Pittite faction with all the others. Now the Grenvillities, Addingtonians, Canningites, Portland-followers and those loyal to Pitt who never defected were all supporters of the same government and could clearly be identified as a single political party.

Throughout the 1822 parliamentary session the government did indeed appear more at ease with itself than at any other time during the last decade. The more comfortable majorities as well as a more amicable relationship between Liverpool and King George made all ministers feel more confident and relaxed. There were still difficult matters to deal with. Agriculture was still a thorn in the side of the administration as over-supply had depressed prices in spite of the Corn Laws passed in 1815. This led lobbyists to demand further protectionist measures such as minimum guaranteed prices for home-sold grain, not just those imported. Liverpool, having been principally opposed to the import tariffs imposed seven years earlier and only swayed under the pressure of the moment, would not relent to these further demands. Protecting agriculture at what would have been the expense of industry was not something he was prepared to do. It cannot be said for certain whether, without the Grenvillites, without the confidence of the King, without having relinquished the burden of fighting against the possibility of a royal divorce and against constant rioting, Liverpool would have made such a stand in favour of his free market principles. All that can be said is that the Liverpool of 1815 hadn't but the Liverpool of 1822 had, and the farmers would, for the time being, have to wait for the invisible hand of the market to correct their situation.

However, the government was to face one more painful blow in the summer of 1822. Castlereagh, who had now inherited the title of Lord Londonderry following the death of his father in 1821, had become increasingly depressed over the previous couple of years. Following his settlement in Vienna he had taken over leadership of the House of Commons – notoriously the weaker chamber in terms of support for the government. He represented the administration in most of the major debates that took place in the Lower House and therefore came under great personal criticism from the opposition benches, from the press and from the public. Arguably he was more demonised for government mistakes or the adverse state of the country than was the Prime Minister. Add to this the heavy workload he had to manage in his role as Foreign Secretary and the mental strain he was under became unendurable. There has been suggestion amongst historians that Liverpool saw Londonderry as his successor[24] when eventually he retired, as the latter had been one of the former's most steadfast supporters alongside Melville and Sidmouth, neither of whom had any appetite for the top job. However, this possibility came crashing down around Liverpool when, in

August 1822, Londonderry committed suicide. He had been unwell for some time, probably due to the strain he was under in work, and had suffered bouts of madness. Those close to him had suspected that suicide attempts may be drawing near and so steps had been taken to remove sharp objects from around him. However, he managed to locate a pen knife and slit his own throat.

It was unfair that Castlereagh took the blame for the government's policies but in his role as Leader of the House of Commons he was the individual most visibly associated with them. His unpopularity was such that shortly after his suicide Lord Byron wrote in verse:

> Here lie the bones of Castlereagh
> Stop, traveller, and piss

Personally for Liverpool the loss was devastating. Practically, though, he now needed to find a new Foreign Secretary and someone who could take the responsibility of almost single-handedly taking on the opposition in the House of Commons. The Foreign Secretary was then, as it is today, one of the highest offices of state although the holder back then was arguably second highest ranking minister, even over the Chancellor. The only two individuals who could be considered from within the current Cabinet were Peel, who was able although not overly-experienced, but he was proving to be an effective Home Secretary and Liverpool saw no reason to move him; or Wellington, but he had made it clear to Liverpool upon first joining the ministry that he did not see himself as a party man and wanted to reserve the right to join a non-Tory government at some point in the future if he so desired. The Foreign Office would undoubtedly require Wellington to toe the party line and this would not be fair to him. Besides, the Duke necessarily sat in the Lords and the government still needed an extra man to fight their corner in the Commons now that their only orator of any ability was permanently removed. Again Liverpool turned to the one man he seemed unable to escape being in need of. How he must have wished that there was another alternative but to go crawling back to Canning, but the latter hadn't left for India, the position of Governor-General still being occupied. The King would be an obstacle but if he wanted his administration to have a chance at survival he would at least have to consider bringing Canning back to the fold.

Canning still had his heart set on India but the chance to appropriate all the positions that had belonged to his old enemy (Foreign Secretary, Leader of the House of Commons), a man who had once shot him, must have been tempting. Liverpool met with the King, who in turn was outraged at the prospect of bringing Canning into his government. However, when he realised that there was no ministerial support for his position he quickly, albeit reluctantly, decided to endorse the plan[25] rather than see the ministry dissolved and replaced with Whigs. In mid-September 1822 George Canning returned to government once again, as Leader of the House of Commons and Foreign Secretary. Liverpool now had the best team possible in both Houses, although the Commons was still admittedly shy of talented debaters. Further to this it was decided that Vansittart would retire from his position as Chancellor of the Exchequer in exchange for a peerage and he was replaced by Frederick Robinson. Now Liverpool's Cabinet consisted of four future Prime Ministers all in senior positions: Canning as Foreign Secretary; Robinson as Chancellor of the Exchequer; Wellington as Master-General of the Ordnance; and Peel as Home Secretary. These individuals – allies in government and successors to the premiership – would prove to be difficult to manage and would find it next to impossible to work together whilst keeping their egos in check. Liverpool agreed with Canning on most areas of foreign policy and therefore had little to do in terms of negotiating a unified position with him in his primary area of responsibility. However, Canning's influence strayed beyond the bounds of the Foreign Office. He was influential in getting Robinson – a known Canningite – into the Exchequer and in securing Robinson's old position of President of the Board for another of his supporters, William Huskisson.

In the opinions of the rest of the administration, Canning was already making the waves that they had feared. In the space of a month he had transformed the composition of the Cabinet by pushing Liverpool into accepting his followers almost as a condition of his return. Liverpool was too tired to put up a fight and knew that he needed Canning. His Cabinet, though, were far more willing to assert themselves and over the months that followed, Canning's determination to implement reform in areas of the constitution far removed from the remit of a Foreign Minister (such as Catholic emancipation and parliamentary reform) were met with resistance from the traditionalist wing of the government, led by Wellington. Peel was caught in the middle, being apparently pro-reform in some areas but considering government unity more important than any single issue.

The ten years until the end of 1822 were a distressing time for the nation with all the ills that Liverpool's administration had to work against, but the Cabinet had been incredibly united. This was the one thing that could have kept such an unpopular administration in office for so long. The loyalty of Vansittart, Sidmouth, Wellington and Castlereagh had kept Liverpool afloat. The five years from 1822 would be notable for being the exact opposite: the country entered a new age of prosperity, the opposition became dejected, the government enjoyed widespread popularity but the Cabinet was disunited and marred by ill-feeling. Wellington in particular took exception with Canning and felt disturbed by how much he felt that Liverpool worked with the Foreign Secretary[26] above the rest of the Cabinet, often appearing to make decisions on behalf of the government between just the two of them.

In February 1823 a budget was presented to the House of Commons which proposed widespread tax reductions, thereby alleviating the burden on the masses and increasing the government's popularity. As the price of grain increased the agriculturalists also became happier and the sessions saw little in terms of objections to policy from the opposition. The following two years saw further growth in the economy. All the while Canning's acclaim grew as, owing to his role as Leader of the House of Commons, he was invariably associated with all government legislation that passed through this chamber, almost all of which was popular.[27] In the spring of 1823 France occupied Spain in spite of strong rhetoric from Liverpool and Canning that Britain was opposed to the move (albeit that they would remain neutral unless British interests were directly threatened – they were well aware that the country's recovery was fragile and they were in no position to finance another war). It was the one bitter pill that they had to swallow in the midst of an otherwise positive year. Not all members of the Cabinet were able to accept the policy of British neutrality in the affairs of the Iberian Peninsula as easily as Canning had. Wellington, having risked his life fighting to drive the French out of Spain and Portugal just ten years previously now had to watch on whilst Foreign Policy decisions were taken by his Prime Minister, to whom he was loyal, and Canning, to whom he was already beginning to feel increasingly embittered.

However, Canning did not stand idly by in accepting French conquests. He used all the diplomatic means made available to him to ensure that France was kept out of South America, where acquisition of colonies had become a strong desire of the French following the removal of Spanish sovereignty from most of that faraway continent.

In the spring and summer of 1824 Liverpool's health started to give way and speculation became rife over who his successor would be. Wellington had become the royal favourite over the preceding years, not least because the King still despised Canning and was aware that Wellington now shared his sentiments, but also because the Duke of York, heir apparent to the throne, saw him as the royalist voice in the Cabinet. Wellington had previously refused to discuss the possibility of overthrowing Liverpool, stating unreservedly that he was loyal, but had admitted that he would put himself forward as a candidate if necessary to prevent Canning from being considered.[28]

The two would further fall out over the issue of Catholic emancipation, against which Wellington was vehemently opposed but which Canning was passionately in favour of. In March 1825 Sir Francis Burdett MP proposed a Bill into the House of Commons 'for the Removal of the Disqualifications under which his majesty's Roman Catholic subjects now labour'.[29] Sir Robert Peel, the Home Secretary, was the minister responsible for arguing the government's position on the Bill, although as always within Liverpool's ministry there was no official position. Peel was personally opposed to it but realised early on in proceedings that there was a majority in favour of it in the House of Commons. The Bill was to be voted on towards the end of April and Peel made up his mind that if it passed he would resign.[30]

Liverpool was also aware of the strength of feeling for the Bill in the Commons, but was equally aware that it would be defeated in the Lords. He was personally opposed to the principle of emancipation but started to feel that the tide was turning and that it would only be a matter of time before a similar Bill finally passed through both Houses. Therefore, he believed, there was little point in resisting it now, but he could not bring himself to argue for it. His logic brought him to the conclusion that perhaps it was time for him to retire from office also.[31] Once the Bill passed through the Commons on 29 April, Liverpool put the consequences for both himself and Peel (who had made the Prime Minister aware of his intentions) to Wellington, who then spent the following month trying to dissuade both from abandoning their posts. The Bill was ultimately defeated in the Lords in May but the ramifications of this put further question marks over Liverpool's position. The Prime Minister had spoken out against the Bill in the House of Lords which had caused Canning great annoyance. The Foreign Secretary requested a Cabinet meeting almost immediately afterwards in which he declared that the government would finally have to take a stance on the matter, which Liverpool knew meant isolating either one half of the Cabinet or the other. Canning and the Catholic question looked set to tear apart yet another administration. However, it all ended rather timidly when, at the meeting of Cabinet, his ministerial colleagues informed Canning that to push the issue would be to destroy the government, following which he made his point of view known but pushed the matter no further.

The year 1825 would end with a bad harvest which had far-reaching consequences. The 1815 Corn Laws still kept grain prices artificially high but now there was not enough of it to go around. Alongside this there was a downturn in industry which meant that fewer people had enough money to afford their basic staple foods. There was pressure from agriculturalists to extend the Corn Laws further to compensate them for the bad harvest, and pressure from the rest of the population to repeal them altogether so that the price would fall and people could afford bread. Liverpool's free trade instincts led him to support the latter position[32] and a general election called for June 1826 was fought largely on this issue. The government returned to office after the election but the summer of 1826 was unusually hot, leading to drought and as another poor harvest looked imminent, grain prices soared. In September the government authorised the reintroduction of imported grain in order to allow the starving masses an affordable alternative. In the following session Liverpool intended to suggest a revision to the Corn Laws involving a sliding scale of protection: whereas presently there was a ban on imports if the price fell below 80s per quarter, Liverpool was to suggest a ban below 60s, then limited protection between 60s-80s. However, he soon became very ill and would never have the chance formally to introduce his measures. In December 1826 Liverpool withdrew to Bath for rest and requested that Canning come to see him there. It seems that en route to Bath Canning had convinced himself that the Prime Minister was going to resign and that he would succeed him.[33]

Liverpool seemed to make a recovery at Bath and returned for the 1827 parliamentary session with no talk of resignation. Then, on the morning of Saturday 17 February, he collapsed at home having apparently suffered a paralytic stroke. It took him days to recover his power of speech and weeks before he could walk again. By the end of March it became clear that the business of government could no longer wait and a successor would have to be found. Liverpool was certainly too tired, and probably too aware of the severity of his condition to protest. By April he was removed from office.

The Earl of Liverpool had been known as a kind and selfless individual. He never sought power and high office but assumed them when he felt it was his duty. He loyally stood by his friends even when convinced that they would dessert him. His tenure as leader marks the transition from the eighteenth century method of government – royalist, intransigent, holding a great deal of respect to the settlement of the Glorious Revolution of 1688 – to the nineteenth century method – progressive, reformist, acknowledging the rights of more than just the privileged few.

There is no doubt that, almost certainly in spite of his character, he presided over times of severe oppression including heavy taxation, the suspension of habeas corpus and Peterloo. His legacy is often dismissed as non-existent given that the two issues he spent the majority of his tenure fighting over – Catholics and Corn – both eventually had legislation passed that reversed completely Liverpool's position, and today the majority of people celebrate freedom and diversity on the one hand, and free market principles on the other as cornerstones of UK society.

However, when reviewing Liverpool's successes and failures it must be done in the context of the time. In the early nineteenth century the industrial revolution was just commencing, Britain had come away from decades of war and the masses were crying out for liberation. The atmosphere was unstable and could quite conceivably have resulted in revolution. Liverpool led the country for fifteen years, an incredible feat in itself and one that demonstrates, at the very least, adept political skill. Even more spectacularly he guided the country through fifteen years of turmoil and Britain was undoubtedly in a better position economically and socially at the end of his tenure than it had been at the beginning.

Liverpool is often depicted as the villainous Prime Minister in charge during Peterloo – which is true and he deserves little protection from this accusation – whilst historians often forget that he also presided over Waterloo. Whereas he takes the blame for the ills of his decade-and-a-half in power, he receives little credit for the positives such as the post-war settlement in Vienna (which is usually attributed to Castlereagh), introducing legal reforms (the credit for which often goes to Peel) or protecting South America against French imperialism (which history remembers Canning for). In reality, under Liverpool the writ of the Prime Minister ran throughout every government department and he should be judged on the successes, as well as on the (not insignificant) failures.

George Canning
(1827)

Sir, your father broke the domination of the Whigs. I hope your
Majesty will not endure that of the Tories

George Canning to King George IV, 12 April 1827

It is the Opinion of some wise Men, that the King cannot follow a
more fatal Counsel that to confine himself to any one Party of his
subjects

Daniel Defoe's *Tory*, 1692

BY THE END OF MARCH 1827 it had become clear that a
successor would be needed for the deteriorating Lord
Liverpool. It was therefore in a chaotic and, for the majority of
members of the government, completely unprecedented
atmosphere that ministers and backbenchers alike started to
rally around their favourites. Catholic emancipation was still
the polarising issue of the day and so two factions developed
within the Tory party: the *Ultras* who were Protestant and non-
reformist in principle; and the *Liberals* who were in favour of
emancipation and therefore seen as pro-Catholic.

Canning became the champion of the Liberals, whilst
Wellington was a favourite for the Ultras,[1] although he outright
refused to request office or to allow others to campaign on his
behalf. Canning's chances of becoming Prime Minister had
improved markedly since his return to the Cabinet five years
earlier. King George had been very impressed with his
handling of foreign policy, particularly with regard to South
America and Portugal. During Liverpool's absence Canning
had also expertly steered the Prime Minister's Corn proposals
through the House of Commons, which had won him much
admiration on both sides of the Chamber.[2] Wellington dreaded
the thought of Canning as Prime Minister and did his utmost to
dissuade the King from appointing him, without intriguing for
office for himself. Canning, on the other hand, was happy to
make it clear to anybody who would listen that he both coveted

the position and saw himself as the natural successor to Liverpool.

On 28 March both Wellington and Canning were summoned to visit the King at Windsor for separate talks. In Canning's meeting, King George informed the Foreign Secretary that he could not do without him but that he could not accept a pro-Catholic at the head of government. Canning told the King that it was either the premiership or resignation for him.[3] The King tried to avoid making such a difficult decision by instructing the Cabinet to appoint a leader of their own. However, on 31 March he was told that such passing of the buck was not an option and so the political stalemate looked set to continue. The three senior men in the government were Canning, Peel and Wellington but their positions were worlds apart from each other. Canning was for the premiership or nothing. Wellington did not necessarily desire the top job but was prepared to take any course of action to keep Canning out. Peel would serve under another 'Protestant' minister, but not Canning. He did not put himself forward because he knew that Canning would never serve under him and he believed that a ministry could not survive without him.[4]

In order to break the deadlock Canning offered Peel several tempting enticements to lure him into support. These included the post of Foreign Secretary (a promotion that also meant relinquishing his current responsibilities for Ireland, over which a Protestant Home Secretary and a pro-Catholic Prime Minister were bound to fall out), a peerage and even the leadership of the House of Lords. Peel was steadfast. Meanwhile Protestant peers were approaching Wellington, encouraging him to push for the premiership but the proud Duke was adamant that the King should be allowed to make up his own mind, probably naïvely confident that King George would not consider Canning. In spite of Wellington's refusal to intrigue overtly for the top job, Canning still believed him to have stirred up the Lords in their pushing for him.

On 9 April 1827 the King sent Peel to suggest to Canning that the Cabinet all agree to serve under Wellington. This proposal was not even considered before it was rejected. When he discovered that his plan was dead in the water, King George bowed to the inevitable and summoned Canning with instructions to find an administration that could function.

Canning wrote to Wellington telling him that he had been tasked to form a ministry and expressing the hope that the Duke would join. Wellington replied asking who would lead the new government. Canning's return letter stated that it was generally understood that the King entrusted the forming of an administration to the person expected to be at the head of it and that this was so obvious that he hadn't felt the need to state it explicitly. Wellington claimed that he had been insulted by the tone of Canning's letter[5] and resigned both from the Cabinet and as commander-in-chief. The truth is that a man of Wellington's fortitude was difficult to offend and being insulted by Canning's choice of words was a convenient excuse for him to take a course of action that he had always intended to pursue should Canning be appointed Prime Minister anyway. Peel also immediately resigned and within a few days so had Westmorland, Melville (who, incredibly, was pro-Catholic but felt the temptation of a good bandwagon as much as the next person), Eldon and Bathurst. In total over forty government supporters deserted at the news of Canning's promotion.[6] His only option now was to court the Whigs.

On 12 April 1827 George Canning met with the King to confirm his position and then, later in the day, he entered the House of Commons for the final meeting before the Easter recess, now as First Lord of the Treasury. It was the culmination of decades of ambition. His old friend and supporter Frederick Robinson was rewarded for his loyalty by being elevated to the Lords as Viscount Goderich and taking the lead in the Upper House, while many of the other Cabinet spaces were filled with Protestants in an attempt both to stir up support in Parliament and to appease the King. Canning took the responsibility of Chancellor of the Exchequer for himself.

Meanwhile the moderate Whigs made it clear that they would support Canning without guarantees of office, elevation or even commitments on specific policies.[7] It was enough for them to see the Ultras out of favour for the time being. At the end of April Lord Lansdowne, now a moderate Whig leader, came to an agreement with Canning over the appointment of some junior ministerial positions to some Whigs in exchange for their support. Hard-line Whigs led by Earl Grey would still be in official opposition to the government, but the numbers were now a little more favourable for the incoming Prime Minister.

When Parliament reconvened in May the topic on the political agenda was parliamentary reform. This was something that Canning and the Ultra Tories had in common in that they were all opposed to it but the Whigs were generally in favour. The imbalance in representation, with county areas being heavily represented but highly populated and growing towns having no representation in some cases, was something which many MPs felt needed addressing. The government, being a coalition, was easy to criticise from the outside using reform as ammunition and many Members attacked the new administration for having no consistent policy in this area.[8] At the end of May Parliament voted on disfranchising the constituency of Penrhyn and transferring the seat to Manchester. Canning came out in staunch opposition to the measure but was defeated largely down to the efforts of his own Whig ministers. Coalitions, he was learning, are not easy to manage.

His health deteriorated through the months from May-July and during the summer recess he intended to get as much rest as possible so as to be ready for the inevitable attacks from the hard-line Whigs and Ultra Tories that would come in the new session. His condition got worse throughout July and on the 30th he went to bed and never left his room again. On 8 August 1827 George Canning died.

To this day Canning is the shortest serving Prime Minister in the history of the United Kingdom. His assent to the premiership was the result of decades of both hard work and hard conniving. He had played a significant part in the story of every administration from the turn of the nineteenth century until his death a quarter of a century later and, more importantly, he had played a significant part in the story of their downfalls. For Addington, Canning had been the thorn in his side, the man who had never gotten over Pitt's resignation and the author of *The Pilot That Weathered The Storm*. For Pitt, during his second tenure, Canning had made a speech attacking the previous administration which Pitt had worked so hard to coerce into his own. Upon Pitt's death Canning had worked tirelessly to destroy the Grenville-Fox coalition, successfully in the end.

He made life difficult for Portland's government from the inside, first of all by insisting on Castlereagh's removal and then by duelling with Castlereagh (and subsequently being shot in the thigh). When Perceval became Prime Minister, Canning refused to serve and spent the next few years making snide remarks in the Commons about the government. Once Perceval was assassinated and Liverpool took office, Canning initially refused to serve yet again and even introduced a motion to force the government to discuss the issue of Catholic emancipation, contrary to Liverpool's policy of no policy. He then became Ambassador to Lisbon from 1814-16 before returning to Britain as President of the Board of Control until 1820. Even then, though, he would continue to make life difficult for his colleagues, resigning in 1820 out of loyalty to Queen Caroline. The point that Canning was more of a hindrance to his friends than he was a help is an easy one to make. However, what is also apparent here is that he was a man of principle. Arguably too eager to resign if he didn't get his own way, he was at least prepared to follow his convictions rather than to sell a point he didn't believe in. Looking back two hundred years later it is clear that his positions on issues such as Catholic emancipation and the abolition of the slave trade were just and right. Viewed from the point of view of his contemporaries, he came across simply as disloyal and a nuisance.

In the end, Canning achieved what he had always coveted – the position that William Pitt had held and that he saw himself as the natural heir to. That it was to be the shortest tenure in history means that his destiny was to achieve it more as a token gesture than as a chance to wield any real influence. Canning is remembered by history as a forceful debater, as a man who got angry during arguments – angry because he was emotional, emotional because he cared. He was opinionated and unafraid to express himself. He is remembered as being extremely influential, clever at writing verses, needed by every government and with the ability to destroy them if he felt he should, but, owing largely to the brevity of his tenure, he is not remembered as a great leader of the Tories, or of the nation.

Frederick Robinson, 1ˢᵗ Viscount Goderich

(1827 – 1828)

The country will…support us, particularly if we exert ourselves
bona fide to get rid of, or at least to nullify, the odious distinctions of
Whig and Tory

Viscount Goderich, September 1827

Let us not divide under this or that Ministry, under this or that
Faction or Party; but let us all unite

Daniel Defoe's *Whig*, 1692

ON 8 AUGUST 1827, the same day that Canning died, King
George IV summoned Viscount Goderich (Leader of the House
of Lords under Canning) and William Sturges-Bourne
(Canning's Home Secretary) to see him. The upshot was that
the King expected Goderich to replace Canning immediately as
Prime Minister, so as to remove the chaos of an interregnum,
with a similar ministry to the one already in place. The next few
weeks saw the Whigs and Liberal Tories vying for the positions
opened up by the numerous promotions caused by Canning's
death. Whigs could not abide the idea of higher positions being
awarded to Tories, Tories felt the same about Whigs. All the
while the King made things more difficult by forcing
appointments on his Prime Minister when they were supported
by neither side, or vetoing them when supported by both.[1]
Consequently it was 1 September before the Cabinet was
finally settled upon.

It seems like such a wasted effort on reflection because
due to the length of the parliamentary recess (Parliament
usually broke up in July and did not reconvene until the new
year, save for exceptional circumstances) even though
Goderich's short premiership would be longer than Canning's
in terms of days served, he would never attend Westminster as
leader of the government. The new administration had plenty
to be optimistic about at the end of 1827. The price of corn was

steadying, the economy was undergoing a revival, the government had cut the cost of the armed forces thereby saving the taxpayer money and they had devised a proposal for property tax[2] to replace levies on various goods and imports, which should help to boost trade.

However, there was also much to feel pessimistic about, almost all of which was out of Goderich's control. In the July of 1827 Canning's government had signed a tripartite agreement with Russia and France committing all three nations to act militarily to keep Greece and Turkey from continued fighting. Those two nations had been at war with each other but with other Islamic nations such as Egypt entering on the Turkish side, the European nations felt obliged to represent Christendom with a show of solidarity towards Greece. None of the signatories had any appetite for war but it was hoped that an official treaty would deter both sides from continued hostilities. It didn't.

As Turkish and Egyptian ships moved towards Greek Peloponnese a British fleet was despatched in September to blockade Greece in order to prevent any possible attack. Admiral Codrington was in charge of the fleet and for weeks he held firm watching the invading ships terrorise the islands before him without ever attempting to pass his blockade. Largely due to the difficult communications of the time but also in part due to Goderich's wanting to discuss every possibility several times over, by halfway through October Codrington had received no instructions as to how to proceed. So, on 20 October, he moved his fleet towards the Turkish one, apparently hoping to scare them away. The British fleet sailed into Navarino Bay where a full scale engagement took place and the Turks and Egyptians were decisively crushed. When the Cabinet learned of this they were horrified. The King, elated, decided to bestow upon Admiral Codrington the Grand Cross of the Bath[3] and so all of a sudden ministers found that they would be forced to defend Codrington's actions, rather than rebuke him, because the King was endorsing them. All throughout the government had no idea (and what is worse they *appeared* as though they had no idea) how to react.

Goderich started to become fearful of facing Parliament[4] and devised a plan with his friend Lord Lansdowne to strengthen the administration so as to make the experience a little easier. The idea was that they would bring Lord Holland into the Cabinet, which would please the Whigs, and also Lord

Wellesley, which would suit the Tories. Having one on each side of the divide meant that everyone would be happy and the government would be stronger. The only alternative in his mind was to resign. However, entirely by accident resign is exactly what he did. The chronology of the bizarre saga is as follows:

On 8 December Goderich's plan of bringing Wellesley and Holland into the government was rejected by King George. Then, on 11 December, he wrote to the King to insist upon the appointments, explaining how inadequate he felt in his current position without such support. It was supposed to come across as a demand for the assignments but the King interpreted it as a letter of resignation[5], which he happily accepted!

At this time rumours abound that the hard-line Whig leader Lord Grey had already drawn up a Cabinet of his own ready to take office once Goderich had fallen. The news of this evidently found its way to the King who, realising that the present half-Whig government was preferable to a new entirely-Whig government, decided to reverse his decision and restore Goderich within a week of removing him.

Parliament was due to meet on 22 January for the beginning of the new session but by the new year the government had not even settled on a speech. In-fighting continued as two Cabinet ministers – William Huskisson (Secretary for the Colonies) and John Herries (Chancellor of the Exchequer) – were at odds over who should be appointed Chairman of a government-created finance committee.[6] Goderich, again unable to settle the matter himself, put the stalemate to the King in a meeting on 8 January. King George again assumed that Goderich was telling him that he could not control his Cabinet and he came away with the impression that the ministry was no longer able to function. He therefore decided during the meeting to accept Goderich's resignation. So Goderich 'himself had never offered a resignation, yet his resignation had twice been accepted!'[7]

Goderich had been a weak person, accidentally elevated to a position of power on the basis that he had been good friends with a previous leader, whose death within four months of forming a government had left the King to hope that he could keep the same ministry and not have to go through the vetting process again. The fact that he accepted two resignations that had never been offered shows that even the idle King George IV realised early on that Goderich was not suitable for the position of Prime Minister. It can only be speculated how he would have fared had he stayed on for long enough to face Parliament, but given the evidence of his handling of his Cabinet it cannot be assumed that it would have been a positive experience. He was not robust enough to manage the powerful individuals that worked within his government so he is unlikely to have managed his equally powerful political enemies much better. By all accounts he felt much happier once the burden of office was removed from him and taking him away from such a difficult responsibility was one of the better judgements made by George IV. However, the Canning/Goderich saga experimented with putting the Tories into coalition with the Whigs, whilst facing opposition from factions of both parties. So the question facing the Tories at this time was the same as the one facing the country: where will the next leader come from?

Arthur Wellesley, 1St Duke of Wellington
(1828 – 1834)

God deliver me from my friends! I'll take care of my enemies
myself

The Duke of Wellington, November 1828

As long as the Government can maintain it self, and will maintain
me, 'tis sure of me: But I have liv'd too long at Court to die a Martyr

Daniel Defoe's *Tory*, 1692

THE DAY AFTER GODERICH'S 'RESIGNATION' the
Duke of Wellington was asked by the King to form a
government. At this point he must have been feeling very much
like a last resort but his sense of duty was too strong even to
consider not accepting. He had looked on, horrified, as the
people who stood against everything he believed in had been
admitted into influential government posts because of
Canning's need for support and Goderich's naïve experiment
to unite Whigs and Tories forever.
　　　　Now the Duke had the opportunity to undo all that by
bringing the Ultras back into power. The first person he enlisted
was Robert Peel, who was to return to his previous role as
Home Secretary as well as Leader of the House of Commons.
Henry Goulburn became Chancellor of the Exchequer. All
other positions were filled by Ultras or Canningites. The King's
speech, largely worked on by Wellington, included a
condemnation of the events in Navarino; already the
administration was prepared to be stronger that its immediate
predecessor. However, so was the opposition. Whereas under
Canning and, it would be safe to assume, under Goderich, the
opposition Whigs were reserved (formally opposed to the
government but appreciative that the result of their pushing too
hard may be that the government falls and is replaced by the
Ultras), now that their bitter enemies were back in power they
had nothing to lose from an all-out attack. They painted a

picture of Wellington as a military despot[1] – seizing political power in a quasi-legitimate manner, but still little better than the French Generals of thirty years earlier.

Early in 1828 Lord Russell, a future Prime Minister himself, introduced a motion calling for the repeal of the Test and Corporation Acts. These Acts in essence prevented Protestants of non-Anglican denominations from holding public office in England. This was dangerous territory for the new administration. Wellington was a passionate establishmentarian who saw nothing wrong with privilege for those within the elitist sphere. However, feelings against Methodism or Scottish Presbyterianism, for example, were not as strong as anti-Catholic sentiments. Therefore the motion was likely to be carried and the government, if opposed to it, would be embarrassingly defeated at an early juncture. That said, to support it and then oppose the Catholic Question when it would invariably come up again at a later date could lead to charges of inconsistency. In the event Wellington made the government position to support the motion in order to avoid immediate embarrassment. Although it passed the Commons safely[2] and looked set to do the same in the Lords, its reading in the Upper House was not a comfortable experience for the new Prime Minister. He was attacked by the minority who opposed the Bill as having abandoned his own principles, which for years had defended the system he was now proposing to undo. Many of these critics were good friends of the Duke, which made the attacks all the more painful.[3] Once the Bill had passed it had achieved both of Russell's primary and secondary aims in proposing it: to remove unfair discrimination against non-Anglican Protestants; and to hurt the government.

It was rather portentous that despite a large and influential number of ministers opposing the repeal of the Test and Corporation Acts in principle, supporting it in spite of their reservations was the only major issue on which they could unanimously agree in that first session of Parliament. The other prominent matter which caused divisions were Corn and parliamentary reform. Regarding the former, Wellington was naturally disposed towards protectionism but once again aware that a significant faction within his ministry was eager for liberalisation of the market. In the end it was settled that a further law would be passed, reducing the price below which protection would be afforded to farmers but keeping it there nonetheless.[4] The second issue of parliamentary reform cropped up because of the disfranchisement of Penrhyn voted on during Canning's tenure. The constituency had lost its representation in Parliament because of corruption from the officials working there. By 1828 the time had come for Parliament to make a decision as to what would happen to Penrhyn's representation. It would have to be transferred somewhere else but the question was *where*?

The Prime Minister was in favour of having it moved into the next borough but a sizeable number wanted to see it transferred to Manchester, as increasing numbers of Members recognised the importance of growing cities and their needs for representation.[5] On both of these issues the factions within the administration that stood opposed to Wellington were Canningites, namely Huskisson (a favourite of both Canning and Goderich), Lord Palmerston, Lord Dudley, Charles Grant and William Lamb.

After the Penrhyn episode (which went the way of the Canningites) came a vote on taking similar action against another corrupt constituency – East Retford. In this case a Whig peer openly paid the few freemen eligible to vote to support his candidate and had done for many years. It didn't become an issue until the seat became contested in the 1826 election and the extent of the corruption became widely exposed. Again the Duke felt that expanding another county constituency was favourable whereas the Canningites voted to enfranchise the nearby city of Birmingham in its place. This time they were defeated and following the vote Huskisson offered the Prime Minister his resignation, evidently believing the Duke needed him and would beg him to stay. Huskisson's conviction was that once he had managed to force Wellington to grovel he would have greater leverage over him in future.

The Duke did not buckle, though, and informed Huskisson that he would take his letter of resignation to the King. Over the next few days Palmerston and Dudley were both despatched to convince Wellington that accepting Huskisson's resignation was a mistake and he should change his mind.[6] When the Prime Minister did not capitulate, they informed him that if Huskisson went they would also be forced to go. Wellington was happy to accept all their resignations and, along with Huskisson, Palmerston and Dudley, Grant and

Lamb also left office. The Ultras were now finally free of their Liberal Tory balls-and-chains.

Whatever feelings of success this episode may have stirred inside Wellington and his supporters was to be short-lived. The 1828 session ended in embarrassment. In order to replace the Canningites, Wellington necessarily had to promote from within the comparatively narrow Ultra Tory faction. Various appointments were made including William Vesey Fitzgerald to the office of President of the Board of Trade. This seemed a relatively insignificant assignment at the time it was announced. Since the passing of the Succession to the Crown Act 1707, MPs were required to resign their seats and seek re-election from their constituents in order to accept an appointment to a government office. This was one uncharacteristically democratic process at a time when a tiny minority in the country was enfranchised. This practice was not eradicated until 1926.

Fitzgerald subsequently resigned his seat in County Clare, Ireland, and sought to be returned as a minister of the Crown. However, he was challenged by a leading Irish Roman Catholic named Daniel O'Connell. By law Catholics could not sit in Parliament at Westminster and so until this point in history it had seemed pointless for any Catholic to stand for election. However, O'Connell became aware that although he could not claim a seat in Westminster there was nothing to in law to prevent him from standing.[7] Due to the demographics of Ireland being strongly Catholic, and Priests from all over County Clare campaigning on his behalf, O'Connell won the by-election comfortably. So the democratically elected representative of the people was now unable, by law, to represent the people. The consequence was that the government of the United Kingdom once again had to address the Catholic Question.

Incredibly, Wellington decided that the time had come to grasp the nettle and make the relevant concessions to allow O'Connell to take his seat (including taking a different Oath to the usual Oath of Supremacy sworn by Anglicans pledging allegiance to the monarch and the Church of England). The Prime Minister was now convinced that change was inevitable but Peel was against, as were most of the Duke's own supporters and, of course, the King.[8] There was no way for the Prime Minister to support pro-Catholic changes to the constitution without giving the appearance of having abandoned his Protestant principles. It was Peel that was the most important for the Duke to convince. 'Orange Peel' had prided himself on his steadfast Protestant position whenever this question had arisen throughout his career. Now he was the Prime Minister's second-in-command and the Leader of the House of Commons. If he was against the Duke then the government really was in trouble. Wellington's change of heart regarding emancipation may seem like a sign of indecisiveness or willingness to sacrifice his convictions for power. Neither accusation is easy to refute given the circumstances but another explanation makes far more sense. The fact was that for Wellington the ability of the King's government to function as effectively as possible was priority number one. Although he was principally opposed to emancipation, neither this nor anything else mattered more than the effective execution of government. O'Connell's actions had made the governing of Ireland impossible without emancipation and therefore it must be delivered. He spent the next eight months trying to convince Peel of his viewpoint.

In the end this argument found its way through. Peel still did not consider himself pro-Catholic, but he accepted that the harm done in leaving the issue unresolved was greater than the harm in legislating in favour of emancipation. Whereas initially he felt that his position in the government was incompatible with proposing emancipation on the basis that he had argued so passionately against it in the past, Peel was further convinced by Wellington to remain on the basis that the administration couldn't survive without him.[9] The King was much more intransigent in his opinion but, in the end, much more easy to overcome as an obstacle. If one thing was known about George IV by those ministers who had served him for the best part of two decades, it was that he wanted an easy life. The events with the King played out as follows:

After winning Peel round to the benefits of emancipation at the end of 1828, Wellington's Cabinet worked on a plan to make the principle more tolerable for the monarch, including introducing safeguards for the establishment. By March 1829 they had failed and so, after a meeting on 3 March between King George, Wellington, Peel and Lord Lyndhurst (the Lord Chancellor) in which George outright refused to support their proposals, all three tendered their resignations.[10]

By the following day they had all received letters from the King asking them to retract. So, on 5 March 1829, Robert Peel was able to introduce into the House of Commons a Roman Catholic Relief Bill, on behalf of the government, unanimously supported by the Cabinet and accepted by the King.

In spite of the large majorities that the government could expect for its Bill, given the support from the Whigs and the Liberal Tories, including the Canningites who had resigned from office the previous year, the debates were fought with anger from the minority opposing the measures. On 10 March Wellington spoke in the Lords in support of his measures for the first time. On this occasion the Earl of Winchelsea rose to criticise the government, request a general election and suggest further parliamentary reform (believing that the population of the country was anti-emancipation, he calculated that by making Parliament more representative, the House of Commons would never again pass such a Bill). The Duke responded with little difficulty but Winchelsea persisted and, over the next few days he wrote open letters which found their way into newspapers suggesting that the Prime Minister intended to allow Popery into every aspect of government. The Duke demanded satisfaction and so within days the Prime Minister of the United Kingdom met one of his own backbench Lords at Battersea Fields for a duel. In the event Winchelsea refused to raise his pistol. Wellington shot and missed,[11] whether deliberately or not is impossible to say. The fact that the Duke rose to the bait and fought a duel whilst holding the highest office of state, rather than let such a relatively minor insult pass, suggests that he was feeling under strain at this point in time.

The emancipation legislation passed into law and once it did Wellington looked forward to a period of stable government having now solved the issue that had caused disruption to the people of Ireland and the various governments of the United Kingdom for decades. However, contrary to ending the tensions between Catholics and Protestants, the granting of emancipation only indirectly served to intensify them. On 15 May 1829 O'Connell arrived at Westminster to claim his seat in Parliament. Had the ministry handled the situation better then nearly a century of conflict may have been avoided, but they didn't. Rather than allowing O'Connell to go about his business quietly, MPs insisted that because he had been elected before the Emancipation Bill he must take the old

Oath of Supremacy, not the new one built into law only recently.[12] O'Connell refused and was therefore forced to seek re-election. He would be unopposed but he campaigned heavily on a message that the Union would never accept Catholics and so the people of Ireland must from now on work endlessly to repeal the Act of Union and gain their independence. Irish Republicanism would soon be a national institution.

The 1829 session closed without further noteworthy incidents, although civil discontent was rife throughout the country due to various factors: many people were unhappy with the emancipation granted to Catholics; they were disillusioned with politics, having seen blatant corruption in areas such as Penrhyn and East Retford, which were believed not to be isolated incidents; agriculturalists were dissatisfied with the protection for grain having been reduced the previous year. The Duke was not overly concerned by reports he received of popular dissatisfaction, believing them to be exaggerated. However, due to the occurrence of a completely unrelated event they would lead to the downfall of his ministry by the following year.

In June 1830 King George IV died. With no legitimate children of his own it was his brother, William, who succeeded him as King William IV. William was generally seen as a refreshing change from the idle George. He was instinctively less inclined to Toryism than his brother, but made it clear from the outset of his reign that he intended to keep the same ministry that George had left, paying great reverence to the Duke.[13] However, circumstances would also play a part in the fate of the ministry and the indirect consequences of George's death meant that Wellington's administration was living on borrowed time. Under the law at the time, once a monarch died a general election had to be held within six months. The government in this instance decided to go to the country almost immediately and so an election was scheduled for the end of July.

The government's strategy for the election was to target seats currently controlled by Canningites so as to remove them from Parliament to be replaced by a more loyal breed of Tory. However, it was not to be and the result of the election was that the government clearly lost support in the Commons. Wellington realised that he needed to strengthen his government if it was to survive. In spite of the blatant manner in which he had tried to eliminate the Canningites during the election, the Duke must have been aware during the summer of 1830 that he now needed to court them to make his ministry viable. Of the big names within that faction, Huskisson was widely seen as the leader and an opportunity for a reconciliatory discussion presented itself in the early autumn.

On 15 September 1830 the Liverpool-Manchester railway line was opened for use. As MP for Liverpool, Huskisson was present at the opening and due to ride on one of the trains that would convoy from Liverpool to Manchester that day. As Prime Minister, Wellington would do the same, though on a separate train, in order to show his support in an official capacity. Sixteen miles into the journey the convoy made a scheduled stop to take on water. As a safety precaution all passengers were advised to remain within their carriages but a few dozen people did get out for various reasons. Huskisson was one of them and at this time he approached the Duke's carriage to speak to him. Whether the pair could have been reconciled is impossible to tell but it is a clear sign of the Prime Minister's fortunes that he would never have the opportunity to try. During the encounter George Stephenson's *Rocket* came along the line at a speed fast enough to frighten the crowd into dispersing. Huskisson tried to get out of the way and failed, having his leg crushed and ultimately dying of his injuries.[14] He was the one and only fatality. Contemporaries felt that Wellington had been politically fortunate that the only person to have been killed was 'his most dangerous opponent, the one from whom he had most to fear'[15] but given what became of the Duke's government in the following weeks perhaps the truth is that reconciliation with Huskisson may well have been an opportunity missed.

Shortly afterwards the Duke made overtures to Palmerston for an alliance but the latter was insistent on bringing all of his followers back into government which would have had the effect of diluting Wellington's influence to the point where it would be negligible. The result was that negotiations broke down and the government was to soldier on. Morale was becoming a problem, though. Peel, who alone had been expected to take on the increasingly burdensome task of defending the government in the Commons, was becoming particularly dejected. When Parliament was opened by the King on 2 November there was no mention of parliamentary reform in his speech. The Whigs immediately responded by asserting the need for it, claiming that discontent throughout the country could be settled by it. Wellington responded by steadfastly refusing to support any measure in favour of changing the system currently in place.

On 9 November the Duke was due to attend the Lord Mayor's banquet along with the King and Queen. As the date approached, though, rumours were circulating of a plot to attack or even kill him. Henry Hunt, the individual who was due to be arrested on 16 August 1819, leading to the Peterloo Massacre, was ostentatiously pronouncing to hostile crowds the inadequacies both of the current political system and of the government's ability to change it.[16] As more and more reports reached ministers all suggesting the same thing – that an attack was going to happen and that widespread disorder would inevitably follow – the Duke advised the King not to attend and made the decision himself to withdraw from the event. Whether due to Wellington's decision not to attend or because rumours were exaggerated, in the event aside from small-scale clashes between the military and public the night passed rather uneventfully. However, the fact that disturbances had occurred at all seemed to substantiate Whig claims that reform was necessary and the fact that there had been no attack on the Duke led to allegations that he had overreacted and even acted out of cowardice.[17]

On 15 November Parliament debated the government's Civil List – effectively Members were being asked to ratify the proposal for royal expenditure including the King and Queen's personal allowances. The vote was widely viewed as one of confidence in the government, which was defeated by 29 votes.[18] Wellington had been at home at the time of the vote and it was Peel who delivered the news to him personally, along with advice that the government must immediately resign. Wellington may well have wanted to fight on but he could not without Peel, who was resolutely committed to resignation, having suffered from overwork for too long. So, for the first time since Lord Grenville had taken office over two decades earlier, a Whig was to ascend to the Prime Ministership of the United Kingdom as a disappointed William IV sent for Lord Grey to form a ministry of his own.

It was clear from the outset that the Whigs would pursue an agenda aimed at achieving some form of parliamentary reform. After all they had spent almost the entire legislative session pushing for it and Wellington's comments opposing reform during the King's speech debate was seen by many contemporary observers as having represented the hammering of the final nail into his Prime Ministerial coffin. However, nobody expected the extent to which the new government would attempt to take reform. On 1 March 1831 Lord John Russell, the individual who had caused Wellington problems during the early days of his first session in power by calling for a repeal of the Test and Corporation Acts, and who was now a member of Lord Grey's government, introduced their proposals to Parliament. It stunned the Tories and all they could do was laugh uncomfortably, forcing themselves to believe that the measures were political suicide, evidently misjudging the mood of the nation. Russell was suggesting disfranchising sixty rotten boroughs and reducing the number of representatives in a further forty-seven from two representatives to one. All in all 168 Members would lose their seats.[19]

Peel alone appeared to recognise the significance of the motion, apparently aware that any attempt of his own to introduce a smaller-scale reform aimed at appeasing all parties would look comparably ineffectual. Peel led the opposition against it in the Commons whilst Wellington took the lead in the Lords. The Ultras, generally opposed to the Bill, were ready to accept their leader back with open arms but the Duke was cautious having been burned by them once. He needed to rally support somehow, though, because the Reform Bill was coming to the Lords having passed the Commons on 21 March by 302 votes to 301.[20] The victory of this Bill was devastating to Tory peers who relied on the establishment's status quo to maintain their privileges but the narrow margin produced some comfort because the Lords as a body was likely to be less in favour of the measures than the Commons.

As the Bill went through Committee stage General Isaac Gascoyne, a Tory Ultra, attached an amendment stating that there must be no changes to the number of seats in England or Wales, which almost defeated the purpose of the Bill itself. The amendment was carried by a slim majority on 20 April[21] but the government could not accept this and asked the King to dissolve Parliament. Ministers, MPs and Lords all discussed the matter in a fiery confrontation on 22 April and tempers were only calmed by the arrival of King William himself at Westminster, declaring his intention to respect the requests of his ministers and call an election. On 28 April polling began and by 1 June the historic election came to an end. The Tories, who had won a majority the year before, were now devastated by a public who supported reform. Across the country Ultras were swept aside or else refused to stand in order to avoid the inevitable embarrassment. The Whigs returned with a majority of around 130 seats. Political pain was accompanied by personal grief for the Duke as, on 24 April, his wife died. Then, on 27 April, rioters smashed the windows of his house and were seemingly intent on destroying the entire building, in spite of his wife's body still lying inside, only being dispersed by warning shots fired into the air by his staff.

When Parliament reconvened in June the Whig government, bolstered by increased numbers in the Commons and the knowledge that the electorate supported their policies, introduced a Reform Bill into the Commons for the second time and on this occasion it was passed comfortably. Before seeing it debated in the Lords Wellington canvassed the Tory Ultras. He was still sure not to commit any promises to them in terms of Cabinet positions should he return to power but in this instance he needed their support. At the beginning of October the Lords debated the Reform Bill. Over five days passionate oratory on both sides enraptured a packed House and in the end the Bill was defeated, almost inevitably. Lord Grey requested a temporary recess while the Cabinet discussed options. During this time the Prime Minister implored the King to create at least forty Whig peers to allow him to overturn the majority in the Upper House. Riots spread up and down the country which Grey argued was evidence that the public needed to see reformed institutions, whereas for Wellington it was evidence of agitators deliberately stirring up unrest and therefore reform should be resisted in order to keep these criminals out of Parliament.

In the end the King refused to create the number of peers required to ensure a Whig majority and so the only option left to the government was to reintroduce the Bill with some concessions to win over the moderate Lords. The concessions included Gascoyne's amendment from the previous year (although Gascoyne had lost his seat during the general election) to keep the number of seats in England and Wales the same, albeit some would be redistributed within these regions. This was enough to do the trick and on this occasion the Bill passed through the House of Lords, once again ready for the Committee stage. The atmosphere was an uncertain one. Wellington had opposed the Bill with all his being, convinced that reform would lead to revolution; the waverers had won the day for the Whigs but the real test would be at the Committee stage and if the Bill did not pass unchallenged what would happen then? Would another election be held (there had already been two in as many years)? Would the King create forty or fifty Whig peers? Would revolution break out either way?

On 7 May 1832 an amendment attached by Lord Lyndhurst which postponed discussion of the disfranchisement of rotten boroughs was carried. Lord Grey had now had enough of the filibustering tactics of the opposition. He gained the consent of his Cabinet to go to the King and demand the creation of fifty new peers or else they would resign. Once he attended Windsor and presented his ultimatum to William, the King accepted his resignation and sent the trouble-causing Lord Lyndhurst to instruct Wellington to form a ministry. The next few days saw Wellington sounding out the leading Tories on their willingness to serve, but found few positive responses. Peel wouldn't on the basis that a new government would have to enact some sort of reform and having already backtracked on emancipation he worried that this would become his reputation if he took the same course of action on this issue.[22] Many members of the Duke's former administration took the same line. Wellington, though vehemently opposed to reform, was willing to accept it if it meant that a stable Tory government could continue. Many of his allies were less strident opponents of the principle of reform, but were less willing to buckle owing to their unwillingness to appear weak.

The Duke informed the King that he could not form a government and Grey was invited back. On 17 May Wellington defended in the Lords his attempts to form an administration and criticised the Reform Bill. An outraged Grey demanded that the King create his peers to settle the issue once and for all, which William agreed to but in the end it was unnecessary. Wellington, having given up hope, stopped attending the debates and Tory opposition melted away. On 4 June the Great Reform Bill passed into law.

Wellington would return to the Lords once the Reform Bill had passed, seeing it as his duty to keep serving the country for as long as he had the capacity to do so. However, the passing of the Bill left him thoroughly depressed about the state of the country. Aside from disfranchising scores of rotten boroughs, the Great Reform Bill also enfranchised many more voters. Now one in seven males were eligible to vote[23] and so to give the new electorate an opportunity to express itself a general election was called for in December, the third in as many years. The result was a disaster for the Tories. Of 650 seats they won somewhere in the region of 150. The Whigs were now by far the dominant party, with the Tories being roughly equal in numbers to followers of Daniel O'Connell and his Radicals.[24] Although the Tories continued in formal opposition, Wellington saw as his mission a more pressing priority of defeating the Radicals than defeating the government. In his world, where the ability of the King's government to continue functioning was the priority over and above everything else, the Radicals were the biggest threat to everything he held dear. The way he saw it the Whigs were ideologically flawed but at least they wanted to make changes within the framework that he cherished. The Radicals wanted to dismantle that framework altogether.

Due to the numbers of Tories now in the Commons the idea of a Tory government was not a possibility. Therefore if the Whig government fell, chaos and disorder would surely descend on Britain. The only option open to Wellington, in his mind, was constructive opposition; challenging the government when he felt that they were wrong but not aiming to see them fall. The Ultras were dismayed by this, wanting to take the fight to the Whigs rather than what they saw as rolling over. However, with nobody else in the Lords to lead them they had little choice but to fall behind the Duke.

In the Commons, Peel coincidentally followed the same strategy, without a meeting of minds to have planned it,[25] and the Ultras there followed his lead for much the same reasons. Peel's rationale for his actions was different to Wellington's; he wasn't concerned about anarchy if the current ministry collapsed, he was concerned that the Tories were not currently strong enough to lead. Therefore he had to bide his time to attract supporters away from the Whigs and Radicals.

When in each other's company, Peel and Wellington were amicable and they would strategise where necessary but there was a tension there that had not existed during the times of Liverpool, Canning and Goderich. Wellington still remembered that Peel had insisted on resigning when his own ministry had a chance to fight on in 1830 and he had refused to join a new ministry led by the Duke when the King requested them to in 1832. Peel felt that Wellington regarded him as shying away from his duties because of these incidents, which may well have been true. Ostensibly the two would remain loyal to each other for the rest of their lives, whatever private feelings they may have had.

Early in the 1833 session the newly-strengthened Whig government introduced an Irish Church Bill into Parliament, intended to help calm lawlessness within that country by reducing the burden of the Church of Ireland on the populace. At this point in time all Irish earners paid tithes to a Church that the vast majority did not belong to and emancipation had done little to quell discontent in the Emerald Isle. This latest sop was intended by the Whigs to go hand-in-hand with a tougher enforcement of the law to end trouble there forever. For the Duke, the legislation was unacceptable but his growing fear that revolution in Britain was growing ever nearer led him to be cautious when attempting to defeat the government. Consequently he advised his followers to abstain from voting against the measures, which they did, then attach a series of amendments to the Bill at Committee stage[26] to make the legislation impotent, which they also did. The Whigs eventually accepted the ridiculous additions on the basis that the principle of the Church of Ireland not being immune from reform had been recognised, so in future it could be revisited. The government could claim that they had passed their legislation through both Houses and were therefore viable and able to continue in office. The Ultras could rest assured that no actual changes had been enacted.

The fact that the Whig government was less able to carry out the sort of political reforms that it had hoped to led to the ebbing of morale on their side. At the end of the 1833 session the Duke felt that his strategy had been vindicated against the wishes of the Ultras and so, going into 1834 he once again took to reining them in when it came to attacking the government in the Lords, whilst leaving Peel to do the same in the Commons.

In the autumn of 1833 the Duke was offered the Chancellorship of Oxford University in spite of not having had a university education. By all accounts he modestly replied that he was not qualified and implored the University to find someone else but when they insisted that there was nobody, Wellington accepted and was elected unopposed in January 1834. When news of this reached Peel he was understandably dismayed.[27] He was an intellectual of high public standing; he had attended Oxford University himself in his youth; he had represented the Oxford University seat in Parliament until the Catholic emancipation affair in 1829 when he had felt compelled to resign having spent a career opposing emancipation and then about-turning on the issue. The fact that he had not been considered cemented in his mind the suspicion that he had not been forgiven by his old constituents. The fact that it was Wellington who had convinced him to change his mind on the Catholic Question, and yet he was being honoured while Peel was being snubbed, only served to increase his private resentment of the Duke.

Throughout 1834 the government slowly began to crumble. They were not as effective in the legislature as a group with such a large majority should be and they were divided as to how reform should happen. In May the Cabinet agreed, after pressure from Lord Russell, to set up a commission to examine the possibility of siphoning excess revenue from the Church of Ireland for spending elsewhere. Some ministers felt that Church revenue should stay in the Church and resigned on principle. Among those abandoning the government was the Irish Secretary, the future Conservative Prime Minister but then-Whig Edward Stanley; and the ex-Tory Prime Minister but now-Whig Earl of Ripon (previously Viscount Goderich). The ministry was finished and, on 8 July, Grey resigned. The King sent for Lord Melbourne, a minister in Grey's government who, before his elevation, had been the Canningite William Lamb who had abandoned Wellington's administration when Huskisson had held him hostage over reform in 1828.

There were still several weeks left in the parliamentary session and the Duke felt that he could use this time to prevent the government from enacting anything new, using his influence to defeat proposed legislation to allow Protestant dissenters into Oxford and Cambridge Universities. The parliamentary session ended on 15 August and the Duke prepared for a quiet recess, those of the 1830, 1831 and 1832 sessions having been disturbed by the effects of general elections and 1833 being dominated by correspondence with Oxford University about his Chancellorship. Such was the conviction of Members of both Houses that nothing of significance would occur that Peel left for Italy in October with his wife and daughter.

However, it was not to be. On 10 November Earl Spencer died meaning that his son Lord Althorp would inherit his title.[28] This would not normally be a significant event but Lord Althorp was the Whig Leader of the House of Commons and his inherited peerage meant elevation to the Lords, which could not in those days be discounted or postponed. The government was as lacking in strong debaters in the Commons as Liverpool's had been and when the new Prime Minister, Melbourne, presented the news to William IV the King saw no possibility of the administration continuing.[29] He dismissed his ministers and sent for Wellington to begin a new government. The Duke met with the King and told him that he could not form a government but that the time had come for the Tories to be led by Peel.[30] His reasons for deferring to his old ally were threefold. Firstly he was of the firm belief that any future government had to be led from within the House of Commons. Recent Whig reforms had consistently attacked the establishment and Wellington was convinced that more was to come, maybe even revolution. Either further reforms would come restricting the powers of the aristocracy or else a revolution would destroy them forever. Secondly, the Duke was getting older and already starting to be hampered by hearing difficulties. Although he was committed to serve his country until he could no longer, he felt that a younger man would have greater capacity. Thirdly he had been in that position before and had found that he commanded no greater amount of respect for all his military achievements. He could not keep recalcitrant Tory Lords in line and perhaps somebody with less of an uncompromising reputation would be better suited to drawing in moderate Members.

The King concurred but the problem was that Peel was somewhere in Italy. Wellington agreed to undertake all responsibilities of State alone on a temporary basis until Peel returned. Within nine days one of the Queen's officers had left

London, sailed to France, travelled to Italy, found Peel and got his agreement to form a ministry.[29] The Iron Duke was now no longer leader of the Tories.

Wellington had led his party for six years, the majority of which had been in opposition. He is remembered by history as a reactionary on the basis that he opposed changes to the establishment including parliamentary and electoral reform. This is certainly the case and there is little disputing that throughout his career Wellington was an obstacle to change. However, as Prime Minister he introduced Catholic Relief legislation, the most radical piece of pro-Catholic legislation in history. This in itself, though, is another cause for criticism. Wellington had been personally opposed to Catholic emancipation, yet he supported its passage. In doing so he has left himself open to charges on having no principles, or at least of easily abandoning them. Contrary to this, though, Wellington was very much a man of principle. In all his political career he had one overriding principle which for him far outweighed all other concerns. This was that His Majesty's Government must be allowed to continue. Once this is understood, Wellington as a politician is understood. The King's government should not be brought down or else revolution may easily follow and if that meant swallowing distasteful legislation then so be it.

So it was that by disposition the most reactionary Prime Minister of the times passed one of the most progressive pieces of legislation ever. However, even this was not enough to get the public on-side. Nearly two decades after Waterloo when the glory of that battle was long forgotten, riots swept the country and the Duke's house was targeted. In 1833 crowds pelted him with stones as he rode his horse. He was not loved and the result of the 1830-32 elections show that he was out of touch with the public, a relic of a by-gone era. His role was to keep the party going long enough for a new name to grow in stature to the point where he was ready to take the reins and then the Tories would undergo one of several transformations to come over the years.

From Tories to Conservatives

THROUGHOUT THE PERIOD IN OPPOSITION Sir Robert Peel had been undergoing a personal transition which would go on to infest every facet of the Tory Party, forcing it to undergo the same alterations. After Wellington's ministry had fallen many Ultras blamed Peel, like Wellington privately did, for the fact that he had not wanted to fight on. His motives will undoubtedly have been complex, as these decisions rarely come down to a single issue. He had found it difficult carrying the government in the Commons; he had lost his sense of identity after changing his views on Catholic emancipation; he wasn't entirely sure how he felt about parliamentary reform and therefore could not credibly make a stand either way on the issue.

For Peel this period saw the beginning of an intense personal dislike of the Ultras. As much as he resisted the Radicals he felt that the hard-line Tories were almost as much of a problem. 'He despised what he saw as their amateur and selfish approach to politics. He rejected their refusal to look beyond their own park gates to the interests of the nation as a whole and consult the greater good'[1]. If the Ultras had only opened themselves up to the possibility of change, then they would never have caused Wellington so many problems and that government need not have fallen. If they had only accepted that some measure of reform was necessary then the Whigs would never have introduced their radical changes into Parliament, forcing widespread changes on institutions that may not have been considered otherwise.

Once Peel had been sent for, to commence his own administration, he recognised the need for a broader based government than the Tories had previously been used to. He had spent his time in opposition trying to secure defectors from the government by constructive opposition to particular policies and ideally he would have liked to have had more time to continue building his support, but time was not on his side and now he had to make the most of the situation at hand. So Peel set his mind to reforming the Tory Party, making it more viable to the electorate but also more attractive to dissident Whigs. The term 'Conservative' had been used sporadically over the previous few years to identify the more moderate

Tories, a group distinct from the Ultras but not necessarily the Canningites, many of whom, such as the Earl of Ripon, had happily joined the recent Whig ministry.

Peel was happy with the term, which meant dropping the Tory brand whose reputation had suffered over the past few years. There were several important developments during the December of 1834 that allowed the transition from one party to another party to take place. On the 9th, Peel arrived in London, met the King and formally accepted his invitation to form a government. He now needed to set about finding ministers. In the spirit of widening the base of the party he contacted Edward Stanley, who had been Irish Secretary in Lord Grey's government but had left due to disagreements over policy. Stanley was now floating in a chasm between Whig and Tory, which actually suited him for the time being. He saw himself as a future Prime Minister (indeed he would be) but saw no reason to assist Peel, who he now saw as a rival for the top job, and he was convinced that the new government would be the same old Tories, in which case he wanted to keep his distance. There is little doubting that Stanley saw his position between the two parties as one of advantage as he could draw support for both if ever he made a bid for the premiership. What would today be called 'stealing the centre ground' was first considered during this period. This is important because more than one historian has commented that what Peel did next was borne out of 'a need to pre-empt Stanley…'[2]. This theory may hold some water but it is unlikely. Peel accepted the seals of office from King William on 9 December and wrote to various individuals offering them places in his Cabinet immediately afterwards. Stanley replied to Peel declining his invitation on 11 December and by the 13th the new Prime Minister had constructed his Cabinet. On 18 December what we now know as the Tamworth Manifesto was published, outlining the government's position. Events here moved so quickly that the argument that Peel's manifesto was designed to combat the threat from Stanley can be discounted. This was a position that Peel had held for many years and now he was given the platform to express himself. An explanation of what happened is thus:

In order to accept government office in the nineteenth century MPs had to seek re-election from their constituents. Therefore Peel would need to be re-elected to Tamworth.

However, he had wanted more time in opposition to attract Whig defectors and now that this was not an option, the only way to create a viable government would be to increase the numbers of Conservatives in the Commons by calling a general election. So he decided that upon being elected back as MP for Tamworth and, thereby, being ratified by the electorate as Prime Minister, he would ask the King to dissolve Parliament and hope for a stronger position after a general election. Therefore, he decided to put a personal manifesto out to the electors of Tamworth explaining his position, which was not unusual except that in this instance he was trying to use it as a manifesto for a new political party. What made it more unusual was that it was widely known that this local election would lead to a national one and that this particular manifesto would therefore be the party position going forward. The result was that Peel's Tamworth Manifesto was printed nationally, finding its way to the furthest reaches of the Kingdom and it now represents the beginning of the Conservative Party.

In drawing up the manifesto the major issue that Peel had to address was the Reform Bill. His attitude towards this piece of legislation would define his political position. He could renounce it and pledge to do all in his power to reverse it which would win over the Ultras but alienate most of the electorate, which had been demonstrated by the poor results that the Tories saw in the 1832 general election. He could promise to carry on further reforms, but this would be inconsistent with his own position, or he could promise to defend the system as it was and pledge to commit to change wherever he felt that it was necessary. The section of the manifesto dedicated to the Reform Bill stated:

> With respect to the Reform Bill itself, I will repeat now the declaration I made when I entered the House of Commons as a member of the Reformed Parliament – that I consider the Reform Bill a final and irrevocable settlement of a great constitutional question – a settlement which no friend to the peace and welfare of this country would attempt to disturb, either by direct or by insidious means.

Here Peel clearly lays out his intentions: the Reform Bill settled the issue of corruption and therefore it should not be touched.

Next, Peel went on to address the consequences of the Bill for public servants and how he sees his own duties being undertaken in the new Parliament:

> Then, as to the spirit of the Reform Bill, and the willingness to adopt and enforce it as a rule of government: if, by adopting the spirit of the Reform Bill, it be meant that we are to live in a perpetual vortex of agitation; that public men can only support themselves in public estimation by adopting every popular impression of the day, - by promising the instant redress of anything which anybody may call an abuse – by abandoning altogether that great aid of government – more powerful than either law or reason – the respect for ancient rights, and the deference to prescriptive authority; if this be the spirit of the Reform Bill, I will not undertake to adopt it. But if the spirit of the Reform Bill implies merely a careful review of institutions…I can for myself and my colleagues undertake to act in such a spirit and with such intentions.[3]

In this long paragraph Peel begins by stating that he will not become a slave to public opinion and that he will not address every grievance that the electorate or the general public feel that they have with particular institutions. His own judgement will decide what should, and what should not, be addressed by the State. Here he sounds incredibly similar to Edmund Burke, often seen as the father of modern conservatism, in a speech he made to the electors of Bristol some sixty years earlier. On that occasion Burke remarked that 'your representative owes you, not his industry only, but his judgment; and he betrays you, instead of serving you, if he sacrifices it to your opinion'[4].

This goes to illustrate that the principles of the Conservative Party were partly founded within the Tamworth Manifesto. Further into the paragraph Peel goes on to set out his position that if the Reform Bill means that careful review should be undertaken of all institutions then he will carry its spirit through. In other words he was open to change, if it is purposeful and steady, but not sweeping changes to stable institutions and not change for the sake of it.

This provided a slight crisis of identity for the new Party. In his fictional work *Coningsby*, based around the events of the time, the future Conservative Prime Minister Benjamin Disraeli commented that 'There was indeed a considerable shouting about what they called Conservative principles; but the awkward question naturally arose, what will you conserve?' The fact was that the Conservatives were for protecting established practices and institutions whilst leaving themselves open to the possibility of change. So would it be the case that they would 'protect the prerogatives of the Crown, provided they are not exercised; the independence of the House of Lords, provided it is not asserted; the Ecclesiastical estate, provided it is regulated by a commission of laymen? Everything, in short, that is established, as long as it is a phrase and not a fact'⁵?

The fact was that the Tories were displaying an adaptability that would allow them to survive through the centuries. This rings with what Defoe said about his Whigs and Tories 150 years earlier: the new Party, much like the old faction, recognised that to the public, they must, to some extent, follow their opinion. The problem was that this necessarily meant changing and change inevitably means leaving someone behind; in this instance the old establishment. The sort of Tories that had followed Wellington and Liverpool, even Perceval and Pitt, now found themselves no longer wanted by their party, nor able to identify with it.

Perhaps the conversation between Tadpole and Taper in *Coningsby* was not far off, or certainly would not appear too far removed from the truth to the old Tories who had just seen their world transformed:

> 'Hush!' said Mr. Tadpole. 'The time has gone
> by for Tory governments, what the country
> requires is a sound Conservative government.'
> 'A sound Conservative government,' said
> Taper, musingly. 'I understand: Tory men and
> Whig measures.'⁶

In the modern world such a change of tack can be spun as smart political strategy. Indeed many saw it as such at the time but it does smack with the feeling of abandoning principles. The truth is that it was more of a generational issue: the old Tories held on to outdated values and although they shared a Party with their younger colleagues they no longer held shared ideals. The new Conservatives were being true to themselves but being politically astute by trying to carry as many supporters with them as possible. So now the story unfolds into the middle third of the nineteenth century, with the leadership tenure of Sir Robert Peel.

Sir Robert Peel
(1834 − 1846)

It may be that I shall leave a name sometimes remembered with expressions of goodwill in the abodes of those whose lot it is to labour

Sir Robert Peel, June 1846

As for your Fashion of Government, Mr. Tory, I hope it is either gone to the Grave with King Charles, or to France with King James; and could heartily wish you would follow it to either place

Daniel Defoe's *Whig*, 1692

PEEL SOON ESTABLISHED that the only hope for his government to survive would be if he could increase the number of Conservative MPs, which meant calling a fresh election. In the spirit of building a broader based administration he approached various dissident Whigs, including Stanley, but they were not agreeable to joining him and in the end Peel's Cabinet was far more similar to Wellington's than he would have liked.[1] The Iron Duke himself returned as Foreign Secretary and William Gladstone, the future Liberal Prime Minister, entered the Conservative government as a junior minister.

Peel set out his Tamworth Manifesto, which was endorsed by the whole Cabinet, in order to seek re-election but as the only candidate standing in the Tamworth by-election caused by his resignation, he was returned unopposed. Parliament was subsequently dissolved at the end of December for a general election to be held throughout January. The result was that around 290 Members could support the Conservative government. Of 658 MPs this meant that they were still not a majority party, but it was a considerable improvement on the 150 or so from the 1832 election.[2]

Peel decided that his government must work within the principles of the Tamworth Manifesto if it was to survive. That is, protect institutions but propose limited reforms of them. The strategy, he believed, would draw in moderates whilst dividing his opponents between those who opposed any reform and those who wanted radical changes. He set his sights to reforming the Church of England as a means of protecting it from radical overhaul. The Church at this time was extremely unpopular, being seen just as corrupt as politics had been before the Reform Bill. Peel was always an antidisestablishmentarian but if he was going to stave off the arguments that the Church should be disestablished he knew it would need to change. Abuses were all too common, as is often the case when an institution is so heavily protected by the State.[3] He set up an Ecclesiastical Commission to report on the problems and the options.

However, Peel's hopes of uniting moderates whilst dividing his opponents didn't materialise during the 1835 session. Daniel O'Connell, the leader of the Radicals and the man whose election to Parliament had brought about Catholic emancipation, formed a limited alliance with the influential Whig Lord John Russell. The objective was simple: to bring down the government. This meant tactical voting in the Commons. Consequently throughout February and March the government suffered a series of defeats which seemed to be getting increasingly heavy. On 8 April 1835 the Cabinet was agreed that they must leave office, having been defeated on a vote about Irish Tithes on the 7th. They resigned with immediate effect seeing no other option available: they could not keep going as they had been proved impotent in the legislature; they could not call a general election in the hope that this would change the constitution of the Commons, as the result would certainly be the same as it had been three months earlier; they could not form a coalition having already tried and failed with Stanley and being principally opposed to the Radicals and the Whigs.

Peel returned to opposition as the King reluctantly sent for Melbourne. Peel must have known that he had taken office too soon. Had he remained in opposition for longer he could have continued with his strategy of picking off those disaffected with Whig policy, eventually building a majority for himself. Now that the burden of office had been removed he could return to this strategy. He was able to turn his hand to his opposition tactics immediately as the Whig government introduced a Municipal Corporations Bill into the House of

Commons. The spirit of this piece of legislation was to reform local government by making it more democratic and accountable. Peel supported it in principal and was happy to criticise particular sections which he saw as needing improvement whilst supporting the idea of reform. Because of his endorsement the Bill passed through the Commons but when it got to the Lords it was trounced by the Tory Ultras who sat there. Wellington did not possess the limited influence over them that he had wielded even twelve months earlier; they had a free rein.[4] They had no time for Peel's moderation or his strategy to pick off supporters from a group that they detested anyway. All Peel could do was stand by and watch as they ignored his design and undermined his leadership.

In August 1835, while the Ultras in the Lords were attaching whatever amendments that suited them to the Municipal Corporations Bill, Peel left London, effectively abandoning the parliamentary session. His rationale was to distance himself and his Conservatives in the Commons from the Ultras in the Lords. Once the Upper House had finished mauling the Bill it got sent back to the Commons for review. Now Peel returned to Parliament to reassert himself. On this occasion he worked closely with Lord John Russell to put together a Bill accepting some of the Lords' amendments but rejecting others. He had now shown the country that he was prepared to work with his opponents, putting political opportunism aside for the greater good, and he had shown the Lords that the Commons was united.

At this point in history the House of Lords still had the power to reject any legislation that was attempted to pass through their chamber but the threat of the King creating an unspecified number of peers to overrule them had been ever present in the backs of their minds since the Reform Bill saga and so a compromise on the Municipal Corporations Bill didn't seem such a bad deal. Meanwhile, during the same session Stanley, who had sat on the government's side of the House of Commons, more because there was no in-between option, had come to blows on several occasions with Daniel O'Connell, the Radical leader who found himself also on the government benches for no other reason than that he was not a Conservative. By the July of 1835 Radicalism within the government had become too prominent for Stanley's comfort and he made the symbolically significant gesture of taking his seat on the opposition benches, albeit he still would not formally align himself with Peel out of suspicion of the Ultras.[5]

The 1836 parliamentary session was a slow one. This was partly because the government found it difficult to introduce new legislation given that the Prime Minister, Lord Melbourne, was naturally cautious about change but the Radicals (who the government needed for support) wanted overhaul of the institutions. Consequently they were divided on what to do: they were aware that any controversial legislation would be defeated in the Lords anyway and they didn't want to create reason for their supporters to defect to the opposition, which was now almost as large as the government in the Lower House. What the session did see was Peel and Stanley voting together on the legislation that was considered and introducing joint amendments on it. The two worked together on many of their proposals and Peel must have known that he was getting closer to drawing Stanley into his official opposition; into his new Conservative Party.

During the recess Peel and Stanley strengthened their alliance as the latter started to realise that they were of a similar mindset on many policy areas. The pair agreed on a united strategy for the upcoming session[6] which relied on keeping the Ultras from attacking the government too heavily (which could have the effect of uniting Radicals and moderate Whigs more firmly in their need to defend themselves) whilst allowing the Radicals and Moderates on the government benches to divide themselves, which would invariably happen as they disagreed on almost every issue.

Things seemed to go as planned during the session and Melbourne increasingly turned to the Conservatives for support, unable to rely on the Radicals, which accentuated the fractures in the government. However, political events are rarely straightforward and often the unforeseen guides things much more powerfully than controlled circumstances. On 20 June 1837 King William IV died and his niece, Victoria, became Queen. This time there was to be no waiting around for a general election and Parliament was dissolved on 17 July. The result of the election was a gain in seats for the Conservatives, who now controlled over 300 and were only 30 or so short of the Whigs.[7] The momentum was moving towards Peel but even so he must have felt frustrated. The new Parliament could potentially last for seven years which meant that the government may hold on for a long time. Had William survived for longer, with public opinion gradually shifting in his direction, Peel may well have won a majority at the election.

There were two positives to take away from the events that followed, though. After returning from an autumn holiday in Germany, in time for the start of the new parliamentary session due in November, Peel gathered all of his Conservative MPs together at his house on the morning of the Queen's Speech as a means of reinforcing their collective sense of identity. Stanley and his chief Lieutenant James Graham both attended. They were now officially united with Peel. The second reason for optimism was that the Radicals and Russell argued over several issues raised in the Queen's Speech, which signified to Peel that a rift was on the way. Towards the end of December news broke that there had been a rebellion in Canada, which would prove to be a fine issue on which Peel could test his long term strategy.

Parliament was recalled in mid-January 1838 and the government proposed suppressing the Canadian rebellion (which Peel could fully support) and sending Lord Durham across the Atlantic to negotiate a lasting solution (which Peel could not endorse). The problem was that Lord Durham was underqualified for such a task and his natural inclinations would have him negotiating away all of the Crown's influence in the colony. The Radicals were also at loggerheads with the government on the issue. Being led by O'Connell who had made it his *raison d'être* since being refused his seat in Westminster when he first arrived in 1828 to release Ireland from the shackles of British colonialism. Therefore he saw no reason not to repeat the formula elsewhere. To him, Britain had no place in Canada and he would vote against the government if it tried to suppress a rebellion which was, to him, just a reflection of public sentiment.[8] So the choice for Peel was whether to support the government that he was officially opposed to, or to oppose the government even though it would mean aligning himself with the Radicals. Either way a major faction on the government side would feel aggrieved but by the same token the mistrust between Radicals and Whigs would increase. In the event Peel decided to support the government in quashing the rebellion and if Durham was despatched also, then this was unfortunate but so be it.

Throughout Peel kept to his long term strategy: defending cherished institutions; resisting Radicalism; accepting reform where it is evidently necessary. In other words enough Conservatism to keep the Party faithful happy whilst accepting enough reform to attract some moderate Whigs. All the while he saw his real opponents as the extreme Whigs and the Radicals.

On 12 May 1838 a dinner was held at the Merchant Taylors' Hall for 300 Conservative MPs. The Conservatives looked more like a modern Political Party now than at any other time in their history. Peel gave a speech in which he assured his supporters that the country was behind them, their strategy was working and that they should stick to it to reap the rewards. The 1838 session then ended uneventfully and by the start of 1839 the Conservatives were edging closer in number to the Whigs and Radicals in the Commons. The government was in trouble as crisis after crisis hit and its support diminished. The suitability of the Corn Laws was once again questioned as agitation in the country grew for their abolition. This issue split the Whigs and the Radicals again with the former in favour of keeping them and the latter in favour of affordable bread. Again Peel would support the government in order to protect them from their own followers, hardly able to foresee that this issue would one day cause him to realise his own crowning achievement whilst simultaneously bringing about his political downfall.

The final crisis for the government arose at the beginning of May. Slavery had been abolished in Britain since 1806 and unlawful in the rest of the Empire since 1833 but a system of slave 'apprenticeships' had been introduced as a transitional measure.[9] The reality was that 'apprenticeships' were little different to actual slavery: former slaves were encouraged to remain on their plantations and in return, if they worked for 40 ½ hours per work for free, they would be paid for every hour they worked over and above this threshold. The idea that they may be paid anything at all must have been an attractive one to people who had never known anything but absolute slavery, however the system required an uneducated workforce to be able to calculate for themselves the number of hours they worked each week. Melbourne wanted to intervene to ensure that the spirit of anti-slavery was being adhered to, whereas Peel suggested further enquiries were necessary before action was taken. The government carried the day but with a tiny majority. Melbourne had lost his confidence: he was tired of fighting the opposition as well as simultaneously fighting his own Radical 'supporters' and so, on 7 May, he resigned. However, the Queen was very fond of Melbourne. Ascending to the throne at the age of eighteen, Victoria had been very impressionable: she had led a sheltered life guarded closely by an overbearing mother; her father had died when she was a child meaning that she had had little exposure to men. Melbourne had schooled her in politics and had become a form of father figure to her. So it was a greatly saddened Queen who sent for Peel on 8 May. Upon his arrival Peel informed her that the Conservatives were still a minority in the Lower House and therefore to make up a government he would need publicly to have her support. To that end he requested that she replace some of her ladies-in-waiting, the majority of whom were seen as Whig sympathisers and a significant minority of whom were close relatives of leading Whigs. This was partly a symbolic gesture of unity with the new ministry but also it was driven by concerns that Victoria may be influenced by those who had her ear regularly and this in turn could cause a conflict with the government.[10]

The Queen refused, believing that it was quite improper for Peel to have asked. She later told Melbourne that 'Sir Robert Peel has behaved very ill, and has insisted on my giving up my Ladies, to which I replied that I never would consent, and I never saw a man so frightened'. She went on to justify her intransigence ('the Queen of England will not submit to such trickery'[11]) and apparently what appeared to be a trivial issue became one that both sides saw as non-negotiable. On 10 May Melbourne was instructed to return to office, which he did. In a sense the Prime Minister was given a new lease of life insofar as his administration had looked dead in the water just a few days earlier but now looked able to soldier on. However, the saga really served to confirm to most observers that the real influence in Parliament was held by Peel's Conservatives: the government would continue or fall depending entirely upon which better suited Peel.

So the government staggered on while Peel played a waiting game. His only chance at forming a successful ministry would be to defeat the Whigs decisively at a general election. A large majority in the Commons (and this alone) could give them a fighting chance given that the Queen was firmly on the side of the Whigs and that Wellington, old and hindered by substantial hearing-loss, was now unable to be relied upon as their bedrock in the Lords. Peel had led the Conservatives through two general elections and each time they had improved their results from the low point of 1832. The general feeling was that the next would see them victorious.

Immediately into the 1840 session the opposition moved a want of confidence motion in the government. There were several days of debates before the government defeated it by a majority of 21 votes on 31 January. Melbourne's administration had been given a reprieve but it was able to achieve nothing through the rest of the year. In fact it was the Conservatives who drove the agenda, introducing (ultimately unsuccessful) motions to combat electoral abuses in Ireland, which resulted in O'Connell taking personal offence and establishing a National Association for Repeal to give further strength to his calls for repealing the Act of Union. All the while the Conservatives found that they now had an issue that they could rally around and, more to the point, those that had wanted for several years to attack the government were now allowed to do so.

In 1841 the political scene was rife with tension: everybody could sense that the government was living on borrowed time but when and how the end would come was uncertain. In May Lord Russell introduced a motion to be included in the Chancellor's Budget which would reduce the import duties on sugar. This was comfortably beaten and was followed by a widespread assumption that the government must resign. When they didn't Peel announced another resolution of no confidence in them. On 5 June 1841 the results came in that the government had been defeated by 312 ayes to 311 noes.[12] Not for the last time a British government would be defeated on a vote of no confidence by a single vote.[13]

Two days later the dissolution of Parliament was announced and Peel prepared for his third general election as Conservative Party leader. The result was that the Conservatives retuned to the Commons with a majority of around eighty MPs. In spite of this Melbourne's government did not resign straight away and so when Parliament reconvened in August the Conservatives moved yet another vote of no confidence. This time the government was defeated by 91 votes and Melbourne had no option but to resign.

Peel was summoned to meet the Queen on 30 August. She still rued the loss of Melbourne but at least this meeting with her new First Minister went better than their last, two years earlier, with Victoria recording that 'the first interview with Sir Robert Peel has gone off well' in a letter to Melbourne. He could not expect to replace his predecessor in the heart of the sovereign and indeed, whereas she had seen Melbourne every day as long as he was in London, Peel 'wanted to come to-morrow' but the Queen told him not to bother and that he could return the day after if he so wished.[14]

Peel now had the office with the power that he had been working towards for at least the last seven years. He inherited a struggling economy and increasing pressure from the working classes for assistance in improving their standard of living. He had given economic matters a great deal of consideration during his years in opposition during which time he had become heavily influenced by free market ideas (the Corn Laws, on which he was still unsure of his own position, was the one exception to his now anti-protectionist instincts) and therefore wanted to reduce or remove import tariffs on many goods which he saw as a barrier to trade. However, he also wanted to manage a budget surplus and so had to consider to what extent Treasury income would be affected. His conclusion was that an income tax would have to be imposed, which would allow his tariff reductions, thereby liberalising trade and in turn probably produce a greater revenue for the Treasury than the tariffs themselves yielded. It would also produce an immediate yield of its own to cover the budget deficits run up by the previous Whig government, or at least that was the theory.

Peel was aware, however, of the political risks that a Bill proposing income tax could be defeated by the opposition combined with his own supporters; that those who were required to pay it would resent it; that it would stir up discontent in a fragile Ireland if their citizens were forced to pay it, and it would cause discontent in an increasingly hostile England if the Irish weren't included.[15] The greatest political risk, though, lay in the Corn Laws. How could a government reasonably impose a widespread income tax, justified on the basis of removing barriers to trade by allowing tariff reductions, without revisiting these most protectionist of regulations? Lord Ripon, now President of the board of Trade and one of three former Prime Ministers in the new Cabinet along with Peel and Wellington (the latter without portfolio), was asked to examine the Corn Laws in particular. Both Peel and Ripon acknowledged the need for reform in this area but again were aware of the complications: agriculturalists were opposed to reducing protection; many in the Commons and the Lords felt the same.[16]

So in the first two months of the 1842 session the government was able to present its proposals to Parliament: at the start of February Peel introduced a new Corn Bill to the House of Commons which was to reduce, rather than remove, the levels of protection available on grain and in March the ministry put forward a budget announcing an income tax of seven pence in the pound with exemptions for Ireland. The Prime Minister began to feel stronger justification for his free market principles as unrest started to grow throughout the country during 1842. Bad harvests had combined with a lack of competition in the market for meat to result in the price of food being abnormally high. Meanwhile wages were depressed meaning that the people were going hungry. Having introduced the first Police Force when he was Home Secretary under Wellington, Peel could never be accused of being soft on civil disobedience, but in this instance he felt that he could also tackle the causes of it.

By the spring of 1842 the government faced a perfect storm of unrest from almost every section of society. The working classes, finding themselves either unemployed, on reduced hours or being paid poor wages (initially attributed to over-supply of the labour market) found that they could not afford bread. The Chartist movement had been established many years earlier to push for universal (male) suffrage to give a voice to these same individuals, but now the movement snowballed, fuelled by the poverty that had overwhelmed the working classes that year. At the same time the Anti-Corn Law League had been established to push for the removal of grain tariffs in order to bring down the price of bread (reductions in the levels of protection was not enough, they wanted absolute removal of tariffs). This League was overwhelmingly comprised of middle class individuals and at this point saw its opportunity to put pressure on the government: mill and colliery owners deliberately kept wages low, using the economic difficulties faced by the working men to prove their point to the government that the price of food needed to be reduced and removing grain tariffs was the only way to do it. At the same time agriculturalists, supported by many in the aristocracy, were unhappy with the reduction in the levels of grain protection and were agitating for the return to the previous levels.[17]

In the early summer of 1842 Chartists went round the northern counties closing mills and pits through violence, aiming to bring the country to a standstill until their demands were met. In the August Peel sent an army battalion north from London and within a week or so order had been re-established.

There was no doubting that the agitators needed punishing but as far as the government was concerned those that had caused the violence were more to blame than those who had committed it. The Chartists had breached the peace but they were acting through economic motives and through a genuine fear that they may not be able to feed their families. League members, however, had deliberately kept the working men poorer through political motivation, which was inexcusable. The government started to gather evidence that could directly implicate mill-owning League members as being criminally responsible for the riots and, although ultimately they would be unable to secure convictions, they could successfully denounce the League as a dangerous organisation.

By the end of 1842 Peel's government was in a difficult situation: they had removed or reduced import tariffs on several commonly used goods on the basis that it would encourage trade and therefore improve revenue to the Treasury; they had introduced the income tax, again to increase the income to the Exchequer. All of this had been done in order to realise a budget surplus which the Conservatives saw as essential. However, whereas the removal of tariffs had immediately cut that source of income, the consequent boost in trade was not instantaneous. Furthermore, the income tax had taken time in being established and so a full year's collections were not possible. Together these factors meant that by the end of the 1842 financial year the government was facing yet another budget deficit.[18]

Just to add to the stress of a yet-to-be vindicated economic policy, widespread social unrest and opposition from almost every conceivable faction, Peel's personal safety was

called into question at around this time. In January 1843 Peel's
Private Secretary, Edward Drummond, was assassinated by a
man who had believed him to be Robert Peel. His murderer,
Daniel MacNaghten, was eventually acquitted on the grounds
of insanity but for Peel the spectre of conspiracy festered in his
mind and the public at large speculated on the possibility of
another Prime Ministerial assassination just over three decades
after Spencer Perceval's unfortunate demise.[19] It was in this
atmosphere that Peel decided to delay any further tariff
reductions until the government started to realise the benefits
of liberalised trade, trying to navigate a narrow path between
the protectionists and free-traders, now convinced that straying
too close to either side could lead to his death.

Having predicted during the debates of 1842 that the
new income tax would produce a budget surplus of £500,000,
the government, at the beginning of 1843, had to acknowledge
that the reality had been a £2 million deficit.[20] This should have
provided ample opportunities for attack from the opposition
but during the May 1843 budget debate, Peel and his Chancellor,
Henry Goulburn, skilfully defended their decision to continue
with their present course. Peel argued that had the income tax
run for the whole year then there would not have been such a
large deficit; had the tax not been imposed at all then the
country would be in financial ruin; and 1842 was an abnormally
poor year due to a succession of bad harvests which had already
been improved upon the previous autumn. As soon as
financially practicable the government would continue with
tariff reductions.

1843 was to prove a difficult year. Aside from the
trouble felt in England, Daniel O'Connell wasn't about to let
the government forget about Ireland. He was still overseeing
his Repeal Association and pushing for the objective of
repealing the Act of Union as hard as ever, apparently
convinced that 1843 could be his year.[21] Membership of the
Association boomed and gatherings took place all across
Ireland. Peel hated the thought of doing nothing but attacking
O'Connell could turn him into a victim in the eyes of the British
people. Consequently he condemned the policies of the
Association but would not act harshly against its supporters.
Evidence was gathered against O'Connell throughout the year
to remove him by legal means and, by mid-October, he was

arrested for treasonable conspiracy after Repeal Association placards were discovered calling for a 'Repeal Cavalry'.

Further problems arose much closer to home. In November James Graham, the Home Secretary, introduced a Factory Bill on behalf of the government which raised the minimum age of child labourers in factories from eight to nine years. Lord Ashley, a Conservative who had campaigned for years on the issue of the rights of children attached an amendment reducing the number of hours worked by children and women in one day from twelve to ten. Many Conservatives supported this amendment on an humanitarian basis, but ministers did not, as the lost hours would affect the still-fragile economic recovery. Agriculturalists generally voted in its favour out of spite towards the Anti-Corn Law League,[22] many of whom were factory owners, who had affected their livelihoods so much over the last few years. At first reading the amendment was carried but in May of 1844, at its second reading, Peel made it clear that he would resign if it passed. The recalcitrant Conservatives duly fell in line and supported the government. The whole episode served only to demonstrate that Peel's personal authority had waned since coming to power, albeit that there were no viable alternatives so with the threat of resignation he could still not get his way.

Apart from dissention within his own ranks (with arguably the most scathing attacks coming from the future Conservative Prime Minister Benjamin Disraeli[23]) 1844 looked a more promising year than Peel had yet experienced as Prime Minister. The previous year had seen a good harvest, Ireland was quiet and there was little discontent in England. The Corn issue remained silent during the session that year due to a wide held belief that the government would not act either way on it (neither increasing protection nor removing it). So it was dissention within his ranks that defined Peel's Conservatives at this point in time. In late June 1844 the government introduced proposals to the Commons aimed at lowering the price of sugar. The essence of the motion was to bring down tariffs on imports from non-imperial sources to just above those from imperial colonies. The idea was that bringing down tariffs would reduce the price but by keeping it just above the rate charged to areas within the Empire the country could still be seen to be doing right by its friends. As with almost all of Peel's legislation it was a compromise, and as with much else it pleased nobody. The vote cut across party lines and protectionists angry at tariff reductions joined forces with free-traders annoyed that tariffs would remain, which resulted in a defeat of the government.

In the immediate aftermath Peel felt that he must resign[24] but he began to soften over the following days. In the end the administration put forward an amended Bill, which passed by a slim majority after Peel made a speech in its debate criticising his party for its disloyalty. The new motion had passed but party morale had been damaged. By attacking his friends during the debate Peel 'handled the whole episode as badly as any in his long parliamentary career…the relationship between Peel and his party could never be the same again'.[25]

Thanks to the improved economy, the income tax and the new tariff reforms, the 1844 financial year saw a budget surplus of £3 ½ million. In the 1845 budget, Peel proposed reductions on more tariffs (including sugar) amounting to over £3 million of income to the Treasury, in exchange for the House allowing the income tax to continue for at least the next three years. These proposals passed through without major incident, other than that the Prime Minister was reliant on Whig support to make up for dissident Conservatives. What was noteworthy were the other events of the twelve months following the passage of the 1845 budget, which ultimately decided the fate of this government and provided the backdrop against which history would remember Sir Robert Peel, the Prime Minister.

During the summer of 1845 agriculture struggled generally but a plague swept through potato crops all across Europe. This wasn't as much of an issue as it could have been in most countries but if the disease hit Ireland, which was completely dependent on the crop as a staple food in the way that England was on bread, then the situation would be disastrous. It was autumn before it was confirmed that this was indeed the case and the Prime Minister was faced with a nation about to starve. In November the government introduced some desperate measures including a ban on the use of grain for making alcoholic drinks such as beer; removing duties on food imports from the colonies; and buying American maize by the shipload for distribution throughout the isles. This was an inventive initiative which didn't undermine any of the markets since there was no market for maize at this time. Its only flaw was that it was on too small a scale. The government purchased £100,000 worth of maize from the USA to replace £3 ½ million worth of lost potatoes. Something more was needed and perhaps the Irish Potato Famine pushed Peel more quickly down a road that he was already heading,[26] but for whatever reason in the winter of 1845 the Prime Minister felt that there was a clear course of action that had to be taken, and this involved him committing political suicide.

At the beginning of November Peel called a Cabinet in which he stated his belief in the need now more than ever for cheaper food. He therefore wanted them to consider the question of removing tariffs on foodstuffs in general, not just those imported from the colonies. He never actually mentioned the Corn Laws, but the Cabinet felt that this was what he was suggesting and overwhelmingly they expressed the view that the Laws must be maintained. At a second meeting at the end of November Peel announced that he felt the Corn Laws should be suspended, but that he could not credibly do it and so perhaps he should go. Again his Cabinet spoke out against repeal, even on a temporary basis, but also said that they wanted him to stay.

In the end he managed to convince ministers to support his proposals out of loyalty to him but, realising that they did not share his convictions,[27] he wrote to the Queen advising her that he was unable to see Repeal through, that it was necessary for the future of the country and that she must therefore find another Prime Minister. Stanley could still command a majority of Conservatives but he was a protectionist at heart and so Peel could not advise Victoria to send for him. Instead, in an audacious move, he told the Queen that she should hand power to his political enemy; that the Whig Lord John Russell, a recent convert to the ideals of free market capitalism, was the man to steer the country through its present storm. In mid-December Lord Russell was asked to form a government. He consulted with his Whig colleagues including Lord Palmerston and Lord Grey and, on 18 December, he accepted. By 20 December he returned to the Queen to inform her that, actually, he could not put together a Cabinet, so Peel was sent for once again. He accepted the Queen's request that he form a government without further consultation, a welcome contrast to the dithering manner in which Lord Russell had handled the same request a few days earlier.

Peel now had a new resolve, he could no longer be a victim to the fickle whims of his fellow parliamentarians. The Queen and the country needed him and so he would now do whatever it would take to see his mission through. He summoned his Cabinet to a meeting at Downing Street on the evening of the same day that he had met Queen Victoria and told them all that with or without their support he was going to Parliament to propose repealing the Corn Laws. This statement was initially met with silence. Then Stanley spoke out that he must at once resign. Wellington, on the other hand, was in favour of the Corn Laws but over and above anything else, as we have seen from his time as leader of the Tories, he was faithful to his sovereign. And the Queen needed her ministers. He was seventy-seven years old, he was deaf but he would forever be loyal.[28] Those ministers who needed to consider it further were brought round by their distaste of the thought of handing power to the Whigs.

At the end of January 1846 Peel produced his proposals to Parliament and they went much further than any had expected. It wasn't just the Corn Laws that were to be repealed. Peel was suggesting removing almost all remaining tariffs, making Britain a free trade nation even though nowhere else in the world had yet done the same.

The Bill was debated in February and, on the 16th, Peel gave an impassioned speech in which he called on the House to show Britain as a leader of the world and not to shrink from this opportunity, whilst also pointing out that wherever tariffs had been removed (by him) prices had fallen and so with a famine hitting Ireland they could hardly justify keeping food prices artificially high. The Bill passed its first reading by a margin of 97 votes. Although 231 Conservatives voted against, more than twice as many as those that voted for.[29] The Party was now split between followers of Peel and followers of protectionists such as Stanley in the Lords and Bentinck (grandson of the former Prime Minister, the Duke of Portland) and Disraeli in the Commons.

Disraeli's attacks on Peel, always difficult, now really mounted.[30] The concern for the government became that even if the Bill passed the Commons, Ultra Tory opposition in the Lords would undoubtedly be even stronger. The Bill passed its second reading in the Lower House by 88 votes at the end of March and so went on to committee stage. So far, so good.

However, in politics battles are never fought in isolation. One of the effects of the Potato Famine was mass disorder in Ireland, fuelled by hunger. In order to deal with this the government introduced into the House of Lords an Irish Life and Property Bill, which would give the state the power to deploy police and impose a curfew in Ireland. It passed there comfortably and went to committee stage at the same time as the Corn Bill. Disraeli and Bentinck saw an opportunity, with the Irish Bill, to defeat ministers,[31] thereby bringing the government down and, in turn, preventing the Corn Bill from passing into law.

It was the Corn Bill that returned from committee stage first, into the Commons for the third reading in May. 15 May 1846 was notable for a tense and hostile atmosphere in the Commons. Peel and Disraeli traded insults in which Peel implied, but did not prove, that Disraeli was being dishonest about having requested a Cabinet post for himself after the 1841 general election and Disraeli accused Peel of 'petty larceny'[32] of other people's ideas. In the event the Bill passed onto the Lords by 98 votes. Whatever the outcome, by pushing the Bill this far Peel had signed his own political death warrant.

June saw the Corn Bill debated in the Lords, whilst the Irish Bill entered the Commons. The scene was now set for an incredible political battle. The government chose Wellington to introduce the Corn Bill in the Upper House, mainly because nobody else of decent stature was willing. The Duke was not an ideal choice because he was personally opposed to almost every measure contained in the Bill, but he did his duty commendably, stressing to the Lords that it was their responsibility to accept the will of the Commons.[33] The debates continued.

Meanwhile, in the Commons, the debates on the Irish Bill opened and it soon became clear that the government did not have as much support as they should. The Whigs, desperate to destroy the administration, had been forced into supporting the Corn Bill by Lord Russell but now in the Irish Bill they had an issue on which they could defeat the government and conceivably seize power themselves. The dissident Conservatives simply wanted revenge for having the Corn Bill forced upon them, even if it meant years out of office.

The debates on the Irish Bill through June were ferocious. Bentinck accused Peel of having no right to lecture the House on Irish affairs, claiming that the Prime Minister had caused George Canning's death in 1827 by refusing to support him on emancipation, only to change his mind a year later.[34] Peel was greatly offended but could do little to counter the attacks that were now coming in from all sides of the House. In the early hours of 26 June the vote on the second reading of the Bill took place and the government was defeated by a sizeable majority. However, a few hours earlier the Lords had passed the Corn Bill into law.[35] Peel had achieved his objective, but it had come at the expense of his government. The Conservatives now followed Stanley, turning away from Peel either on the issue of Corn, Ireland, being accused of disloyalty by him in 1844, or any number of other matters that during his twelve years as leader he had done to offend individual Party members. He knew his position was no longer tenable but took satisfaction in having answered the Corn question once and for all. On 29 June 1846 Sir Robert Peel announced to the House of Commons his resignation as Prime Minister.

He had led his Party for 12 years at the beginning of which he had, in effect, created a brand new Party, leaving behind the dinosaurs of the Tory Party and attracting some moderate Whigs to make a broader-based group. He led the Conservatives through three general elections, although he only won one. Peel is best known today for something he did before becoming leader – establishing the Metropolitan Police as Home Secretary. His greatest achievement during his 12 years at the top was also what led to his downfall – repeal of the Corn Laws.

The main problem for Peel wasn't that he tackled such a contentious issue head on. True, this would have been difficult for anybody; emotions ran high on both sides of the debate and whichever way he campaigned he would find around half the country opposing him. Politically the easiest option would have been to have sat on the fence (and indeed this is what he had done in opposition) but once he had made up his mind about the merits of any course of action it was not in his nature to do this. No, the real difficulty for Peel was that having spent decades advocating protectionism, his change of mind led to charges of betrayal from his supporters. It was such an easy charge to make, given that he had done exactly the same thing on another emotive matter – Catholic emancipation – a decade-and-a-half earlier. On both occasions Peel had been won round by the merits of the arguments. This is something quite alien to us in the twenty-first century, who have become used to politicians being entrenched in their own views –

uncompromising and unwilling to concede that they were wrong in the fear that it could be politically damaging. There is good reason for this fear. Peel is an example of how a person acknowledging that they were wrong can lead to their political downfall. However, history has vindicated him on both issues: nobody thinks of prejudice as acceptable today and protectionism is regarded as harmful to trade, expensive for consumers and damaging to third world economies that rely on exports.

Once convinced by virtues of a particular course Peel was prepared to pursue it regardless of the damage it would do to him personally. In the sense that he lost office almost immediately after his u-turns on both occasions it could be said that they were mistakes. In the sense that history remembers him as a man of integrity and that even as soon as four years after leaving office, on his deathbed in 1850, crowds of well-wishers gathered around his home to hear of any news,[36] perhaps those involved in the politics of today could take some lessons from Sir Robert Peel.

Edward Smith-Stanley, 14th Earl of Derby
(1846 — 1868)

We ought to adhere, as far as possible, to our policy of making every
obstructive motion come from the Liberal side of the House

The Earl of Derby, 28 May 1860

I have heard that Henry the Fourth of France, who was esteem'd a
wise and politick Prince, thought it very good King-craft to caress
his Enemies

Daniel Defoe's *Tory*, 1692

THE DAY AFTER PEEL'S RESIGNATION, Lord Russell assumed office as Prime Minister and the Conservatives, as they had expected to be, were moved to the opposition benches. Lord Stanley seemed like a natural leader for them to fall behind having been a senior member of the Cabinet since 1841, had his own personal following since the mid-1830s and been opposed to the repeal of the Corn Laws along with the majority of the Party.

   After the previous general election Peel had commanded around 340 MPs. Now in opposition there was a clear difference between Stanley's Conservatives and the Party that Peel had led: only around 230 MPs (roughly the number that had voted against Repeal) could now be directed by the Party leadership.[1] The 112 MPs that had voted with Peel now knew not where they belonged. On most major issues they were closer to the Conservatives than the Whigs[2] (and indeed they duly moved to the opposition benches after Peel's resignation) but on the matter of free trade they were a clearly distinct group. They started to refer to themselves as 'Peelites' and tried to forge a separate identity from the Protectionist Conservatives,[3] under the leadership of Robert Peel. The problem was that Peel was nowhere to be found. He still turned up to vote in the Commons but, having relinquished the burdens of high office, he had started to enjoy the pleasures of family life, of spending time in his constituency home, and seemed to have no appetite to take those burdens back.[4] Stanley's strategy in these early days was to continue as normal in the belief that the Peelites would eventually accept themselves as Conservatives once the emotions of 1846 had died down. He neither wanted to flatter nor offend them but simply pretend that they were not a concern.

Considering the unforgiving manner in which the Conservative majority had just deposed of their previous leader over a single policy area, it would be safe to assume that the new opposition under Stanley would fight tooth and nail to protect British industries, in spite of his strategy of appeasing the Peelites. But this is not what happened. As soon as they assumed office the Whigs introduced a Sugar Bill aimed at liberalising the market for sugar, which as we have seen currently favoured the colonies and was highly controversial (Russell's ministry was brought down in 1841 after a vote on sugar and Peel attempted to reduce tariffs on the product in 1844 but was defeated). Conservatives in the Commons were decisively defeated in their opposition to the measure by the combined force of Peelites and Whigs.[5] Stanley, observing from the Lords, instructed the Party in the Upper House to allow the Bill passage once it was presented there: they still had a majority and so could defeat it if they worked hard enough but he had now come to the conclusion that the only way to defeat free trade in the long term would be to let those in favour of it have their experiment, which would undoubtedly expose all its flaws.

Not all of his followers could accept such a concessionary policy: Bentinck, who had taken the lead against Peel's Repeal legislation in the Commons, attacked Peelites and free trade at every opportunity. He managed to offend William Gladstone to the point where this most amenable of Peelites to the idea of reconciliation ended up keeping his distance.[6] Stanley's efforts to keep Bentinck in check succeeded only in annoying him. The new leader was discovering quicker than most that there is no easier way to alienate everybody one needs than to try to lead them.

The autumn of 1846 saw further potato blight on a much larger scale than had occurred in 1845. Ireland was now starving. The government introduced measures such as pressuring landlords to reduce rent for Irish farmers in order to ease their financial burdens. Stanley opposed this but offered no alternative measures, apparently deciding that if he did so he may be forced to test them one day.[7] For the time being he would not make any ostensible policy announcements which could either restrict his actions in future or else assist the government in what to do today.

When Parliament opened in January 1847 he made no open criticism of the Queen's Speech. This set the tone for the rest of the parliamentary session. The Conservatives were dispirited and disorganised. Where Stanley took a stand that would appeal to the Peelites the Ultra Tories abandoned him but when he spoke to his Conservative supporters the Peelites would have nothing to do with him. Parliament dissolved in July and all parties prepared for a general election in which they all had everything to lose: the Peelites needed an increase in numbers based on public support for their free trade ideas in order to show the Protectionists the errors of their ways; the Conservatives needed to destroy the Peelites in order to give themselves a fighting chance at ever governing again; and the Whigs needed nothing more than a retention of the status quo in order to return to power – a split opposition suited them perfectly. Even at this late point in history Party loyalties were not easy to discern in all cases but the result of the general election was roughly 250 Conservative MPs, 80 Peelites and 330 Whigs.[8] All in all the Peelites suffered most but the Whigs were clearly the governing Party for the foreseeable future.

The only other notable incident during the 1847 general election was the victory of the Whig Lionel de Rothschild in the City of London constituency. Rothschild was a practising Jew, banned from sitting in Parliament by law and so his election, much like that of Daniel O'Connell nearly twenty years earlier, threw up a great constitutional question. The Whigs were in favour of amending the law to allow Rothschild to take his seat but Stanley was fervently opposed. The matter highlighted further something that Stanley was already well aware of, which was his lack of strength in the Commons. Who could he rely on to lead his Party in the Lower House? Disraeli invariably held the House captivated whenever he spoke as he was always entertaining but he commanded no personal following. Further to this he could not be trusted to support the Party leadership: he had turned on Peel and was now going his own way on Jewish emancipation. Throughout his career

Benjamin Disraeli would be known to pick up or abandon ideas whenever they suited his political needs.[9] At this point in time the Conservatives needed unity and the majority opposed granting concessions to Jews. However, the issue was too close to his heart for him to toe the Party line. Disraeli, as his name suggests, had been born into a Jewish family but his father had him baptised by the Church of England at the age of eleven.[10] The reasons for this are unclear in the sense that neither Benjamin Disraeli nor Isaac D'Israeli ever recorded why the decision was made, but it is extremely clear why when one considers the prejudices that Jews, and indeed any minority group, faced in Hanoverian and Victorian England. By converting him, Isaac was giving his son a fighting chance of climbing through the echelons of society to the heights he eventually attained. So once again Disraeli prepared to drive a wedge into his Party, a Party which the leadership was trying to unite. Thus he was a liability in the eyes on Stanley in 1847.

Bentinck was another possibility. He had his own following and he was Protectionist by nature. However, he and Stanley had fallen out over the latter's efforts to rein Bentinck in during his anti-Peelite campaign of 1846. Even if they could get onto decent terms again the Conservative leader was all too aware of how venomous and dangerous Bentinck could be when he wished. Further to this Bentinck was also in favour of Jewish emancipation, though for less personal reasons than Disraeli. Stanley felt, therefore, that it may be better to keep both marginalised at this time.

When it came to the discussion of the Jewish Disabilities Bill on 16 December, Disraeli spoke in favour of the measure, criticising opponents not for their principles, not for their opposition to fairness, but on what he perceived as the flawed basis of their own faith, claiming that Christianity was merely an extension of Judaism. He famously asked the rhetorical question 'where is your Christianity, if you do not believe in their Judaism?'[11] The Commons was stunned. Before the same debate Stanley had implored Bentinck that if he must vote for the Bill he do so without causing a fuss.[12] This plea fell on deaf ears. Bentinck spoke out in the debate about how the Bill was principally and morally favourable. The Bill passed its first reading but the vote of a majority of Protectionists against it was seen by Stanley as a further rejection of Bentinck as their leader.

In January 1848 Stanley decided to grasp the nettle and appoint a Party leader for the Commons. The idea was simultaneously to demonstrate that the Party was not dependent on Bentinck and Disraeli by appointing someone else and to reunite the Conservatives under a single banner as the old habit of falling into smaller factions was starting to take hold. Bentinck commanded around fifty followers, Peel still had around eighty. In February Lord Granby, eldest son of the Duke of Rutland, was appointed to the position but by March, realising the size of the task, he resigned. Bentinck no longer wanted to be Commons leader but he had assumed that if he wasn't, Disraeli would be. By passing over Disraeli, Stanley had simply pushed both men further away.

It was a mistake he would not learn from: he decided to stagger on through 1848 without an official leader because on most of the business to be conducted that year he and Bentinck agreed so he could rest safe in the knowledge that the Party would act as a Party, if only by chance. The Jewish Disabilities Bill had already passed through the Commons (Stanley defeated it in the Lords) and measures such as the suspension of habeas corpus in Ireland (which was still suffering from famine and, therefore, increases in crime) were popularly supported by both parties. As long as he and Bentinck were on the same page he need not appoint a *de jure* leader of the Conservative Party in the House of Commons.

However, in September 1848 Bentinck died unexpectedly of a heart attack so once again the issue was seen to need addressing and, once again, Stanley passed over Disraeli. He wrote to John Herries – a 70 year old MP of mediocre ability – offering him the position towards the end of December. On the same day he wrote to Disraeli explaining that he – Disraeli – simply didn't have the support needed to lead but expressing the hope that he would do his duty under Herries.[13] Stanley misjudged the positions of both men. Within a day he had received a reply from Herries rejecting the leadership (but suggesting a Shadow Cabinet of several individuals instead) and a letter from Disraeli rejecting subservience to Herries.

Stanley had to act quickly. He had learned from Peel's mistake that snubbing Disraeli could be fatal and arranged to meet him in January 1849. He offered him a role as part of a triumvirate leadership with Herries and Granby and, although Disraeli initially declined this offer, he soon fell in line once he realised that he would probably never get another chance.[14] Stanley's concerns about Disraeli's reliability were soon proved to be well-founded. Disraeli, believing that the Peelites needed to be brought back into the Party, started to suggest throughout 1849 that he wasn't, nor had he ever really been, a Protectionist. His quarrel in 1846 had been with Peel, with specific measures and with his betrayal of his Conservative supporters. Stanley quickly became annoyed at what he saw as a similar betrayal of him by Disraeli as that which Peel had committed three years earlier. Protectionist MPs started to distance themselves from him and Stanley reprimanded him for his initiative. By the end of the year a suitably chastised Disraeli was duly advocating the need for increased protection.[15]

       The opposition was now ready to launch co-ordinated attacks on the government. The 1850 session saw representatives in both Houses moving proposals for increased protection, or at least a reduction in the tax burden on previously protected industries such as agriculture as a means of alleviating the hardships felt there. The fact was that the removal of protection had reduced prices but the increase in demand that had been anticipated as a consequence had not yet been realised. Therefore the poor were better off but industry was suffering. This strategy succeeded in giving the Conservatives a sense of identity and purpose as well as increasing their morale after the lacklustre sessions of the previous two years. However, it was unsuccessful in defeating the Free Traders in Parliament. Stanley was now prepared to attack but he needed an issue on which he could strike and win. Free trade versus protection was not it.

       Fortunately the government handed him such an issue on a plate during that session. In 1847 tensions between Jews and Christians in Greece had heightened due to Christians, who wanted to burn their traditional effigy of Judas, having restrictions placed on them by the Greek government for fear of offending the Jewish community. Some Christians took this badly, some burned their effigies anyway and were criticised or punished and agitation grew. During the unrest that followed a Jewish Portuguese man living in Greece named Don Pacifico found his possessions destroyed by an anti-Semitic mob. He had appealed to the Greek authorities for compensation, to no avail. Don Pacifico had been born in Gibraltar, making him a

British subject and so he approached the Foreign Office for support. The bellicose Foreign Secretary, Lord Palmerston, responded unilaterally by sending a Royal Naval fleet to the area to seize Greek assets up to the value lost by Don Pacifico, which resulted in the blockade of Athens.[16]

In June 1850 Stanley attacked the government without restraint in the Lords for this dangerous course of conduct.[17] Where domestic politics failed, foreign politics would succeed. Many Peelites and Whigs joined the Conservatives in their criticisms of the government. Stanley's motion condemning the administration was passed but the Whigs were not defeated. Within days they had presented their own motion in the House of Commons to debate the matter and on this occasion the Lower House voted for the government meaning that, effectively, nothing was decided upon. What events had done was to demonstrate to Peelites that they and the Conservatives did have some shared values and that trade was not the be all and end all of politics.

Just to confuse matters further for the two factions, at the end of the month Peel was thrown from his horse in London and, on 2 July, died of his injuries.[18] What was the future of the Peelites without their leader? It would be years before the answer to that question became clear. Meanwhile the government kept making political gaffs on which the opposition happily capitalised. Pope Pius IX organised the Roman Catholic Church in Great Britain into twelve bishoprics headed by an Archbishop of Westminster. There was nothing illegal in this and in fact the Pope felt that the measure would be supported amongst the political classes. Towards the end of 1850 Lord Russell denounced the Pope's actions as disrespectful and likely to incite violence. In doing this, Russell managed to alienate many of his fringe supporters.[19] Catholics were offended and supporters of civil liberties felt that speaking out against the Pope's actions was tyrannical. The Conservatives were divided on the matter but, under Stanley's direction, they remained silent and let the government tear themselves up over it.

At the Queen's Speech at the opening of the 1851 session, Stanley focused on agricultural relief, allowing the Whigs to do all the criticising on the Popish front. In mid-February the Radical MP Peter Locke King introduced a motion proposing the redistribution of constituency seats between counties and boroughs. In a shock move the Conservatives were instructed to abstain in order to demonstrate the divisions between the Whigs and the Radicals. The government, officially opposed to the measure, was defeated. Lord Russell found this unacceptable and resigned as Prime Minister. On 22 February 1851 Queen Victoria sent for Lord Stanley and asked him to form a government.[20] Accepting would mean governing with a minority and certain defeat. Declining would mean admitting that he wasn't popular enough to carry the confidence of Parliament. So Stanley did neither. He advised the Queen that he would stand by her if necessary but that she should explore a Whig-Peelite coalition first. His belief was that either the Peelites would accept and then he could spend his remaining time in opposition turning them against the Whigs, or they would decline and he could, in future, be confident of their support. By 25 February negotiations between Whigs and Peelites had broken down and Stanley was instructed to form a government.

The following two days were painful for the Conservatives as the Peelites in general (and Gladstone in particular) refused to serve with them[21] and Stanley could not find an acceptable ministry made up from the existing MPs and Lords. It all ended with an embarrassed Stanley informing the Queen that, despite his pledge to stand by her if the Whigs were unable, he could not keep his promise.

The Whigs were back in power on their own, though they were still unpopular due to Russell's anti-Popish comments alienating Radicals and Peelites and their vehement free trade policies incensing Protectionists.

On 30 June Stanley's father, the 13th Earl of Derby, died, meaning that Stanley now inherited that title. The newly elevated 14th Earl of Derby now focused on how he could successfully govern when next presented with the opportunity. Having failed to gain the support of the Peelites in the February his determination became winning over moderate Whigs. On the three major issues facing Parliament he devised a coherent Party strategy: protection could not be reversed in the lifetime of the current Parliament – opinion in the Commons was too strongly in favour of free trade. He felt that the issue should be avoided, that Conservatives should not advocate protection in case they had to abandon it in future. If a further election returned another pro-free trade Commons then the Party must accept that protection is a dead policy. On the issue of Catholicism, Stanley once again advocated a policy of staying silent and allowing the government to create enemies with its own position. Finally, on the issue of parliamentary reform, he was personally opposed but was concerned with the number of urban voters who were enfranchised to elect rural MPs. A better drawing of boundaries may not be such a bad idea and so the policy was to oppose widespread reform but leave themselves open to incremental change.

Then Russell's administration managed to stumble yet again. In December 1851 Palmerston was sacked from the Foreign Office for pledging British support for the actions of Louis Napoleon, who had overthrown the French government and declared himself Emperor.[22] The official stance of the British government was neutrality and so Palmerston had to go for his presumptuous gaff. Heading into the 1852 session it looked like Palmerston and Russell may clash in Parliament, which could bring the administration to its knees. This is exactly what happened: it was only February by the time Russell resigned in the face of opposition from Peelites, Conservatives and Palmerston (who remained popular in the country where his handling of foreign policy was viewed as patriotic, rather than overly-aggressive as it was interpreted in Westminster). On 22 February Derby was yet again asked to form a government and was this time in a position to accept.

Much to the dismay of the Queen, Derby informed her that he would offer Lord Palmerston the Chancellorship of the Exchequer as a means of keeping him on favourable terms with the new government whilst keeping him away from the Foreign Office where he had done so much damage over recent years with Don Pacifico and Louis Napoleon. When Palmerston declined Disraeli was awarded his first ministerial position as Chancellor, whilst returning as leader of the House of Commons.[23] This was a necessary appointment as Disraeli represented just about the only talent that the Conservatives possessed in the Lower House but within weeks of assuming office his unpredictability manifested itself once again. The government was broadly agreed that no move should be made in favour of protection whilst they were in the minority, nor against it until the public could have their opinions heard by means of an election. Disraeli was of the opinion that protection was dead and that the Conservatives would fare better in an election if they dropped it. In his first budget speech as Chancellor he praised the effects of free trade, effectively setting the government's stall in that camp, although not explicitly saying so. He was reprimanded accordingly and so the government proceeded unsure as to what could and could not be said regarding trade and tariffs. The fact that their policy would be determined by the outcome of a general election begged the question, When would that be?

Clearly a government so overwhelmingly in the minority could not go on for long without seeking reinforcement through an election but Derby was firmly of the belief that they should hold on for as long as possible before requesting a dissolution.[24] The reason for this was to demonstrate to the country that the Conservatives could be trusted to govern, which required time. In the event the government fought on until the end of June, dissolving Parliament on 1 July 1852.

As results from around the Kingdom filtered in throughout the summer it looked as though the Conservatives had made gains, but were still going to be in the minority in the Commons. There were around 290 Conservatives, 40 Peelites and 320 Whigs.[25] Derby intended to stay in government, calculating that a reconciliation with the Peelites may give him a majority, but he accepted that he would have to embrace free trade policies.

During the summer France announced that it was holding a national referendum to declare Louis Napoleon as Emperor Napoleon III.[26] Derby saw this as potentially provocative and ordered increased military expenditure, charging Disraeli with the task of finding the money to cover it. The Chancellor, who had intended to give tax relief to agriculturalists[27] as compensation for the losses they were incurring due to cuts in protection, was consequently aggrieved at this order from his superior.

On 14 September the Duke of Wellington died, aged 84, and the Cabinet reassembled in London to make arrangements for his funeral but taking the opportunity also to discuss forthcoming political matters. Parliament would reconvene in the November, all the while the Chancellor was put upon with more demands from his Premier: to increase numbers in the navy; the army; the marines; to abandon plans to abolish advertisement tax.[28] What Disraeli had hoped would be a revolutionary and popular budget was turning into a guaranteed unpopular proposal: more spending funded by more taxes.

On 3 December Disraeli announced his budget to the House of Commons and for the next two weeks it was debated in that chamber. It soon became clear that Peelites, Whigs and Radicals would not be supporting it. On 16 December that budget was defeated in a vote.[29] The following day Derby visited the Queen and informed her that he had no choice but to resign. Lord Aberdeen, a Peelite, was invited to head a coalition government made up of his own faction and the Whigs.

Once more Derby found himself in opposition and, just like both on his last occasion there and his tenure as Prime Minister, the strategy he pursued was one of inactivity to allow factions of the government to tear themselves apart. It was hardly an inspiring policy, giving little cause for his own backbenchers to feel united or to experience the highs of successful attacks on their opponents, but it was understandable given the composition of the present ministry. Throughout the 1853 and 1854 parliamentary sessions Derby rarely visited London. He was still the leader of the Conservative Party but both personally and professionally he felt too depressed to attend.[30] On the occasions that he did present himself to challenge the government his following was not strong enough to grant him success. The Conservative Party was falling to pieces but the ministry did, as Derby had predicted, start to turn on itself.

In February 1854 Peelites and Radicals in the Commons attacked their own front bench on their policy towards the ongoing conflict between Turkey and Russia in which Britain had ostensibly refused to take sides whilst discreetly arming the Turks. Policy was unclear and the backbenchers were unhappy. Eventually the government did officially declare war on Russia on 28 March. Derby spoke out in support of this measure against what he saw as a tyrannical Russia.[31] The Crimean War had begun and with it came a renewed surge of unity among the Conservatives: the government had bungled their way into the war and happened to come out on the right side but the Conservatives would patriotically resolve to see Britain victorious in spite of, rather than thanks to, a weak Whig government. However, it was

Disraeli who was organising the foot troops of the Party, Derby still scarcely making himself available.[32]

The war raged on over the winter with the British troops landing in the Crimea and the British navy having some early successes at sea. However, only 25,000 troops had been sent, which was widely accepted as being inadequate to achieve anything on Russia's doorstep[33] and as winter set in the British military began to suffer. In January 1855 the ministry started to attack itself over its conduct of the war. The opposition watched as the government tore itself up. It was a motion passed in the Commons that same week demanding a Select Committee enquiry into the state of the army before invading the Crimea that broke the administration. On 30 January Aberdeen visited Windsor Palace to tender his resignation and, on the 31st, Derby met with the Queen who asked him to form a government. He accepted on the condition that Palmerston could join, to which the Queen agreed.[34] However, Palmerston claimed that he could not serve with the Conservatives while carrying with him the support of those that currently looked up to him. Once again Derby had to inform Victoria that he had failed to put together a Cabinet.

He hoped that he may still be recalled once Parliament realised that nobody else had the support of a majority either. The Queen offered the commission to Lord Lansdowne, who could not form a Cabinet.[35] In the end she reluctantly approached Palmerston. The 70 year old Viscount managed to secure the support of the Whigs and Peelites by convincing them that it was him or Derby at the helm. Thus, in February 1855, he took office as Prime Minister.

Most expected Palmerston, owing to his age and growing blindness and deafness, not to be able to last long as Prime Minister. Few could have expected him to have dominated British politics for the following ten years. He survived his first year by a combination of luck and pluck. In March 1855 Tsar Nicholas of Russia died and Palmerston convinced Louis Napoleon, also engaged in the war against the Russians, not to sign a peace agreement that was on the table but to continue fighting.[36] Eventually, in 1856 the Anglo-French alliance secured a more favourable peace including a demilitarised Crimea. The episode did not come without its casualties: remaining privately committed to fighting Russia and pushing them into a weaker negotiating position whilst ostensibly claiming to be labouring for peace left Lord Russell, back in the Cabinet at the Colonial Office and charged with negotiating an end to hostilities with France and Russia in Vienna, in a bind. His job, it seemed, was deliberately to bungle peace negotiations.[37] Derby locked on to this contradiction and attacked Russell, hoping to bring down the government. However, Palmerston's sense of self-preservation was too strong. He threw Russell to the wolves and the Colonial Secretary duly resigned on 16 July 1855.[38]

1856 was another lacklustre year for the Conservatives as well as the government. By the December Derby's closest advisers were once again informing him that he needed to assert himself, as his Party was losing direction and discipline in his prolonged periods of absence. In 1857 he tried to reassert his authority and rebuild the Party. He held a meeting with Gladstone, now a leading Peelite, in the February to discuss reconciliation between the factions. Although Gladstone was eager to come back to the Conservatives, Derby was aware that his own supporters may despair on seeing a return of the Peelites who had offended them so much over the previous decade. The meeting was inconclusive.

At the end of February Derby got his chance to demonstrate how vulnerable the government was. The Chinese authorities had seized a British registered pirate ship, the *Arrow*, and imprisoned some crew members for crimes of piracy. Sir John Bowring, the Governor of Hong Kong, decided to retaliate to what he saw as an affront to Britain by attacking a Chinese compound. Derby used this as his premise to attack Palmerston's government in February and March and was supported by his Conservatives and Gladstone's Peelites. When a motion was proposed in the Commons denouncing the government, Disraeli asserted that it should be viewed as a vote of confidence. The motion was carried on 3 March[39] and Palmerston subsequently announced that Parliament would be dissolved by the end of the month.

The result of the election was a decisive Whig victory. The Conservatives returned around 260 MPs, far fewer than the 290 from the 1852 election but they could take solace in the fact that all those returned were loyal and would require less controlling than the rebellious intake of five years prior. Another positive was the almost entire obliteration of the Peelites. A few leading members such as Gladstone still returned to the Commons but without a sizeable faction they would be forced to choose a Party with which to align themselves.

However, there was no escaping the return of the Whigs under Palmerston. Made up of Liberals, Moderates and Radicals he now officially commanded around 350 MPs, although the reality was that they would probably be as factious as those who had voted with the Conservatives over the *Arrow* crisis.

The new 1857 session from May passed off quietly. It was January 1858 before sudden storm clouds enveloped the government and brought it down. On 15 January an Italian named Felice Orsini attempted to assassinate the French Emperor Napoleon III in Paris. He had travelled to France from the UK carrying grenades made in England.[40] Understandably relations between Britain and France soured. The French Ambassador wrote to the government demanding assistance in prosecuting such individuals in future. The government did not formally reply but responded to the crisis by introducing a Conspiracy to Murder Bill, toughening the penalty for anybody committing existing offences as a means of appeasing an increasingly hostile France.

Derby pledged Conservative support to Palmerston for his measures while the Whigs decried them as surrendering British sovereignty – amending British laws because of French demands. On the first reading in February the Bill was passed. However, a Radical amendment, proposed for the second reading, denounced the government for not responding to the French Ambassador's letter asking for assistance, as it now looked like the changes proposed to the law were a result of the demands made by him.

The Conservatives saw an opportunity given that they knew from the first reading that the Whigs were voting against the Bill – it had only been carried with Tory support. They overwhelmingly voted in favour of the Radical amendment, embarrassing the government. On 20 February an humiliated Palmerston resigned the premiership.[41] On the same day Derby was called to a meeting with the Queen during which he advised her, as in 1851 and 1855, to explore other options before asking him to head a government. His apparent lack of ambition in assuming office was a great source of frustration for his supporters but the following day he was informed by the Queen that she required him to take over.

Derby subsequently approached Gladstone and the Whig Duke of Newcastle to try to broaden his administration[42] but when both declined he was left with a Cabinet made up of similar individuals to the one he had led six years earlier. The crisis with France was settled by Lord Malmesbury, Derby's Foreign Secretary, writing a reply to the French Ambassador's letter to the previous government which re-established cordial relations. Now the Prime Minister could focus on trying to govern by dividing his many enemies in Parliament. His first significant piece of legislation was to be an India Bill, aimed at reorganising the governance of that colony. Palmerston led the opposition in their criticisms of the initial proposal put forward but Derby was successfully able to draft in leaders from the other opposition factions to rally against his opponent. Lord Russell, between whom and Palmerston there was no love lost (Russell having been thrown to the wolves by Palmerston when he served under him as Colonial Secretary in 1855 and Palmerston having been sacked by Russell over the Louis Napoleon crisis when he was Foreign Secretary in 1851), had his own substantial following in the Commons and thus was invited to help draft a compromise Bill which would be acceptable to his supporters.[43] Gladstone, still a leading Peelite albeit with very few followers, agreed to support a compromise measure on the basis that an early defeat for the government would inevitably lead to the return of Palmerston, which he could not tolerate.

Shortly afterwards, a motion aimed at censuring the government over a rebuke sent to the Governor General of India about his threat to confiscate property belonging to the indigenous population, was defeated in spite of support from both Palmerston and Russell. Despite their both opposing the government on this measure they still could not bring themselves to work together and so Derby's administration kept going, marching over the divided opposition with ease.

His next challenge came when Lord Russell introduced an Oaths Bill aimed, much like the Jewish Disabilities Bill he had introduced unsuccessfully when he was Prime Minister eleven years earlier, at allowing Jews to be admitted to Parliament by removing Christian wording from the Oath. For eleven years Lionel de Rothschild had been the elected representative for the City of London yet unable to take his seat. The Bill passed through the Commons with Disraeli being characteristically passionate in his support of it[44] and, accepting that he had to remain open to change, Derby gave it his backing in the Lords. His support wasn't enough, though, and the Bill was rejected in the Upper House. Realising that there was the potential for a clash between the two Houses, Derby managed to negotiate a compromise which would allow each House to determine the composition of its own membership. Thus the Parliamentary Oaths Act amended the Oath for the House of Commons whilst preserving the constitution of the House of Lords.[45]

Throughout the recess of 1858 Derby made plans to introduce a Parliamentary Reform Bill the following session. He drafted a committee of leading Cabinet members to discuss the issue. By the start of 1859 they were prepared to propose extending the franchise to a greater population, ensuring that freeholders in boroughs could only elect members for their boroughs and not for the counties, and redistributing seats based on the population as at the 1851 census. Two Cabinet members resigned[46] but Derby was steadfast.

The Reform Bill was introduced to Parliament on 28 February and with a divided opposition Derby was hopeful of success. However, during March Lord Russell, now unashamedly intriguing to lead the Whigs thereby displacing his old rival Palmerston, introduced a hostile amendment neutralising the government's proposal to transfer county votes into boroughs. The Conservatives made it clear that if Russell's amendment passed they would dissolve Parliament.[47] Palmerston now had a choice between handing a victory to Derby and handing one to Russell. He eventually decided to support Russell's amendment and the government was defeated in a vote on 1 April. On 4 April Derby announced that the Queen had agreed to dissolve Parliament but warned against the numerous factions now occupying the Commons as being obstructive to the governance of the nation. As long as nobody could hold a majority, nothing could ever be settled upon. How soon the House would heed his words.

The election resulted in a gain of just over 30 Conservative MPs taking their total to about the 300 mark. However, they were still short of a majority with the various Whig factions totalling in excess of 350. Once again Derby's only hope was to keep them divided. However, the night before the new Parliament met for the first time, a group of over 270

Whig MPs met at Willis's Rooms in London. Followers of various factions including Whigs, Moderates, Radicals and Peelites had been called there by Russell and Palmerston who appeared on a stage together both claiming that they would serve under the other in a government if the factions could agree to unite. They proposed that on the evening of the Queen's speech their new united Party should propose a want of confidence vote in the government to defeat them with immediate effect. Overwhelmingly, the plan was supported and on that night the Liberal Party was born.[48]

The following day, 7 June, Parliament met for the Queen's Speech and the Liberals moved their motion. The next three days saw impassioned debate on both sides before the government was defeated on 10 June. The following day Derby resigned. Following much speculation as to who was to lead the new Liberal coalition, Palmerston took the premiership with Russell taking over the Foreign Office and Gladstone, the most senior of the Peelite contingent, coming in as Chancellor of the Exchequer.

The remainder of the 1859 session passed quietly with events abroad comprising the only significant matters for discussion. Italian states were fighting for their independence, with the help of France, against Austria. Derby procrastinated on the issue, hoping at some point to exploit divisions between the Liberal factions. There were plenty of differing opinions to abuse. Orsini, the Italian who had attempted to assassinate Napoleon III in 1858 had done so to bring attention to his campaign for Italian independence. It had worked in spite of failing to kill the Emperor, as Napoleon took France into the war against Austria. Some felt the French justified and wanted to support them, some felt that the war was a veil for French expansionism and this should be opposed, some argued for neutrality.

Once the 1860 session opened Derby's patience appeared to have paid off: the government announced a trade agreement made with France freeing up trade on various commodities in the February, then in the March it was confirmed that France was going to annex Savoy and Nice.[49] Suddenly fears over French expansionism seemed validated and the government were exposed to charges of being manipulated by Napoleon – given an attractive trade agreement to soften them up before France stomped its authority over Europe. Meanwhile the Liberals created further divisions within their own ranks when Lord John Russell introduced another Reform Bill (having defeated the Conservative proposal of a year earlier) which was opposed by the anti-reform Palmerston. Derby, it seemed, simply had to watch and wait for his opponents to destroy themselves. Russell withdrawing his Reform Bill in June was one of the great victories of that year, because Palmerston had opposed Russell and the Whigs, which gave Derby a hope that the Prime Minister may yet cross the threshold and join the Conservatives.

Encouraged by this thought, the Conservatives held confidential talks with Palmerston in which they pledged not to bring down the government but only to oppose the Liberals on specific measures (those which would drive a wedge between Palmerston, Gladstone and Russell) on condition that no radical cause was pursued. The Prime Minister was happy with this arrangement, seeing it as an opportunity to guarantee himself support when a clash with Gladstone inevitably came.

The strategy initially worked with Palmerston and the Conservatives working together to pass or defeat various Bills during the 1861 session, meanwhile Gladstone threatened to resign twice.[50] However, Gladstone's budget passed the Commons in April in spite of it being far more adventurous than Derby had expected, which he felt constituted a breach of their agreement on Palmerston's part. More pressingly the Liberals had united to get the budget through in the face of Conservative opposition and they now looked far less fragmented than they had at the start of the session.

Foreign affairs moved from Italy to America as the U.S. Civil War broke out that year. The government advocated neutrality, which was largely supported by the opposition if for no other reason than that public opinion was divided over which side should be supported. Some believed in the right to self-determination so if the Confederacy (South) wished to secede, who was the Union (North) to declare war and stop them? Some felt disgusted at the slavery still practiced in the South decades after Britain had ended the practice and therefore felt that they had more in common with the North. So neutrality it was, at least as long as Palmerston's health held out and he remained in office (he was now 77 years old). Reminders of mortality were never far away at this time – Prince Albert died in December 1861 leaving the Queen a widow. He had been 35 years Palmerston's junior.

1862 saw clashes between Gladstone, the Chancellor of the Exchequer and Disraeli, his predecessor to that office. These two men would be fierce political rivals for the rest of their lives and this is the time when it started. Disraeli attacked Gladstone for what he believed to be government over-spending while Gladstone was revelling in his public popularity having reduced income tax and various duties. As the Chancellor took popular opinion as a measure of success his opponent criticised him for playing a dangerous game with the nation's finances, as he believed that the sums simply didn't add up. Derby had to rein in his number two throughout this period: Palmerston was looking frailer by the day so there was every chance that the Conservatives could be called to government and he could not guarantee that in that scenario expenditure would be cut. In Derby's eyes attacks on the government must focus on foreign policy. The old animosity between Palmerston and his Foreign Secretary Russell was back so they could attack the government on this front, fanning the flames of distrust between two senior Cabinet members without worrying about whether it would affect them if they ever took office. This was mainly because they disagreed with almost all of Russell's diplomatic efforts and so in the event of a Conservative government they would happily pursue a different course. Indeed the Foreign Secretary gave them plenty of ammunition: firstly he advocated recognising the Confederate States of America as an independent country in spite of both Palmerston and Derby's positions of neutrality;[51] next when Greece overthrew its ruler and started searching for a new monarch Russell offered ceding the British protected Ionian islands to the Greeks as a gift without consulting Parliament;[52] then when Prussia and Denmark looked set to go to war over Prussian attempts to annex Danish land, Russell was completely unable to negotiate a settlement, largely due to his inconsistency over which side he supported.

Just before the opening of Parliament in January 1864, Russell argued in Cabinet that Britain should act militarily on behalf of Denmark if the German Confederation invaded. When the Cabinet disagreed it left the government pursuing an undetermined foreign policy which was opposed by the

Foreign Secretary. At the beginning of February Derby spoke in the Lords giving an abridged history of Russell's foreign diplomacy, the implication being that it was nothing short of a disaster for Britain. Having had to give up on supporting Denmark, Russell tried to arrange a conference of European powers to negotiate a settlement. In July Conservatives put forward motions in both Houses of Parliament criticising the government's handling of the Denmark-Prussia affair, which was carried in the Lords but defeated in the Commons. The opposition was inching closer to toppling the government.

During the second half of 1864 Derby became severely ill and was bed-ridden for months. He made the journey back to Parliament for the beginning of the 1865 session to find that he was on the same side as the government over the initial issues debated (support for Canadian states' plans for Federalisation as a means of defence against what was believed would be an aggressive and expansionist U.S.A should the Union win the Civil War, which looked likely; and opposition to the disestablishment of the Church of Ireland, proposed by a backbench Liberal). Then, just as his health was improving, Palmerston's deteriorated. This caused much speculation. A general election had not been held since 1859 so one had to be called within twelve months based on the then-septennial maximum parliamentary terms. Would Palmerston be leading the Liberals into the election? Someone would have to succeed Palmerston at some point, who would that be? If Russell succeeded the Prime Minister then the Radicals would probably desert having been horrified by his foreign policy, but what if Gladstone took over? He was now a champion of the Radical cause, becoming known popularly as 'People's William'.[53] He would horrify traditional Whigs, but these characters were few and far between at this point in time. The worry about Gladstone was that he could, realistically, be successful.

Parliament was dissolved in mid-July 1865. In the years leading up to the general election the Conservatives had won several by-elections, taking their total number of MPs up to around 310. By the end of the election they were once again down to 290.[54] Derby had spent almost two decades as leader of the Conservative Party, gradually building their numbers in opposition and, briefly, minority government to the point where they would one day have a majority. Now at the beginning of another seven-year Parliament, hopes of this looked dashed. The strategy of restrained opposition had failed and the Conservatives had every right to feel dejected. Derby himself was 66 years old and would probably never again get a chance to lead the country. Disraeli was 61 and was becoming downhearted at having spent a lifetime in opposition.[55]

Then, in mid-October, Palmerston died within days of his eighty-first birthday and immediately the political landscape changed. Palmerston had personally been extremely popular but the Liberals could now no longer rely on this popularity to carry them. Russell assumed the premiership while Gladstone remained at the Exchequer. With Palmerston out of the way Russell was free to push his agenda of parliamentary reform, much to the delight of the Conservatives who viewed it as Russell's political suicide.

So once more a newly spirited Derby urged his Conservatives to exercise restraint and let the government bring about its own downfall. However, the dogs smelled blood and were desperate to break the leashes that had bound them for two decades. When Gladstone presented the government's reform proposals in March 1866, Disraeli attacked the Chancellor as being a traitor to his party, thereby criticising the government without actually taking a stance on reform on behalf of the Conservatives. It was Liberal MPs who forwarded a hostile amendment in the April calling for the postponement of Gladstone's measures to extend the franchise until the matter of redistributing seats was settled. Eventually the motion was defeated but only by five votes as Liberals turned on their leaders *en masse*. Another half-dozen amendments were moved on the Bill over the coming months. Conservatives became increasingly hostile towards the government, unleashing twenty years of frustration on their opponents. In mid-June a final amendment was moved by a Liberal MP which defeated the government due to support by the Conservatives and a significant proportion of Liberals. On 26 June Russell's Cabinet resigned.

The next day Derby accepted the Queen's request to form a government, becoming the first person in history to become Prime Minister on three separate occasions.[56] The following week saw the dissident Liberals that had helped to bring down the last government refuse to serve under Derby meaning that in 1866, as in 1852 and 1858, Derby would be leading a minority government. Disraeli returned as Chancellor of the Exchequer and Derby's son, Lord Stanley, was appointed Foreign Secretary.

The new government would receive no honeymoon period despite the prorogation of Parliament being only six weeks away. On 23 July 20,000 reformists, angry at the defeat of the Liberals' Reform Bill, marched to Hyde Park for a gathering.[57] The police closed the gates to the park at the government's instruction and public disorder followed with the crowd breaking down the gates and accessing the park. Derby denounced their actions in the Lords and, when another meeting was called for the following week, he insisted that they find another location.

The government was still standing at the end of the session in August and during the recess Derby, prompted by Disraeli,[58] mulled over the issue of reform and, more specifically, how to achieve a lasting settlement that would stop the issue from dominating the legislative agenda as it had done for the last thirty years. In November he proposed in Cabinet that, rather than introduce a Reform Bill, which may be defeated and force an election, the government should introduce separate resolutions for the individual issues that needed reform, for agreement in Parliament. These could then be accepted or rejected in isolation and reform could move forward on whatever was taken up in the end. His idea was to expand the franchise; enfranchise the labouring classes; revise the distribution of seats; revise the boundaries of existing seats; and consider the introduction of secret ballots (all polling at this time was public) amongst other things.

However, when the administration faced Parliament at the beginning of February 1867, it was clear that the opposition would not be satisfied with proceeding by resolutions, apparently expecting a Reform Bill to settle the matter[59] sooner rather than later. In the face of overwhelming Liberal support for such a measure the government had to reconsider their options. They began discussing what should be included in such a Bill that wouldn't result in their downfall as it had so many other administrations over recent years. By the end of February all proposed resolutions were voluntarily withdrawn by the government before the opposition had a chance to force them to do it.

Derby and the majority of the Cabinet were in favour of extensive reforms of all the factors raised in their various resolutions for two reasons: it would make their Bill different enough to the Liberal one of 1866 for them to justify their obstruction to that piece of legislation; and it would provide a lasting settlement. However, a minority of ministers, namely Lord Cranborne (who would become Prime Minister one day as Lord Salisbury), Lord Carnarvon and Jonathan Peel[60] (son of former Prime Minister Sir Robert) wanted more limited reforms, much closer to the previous Liberal Bill, or else they threatened to resign.

Derby was distressed by this but ultimately felt that it was better to lose them and have a chance at passing a Bill that the majority of Conservatives and Liberals supported than to keep his Cabinet together and face defeat. The three Cabinet ministers resigned as expected and Derby went on to ensure that the rest of the Conservative Party united behind his plans. In mid-March he informed the entire Party of what the Cabinet's intentions were before going to Parliament and instructed them to give their full support or else force the government out of office.[61]

Disraeli introduced the government's Reform Bill on 18 March. Derby's ministry would live or die by the result. Gladstone led the opposition in the Commons and made several speeches over the following week denouncing various measures contained in the Bill. However, Disraeli was adroitly able to counter his criticisms by reminding the House that Gladstone had supported the majority of those measures in the past: the Whig and Liberal Parties had now introduced so many Reform Bills under Grey, Melbourne, Palmerston and Russell with various alterations to the semantics that very little in the Conservative Bill had not been attempted at some time previously.

Having defeated Gladstone in the debates, Disraeli was able to force the Bill through first and second readings as well as committee stage. The opposition was disunited whereas the Conservatives were one voice. Disraeli's confidence grew by the day, all the while an ailing Derby relied on his number two to take control of events as his health, as well as his position in the Upper House, removed from the debate, denied him the opportunity of doing so. The Bill passed its third reading in mid-July and moved to the Lords. There the Liberal Lord Grey introduced a hostile motion effectively rejecting the Bill. Now

Derby exerted all of his fragile energies in whipping the Conservative peers into support. He gave an impassioned speech on 22 July, which succeeded in steering the Bill through second reading but the exertion put him back into his sick bed. He was therefore absent during the Lords' committee stage, where the Bill passed through, but he dragged himself back for the third reading on 6 August where his Bill became law.

Derby had now seen the issue through just in time for the parliamentary recess but although he had been leader of the Party at the time of the passage of the Reform Bill, it was Disraeli, his chief lieutenant and his successor who deserves the credit for managing the process. Disraeli initially suggested that a new Reform Bill was necessary during 1866, he had controlled debate in the Commons and he had defeated Gladstone.

The recess was a chance for the government to celebrate its recent successes but for much of it Derby was bedridden with illness. Parliament was necessarily reconvened for three weeks from November to December to respond to Fenian outbreaks in Manchester but aside from that the prorogation was relatively quiet. When Parliament returned for the new session on 13 February Derby was too ill to attend. Realising that the stress of high office was killing him, the Prime Minister decided to retire and on 25 February he wrote to the Queen resigning his office. So ended 22 years of leadership. Derby had steered his Party through famine, war, peace, reform, protection and free trade. However, in spite of his long tenure at the helm of his Party and in spite of his returning to become Prime Minister on three separate occasions his leadership can be defined by (incredible as it may sound given these two facts) a lack of tenacity.

Derby was offered the premiership on three occasions before he accepted for the first time. Whenever he lost office, rather than fighting to regain it as his three separate tenures suggests, he actually lost interest in politics. He would return to his Knowsley home, neglect his parliamentary duties and sulk for a while. A long while. Thus after being removed from office in 1852, it was five years later, 1857, before he retook control of the Party, having spent that time bitterly lamenting his failed first premiership. The fact that he returned three times owed more to the fact that nobody of any stature challenged his leadership and Disraeli, clearly the most talented parliamentarian in the Commons, fully supported him, rather than to any importunity on Derby's part.

Further to this, every stage of his leadership, whether in opposition or in government, was marked with inactivity. During the uncertainties of 1851 he refused to take an active stance on Protectionism or the Catholic Question in the hope that the Whigs would argue amongst themselves. During his first premiership in 1852 the hot topic was free trade but Derby would not act on the issue without taking a measure of public opinion via a general election. So his government wandered through aimlessly, not committing to anything for months until an election was held, shortly after which he was removed from office. Then, when in opposition his strategy was to watch and wait, hoping that the Whig government would divide and destroy itself, which it did not. After his second period as Prime Minister and subsequent return to opposition he spent another seven years pursuing this same strategy of passive opposition, hoping that the government's supporters would argue among themselves. In the event it required Palmerston's death to act as the catalyst he needed for that. Only his final term in office can be viewed with any success because he was able to pass the legislation that successive governments had struggled with for three decades.

All in all Derby's strategy of inactivity was a failure. He had three separate terms as Prime Minister but the reality is that of 22 years as leader of the Conservative Party, he had spent around 18 years in opposition. Not drawing blood from his opponents, thereby denying his backbenchers something to feel excited about or united behind, spending years at a time sulking at Knowsley, all these things cost him support in Parliament and support at general elections. His crowning achievement was the passage of a Reform Bill that, actually, was the product of Disraeli's toil. This, though, brings us nicely on to Derby's real legacy and that was to give credibility to a man who would go on to define Victorian politics. When Disraeli made his maiden speech in the Commons he was jeered from all corners of the House. He was eccentric and untrusted, witty and charming but still the son of a Jew with all the stigma that came along with that at the time. However, he had served the only credible leader of the Conservatives as second-in-command for twenty years and so when it came to the point when Derby had to retire, a 63-year-old Benjamin Disraeli was the natural successor as Prime Minister. This could never have been achieved without the ongoing support of the Earl of Derby.

Benjamin Disraeli, 1ˢᵗ Earl of Beaconsfield
(1868 – 1881)

Imperium et Libertas. That would not make a bad programme for a British ministry. It is one from which Her Majesty's advisers do not shrink!

The Earl of Beaconsfield, autumn 1879

Whatever our principles are, you find both them and us prefer'd to you and yours

Daniel Defoe's *Tory*, 1692

ON 27 FEBRUARY 1868 Benjamin Disraeli, the strange and often untrusted outsider who came from a humble class background, was of Jewish descent and wore flowered waistcoats, defied all expectations by kissing the hand of the Queen as her new Prime Minister.[1] He would tell anybody who would listen that he had climbed to the top of 'the greasy pole'[2] and, for someone facing all the disadvantages that he had from his birth, it was a significant achievement. Disraeli returned to Parliament on 5 March for his first session as Prime Minister. Much as before his appointment, he would be facing William Gladstone as the leader of the opposition in the Lower House. The two men were now well into their fourth decade of rivalry, indeed hatred, which had started when both were young Tories unable to connect with each other in the early 1830s.[3] They had each succeeded the other as Chancellor of the Exchequer and would repeat the same with the office of Prime Minister.

As before, Gladstone would prove to be a formidable opponent. Within two weeks of first facing Disraeli in Parliament, the Liberal leader introduced a motion proposing the disestablishment of the Church of Ireland because the majority of that country were Catholic and were therefore being hurt by tithes for which they received no benefit. The proposal took Disraeli completely by surprise. Gladstone was far more pro-establishment and deeply religious, whereas

Disraeli was seen to be Anglican for convenience. Gladstone was seen as anti-Catholic (for example only reluctantly accepting that Catholics should be allowed to study at his beloved Oxford University at the beginning of the 1860s, and opposing that they should be allowed to be appointed to the university's controlling institutions in the early 1870s).[4] Disraeli, on the other hand, had supported the emancipation of Jews suggesting his own liberality when it came to religion. Therefore it is not surprising that the Prime Minister was wrong-footed by this turn from Gladstone. His response was to defend the institution, suggesting that Gladstone was now so influenced by Radical thought that he would eventually turn to the removal of the monarchy. His rambling arguments held no weight and he was eventually defeated in a vote of 4 April. It was clear that calls for his resignation would imminently follow and so the Prime Minister called an Easter recess to buy himself more time.[5]

During the break he consulted the Queen who advised him that she would not accept his resignation before a dissolution. Armed with this assurance, Disraeli met Parliament following the recess determined to see through the session before requesting a dissolution. Aware that the Prime Minister's not resigning meant that an imminent election was inevitable, Gladstone was happy not to push the matter but to keep pressing his Irish issue. This worked better than he could have imagined. Derby's Reform Act from the previous year had enfranchised a raft of working class voters who heard Gladstone's calls for disestablishment as a means of securing equality and felt that they could relate to it. Their logical conclusion was that it was the Liberals who were the Party of equality. Surely, they reasoned, it was they, not the Tories, who were to thank for the enfranchisement of the people. When the election was finally held in November 1868 the results were that roughly 274 Conservatives were returned, compared with around 384 Liberals,[6] which amounted to a doubling of the Liberal majority. At the end of November Disraeli informed the Queen that he would be surrendering office without waiting for Parliament to meet.[7]

It must be disheartening to anybody to lose a general election and be forced from office, more so when the margins were so large. However, for Disraeli his defeat marked the third time that he had been removed from office after a relatively short period, interspersed by years of Whig and Liberal domination. In fact, every Conservative administration ever formed since the Party's inception thirty five years earlier (five in total under Peel twice, Derby twice and the latest under Derby followed by Disraeli) had served less than a full parliamentary term. This raised questions over whether the Party realistically had a future. It was against this backdrop that Disraeli returned to Parliament in 1869, struggling to motivate himself for yet another period of opposition. Gladstone, now installed as Prime Minister, reintroduced his Irish Church Bill early in the session and although Disraeli opposed the measure, claiming it would lead to the break-up of the Union, he was realistic about his ability to make any difference against such an overwhelming majority. The Bill would become law and there was nothing that he could do to prevent it.

In the meantime he had problems closer to home. In April 1868 Lord Cranborne, one of the ministers who had resigned from Derby's government in 1866 over parliamentary reform, had been elevated to the House of Lords as the 3rd Marquess of Salisbury following the death of his father.[8] He considered himself an Ultra Tory and a staunch opponent of Disraeli's leadership. His elevation, a seemingly insignificant event, when combined with another significant title transfer in the Upper House, would shape the power structure of the Conservative Party for the remainder of the nineteenth century: In October 1869 the Earl of Derby died, meaning that his son, Lord Stanley, a hitherto strong ally of Benjamin Disraeli, was elevated to the Lords as the 15th Earl.[9] He was now openly courting the Dowager Marchioness of Salisbury, Lady Mary, who had been the second wife of the late Lord Salisbury, step-mother to the 3rd Marquess. Up until this point relationships between the new Lord Derby and the new Lord Salisbury had been cold. Politically this was understandable on the basis that Salisbury could not stand Disraeli whereas Derby was strongly allied to the Conservative leader. However, personally it is plausible that any animosity stemmed from the reality that it was more than possible that Derby had been having an affair with Lady Mary prior to the death of the 2nd Marquess.[10]

This marriage of Derby's, though, in a perverse way united the two families. Disraeli must have hoped that this would be an opportunity to bring Salisbury into his support, whereas Salisbury would have hoped that Derby could be turned against Disraeli. As it happened, both situations would occur within a few short years, with Salisbury and Disraeli becoming reconciled while Derby became estranged. For the time being both Derby and Salisbury were considered as potential leaders both of the House of Lords and of the Conservative Party. In terms of the leadership of the House of Lords, Salisbury was a strong contender but his hatred of Disraeli turned Conservatives against him, whereas Derby would have had Disraeli's confidence but didn't have the loyal following needed. In the event the Duke of Richmond was instated as leader of the Upper Chamber. Regarding the leadership of the Conservative Party, Salisbury would happily have ousted Disraeli given half the chance but he didn't have as much support as the current leader. On the other hand there was popular support within Party ranks for the replacement of Disraeli with Derby. However, the thought of shunning Disraeli to the point where he removed himself from the leadership of the House of Commons was frightening to most of the Party faithful,[11] who had known nothing but his command of that chamber, which he had held for over two decades.

So Disraeli remained and he spent his time in opposition constructing a Party that would be a force to be reckoned with in future elections. He built up local organisations, empowering them to select their own candidates and ensuring that they had men on standby to react to by-elections or any other such emergencies. Everything was then fed back to a centralised office established during this period to ensure that candidates would be sticking to an agreed Party position. He effectively made the Conservative Party a modern political force. The effects were immediate, first being proven at the next election. In the meantime Disraeli's popularity grew, evidently superseding his opponents when, on 27 February 1872, both he and Gladstone attended a Thanksgiving service at St. Paul's Cathedral to celebrate the return to health of the Prince of Wales, who had been struggling with typhoid over the winter. When the service had ended and the attendees left the cathedral past the surrounding crowds, Gladstone was greeted generally with silence, whereas Disraeli was cheered by most that he passed.[12]

His energies were better spent building the Party in this manner than they were focused at direct opposition in Westminster. With the Liberal majority so large attacks on the government were futile. Aside from this Disraeli's health had been tested whilst in office. Being in opposition could provide him with an opportunity for respite if he was prepared not to over-exert himself in the Commons. Gladstone passed an Education Act in 1870, with little resistance from the Conservatives. The 1871 session was also quiet in Parliament but, as stated, by 1872 the government was beginning to run out of steam while Disraeli's personal popularity increased exponentially. This was partly down to his work in building up local associations to influence the people and partly down to his having written a novel, *Lothair*, his first for twenty-two years, which was an instant hit.

But 1872 would affect the Conservative leader in other ways. In late spring it became clear that his beloved wife, Mary Anne, was quite ill. They spent the summer touring London and its suburbs together before she died in December. Disraeli found life unbearable in the immediate aftermath of her passing but forced himself to continue working as a means of distraction. In early 1873 such distractions would intensify. In the early hours of 12 March Gladstone's Irish Universities Bill was defeated in the Commons by three votes.[13] The Bill intended to extend university education in Ireland by allowing Catholics to attend state-funded institutions as another means of pacifying that troubled nation, along with the Church Bill of 1869 and a Land Bill passed in 1870. Under normal circumstances this defeat would have been difficult but tolerable. However, the government's greatest strength – its sizeable majority in the Lower House – was its greatest problem here. With such a large majority, being defeated in a vote necessarily meant that at least 50 Liberals (half the approximate majority following recent Conservative by-election victories) were voting against the government or abstaining. This was a shattering truth. Gladstone immediately announced that Parliament should be suspended for 36 hours after which the government would give a statement of its intentions.

Gladstone's Cabinet met later that day and quickly decided that their options were resignation or dissolution, Gladstone having placed so much of their reputation in the passage of the Bill. On 13 March Gladstone informed the Cabinet that he had decided upon resignation, which they accepted, and he then went to visit the Queen. Victoria must have felt relieved when the Prime Minister told her he could no longer remain in office. She had found him awkward at best and insufferable for the most part, a stark contrast to the likeable and flattering Disraeli.[14] Gladstone informed the Queen that the Conservatives must be sent for, that they had defeated him on a matter that he had made clear would be considered a vote of confidence in the government and that they must therefore provide an alternative. Victoria gladly sent for Disraeli. Gladstone informed Parliament of his decision and then returned home.

However, when the leader of the opposition arrived for his audience with the Queen he declined the offer to form a government. He advised her that the Conservatives still had a minority that was dwarfed by the Liberals and that he would constantly be humiliated at every division in the House of Commons. He had held office without power once (and had worked closely with Derby who had done the same on three separate occasions) and had no desire to suffer through the same situation once more. He did not say so to the Queen, but privately he knew that he was gradually eroding the Liberal majority. The Conservatives had won no fewer than 13 by-elections in the previous two calendar years. Another positive omen was that he had been cheered at the Prince of Wales' thanksgiving service whereas Gladstone had been ignored. All in all Disraeli concluded that the longer the Liberals held office the greater the damage that would be done to them at a general election. For the past four years, since moving into opposition, Disraeli had allowed the Liberals to cause spoilages to themselves on a greater scale than he himself had bothered to inflict. The reasons for this were fourfold. Firstly, he had spent decades in opposition and his defeat in the election of 1868 meant that he was to be returned there, probably for the rest of his career as far as he could tell. This disheartened him to the point where it was a struggle to motivate himself to lead a hard opposition for the years that followed. Secondly, Mary Anne's sickness during 1872, followed by her death later in the year, had led him to seclude himself as anybody would in similar circumstances.[15] She had been his biggest fan and without her pushing him he now had to inspire himself. Thirdly, the size of the Liberal majority meant that opposition was futile.[16] Even if he could whip his supporters into toeing the Party line on every issue, they would still be demolished by the government every time. Therefore he needed Liberals to turn amongst themselves as they had done on the Irish Universities Bill. Fourthly, he had a genuine held belief that the nation would become sick of Gladstone[17] and that any pushing on his part may come across as opportunistic. He was happy to allow the Liberals to bask in their initial successes, confident that it would lead to their undoing. The only moves he made to capitalise on this was the organisation of the local associations already described, ready to inflict a heavy defeat on the Liberals at the next election. Gladstone, Disraeli informed the Queen, would have to soldier on.

Victoria was disappointed at not being rid of Gladstone once and for all, but accepted Disraeli's argument that a Conservative government in the present House of Commons would be completely neutered. There was still over two years before the end of the septennial term and having a government that weak for that long could be devastating to the country. Gladstone was livid believing, rightly, that Disraeli was playing a political game at his expense. The only reason for someone so ambitious to decline office was to have the opportunity to hold it with even greater power at a future date. He stated in no uncertain terms that if the opposition forced a vote of confidence in the government then they had a responsibility to produce, or at least attempt to produce, an alternative. However, during the course of several three-way communications with the Queen and the Prime Minister as well as private conversations with his own allies over the course of the following day, Disraeli was adamant that he had not defeated the government. The way he saw it, it was Gladstone's own backbenchers that had done that. The Prime Minister could not escape the reality that Irish Catholics in Parliament had overwhelmingly opposed the government's proposals[18] meaning that it had enemies within both religions and on both sides of the Irish Sea. His second course of reason was that he had never suggested that the vote on the Irish Universities Bill should be interpreted as a vote of confidence in the government. Gladstone had done that himself and if the Prime Minister felt some political fallout as a consequence then that was his problem.

On 16 March the Queen instructed Gladstone that he was to remain in office and so he reluctantly reassembled his

Cabinet and agreed to amble through. Disraeli was elated at his triumph and, with the errors that were to befall the Liberal Party over the coming months, what a triumph it proved to be. The government's difficulties began almost immediately. In July 1873 news broke that there had been irregularities in the accounts of the telegraph service for which three ministers, including Robert Lowe, the Chancellor of the Exchequer, were implicated. Gladstone took the opportunity to reshuffle his Cabinet, removing the two lesser ministers and moving Lowe to the Home Office. When it came to filling the vacuum created, he decided that the best candidate to run the Exchequer was himself, alongside his Prime Ministerial responsibilities. There was nothing untoward in this but the problem was that at this point in history House of Commons-based ministers accepting office were assumed to have vacated their seats and were required to be re-elected. Gladstone believed that because he was already a minister and was simply taking on extra responsibilities he would not be required to vacate his seats (he was MP for more than one constituency). Parliament was in recess by this point and was not scheduled to return until February 1874 so he could bide his time on the issue. Constitutional lawyers were hopelessly divided on whether or not the Prime Minister had acted properly but the reality mattered far less than the perception: the fact that he had assumed that an election would not be required added to the impression that he was becoming increasingly autocratic over time and was far removed from the values of the people. On top of this one of the seats that Gladstone held was Greenwich, which it was widely believed the Conservatives would win at the next election. This led to accusations that he had deliberately tried to avoid his constitutional responsibilities in order to protect his majority in Parliament.

Disraeli did very little to capitalise on Gladstone's by-election crisis. The situation did demonstrate to him that the government was crumbling and whatever course of action they took came under heavy criticism. Now he felt it was time to go on the offensive. He wrote an open letter to the candidate for the Bath by-election in the autumn accusing the government of 'plundering and blundering'[19], he visited Glasgow and made a speech to university students there[20] in which he deplored Gladstone's administration. Then, in January 1874, before Parliament was even due to reconvene, it was dissolved. Gladstone realised that he was in trouble and so called an election, hoping to catch the Conservatives off guard. Disraeli only learned of the election when reading a Liberal campaign advert in *The Times*.[21] In a move of desperation the Prime Minister even promised the electorate that a Liberal government would abolish income tax[22], something which was unrealistic and which no credible political party has tried since.[23] Disraeli immediately busied himself with drafting a reply to Gladstone's advert and telegramming senior Conservatives to ready them for the upcoming campaign. The Liberals had hoped to catch the Conservatives off guard and the call for a dissolution was certainly a surprise but the constituency association development that Disraeli had toiled for over the previous five years would now come into its own. The Conservative Party was able to react to such a development with an agility unthinkable under its previous leaders.

More than at any time previously this election was about the party leaders over and above individual MPs. Today we take for granted that the popularity of the leader of a political party has a large effect on the way people vote. In the nineteenth century local candidates who may well have personally known the majority of their small electorates would have determined their own results. The 1874 general election was the beginning of modern polling in that sense: it was Gladstone versus Disraeli, rather than Liberal versus Conservative. The result was a complete vindication of all of Disraeli's strategies: to allow the Liberals to run out of steam; to turn down office-without-power in 1873; to build up local Conservative associations in order to have an efficient party machine at the time of an election. The Conservatives returned 350 MPs, the Liberals and Irish Home Rule supporters totalled around 300. This was the first Conservative majority since the election of 1841 under Sir Robert Peel.[24]

In spite of having been defeated at the election, Gladstone still hoped to meet Parliament before resigning office as had been the custom before Disraeli's resignation in 1868. His main motivation seems to have been to get Parliament to appropriate the £5 million surplus that he had accumulated during his time in office rather than allowing the Conservative government to do with it as they wished. As Mrs. Gladstone argued in a letter to her son Herbert 'Is it not disgusting after all

Papa's labour and patriotism and years of work to think of handing over his nest-egg to that Jew! '

His mind seems to have been turned by the Queen, who wrote to Gladstone explaining that she did not expect to wait three weeks for what would inevitably happen anyway. So, on 18 February, Disraeli had a meeting with Victoria in which he accepted the seals of office. Lord Derby was brought in as Foreign Secretary and Sir Stafford Northcote as Chancellor of the Exchequer, but it was negotiations with Salisbury that dominated gossip in the days leading up to, and immediately after, Disraeli's accepting office. If Gladstone had forever been Disraeli's antagonist without, then Salisbury was undoubtedly the antagonist within. Since Derby's marriage to his step-mother a few years earlier, Salisbury had hoped to realign the focus of power within the Conservative Party. Indeed there had been plenty of support for a Derby leadership bid during the lacklustre years of 1869-72 and Derby himself must have been lamenting the fact that it was not he sitting in Downing Street during that February of 1874. Coupled with this his views had been evolving slowly over time. Disraeli was still affectionately fond of Derby, so much so that he could not see that his old friend had been undergoing ideological transitions. In many policy areas the 15th Earl was now closer aligned to Gladstone than to his own leader.[25] However, he had been offered the post of Foreign Secretary and he was long-sighted enough to take it. Now it was his turn to exert some influence on Salisbury. Using Lady Derby as a go-between, Disraeli flattered Salisbury with compliments of the value of his opinion and the strength of his character. Lady Derby was eager to heal the now-familial divisions between the Stanleys and the Cecils, possibly hoping to establish an alliance for the future governance of the country. In the end Salisbury accepted Disraeli's offer of running the India Office. Choosing his Lady Derby as his representative was an inspired choice by the Prime Minister, but Salisbury was no doubt influenced by other factors. Firstly he was ambitious himself and holding a government post when they had such a sizeable majority would give him enormous influence over a significant number of MPs. Disraeli would not live forever and so this influence could surely one day be converted into outright leadership. Secondly the size of the majority itself meant that opposing Disraeli would be futile so the only option remaining was to align with him.

Meanwhile Disraeli could take further heart from events on the other side of the political divide as, following the heavy defeat of the general election, Gladstone announced that he would be stepping down as leader of the Liberal Party.[26] In reality it would be a year before he was actually replaced and even then it would not be long before he returned, but for the time being Disraeli appeared to have the world at his feet. During the 1874 session he found that without a worthy opponent (Gladstone still turned up but offered no passionate opposition on the scale for which he had hitherto been known) he was able to dominate the Commons. However, he made two mistakes before even taking office, the unforeseen consequences of which would be to force a legislative agenda on his government that he did not want. The first was lauded at the time as a piece of tactical genius, tasting all the sweeter for the fact that it required nothing more than for Disraeli to follow his own beliefs. Seeing the Liberal government pursue a policy of legislating on everything that they possibly could, Disraeli decided that the successive government should give the people a break from burdensome regulation-making. Feeling a certain affinity towards *laissez-faire* he was always more in favour of *encouraging* desirable behaviour than *legislating* for it. He therefore campaigned during the election not to introduce unnecessary Bills into Parliament,[27] thereby allowing the people their freedoms.

At the time this was seen as a masterstroke because the result of the election was a strong Conservative majority. However, this meant that when it came to the Queen's speech the government had little to propose to Parliament for the forthcoming session.[28] The second mistake that Disraeli made was that during his meeting with the Queen to accept the premiership, he repeatedly told her that whatever she wished to be done, should be done, regardless of the difficulties.[29] During the early part of the 1874 session, Victoria made it clear that she felt that Anglican services were becoming too ritualised in a manner similar to Catholic mass and that the government should therefore support legislation aimed at eliminating this. This was a ridiculous position to take but given that Disraeli had promised that her wish was his command, and given that she, being the Queen, had personally read the Queen's speech and therefore knew that there was no busy legislative agenda to get in the way, the Prime Minister felt that he had no excuse with which to avoid the issue.

Much to the Queen's knowledge, the Archbishop of Canterbury was introducing a Public Worship Regulation Bill aimed at removing any Popish influence from Church of England sermons. Disraeli was reluctant but when Gladstone came out in opposition to the measure he knew that he had to support it if for no other reason than to defeat his lifelong rival. Salisbury publicly broke ranks denouncing the Bill, personally feeling that it was dangerous to start legislating over what can and what cannot be done during a church service. Aside from the obvious restrictions on freedoms there was the very plausible possibility that the Church could break up as a consequence.[30] Disraeli privately agreed but with his backing the Bill became law without the government suffering in any significant way as a result.

The recess for Disraeli was marked with ill health. His gout became more severe when it was cold and his asthma intensified when it was damp so the long, hard winters of Britain were positively disastrous for him. As difficult as he found the parliamentary sessions, because the workloads ran him down, the recess was worse because of the weather.[31] The most notable event of the prorogation was that the Liberals finally settled upon a successor for Gladstone, with the Marquess of Hartington, heir to the pecunious Duchy of Devonshire, taking over the reins, albeit reluctantly.[32] Gladstone would now visit Westminster less and less and Disraeli's performances in the Commons became notably different – his command of the House was now more down to his position as Prime Minister than due to any oratorical prowess. Many of his contemporaries put this down to age and ailing health but more than one historian has speculated as to the possibility that it was his greatest adversary that brought out the best in him.[33] With Gladstone gone, Disraeli no longer needed to perform at his best.

Disraeli's performances made little difference to the 1875 session, which passed off quietly as the opposition struggled to compete without Gladstone. His ability now to get away with whatever he wished would be audaciously utilised by the Prime Minister, but to such an extent that it would bring Gladstone running back to Parliament in 1876 to defend his positions. The saga started in November 1875, with Disraeli's purchasing on behalf of the UK shares in the French-built Suez

Canal in Egypt. Half of the shares in the canal were owned by French companies, the other half by Ismail Pasha, the Khedive of Egypt.[34] The canal had been constructed in the 1860s, finally being opened in 1869. Britain had been invited to purchase shares in the franchise at that point but the Gladstone government had declined, seeing it as expensive and pointless. However, by 1874 one in four ships using the canal was British. It had become the principal route of trade towards India, shaving weeks off the journey by sea. This was not just a benefit for tradesmen and the economy, it also made the colony safer by reducing the response time for the army should reinforcements be needed in the event of a mutiny.

Disraeli was not satisfied with leaving such a vital article to British interests in the hands of the Ottoman Empire, partly controlled by French investors or, potentially, to be controlled by the Russians should they usurp the Turks as the dominant power of the Near East. Given that the Russo-Turkish war was only a few years away these concerns were rather prophetic. In the middle of November 1875 Disraeli became aware that the Khedive of Egypt had entered into clandestine negotiations with two French banks to sell his personal shares in the canal in order to fund his lavish lifestyle.[35] Due to Parliament being in recess he had no need to consult or meet, taking the decision unilaterally. Rather than ask the Bank of England for funding, which would take time, raise questions and possibly force the issue of going to Parliament, he instead got Lionel de Rothschild, the wealthy banker-cum-politician who had forced the issue of Jewish emancipation with his election to Parliament, to fund the deal. On 24 November the Prime Minister triumphantly reported to the Queen: 'It is settled! You have it, Madam!'

The country fell behind Disraeli's bold moves and, in spite of Gladstone denouncing the purchase as flashy and vulgar, the House of Commons ratified the measure when Parliament met in 1876. Full of confidence following this great victory, Disraeli made his second audacious move in the 1876 session, which would prove to be the catalyst for Gladstone's return to front-line opposition. In the years leading up to the 1876 session, Queen Victoria had become despondent that most of her regal contemporaries, many of whom were also her relatives, held titular honours higher than her own. Franz

Joseph I was *Emperor* of Austria-Hungary, whereas she was a mere *Queen*. Even more difficult for the Queen to handle was that Alexander II of Russia, who was Victoria's cousin, was a Tsar (Russian for Emperor), meaning that he, too, technically outranked her. The humiliation didn't stop there, though. Kaiser (German for Emperor) Wilhelm I of Germany was ageing and it would not be long before his son, Frederick, succeeded him as Emperor. Frederick happened to be married to Victoria's daughter, Vicky, meaning that in a very short time the Queen's own daughter would be an Empress, looking down on her mother, the deferent Queen.

Victoria became obsessed with appropriating an imperial title of her own and the Suez Canal success only intensified her ambitions.[36] She worked hard on Disraeli through the winter, convincing him that she needed to be both *Regina et Imperatrix*,[37] probably reminding him that he had promised her that whatever she wanted he would deliver when he first took office. She was probably not aware that the Prime Minister had himself written of the possibility of crowning the Queen as Empress of India in *Tancred* nearly thirty years earlier. If ever there was a soul disposed to deliver this most coveted prize, Disraeli was it. The result was the Royal Tithes Bill, announced to Parliament at the State Opening, which the Queen attended in person (a rare occurrence since the death of Prince Albert).

The Liberals were horrified by the Queen's imperial pretensions and Gladstone made a point of attending the debates on the Bill to denounce it in the strongest possible language. In the end his return had several effects. In the short term he inadvertently helped to steer the Bill through as his criticisms, being as stern as anyone would expect from a man like Gladstone, caused all with any sense of patriotism to rally behind their Queen and give her what she wanted. In the medium term he brought out the best in Disraeli once again who, forced to defend such allegations as that he was walked over by the Queen, managed to destroy all before him.[38] Finally, although Disraeli successfully defended his reputation in an official capacity in the sense that he was never accused of anything that was substantiated, the attacks by the Liberals, led by Gladstone, did serve to damage his standing in Parliament amongst the Members themselves. Although the legislation was successfully steered through, from this point onwards Disraeli would not be able to assume that he could get away with whatever he wanted. It was this assumption that had made Gladstone feel compelled to return to fight the government, albeit still not as leader of the opposition.

Foreign affairs would prove to define Disraeli's second premiership, whether it be the Suez Canal, the Queen installed as Empress of India, or his intervention in the Balkans during the souring relations between Russia and Turkey. All of these were driven by a need for Britain to maintain its link to the East and all of which took a prominent role in 1876. In 1875 Disraeli had made it clear that any act of aggression on behalf of Russia towards the Ottoman Empire would be viewed negatively in Britain and could lead to British intervention. In 1876 various Balkan states started to revolt against the Turks, beginning with Bosnia and Herzegovina,[39] undoubtedly encouraged by Russia, and Turkish officials were massacred. Humanitarians were split, Disraeli, who carried the mood of the majority, felt that such atrocities as had happened in Bosnia and Herzegovina should be discouraged whilst also being concerned that an expansionist Russia could crush Britain's control of the seas via Suez. Others, namely Gladstone, felt that the Ottomans were oppressors who should be removed. In reality, Gladstone was a Christian first and an humanitarian second. He convinced himself that Russia was fighting on behalf of Christendom, rather than its own imperial ambitions. He saw in this conflict an opportunity to attack the Prime Minister and he would do so, but not before another twist in that eventful year.

The 1876 session had taken its toll on Disraeli, who was struck by several illnesses throughout the course of the year.[40] He could not bring himself to hand over the leadership to anybody else, as there was nobody as capable despite his age and his various ailments. However, he also could not go on as he was doing, with continuous debate in the House of Commons slowly killing him. He had been a master of the Lower House for forty years. He had famously jostled with Peel, Russell, Palmerston and Gladstone, and been a match for all of them. Now, though, on the advice of his doctors and his friends, he knew that he had to leave the House of Commons. He made his final appearance there on 11 August in which he debated the massacre of 12,000 Bulgarians following a failed insurrection against their Turkish overlords. Victoria happily created him Earl of Beaconsfield (announced on 12 August)[41] rather than see him retire, meaning that he could still lead the government but from the relatively placid House of Lords. The one consequence that he knew would be inevitable from his elevation was that there was nobody worthy to match Gladstone in the Commons, meaning that it would only be a matter of time before that man's mastery of the Lower House naturally led to his return as leader of the Liberal Party.

So it was in the summer that Gladstone, in response to newspaper articles about Turkish oppression in Bulgaria, started to write about the atrocities that had taken place in the Balkans. He sent copies of his resultant pamphlet to a number of media outlets as well as to the Earl of Beaconsfield, who went on to describe it as 'of all the Bulgarian horrors perhaps the greatest.'[42] Of their various clashes over the decades, this, their final one, which would focus on foreign affairs until 1880, would arguably prove to be the greatest that Gladstone and Disraeli ever endured. Gladstone followed his pamphlet writing with pro-Russian speeches, ignoring the oppressive measures employed by the Tsarist regime. He focused on the sufferings of Christian Slavs arguing the case for the right of a people to self-determination, especially when their religion is incompatible with that of their overlords. Gladstone apparently set British rule of Ireland aside in his mind as a completely different set of circumstances.[43] Hypocrisy notwithstanding, Gladstone's anti-Turkish speeches struck a chord with the public. Beaconsfield was naturally inclined against any moves made by Russia but his strategy had been to say as little as possible and let the situation blow over. Gladstone's rabble-rousing meant that pressure was brought on the Prime Minister to address the issue. However, he still felt that a Turkish presence in the region was the best means of keeping Russian expansionism at bay and was, therefore, essential for British interests. If Russia controlled the Turkish Straits then the British Empire would be at the mercy of the Tsar's navy. He therefore responded to Gladstone's speech not by addressing the matter of Ottoman heavy-handedness in quashing rebellions in their own dominions, but by ostentatiously warning Russia not to make any further moves against Turkey. He knew that the Tsar, having stirred up trouble in the Balkans, planned to use Slavish oppression as an excuse to declare war on the Ottomans. By the December of 1876 Beaconsfield had made it clear that any moves made by Russia that may affect

Britain's Empire would result in war. However, to try to ensure that war was avoided, the Turkish Sultan was informed that should his country precipitate hostilities then they would not receive British support.

Turkey and Russia agreed to a brief armistice[44] and Salisbury travelled to Constantinople to represent the UK at a peace summit held involving all interested parties. Negotiations soon broke down in January 1877[45] and, by April, Russia had declared war on Turkey. The government's policy now became neutrality with a reiteration of the previous warning to Russia not to infringe Britain's interests in the Near East. Gladstone, however, was on his soap box at every opportunity. He now had no worthy opponent in the Commons and was quickly asserting his authority on the Lower House, advocating assisting Russia in 'her noble endeavours on behalf of the Balkan Christians.'[46] To add to the difficulties, Lord Derby, the Foreign Secretary, was clearly demonstrating signs of being opposed to war, regardless of how his leader felt.

Throughout the spring of 1877 the Russian army advanced through the Balkans virtually unopposed until it was held up by a Turkish force at Plevna (now Pleven, Bulgaria). Plevna fell in the December and it looked as though the Tsar's forces wouldn't stop until they conquered Constantinople, the Turkish capital. Now Beaconsfield resolved to act, with or without the support of his Foreign Secretary. He ordered a British fleet to pass through the Dardanelles Strait to the Sea of Marmara to protect Constantinople from the Russians. Derby resigned in protest but, within a few hours returned to work when a communiqué from the British Ambassador suggested that the Tsar and the Sultan had entered into peace negotiations, causing the fleet to hold anchor at the Dardanelles.

During the negotiations Russia made impossible demands which would have difficult consequences for Britain including Russian dominance of the Balkans and the Straits. War looked inevitable and the British public was divided over the matter. This crisis may have been the birth of what is now known as 'jingoism', with a popular song being chanted by supporters of assertive foreign policy all over the country:

We don't want to fight but by jingo if we do

We've got the ships, we've got the men, we've got the money
too
We've fought the Bear before, and while we're Britons true
The Russians shall not have Constantinople.

Russia continued to advance on the Turkish capital and so Beaconsfield ordered the British fleet to advance towards the Bosphorus Strait of Constantinople. Meanwhile seven thousand native Indian troops were sent to Malta, ready to invade if necessary. Faced with this prospect the Russians agreed to negotiate a peace, meanwhile Derby resigned once more and was replaced by Salisbury.[47] Now both Beaconsfield and Salisbury had achieved what they had set out to achieve ten years earlier, each using Derby as a pawn. Salisbury had intended to drive a wedge between Derby and Disraeli, which had now been achieved although not by him. The Prime Minister had hoped to use Derby to bring Salisbury into his sphere of influence, which had also been achieved but at the expense of Derby, his hitherto longest-standing political ally.

On June 11 1878 the Congress of Berlin was held to thrash out a peace between the nations of Europe. Beaconsfield and Salisbury both attended personally to represent British interests, with German, Austrian, Russian, French and Turkish ministers also present among others. Beaconsfield, as would be expected, put himself at the centre of attention, impressing all of his European contemporaries to the point where the German Chancellor, Otto von Bismarck, exclaimed that *'Der alte Jude, das ist der mann'*. He unilaterally pushed for Russia to relinquish any influence it held in the Mediterranean, to accept a border for Bulgaria drawn up by him personally and that Cyprus should be put under British control so that the Royal Navy could react quickly to any adverse developments in the region. With Disraeli threatening to leave the conference and declare war should this not be accepted, Bismarck quickly fell in line and the Russians had no choice but to accept.[48] The Treaty was signed on July 13 and Beaconsfield returned home a hero. That summer the Cabinet considered calling a general election but, being only four years into a seven year Parliament it was deemed unnecessary. This would be one of the greatest missed opportunities of the nineteenth century. From this point onwards foreign affairs would continue to define Beaconsfield but now their effects would be adverse. Events on two separate continents would unravel simultaneously and in neither instance was Beaconsfield primarily to blame for British policy. But relations with Afghanistan in Asia and the Zulu Kingdom in Africa were about to take drastic turns for the worse.

In July 1878 the same month as the signing of the Berlin treaty a Russian delegation was received in Kabul. For several years the Prime Minister had been arguing the need for Britain to reinforce its defences of north-west India in case of Russian invasion through the passes there[49] but Afghanistan was officially an ally and the Amir relied upon British support to maintain his independence. However, UK representatives were becoming worried about the Amir's relationship with the Russians and, when a Russian mission was received in Afghanistan, British alarm bells started ringing. The Viceroy of India, Lord Robert Lytton, wrote home to request permission to send his own mission to Afghanistan. This was granted but on the instruction that care was to be taken to avoid war with Russia and that the mission should go via Kandahar. However, Lytton had long since lost his cool. He sent a communiqué to the Amir demanding that he dismiss the Russians and then he sent his own mission forward via the unapproved route of the Khyber Pass. The result was that his delegation would arrive sooner than the British government had hoped and thereby risk a conflict with the Russians. At the border, the delegation was turned away on the instructions of the Amir, as it had been expected to be, which left war as the only option to such an affront. In December 1879 the UK entered into war with Afghanistan, Beaconsfield having the policy decided for him by his Viceroy of India.[50]

Meanwhile in Africa, Britain decided that war could be avoided with a very peculiar policy. In southern Africa the Transvaal Republic, which was a country run by Boer settlers, shared a border with the Zulu Kingdom, which was a country of native Zulus, and the two peoples hated one another. Britain, feeling that war in the region could be destabilising, had annexed Transvaal in 1877 with the plan to make the region a federation under British control.[51] The Boers were unhappy with being annexed but the Zulus were also dissatisfied at being unable to attack their ancient enemy due to the British protection now being afforded them. The High Commissioner of Southern Africa, Sir Bartle Frere, felt that the Zulus needed to be quashed in order for harmony to be brought to the region. Beaconsfield, on the other hand, believed that if the Zulus were treated with respect then they could all co-exist. Towards the late summer of 1878 Frere requested further military support from home in case hostilities broke out. Reinforcements were sent but on the explicit instruction that they were for defensive purposes only. However, Frere sent an ultimatum to the Zulu King demanding that he disband his army and accept a permanent British residence in Zulu. In January 1879, when no response had come, Frere sent his military force into the Zulu Kingdom. Now Beaconsfield was embroiled in two wars that he had not sanctioned.

On 22 January the native Zulus surprised the invading force with an attack at Isandhlwana and 800 soldiers on the British side were killed. So, throughout the late winter and early spring of 1879, Cabinet meetings were dominated with discussions of Afghanistan and southern Africa. Then in the May British forces expelled the Amir from Afghanistan, replacing him with his son who signed an agreement allowing a permanent British presence within his country. At the end of the parliamentary session it looked as though British policy in Afghanistan had been successful, albeit unintentionally so, whereas policy in Africa was a disaster. The problem was that public opinion seemed to be strongly against either war, nobody understanding the need for them. Then, in September, the British representatives in Kabul were massacred by Afghan troops.[52] Beaconsfieldian foreign affairs were soon turning into a shambles. Although Britain could congratulate itself on an unprecedentedly extensive Empire, the lives lost in its maintenance were proving costly.

When Parliament opened in 1880 the Cabinet were resolved on allowing the term to run the seven year maximum, but then early in the session Beaconsfield changed his mind and called an election for March.[53] It proved to be his final defeat. He spent the campaign in retreat, making no public appearances and nothing in the way of campaign manifestos. Gladstone, conversely, had spent the last year campaigning personally for a by-election in Midlothian which he had convinced himself that he should stand for because of his belief that if he could be endorsed there then perhaps he could take back the country from Beaconsfield.[54] He had won the seat in late 1879 by talking day-in-day-out to vast crowds who had gathered in various places to hear him. The journey from his home in Hawarden to Midlothian necessarily meant stops at various northern-English and Scottish stations, where there would be further crowds to perorate to, meaning that he had already covered half of the country in a campaign just a few months prior to the general election.

It wasn't just Gladstone's energetic campaign that defeated the Conservatives and it must be remembered that although he was suddenly popular, he still was not in any official capacity leader of the Liberal Party, that authority being held by Hartington. The result of the 1880 election was a reflection on the Conservative government. In the early years they had passed The Artisans' Dwelling Act (affording loans to local authorities to build working class housing), the Public Health Act (ensuring a minimum standard of sanitation nationally) and they had legalised peaceful picketing, thereby giving trade unions their first endorsement. Together these pieces of legislation had laid the foundations for the fair and just society strived for by so many politicians in the twentieth century. However, by the later years the country had suffered poor harvests, economic depression and two unpopular wars. So the electorate returned a Liberal Party majority of more than 100 MPs.[55] On 21 April Beaconsfield resigned as Prime Minister and told the Queen to send for Hartington, which she did on the 22nd. However, Hartington informed the Queen that although he was technically the leader of the Liberal Party, it was Gladstone that had won the election: no government could be formed without him and he would not take a subordinate position.[56]

Beaconsfield spent the remainder of the 1880 session enjoying his home at Hughenden which, although he had lived there for decades, he had never spent time at during the summer. He left Hughenden in January 1881, apparently refreshed and ready to return to politics. He attacked the Gladstone government at every opportunity throughout February and March in the House of Lords and often attended the Commons to watch debates from the gallery. Then, at the end of March, he caught a chill, which turned into bronchitis and he was bedridden throughout April. He had convinced himself that he would not recover from this illness and indeed Easter Monday, 18 April, would be his last full day. He died in the early hours of the 19th.

Disraeli had been leader of the Conservative Party for thirteen years although, given that he was leader of the House of Commons from the late 1840s he had been an essential cog in the Conservative machine for over three decades. He had, during his last premiership, arguably done more for the plights of the working classes than any of his predecessors, including his old foe Peel. The legislation he had enacted (in spite of appealing to the electorate on a platform of minimal legislation) had allowed for the creation of social housing, thereby clearing inner-city slums; created the first Friendly Societies, thereby protecting people's savings; lowered the working hours in factories, thereby giving employees their first elements of protection; improved public sanitation; passed a Clean Water Act, cleaning the rivers to provide better quality of water for the people. He had ensured that institutions had to serve the benefit of the country as well as themselves and established the principle that organisations could not cause harm to others for their own profit.

He had created a sense of nationalism previously unknown with his (controversial) expansionist foreign policy. Up until this point in history statesmen and MPs referred to the policies of *England*, of *English* principles and the Empire of *England*. From this point in history onwards people started to recognise that a third of the world was governed from London, made up of representatives from all the British Isles. Union Flag-waving jingoism took flight, the British Empire was acknowledged and people in Scotland and Wales started to feel more *British*. Ireland was still a special case.

All that said his foreign policy was controversial and it came at the expense of the liberty of many other peoples. Also, as we have seen, much of it wasn't actually Disraeli's own policy. When it came to Turkey, he had driven policy and carefully controlled the outcome of the Congress of Berlin. But when it came to Afghanistan and the Zulu Kingdom, he had been forced into a policy against his will and, ultimately, these cost him his position as Prime Minister. During his political life he had supported emancipation of both Jews and Catholics and had pushed for the civil rights of these groups, which had been very controversial and required much political courage. He had even mused on the possibility of giving rights to women to vote and represent the people, decades before this would become law and something which his nemesis Gladstone was opposed to.

His legacy to the Conservative Party was widespread. He laid down the principles of One Nation Conservatism which states that too much legislation can be stifling to the freedoms of a people and therefore wants to promote the principles of *laissez-faire*, particularly when it comes to economic affairs. But it also embodies an inclination towards social reform, believing that society will not exist in a contented manner as long as there are clear injustices that the state will not address and so legislation aimed at protecting its citizens is acceptable. This became the philosophy of the Conservative Party, increasingly from the Second World War onwards.

On a more intimate level, he managed to reconcile himself with Salisbury which not only gave his own leadership credibility but strengthened the reputation of Salisbury himself as a team-player, as an experienced statesman and as a Conservative leader, which then allowed him to take over the management of the Party for the following two decades.

From the time of his maiden speech in the House of Commons in the 1830s where he was heckled from the galleries and jeered from the benches (famously abandoning his speech to sit down while shouting that 'the time will come when you will hear me') he was destined to stand out from the crowd. He directly contributed to the downfall of Peel and for twenty years was the right-hand-man of the then-leader Lord Derby. Once Prime Minister he was just as prone to standing out from the crowd as he had been half a century earlier, creating the title of 'Empress' for Queen Victoria, standing off against Russia and causing all of Europe to fall in behind him and embroiling Britain in wars on two continents while pushing the boundaries of the Empire further than ever before. Throughout all of this he never lost sight of his values. In his 70s he was still at heart the young boy who had been ridiculed for his Jewish heritage and his loud clothes. His domestic legislation, all of which was clearly aimed at protecting other vulnerable people who were at risk of being bullied by bigger institutions, was something that he could have looked back on in 1881 with pride.

Joint Leadership: Sir Stafford Northcote & Robert Gascoyne-Cecil, 3rd Marquess of Salisbury
(1881 − 1885)

We shall be quite prepared to do all we can to give proper facilities for the discussion of the Bill with no desire whatever to obstruct it

Sir Stafford Northcote, 26 May 1881

If I had the power I would have thrown out the Bill. I find myself, however, in a small minority

The Marquess of Salisbury, 10 August 1882

Who would have thought…to have seen you and I at Whitehall together in the same interest

Daniel Defoe's *Tory*, 1692

FOLLOWING THE DEATH OF BEACONSFIELD in April 1881, leadership of the House of Lords for the Conservative Party fell to the Marquess of Salisbury, the former Foreign Secretary under the last Conservative government, with few disputing that he was the man for the job. The responsibility for leadership of the Party in the House of Commons was left with Sir Stafford Northcote, who had been Chancellor of the Exchequer under Beaconsfield. Both men had legitimate claims to have been Beaconsfield's number two and both had a reasonable chance of succeeding him. At this time the Lords was still officially equal to the Commons as a legislative assembly (although it was clear to most that the will of the Commons now had to be accepted in the Upper Chamber unless there was good cause for legislation to be revised) so it was not necessarily clear which leader had ultimate authority. However, it was not necessary for either man to have to defeat the other for overall leadership of the Party in any official capacity for several reasons. Firstly, they did not sit in the same chamber and therefore neither had to defer to the other on a daily basis. Secondly, both men needed to work together in order to oppose the Liberal Party in both chambers on most issues, so a contest for superiority was thought to be a damaging prospect, rather than a constructive one. Supporters of both men would vie on their behalf to try to get them a lead over the other but ostensibly the two men worked together and were satisfied, initially, with the Party having no *de jure* leader. Although they would never officially change their stance on this matter, the two men soon started to compete with each other, unofficially.

At around this time a small clique of Conservatives in the House of Commons formed an official alliance known as the Fourth Party, whose intention was to drum up opposition to Gladstone's government, which they were concerned would not be delivered by the official leadership. The group was made up of four prominent Commons orators, namely Lord Randolph Churchill, father of the future Prime Minister, Winston Churchill; future Prime Minister Arthur Balfour, nephew of Salisbury; John Gorst; and Henry Drummond Wolff.[1] Although they hoped to bring down Gladstone, the four men would play a crucial part in the coming leadership battle within the Conservative Party, all of them being clear supporters of Salisbury with little that they found appealing in Northcote.

In May 1881 Northcote was invited to see the Queen during which she apparently expressed to him that she considered him as Beaconsfield's successor.[2] Salisbury, on the other hand, was aware firstly that Northcote was an essential presence in the Commons, the Party having little else in the way of talent there; secondly that the Lower House was increasingly being viewed as the more powerful of the two and certainly where the more fierce debating took place (as opposed to the Lords, which he viewed as dull, having sat in both chambers); and thirdly that his position within the Party was probably not as popular as that of Northcote at this point in time.

The two men worked together as joint leaders in the Shadow Cabinet but their need to outdo each other soon became a contest between the two Houses of Parliament. In 1881 agitation in Ireland was once again on the rise and the Gladstone government's response was to come down tough on rebellious tenants, who were seen as causing much of the disruption in quarrels over rents. Along with the imposition of stricter penalties including the suspension of habeas corpus to punish recalcitrant tenants, the government introduced a Land Bill to try to appease them with what they viewed as their legitimate worries. The Land Bill would, *inter alia*, reduce rates of rent in order to make it more affordable and give tenants minimum fixed terms of tenancy in order to reduce evictions.[3] Now Salisbury and Northcote could, while both being opposed to the Bill, try to assert their own authority over the leadership. Whereas Northcote felt that much could be lost by outright opposition, not least because the Conservatives did not have the numbers to succeed in his chamber, Salisbury was vitriolic in his criticism when the Bill was placed before the Lords. Whereas Northcote suggested some minor amendments in order to limit the damage, Salisbury put forward some powerful amendments abhorred by the radical section of the Liberal Party but backed by such persuasive rhetoric that many peers followed him. Gladstone could have fought Salisbury but in doing so he would have caused a clash between the two Houses, which Salisbury wanted (in order to bring to a head his leadership bid against Northcote) but that Gladstone himself would not countenance. The Prime Minister was very capable but he struggled with chaos. The uncertainty of a conflict between the Lords and the Commons was not something he relished. Instead he thrashed out an agreement, which made Salisbury appear as an able negotiator, and the great constitutional question of where the bulk of the power lay between the two Houses would not be answered for another thirty years.

The next milestone moment in the rivalry between the two leaders came in 1882, when Gladstone introduced an Arrears Bill into the Commons. The spirit of this Bill was to make the government share with landlords any losses caused by defaulting tenants on their land in Ireland only. Northcote advocated compromising once again but Salisbury was intransigent as usual. The strategy had worked for him in the past and the Bill seemed to set a dangerous precedent – forcing the government to share the burden of responsibility when tenants defaulted could lead to them sharing in the losses of all commercial enterprises. Where would it end? He attacked the Bill with his usual venom when it came to the Lords but he had seriously misjudged the mood of his fellow peers. For varying reasons the vast majority wanted to compromise rather than fight. Some felt that the Conservative Party was quickly gaining a reputation for picking fights with the government over Ireland and not talking much about affairs elsewhere; some believed that this was an argument that they could not win; some were landlords in Ireland themselves and would benefit from what was effectively a free insurance policy offered by the government; others still were worried that challenging these measures would be tantamount to provoking civil war in Ireland. All of this, along with threats from Gladstone to dissolve Parliament should the Bill not pass unscathed, resulted in the Conservative opposition falling away and Salisbury being left feeling embarrassed and looking less like a leader than a pretender to the title.[4]

Salisbury then spent the recess away from politics and must have felt that things could not get any worse for him politically. Then came 1883. Early in the session it became known that Northcote had been requested to unveil a statue of the late Earl of Beaconsfield, which would stand in what is now Parliament Square in Westminster. Churchill, in particular, was publicly scathing of this, claiming that it should be Salisbury, rather than Northcote, who should have this honour. Salisbury was embarrassed by Churchill's behaviour, still ostensibly working in coalition with Northcote and now privately probably feeling that he could no longer win a battle for supremacy anyway. Once the statue was unveiled on 19 April, the anniversary of Beaconsfield's death, Churchill again criticised Northcote, claiming that the Conservatives needed a leader that could unite all classes, and the Commons leader was not that man. Again, this was more of an embarrassment to Salisbury than it was a help and the end of the session could not come quickly enough for him.

Northcote looked like a Prime Minister in waiting. His strategy of limiting the scope of government legislation as opposed to Salisbury's obstinate opposition, given the size of the government's majority in the Commons, appeared sensible and measured. Notwithstanding the vicious internal opposition inflicted on him by the Fourth Party, he had widespread support from within the Conservative ranks as they now began to assume that he was the overall leader.[5] Although only three years into the parliamentary term, the Gladstone government looked fragile: Policy over Ireland was failing and in spite of the several acts passed to pacify the populace of the Emerald Isle, unrest was still widespread; Lord Hartington, who had nominally taken over leadership of the Liberals during Gladstone's political hiatus in the 1870s, was widely believed to be dissatisfied with the direction of Liberal policy and rumours of a leadership challenge abound; and the Prime Minister's policy in Egypt had brought him widespread unpopularity. The situation on this last issue was that in the autumn of 1881 an Egyptian Colonel named Arabi had performed a semi-coup whereby he did not remove the Khedive but he forced him to accept Arabi's own policies, which were pro-Egyptian and anti-anybody else. Egypt, thanks to Disraeli's Suez Canal share purchase, was now an essential hub for the British Empire and, therefore, nationalist activities were dangerous for British interests.

Gladstone did not particularly want to get involved but his Cabinet were overwhelmingly overcome with jingoism and his ability to resist their pressure was minimal. Consequently, Arabi was sent an ultimatum to desist or suffer the consequences. When he didn't reply, the Royal Navy bombarded Alexandria in July 1882. This was viewed across the world as a harsh reaction[6] but was nevertheless followed by an armed landing in Egypt in the September, in which Arabi was captured and exiled. So far, so good. However, by the turn of the year General Gordon was despatched by the government to monitor uprisings in Egyptian Sudan and report back. Eventually, the General would take the decision to occupy the Sudan, fall under siege by local forces for nearly a year, be left to his fate by the government and ultimately be killed there. Gladstone would be called the 'Murderer of Gordon' and his reputation would never recover.[7]

During all of this, Northcote simply had to wait to become Prime Minister: the Liberals were self-destructing with unpopular policies on every front; Salisbury had made a hash of his own leadership prospects aided in no small part by Churchill and the Fourth Party; meanwhile his own safe, ginger form of opposition was proving, if not popular, then not as unpopular as those of his rivals.

All of this changed over the course of two situations that developed in 1884. The first involved the National Union of Conservative and Constitutional Associations (NUCCA), which had first been founded by Benjamin Disraeli as a means of bringing greater efficiency to the local running of elections.

NUCCA was effectively a pre-curser to what is now the Party Conference but it was run by an elected Council of the National Union whose role was also to represent the voluntary sector of the Party in their dealings with the professional side. In the February, elected to the Chairmanship of the Council was none other than Lord Randolph Churchill, who immediately turned his attention from attacking Gladstone on behalf of the Conservatives to attacking the Conservative leadership on behalf of the National Union. He demanded that NUCCA be responsible for the financial controls of the Party and selection of the Party leader, an idea abhorrent to both Salisbury and Northcote who believed that parliamentarians should be completely independent to act according to their own judgments. Churchill kept pushing, writing to the pair of them with his demands on several occasions over February, March and April, but the leaders stood firm. Churchill resigned the Chairmanship in May but was re-elected in July, demonstrating to Salisbury and Northcote that the grassroots were fully behind him.

On 26 July 1884 Salisbury met with Churchill to negotiate a peace, which was achieved with smiles on both sides. Churchill could claim that the National Union was being recognised more in an official capacity than it ever had, while Salisbury had held his ground over denying them the ability to dictate Party policy. For Salisbury the real victory was bringing this influential orator back onside, for Churchill it was important to make amends with the leadership in the run up to an imminent general election should he wish to be considered for a Cabinet position. Overall, Salisbury's reputation swelled as a result, as people realised both that his intransigence could be an asset (perhaps Northcote would not have stood up to Churchill so firmly) and also that he had been prepared to compromise, which it had not up until this point been clear that he ever would.[8]

The second situation of 1884 which advanced Salisbury's standing within the Conservative Party hierarchy, was Gladstone's attempt to pass the century's Third Reform Act, with a Bill presented to Parliament in the early summer. When the government introduced their proposals it was clear that there would be a great increase in the enfranchised populace. As far as the Conservatives were concerned the government had no mandate for Reform, given that few Liberals had campaigned on the issue in 1880 and, in any case, they were now four years down the line and so the people should at least be consulted. If the Party held to this line then there would be a clear stalemate, as the Liberals controlled the Commons but they were outnumbered by Tory peers in the Lords. Northcote and Salisbury agreed between themselves that the line to be taken was that they could support Reform but only if the government simultaneously introduced a measure to amend the boundaries of existing constituencies in order to distribute seats more fairly.[9] Reform along with Redistribution, therefore, became the Party line. The Bill passed comfortably through the Commons but was wrecked at committee stage after the second reading in the Lords in July 1884. Gladstone responded by proroguing Parliament.[10]

The following ten weeks saw massive demonstrations both by those in favour of Reform, often with guest speakers from the Liberal side addressing the crowd, and by those in favour of Redistribution, often with guest speakers from the Tory side addressing their supporters. During July it was made clear to Salisbury by those around him that his obstinate approach would be his downfall and that he could not survive the crisis that he was causing. For surely the only way out of this situation was for the government to force the Queen to create the scores of Liberal peers that had been used to threaten Wellington back in 1831. Northcote also started to feel that perhaps they had gone too far and the time to negotiate was upon them. The strategy of outright opposition was all good and well, but it relied heavily on the Conservative Party being united. If Gladstone was to offer any form of concession, no matter how slight, then the fragile opposition would crumble, as their supporters would start to defect. Having made their point, Northcote felt that a negotiated settlement would be the only dignified way out of what was fast becoming a constitutional crisis.

Salisbury, on the other hand, was determined not to focus on what would happen if their supporters fell away, but to ensure that it did not happen in the first place. He went to great lengths to explain to wavering peers exactly why he was opposed to compromise (that the government would promise a Redistribution Bill following the passage of the Reform Bill and then not deliver. This would be greatly embarrassing to those who had stood by him in his insistence that both should be passed together).[11]

Towards the end of October Gladstone did just this. When Parliament reconvened and the same Reform Bill was reintroduced he offered the concerned Tories the promise of a Redistribution Bill as soon as the Reform Bill was passed and negotiations opened up. The Queen, fearing being forced into an embarrassing corner of creating peers that she did not want, put pressure on Salisbury to stand down. It is clear that at this time she felt that his behaviour was not worthy of a party leader and would not have considered him as her next Prime Minister if Gladstone's Liberals were to resign their posts immediately. Salisbury, however, was so entrenched in his position by now that he made it clear to anybody who would listen that if he did not get his way he would remove himself from politics altogether.[12]

Northcote was a loyal colleague and did not want to see Salisbury fall, yet seems to have been absolutely convinced at this point that there was no way back for him. All the Liberals had to do was to offer up enough of a compromise to make Salisbury's stance look ridiculous even to Conservatives and the country would be rid of him forever. Northcote agreed ostensibly to push for the strategy of wrecking the Bill with amendments after the second reading in the Lords, until a Redistribution Bill was introduced, but now he was privately prepared to compromise as were a majority of senior Tory peers. They all started to discuss what to push for and what to sacrifice in future negotiations.[13] When meeting with them in mid-November Salisbury found he was outnumbered but managed to convince them all individually to hold out for a bit longer out of loyalty to him.

Then, on 17 November, Gladstone caved, fearing that the unity of the Conservatives meant that a dissolution was inevitable if he didn't. Northcote and Salisbury met with leading Liberal representatives in a series of talks to discuss what should be included in the Redistribution Bill.[14] For the first time in history some constituencies found that they could only return one MP, but the substance was less important than the fact that both Bills would be steered through Parliament at the same time. All of a sudden Salisbury looked less like a pig-headed lunatic, provoking constitutional crises with his

206 Northcote & Salisbury

unwillingness to compromise, and more like a natural-born leader and master strategist. If an election were to be forced in the near future (the parliamentary term still had almost another three years left) then perhaps he had overtaken Northcote at the right time. However, for Parliament to be dissolved something particularly horrendous would have to happen to the government. Parliament went into recess for the winter but by the time it reconvened in 1885 General Gordon had been killed in Khartoum and the government would have to answer for it.

It was mid-February when the opposition introduced a motion of censure in the Commons criticising the government's lack of action in Khartoum. The allegation was that, having been holed up for a year, there had been plenty of time to send support for Gordon, which would have saved countless British lives that had now been lost. In the debates Gladstone outperformed Northcote, as had become typical whenever they faced off, notwithstanding the fact that his position was far more difficult to defend. The Liberal majority served to support the government, but only by fourteen votes, which was almost as damning as a defeat anyway.[15] Northcote was now becoming increasingly aware that many people considered Salisbury to have overtaken him in the race for overall leadership. He would go on to press his case that the leader should be situated in the House of Commons because of the increasing authority of the Lower Chamber over the Lords, but would it do any good?

Gladstone convinced his Cabinet to keep going but it could not last long. When the government's budget was debated in June the Conservative Sir Michael Hicks Beach forwarded an amendment to beer duties which was carried in the early hours of 9 June. The Fourth Party led the cheers in the House of Commons when the result was announced and at the next Cabinet meeting Gladstone accepted that resignation was inevitable. The Prime Minister announced that he would be communicating with the Queen and the Conservatives began to discuss what course of action they should take. Northcote was convinced that the Party should accept power once Gladstone's resignation was confirmed. Having defeated the government it was their responsibility to provide an alternative. Salisbury was less certain, believing that Gladstone was offering him the same sort of 'poisoned chalice' that Disraeli had declined from him in 1873.[16] The Liberals would be held more clearly to blame for the disastrous British foreign policy of recent years if they were still in office at an election.

Northcote's argument that the Conservatives would be shamed if they shied away from the challenge of office was a strong one and he made it clear that if called, he would expect the Party to fall in line when he accepted the premiership. Salisbury, for his part, over the days following 9 June, realised that if the Queen requested him to form a government, his own sense of duty was too strong to decline. So the Conservatives would be returning to power, the only question was who would lead them? The Party itself was in no position to make up its mind with leading figures split over their allegiances, and neither leader was in favour of a national caucus, particularly since they had spent much of 1884 fighting Churchill over the issue of allowing the NUCCA to select the leader. In the event it fell to the Queen, who traditionally would send for the leader of the opposition when her ministers resigned. The men simply waited to see who she would send for. One of the two would be sent for, the other would go on to be the first leader of the Tories never to become Prime Minister.

Robert Gascoyne-Cecil, 3rd Marquess of Salisbury
(1885 – 1902)

We look upon the integrity of the Empire as a matter more important than almost any other political consideration that you can imagine

The Marquess of Salisbury, 7 October 1885

We Tories…have but one Heart, one Voice, one Purse and one Interest

Daniel Defoe's *Tory*, 1692

ONCE HE RECEIVED HIS SUMMONS to the palace but before actually attending, the Marquess of Salisbury met with Sir Stafford Northcote to discuss the future of the Party. The two men had completely different styles, had disagreed frequently on tactics but had always remained loyal to one another, which had allowed their joint leadership to work effectively. Now Salisbury was to become Prime Minister and Northcote would be forced to take a back seat. Or would he?

The first obstacle that Salisbury had to overcome before even accepting office was to convince Northcote and Churchill that they would have to work together in government, a prospect that neither man relished, but the negatives for which were far outweighed by being permitted to serve in Her Majesty's Government. For Northcote, given that their relationship as leaders had never been conventional and further blurring the usually-clear chain of command, Salisbury offered the post of First Lord of the Treasury. This seems incredible today given that we are used to the Prime Minister also being First Lord of the Treasury. Salisbury's vision was that he would lead the executive, he would make the policy decisions, with the consensus of the Cabinet, he would meet foreign ambassadors and heads of state on behalf of Britain (made easier by his decision also to hold the post of Foreign Secretary) and Northcote would have responsibility for government appointments. Salisbury had the opportunity to take it all given that he had been sent for by the Queen yet he still offered to share some executive power with Northcote. The reality of the situation is that although a goodwill gesture to his long-term colleague was part of the decision-making process, this was also partly about him relinquishing some of his less desirable responsibilities. Listening to junior ministers moaning about why they were overlooked was not something that Salisbury had any interest in. Neither did he have any desire to assess the suitability of candidates for bishoprics. He wanted to get on with the business of government and anything else was a distraction. He would form three separate administrations during his career, serving as Prime Minister for a total of thirteen years but would only hold the office of First Lord of the Treasury for a period of five months during that time.

  Convincing Churchill to join the Cabinet was going to be trickier. There was no doubt that the man wanted it, desperately so, but Churchill was also aware of his own indispensability and, therefore, was prepared to make demands. Firstly he wanted government positions for his Fourth Party allies,[1] which was not a major issue as it only involved finding openings for Gorst and Drummond Wolff. Balfour, as Salisbury's nephew, was to be included anyway (in fact, the ongoing nepotism displayed by Salisbury over the years, which undoubtedly enriched the career of his nephew led to the birth of the phrase 'Bob's your uncle'). Churchill's next insistence was that he could not accept working with Northcote. Salisbury tactfully tackled this issue and the problem of a blurring of the lines of leadership in one fell swoop, by elevating Northcote to the Lords as the Earl of Iddesleigh. Now there would be no question of a dual leadership between the two men with one in each House. Iddesleigh would be quite clearly Salisbury's number two in the Conservative Party leadership, his number two in the government and, now, his number two in the House of Lords. For Churchill the move meant that he could convince himself that he was the leading Conservative figure in the House of Commons, although the actual leadership would be afforded to Hicks Beach. Once the difficulties were all settled Churchill accepted the post of Secretary of State for India.[2]

  Without a majority in the House of Commons there was no point in the new government forming any sort of legislative agenda until after a general election. Their minority

could not be rectified in the short term because the Reform Bill
had passed but local constituencies were not yet aware of the
size of their new electorates. It would be autumn before all
those eligible to vote were aware of their newfound powers of
franchise, meaning that no election could be held until then. In
the meantime the government would have to muddle through
on the domestic front. Foreign affairs was, however, something
that the new administration could act upon without a majority
in Parliament and this is exactly what Salisbury intended to do.
He was of the opinion that almost every Liberal policy should
be reversed, from the embarrassing defeat of Gordon that was
allowed to go without reprisal in the Sudan, to Russian sabre-
rattling once again around Afghanistan, threatening to edge
closer to India. Britain was isolated internationally and the
champion of the Berlin Congress could not allow that to stand.
The new Prime Minister spent the majority of the summer
agonising over events both in Egypt and on the Afghan-Indian
border. In the case of Egypt, Salisbury had been as affronted as
most of the British public over Gordon's death and the
government's lack of action in defending him. However, he
was well aware of the limitations of his position: Sudan was
lost, a re-conquest would take a long time to organise and
execute and the chances were that he would be out of office by
the autumn, replaced by a battle-shy Gladstone. He may well
have thought that reoccupying the Sudan was desirable but it
would have to wait. For now the British would have to be
satisfied with fortifying their position in the northern areas of
Egypt which, in any case, was where the Suez Canal and, ergo,
Britain's real interests lay.[3] In the case of Afghanistan, unlike
Gladstone, Salisbury was quite prepared to go to war with
Russia rather than see Britain insulted. This acceptance of
conflict, and the Russians' awareness of this acceptance in his
mind, meant that he was not someone that they wanted to push
particularly hard. He was as belligerent with the Russians over
Afghanistan as he had been with the Liberals over Arrears and
Reform. In the end a truce was negotiated and signed at the
beginning of September.

However, in politics nothing is ever that simple. At the
Congress of Berlin in 1878 Salisbury had witnessed first-hand
Disraeli's manoeuvring in order to draw up the boundaries of
Bulgaria. Disraeli and Salisbury had been keen to keep that
nation small by creating a new and separate country out of
Bulgarian land named Eastern Rumelia, the idea being that

Russian influence in either nation would not necessarily be as harmful as Russian influence in one larger country. However, the new Prince of Bulgaria had very cool relations with the Russian Tsar, meaning that fears of Bulgaria becoming a *de facto* Russian state were now non-existent and, therefore, a united Bulgaria was not such a bad prospect for Britain. In late September 1885 there was a revolution in the Eastern Rumelian capital, Philippolis, where the Governor-General was overthrown and the position offered to Prince Alexander of Bulgaria, who accepted and declared the two nations united.[4] Serbia immediately declared war on Bulgaria, fearing that an inflated Bulgarian state would threatened their own frontiers. Likewise the Russians, who had protested against the break-up of Bulgaria in 1878 were now horrified at the increased influence of Alexander and eager for a return to two smaller states. The concern now became the possibility of a Russian invasion of Bulgaria and what Britain's response should be. When the Austrian government suggested another pan-European conference to force Alexander to withdraw, Salisbury refused ostensibly due to the value he placed on the will of the Bulgarian people, although it is hard to imagine that he would have taken the same line had the Eastern Rumelians invited a Russian Prince, rather than a Bulgarian one, to govern them.

In November a conference was held in Constantinople and Britain pushed for the Treaty of Berlin to be amended to recognise Prince Alexander as ruler of both Bulgaria and Eastern Rumelia. The Russians, in the event, were unable to convince the other powers to oust the Prince. Serbia invaded Bulgaria in the middle of the month but were decisively defeated almost immediately,[5] meaning that there were no options left for the anti-Alexander faction in Europe.

So, having shown the Liberal government of 1880-85 to have been inconsistent and weak, providing a strong opposition in spite of their minority in the Commons, the Conservatives went into an election in November 1885 as the Party of government presiding over the ongoing crisis in Bulgaria, which was portrayed as a consequence of a flawed Treaty of Berlin, signed by Salisbury. The election was devastating for them, with the Liberals returning 333 MPs to their 251. Irish Nationalists led by Charles Parnell returned 86.[6] Therefore, despite the clear Liberal victory, Parnell had the ability to keep Salisbury in office should he wish to enter into a coalition.

Because of this (decidedly remote) possibility Salisbury felt that he should remain in office to meet Parliament in January, rather than resign immediately and push the Irish Home Rulers into negotiations with the Liberals. His hopes were dashed in mid-December when Gladstone's son Herbert wrote an article in *The Times*, widely believed to be expressing the opinion of his father, stating that if a majority of Irish citizens wanted an Irish Parliament then fairness dictated that this should be granted.[7] This was an incredible *volte face* for a politician who had spent half a century opposing Home Rule even in incremental steps. The fact that it conveniently fell at a time when he needed to outflank Salisbury on the Irish Question in order to obtain power leaves Gladstone open to charges of unprincipled politicking, especially when he had not mentioned the issue during the election campaign. Salisbury was sickened by what he saw as Gladstone's hypocrisy and, characteristically, refused to be drawn on the matter: changing his values just because of the number of people opposing him was not something that he could undertake with a clear conscience.

In courting the Irish Radicals, though, Gladstone was risking the allegiance of Loyalist Whigs and Salisbury could hope to witness the dismantling of the Liberal Party. Apart from the Viceroy of Ireland, Lord Carnarvon (who resigned in January 1886, citing ill health as the reason), the Cabinet were agreed that Irish Home Rule should not be supported if introduced by the Liberals.[8] The government kept their intentions over Ireland to themselves during the recess hoping that the Liberals would tear themselves apart before Gladstone could make a deal with Parnell over Ireland. This didn't happen before the new Parliament met at the end of January and so Salisbury quickly became aware that he was living on borrowed time. At some point he would be defeated by the Liberal majority and have to resign, so Salisbury decided that they may as well introduce some passionately Tory measures to show people that they had not lost their values and give their Party something to unite over. If they were going to lose it may as well be over something worth fighting for. The government introduced a Coercion Bill for Ireland, designed to supress the National League, an organisation fronted by Parnell himself that often took to violence to achieve support for its republican ideals. In doing this, Salisbury was pushing the Parnellites into voting with Gladstone but the staunch unionist Tories were delighted. A Liberal amendment brought the government to defeat on 26 January and the following day the Cabinet agreed to resign.

Salisbury was turned out and Gladstone would have to be called for, causing the Queen yet more anguish. He was by far her least favourite Prime Minister and yet he had returned on three separate occasions. However, things would be more difficult for Gladstone in his third ministry than they had in his first two. Many leading Liberals refused to join the government due to anger over Irish Home Rule, including the 15th Earl of Derby, the inclusion of whom had been an incredible coup for the previous Liberal government once his estrangement from Disraeli had been completed. And more, the fractures within the Liberal Party went deeper than the loss of such fickle supporters as Derby, with Joseph Chamberlain, a very influential Liberal with the grassroots of the Party, resigning from the new Cabinet in March 1886, just weeks after joining, over the issue of Home Rule. Even the ex-leader of the Liberals, Lord Hartington, entered into clandestine talks with Salisbury over how they could work together to ensure that a Dublin Parliament never became a reality. Soon these secret negotiations became public displays of unity as Hartington, leading what became known as the 'Liberal Unionists' openly consulted Salisbury on all important matters,' although a formal uniting of the parties was still nearly three decades away. Both men were adamant that the Act of Union must be preserved. For Salisbury, Home Rule would ultimately inspire other nations within the Empire to move for independence. For Hartington, a Dublin Parliament, even one with limited powers devolved from Westminster, was simply a precursor for Irish independence.

Gladstone moved his Irish Home Rule Bill in the Commons on 8 April. When the Bill came to second reading on 7 June Hartington and Chamberlain led no fewer than 93 Liberals into the 'No' lobby to defeat the government by thirty votes. Gladstone's plans to destroy the Conservatives by wooing the Irish Home Rulers had blown up in his face as more Liberals had defected from him than Irish MPs had joined him. Rather than resign and force the Conservatives to form a minority government as he had tried in 1873 and done in 1885, Gladstone announced on this occasion that Parliament would be dissolved and fresh elections called. This time Gladstone would be unable to keep his intentions concealed until after the election as it would be fought openly on the Irish Question.

Salisbury's determination to bring the Liberal Unionists into a closer alliance with the Conservative Party was exposed during the election campaign as he and his close associates convinced 87 Conservative candidates to withdraw from the election campaign in favour of 87 of the existing Liberal MPs who had voted against Gladstone on the second reading of his Irish Home Rule Bill.[10] This was an audacious display, effectively handing a majority to the Liberal Party on the assumption that those Unionist MPs would eventually merge with his own Party. The result of the election saw 316 Conservatives, 77 Liberal Unionists, 192 Liberals and 85 Home Rulers returned to Parliament.[11] It was an incredible result for Salisbury after only five months of opposition. Following the election the Conservatives would be returned to government but the Liberal Unionists, not quite fully in acceptance of the inexorability of their transition, still sat on the opposition benches with Gladstone's Liberals. They did, however, have their own leaders (Hartington in the Commons and Derby in the Lords) and their own identity. Soon they would establish their own Party funding and on most major issues there was still dialogue between their leadership and that of the Conservative Party. For now, however, they would remain as their own separatist faction, much like the Peelites had been following their split from the Conservatives in the 1840s. Like the Peelites, the Unionists eventual merger with the opposite political Party would take many years to complete.

So strong was Salisbury's conviction that the union of Conservatives and Unionists was inevitable that he actually tried to convince Hartington to accept the premiership with himself serving beneath him. Hartington declined and Salisbury was to return as Prime Minister for the second time. The most notable change in the new Cabinet in comparison with the one that had left office earlier in the year was the promotion of Churchill to Chancellor of the Exchequer and Leader of the House of Commons. He was now clearly second-in-command both of the parliamentary party and of the Cabinet. Iddesleigh was well and truly marginalised, being offered the Foreign Office with Salisbury himself becoming

Prime Minister as well as First Lord of the Treasury. It was August by the time the new Parliament met and so the session was almost over and the government had little to do in terms of domestic affairs. However, they would once again find trials in eastern Europe as a pro-Russian militia kidnapped the controversial Prince Alexander of Bulgaria on 20 August and declared him deposed. Salisbury was convinced that the Russians had played a part[12] and the government openly declared that they supported Alexander's restoration. If Bulgaria fell to the Russians then there was nothing to stop them taking Constantinople and with it the passage to the East. On 7 September Alexander reappeared and abdicated, clearly under duress.

Churchill, displaying yet again his Canning-like quality of being a thorn in the side of any leader that the Party employed, openly deplored Iddesleigh's policies as Foreign Secretary, claiming that Britain was risking a war with Russia over an issue that it had no concern in. Aside from causing friction in the Cabinet, Churchill went further, communicating directly over the course of the autumn with leaders in Germany, Austria and Russia, informing them all that Britain would not get involved if Russia occupied Constantinople; that Egypt was more important to Britain than Turkey; and that the British Cabinet was hopelessly split over what to do about Bulgaria.[13] The candidness of these communications meant that even trying to bluff the Russians into backing down would fail, should Salisbury attempt it, although the Prime Minister was not aware of the *extent* of Churchill's indiscretions.

By the end of 1886 Churchill was planning a spectacular budget full of pledges for spending reductions, quite without consulting the Cabinet first. He demanded substantial economies from all government departments during the course of several tête-a-têtes with individual ministers. However, the millionaire bookseller-turned-politician W.H. Smith, now the Secretary of State for War, refused to see spending reductions in his department at a time when crisis loomed in the Balkans. Churchill sent the last one of several resignation letters to Salisbury, each of which had been intended to force the hand of the premier to cave to his lieutenant. In his letter Churchill implied that had Salisbury and

Iddesleigh the required diplomatic skills, war in the Balkans would never be an issue, so what was Smith concerned about?

This may have been a step too far for Salisbury, who on this occasion accepted the resignation and gained, along with it, a greater Cabinet unity than he had yet known. Churchill leaked his resignation letter to *The Times* expecting to win support, but once they learned of how it had come about almost the entire Conservative Party rallied behind the Prime Minister. Randolph Churchill had gone from being the youngest minister, second-in-command and the most promising talent for the future of the Party to a backbencher with no future left in the space of a few days.

After a Christmas spent trying unsuccessfully to convince the Unionist leader Lord Hartington once again to accept the premiership, with Salisbury serving under him, the Prime Minister settled for a Cabinet reshuffle in January 1887. Ruthlessly deciding that he should remove all potential rivals while he was at it, Salisbury told Iddesleigh on 4 January that his time in Cabinet was over and that he – Salisbury – would once again be taking over at the Foreign Office. In order not to overstretch himself he promoted W.H. Smith to First Lord of the Treasury (thereby demonstrating how he preferred the Foreign Office to the First Lordship) as well as Leader of the House of Commons, one of Churchill's old titles. In a shock move the other role previously commanded by Churchill, the Chancellorship of the Exchequer, was to be taken up by George Goschen, a Liberal Unionist.[14] This appointment required no commitment from the Liberal Unionists generally and was not to be part of a wider coalition but it was indicative of feelings within that movement at that time; clearly more *unionist* than *liberal*.

Iddesleigh was deeply hurt by being removed from office having served for three decades on the Conservative front bench and having been the leader of the Party just two years earlier. Salisbury felt guilty because of their long-enduring working relationship and offered him other positions in the government but they were all refused. His guilt was about to become far worse. On 12 January Iddesleigh finished his last few hours of work in the Foreign Office and walked to 10 Downing Street for a meeting with Salisbury in the early afternoon. The two men were in each other's presence for less than twenty minutes when Iddesleigh died of a heart attack. Having spent decades working together, the two men's relationship ended sourly and Salisbury would have to live with the accusation that he had killed his former friend. The Northcotes successfully barred Salisbury from attending the funeral by explaining that it was a service for family and friends, not former colleagues.[15]

Once the Cabinet was accordingly restructured Salisbury was able to resume his prior preoccupation with foreign affairs, no longer buffered by a separate Foreign Secretary or else hindered by a Chancellor who couldn't accept his own remit. Aside from the growing crisis in Bulgaria, which may lead to a war between Russia and Turkey, with Austria undoubtedly being sucked in against the Russians, there was a growing sense of militarism within France, which was once again inclining towards expansionism with its ministers contemplating recapturing Alsace –Lorraine. Therefore, aside from a war between Turkey, Russia and Austria, France and Germany looked set to resort to arms.

Salisbury, on behalf of Britain, made formal agreements with Austria and Italy not necessarily committing to enter into a conflict alongside them (thereby protecting Britain's neutrality should those nations become aggressors in a war) but promising to prevent Russia or France from over-spilling their own borders. Meanwhile France and Russia were on more friendly terms, raising concerns that a formal *entente* may be on the cards there. The rest of 1887 saw Salisbury delicately balancing the requirements of all the European powers so as not to commit himself in any direction. Russia wanted control of Bulgaria; Turkey wanted to ensure that Bulgaria did not attempt independence from them; Austria wanted to see Bulgaria in any condition other than as a Russian satellite state; France wanted Alsace-Lorraine; and Germany was actively encouraging Britain, Italy and Austria to involve themselves militarily in the Balkans (even though they had no intention of getting involved themselves) because they would have a free hand to attack the bellicose French without fear of reprisals as long as the other powers were already engaged in conflict to the east. Further complicating matters was the fact that Britain was committed by an 1839 treaty to protect Belgium from invasion and there was a strong possibility that in the event of a war between France and Germany the Germans would march through Belgium to attack France, forcing Britain into a war on the side of the French. This made no sense because not only was France the ancient enemy of Britain but Germany, given the strong familial links between the royals of both nations, was a natural ally.

The truth of the matter was that as much as it would suit each of the European powers to see their neighbours go to war with each other, none of the leaders had any appetite for a conflict themselves, meaning that nobody would actually provoke or declare war. As long as the status quo remained, as long as the leaders currently in charge of each of these nations remained in charge, there was not likely to be a war in Europe.

Meanwhile on the home front protectionism reared its ugly head once again. The issue that had destroyed the Conservatives during the middle decades of the century and had looked to have been put to bed by free trade winning the day was now becoming a Party issue once more. The United States of America, which during the 1880s had become as large as Britain in terms of manufacturing and exports, had adopted some heavily protectionist measures which were slowly suffocating British manufacturers. During the 1887 Conservative Party Conference the NUCCA voted overwhelmingly to introduce retaliatory protectionist measures. Salisbury managed to resist but the call for protection would grow over the coming years, with motions being passed at almost every Party conference for the remainder of Salibsury's leadership.

Into 1888 and foreign affairs took another turn for the worse. It is hard to believe, looking back, that it took another quarter of a century for war in Europe to break out. At the turn of the year, Bismarck published details of an Austro-German accord in which both agreed to support the other if war was forced upon them. It was a defensive alliance but the publication of it was clearly intended to make Russia think twice before making any advance on Bulgaria, which would ultimately force Austria's hand. Then in March the German Kaiser, Wilhelm I, died. In doing so he left the throne to his son, Frederick III. Frederick was married to Queen Victoria's daughter, Victoria, and was, on the whole, averse to war. However, he was already suffering from cancer when he took the throne and within months he would be dead meaning that succession would fall to the impetuous eldest grandson of the British Queen, Kaiser Wilhelm II. For the Prussian Empress Victoria, who knew well the rash nature of Wilhelm and the likelihood that he would lead Germany into conflict, the possibility of a war between her mother and her son was a heartbreaking eventuality.

To deal with the threat of a full-scale war involving all of the nations of Europe Salisbury introduced the 'Two-Power Standard' to naval policy, which was to determine the size of the Royal Navy until after the First World War. In essence the policy stated that Britain must have a fleet as least as large as the combined force of its next two closest rivals. It was clear that France and Russia were the rivals in question but keeping the terms vague suited everyone involved.

In 1890 a domestic crisis hit that forced Salisbury to set a precedent that he was completely uncomfortable with. Goschen learned from the Governor of the Bank of England that Barings Bank was dangerously exposed to some failing Argentinian securities. The position was such that Barings was facing imminent collapse unless they could get some outside intervention. Salisbury was committed to the doctrine of *laissez-faire*, however, seeing such a large company go under and the unpredictability of the shock waves that this would produce was unthinkable. London was already the world's largest financial hub and seeing Barings collapse would undoubtedly undermine this. Not for the last time in its troubled history, Barings faced bankruptcy. Not for the last time in history, either, the British government felt compelled to intervene in the affairs of private institutions by 'bailing out the banks'. In the event Goschen and Salisbury managed to negotiate £7.5 million of aid to Barings.[16] £1 million of this was pledged from the Bank of England with the government promising to repay them on any losses incurred on that money in the following twenty four hours.

Meanwhile, Kaiser Wilhelm rid himself of Otto van Bismarck as Chancellor. Then, in 1891, he made a visit to England, the first of many which would occur throughout the 1890s. Although relations between Wilhelm and his English cousins were strained, and although Salisbury never trusted him, believing him capable of destroying the fragile peace in Europe, these events were at the least signs that the two nations could perhaps keep cordial relations under new leadership.

On the domestic front there was an election looming, the septennial Parliaments meaning that it had to be before June

1893 but it was widely expected to occur before mid-1892. Consequently, during 1891, Salisbury started once again to turn his mind to solidifying or even formalising his alliance with the Unionists, going as far as to introduce legislation providing state funded primary school education for all children so as to tempt them in. The Education Bill passed through Parliament in August, supported by Conservatives who were well whipped by their leadership, Liberal Unionists who had fought for the issue ever since mandatory (but unfunded) schooling had been introduced in 1876, and Liberals who could not oppose it for fear either of the electoral consequences or of pushing the Unionists closer to the Conservatives.

The remainder of the session passed off quietly but Salisbury still had another hurdle to overcome before he was able to face the electorate. On 6 October 1891 W.H. Smith, who had held the office of First Lord of the Treasury since Salisbury's only stint there during the winter of 1886-87, died. Replacing him wasn't just a matter of replacing a senior Cabinet minister. Because of Smith's position as First Lord of the Treasury (which aside from Salisbury himself had only been held by Iddesleigh, the widely-considered joint leader at the time_ and because he had also been the Leader of the House of Commons at the time of his death, replacing him meant, in effect, that Salisbury was naming his second-in-command and his successor. Add to this the difficulty the government had in finding individuals who possessed all the skills of an able orator, an effective administrator, a sharp mind, not being liable to attack their own leadership (as Churchill had done), being a member of the Conservative Party (which ruled Goschen out) and happening to be a Member of the House of Commons, rather than the Lords, then the choice was considerably narrowed. In fact, the only option (and one which Salisbury searched around in vain to avoid because he knew that he would come up against charges of nepotism once again) was his nephew, Arthur Balfour.

Uncle and nephew were to be the leaders of the two Houses of Parliament and between them leaders of the Conservative Party for the next twenty years, until the eve of the First World War.

A further electoral difficulty was thrown up when Hartington's father died, meaning that he was elevated to the Lords as the 8th Duke of Devonshire. As leader of the Unionists it had been convenient to have Hartington in the Commons facing off against Gladstone. Now Chamberlain took over as Unionist leader in the Lower Chamber and Hartington's old seat was won by a Liberal in the subsequent by-election. Parliament was eventually dissolved on 22 June 1892 after discussions between the Conservative and Unionist leaderships to determine how long the government should go on for. When the results came in during July the Conservatives returned 269 MPs and the Unionists returned 46. However, compared with 273 Liberals, and their allies the Irish Nationalists returning 81,[17] the Conservatives had lost.

Salisbury opted to meet Parliament rather than to resign immediately but inevitably an amendment was made to the Queen's Speech over which the government was defeated by the majority of 40 that the Liberals held over the Conservatives and Unionists. On 12 August the Cabinet resigned and for the fourth time during her reign Victoria had to send for William Gladstone.

Now in opposition and facing the prospect of Gladstone reviving Home Rule, Salisbury pledged himself to oppose it even if the result was another constitutional crisis brought about whenever a conflict arose between the Commons and the Lords, where the (typically Liberal) leader of the Commons would threaten to have the monarch create enough peers to outvote the (typically Tory) majority of Lords. The Bill was introduced to the Commons in February 1893 and it soon became clear that it would pass through that House. The unionist strategy had to be to defeat it in the Lords. This Bill went further than Gladstone's previous effort because although it proposed to establish a Parliament in Dublin it allowed for Irish MPs in Westminster as well. Salisbury could not understand why the Irish were allowed to affect decisions in England when the purpose of the Bill was to prevent the English having legislative authority over Ireland.

The Bill passed its third reading in the Commons in September after which it was debated in the Lords for the second reading there. Hartington and Salisbury led the opposition to it and saw it successfully defeated by 419 votes to 41.[18] It wasn't even close. Gladstone had once again been beaten. In 1886 he had lasted only months in office against Salisbury's opposition. Now what would have been his crowning achievement was stolen from him by his foe. Almost immediately following the recess and return of Parliament in March 1894 Gladstone retired from politics at the age of 84 having been Prime Minister on four separate occasions (the only man ever to have done so) but feeling that on each occasion he completely failed to achieve what he had set out to.

Gladstone's Foreign Secretary, the Earl of Rosebery, succeeded him as Prime Minister. With Prime Minister and Leader of the opposition both in the Lords, Salisbury and Rosebery clashed much more often than had occurred since Gladstone and Disraeli had taken each other on prior to the latter's elevation to the Lords in 1876. Salisbury had no difficulty in wrong-footing Rosebery at almost every turn. All the while his position grew stronger thanks to the ongoing cordial relations between Conservatives and Liberal Unionists, which Salisbury had assumed would crumble once Gladstone had been removed as a common enemy. Then, in June 1895, the government was censured in the Commons over shortages of supplies for the British armed forces, for which Rosebery as Prime Minister and Henry Campbell-Bannerman as Secretary for War, were held responsible.[19] The government resigned immediately and Salisbury was called for to form his third administration.

His first act was to approach Devonshire and Chamberlain to ascertain whether or not the Liberal Unionists would be interested in a formal coalition, without which the Conservatives would struggle to survive. They both agreed. Devonshire came into the Cabinet as Lord President of the Council, Chamberlain as Colonial Secretary. Further places were afforded to the Liberal Unionists with the Marquess of Lansdowne entering the Cabinet as Secretary for War and George Goschen returning to work with the Conservatives but this time in the much more junior position of First Lord of the Admiralty. Balfour would be First Lord of the Treasury and Leader of the House of Commons with Salisbury once again becoming both Prime Minister and Foreign Secretary.

Salisbury formed this new government with the sole intention of dissolving Parliament so as to improve his standing. The idea was to take on the Liberals while they were disunited following the double blow of losing Gladstone and being forced from office, while at the same time strengthening ties between the Conservatives and the Liberal Unionists by forming a coalition Cabinet and fighting the election as a unionist government. The result was a resounding victory for them: 340 Conservatives (a majority in itself) plus 71 Liberal Unionists on the government side. 177 Liberals and 82 Irish Nationalists made up the opposition.[20]

Immediately upon resuming office, the government was faced with a crisis in eastern Europe yet again. This time the Turks were slaughtering Armenian Christians within the borders of the Ottoman Empire. Salisbury initially tried to instigate a dialogue with other European nations such as Prussia, France and even Russia in order to place some pressure on the Turks to desist. When no other nation showed an interest he started to consider the possibility that the Ottomans had served their purpose. For years he had promoted their existence on the basis that it kept Russia out of Europe. He still wanted Russia out of the straits but perhaps they and the UK should take Turkey by force and split the land between themselves. He was determined to send the Mediterranean Fleet into the Dardanelles Strait to force Turkey to back down or else face invasion and publicly made it clear that this was his intention. However, in Cabinet he came up against outright refusal from Goschen at the Admiralty, who was in turn supported by the rest of his colleagues. Salisbury was isolated and had no choice but to leave the Armenians to their fate, which not only sat uncomfortably with him from a moral standpoint, but humiliated him publicly as his promises of military support now looked like a poor bluff that the Sultan had expertly called.

Salisbury started to question the government's entire military stance. During his last premiership he had initiated the Two-Power Standard but what good was that if Britain refused to use these new battleships?

Just to add to the difficulties Russia and France had signed a formal *entente* whilst the Conservatives had been in opposition meaning that there was a genuine threat of their combined forces being used in a war with Britain; Kaiser Wilhelm was becoming decidedly more anti-British as time went on (claiming that Salisbury had insulted him by refusing to meet him when requested in August 1895); and the US President Grover Cleveland seemed to be agitating for a war with Britain. On this last matter Cleveland had written to Salisbury in the late summer demanding that Britain cede British Guyana to Venezuela, who claimed the territory as its own. Salisbury saw no point in replying immediately as for all he could see the issue had nothing whatsoever to do with the Americans. When eventually he did send a reply it gave a detailed history of the dispute and argued that Britain was not in the business of giving up its subjects to the government of unstable nations for which they do not want to be a part.

With war being a potential, however unlikely, with France, Russia and the United States; relations souring with Prussia who were allied to Austria; and Turkey crumbling with Salisbury desperate to intervene there militarily, Britain was starting to look isolated internationally.

Then events in Africa put further pressure on international relations. In March 1896 Ethiopia defeated the Italian army at the Battle of Adowa, causing the Italian government to fall. Once a new Prime Minister had taken office in Italy he asked for an Anglo-Egyptian force to help prevent him losing all his African lands by marching south and forcing the Ethiopians to reinforce their own position rather than advance further. Between Ethiopia and Egypt lay Sudan. For Salisbury, who had patiently suspended but never completely abandoned his desire to retake Sudan following the tragedy that had befallen General Gordon over a decade previously, this new development represented an opportunity to realise his ambition. Orders were sent to General Kitchener, head of the Anglo-Egyptian forces, to advance as far as Dongola in northern Sudan. This was done swiftly and then Salisbury started to contemplate how to finance a push all the way to Khartoum.

Into 1898 and Russia started to annex parts of China that were of strategic significance to Britain. Realising that his nation was embroiled in either full-scale conflicts or else territorial disputes in Europe, North America, South America, Africa, Asia Minor and Australasia, Salisbury started to become concerned that the Empire had stretched past breaking point. As unpalatable as Russian actions in China were, he could not afford another conflict, certainly not when that conflict would further estrange a nation from Europe, where Britain was looking increasingly alone. He was criticised for not standing up for Britain but Salisbury appeased Russia over China.

Foreign policy at this time was spiralling dangerously out of control, the strains on the Empire were showing and it was only a matter of time before it started to crack and eventually crumble. It may have been with that in mind that

Chamberlain, as Colonial Secretary, started to negotiate in an unauthorised capacity with German representatives for an Anglo-German alliance. When Salisbury discovered this, he duly reprimanded Chamberlain.

On 19 April Gladstone died. He was the last surviving statesman of the great upheaval from the middle of the century when Tories and Peelites split over protectionism. Salisbury acted as Pall Bearer and was evidently deeply moved by the service. If the death of an old rival reminded him of his mortality just at a time when Britain was looking particularly fragile on the world stage, then Salisbury would not have long to lament his situation. In September news arrived in Britain that Kitchener had defeated the Sudanese Khalifa's forces, effectively returning Sudan to Anglo-Egyptian control. At this point the army was just outside Khartoum, which was subsequently captured with little resistance. As soon as the capital was taken Kitchener opened some sealed orders from home that he had been carrying with the express instruction not to read them until the Sudan was once again under Egyptian control. The orders, from Salisbury, were to advance down the Nile as far as Fashoda in the southern area of Sudan, to ensure that the Egyptian and Union flags were flown there and that no other flags were raised. Salisbury's reasoning was due to intelligence he had received that the French were sending an expedition to that same area in order to conquer the source of the Nile, which was strategically important. The last colonial stand-off between Britain and France was about to begin.

Kitchener left immediately, taking a small force on gunboats down the Nile. When he arrived the following day he found the Tricolour flag flying over Fashoda. Two years earlier a French Captain named Jean-Baptiste Marchand had been given instructions to leave the French West Africa territory and lead a small force by land to occupy the source of the Nile in case Britain tried to exert her influence there. It had taken until July 1898 but Marchand had finally arrived there on foot a full two months before Kitchener. However, he had no means of communicating with the outside world and no mandate to leave in order to do so. So he had to sit tight at Fashoda and await further instructions. Kitchener's orders had been to take the territory in the name of the Egyptian Khedive and his force could easily have overcome the small group led by Marchand but cooler heads prevailed, thankfully enough for both sides. A full-scale imperial war was in nobody's interests. Kitchener and Marchand each demanded to the other in person that their respective armies leave, the French claiming that they had conquered the territory first and the British claiming that it had always belonged to the Khedive but for the recent rebellion by the Sudanese Mahdi, which had now been overcome. They then awaited instructions from London and Paris. Kitchener telegrammed the British government, who in turn informed the French of the situation, Marchand having no means of letting them know.[21]

The French knew that they were in trouble. The fact that Marchand was camped in Fashoda with no way of communicating with the outside world was ludicrous. Britain had an army on the ground ready to react immediately to instructions via telegram, whereas any French military support was potentially two years away. Also if Marchand wanted to retreat, he did not have enough supplies to make the two year journey back to French West Africa. Salisbury offered for a British escort for Marchand back to French territory if the conflict could be ended without bloodshed. It took months of diplomacy but eventually this was settled upon. Britain gained control of Sudan and the French avoided a battle that they could not win.

If a war with France had been averted in North-East Africa, a few hundred miles south a completely different set of circumstances were driving Britain towards war. The Transvaal Republic, the Boer nation which had been annexed by Britain under Beaconsfield in 1877 and then reinstated as an independent nation under Gladstone in 1881, had since this time been treating new settlers as second-class citizens. The 'Uitlanders', as they were known (Afrikaans for 'outlanders' or 'foreigners') were often of British descent. They were not allowed to vote; every Boer was compelled to carry a firearm, every non-Boer banned from having one; most of the tax burden fell on the shoulders of the Uitlanders; they were not allowed open-air meetings. Pressure had been building for many years for Britain to intervene on behalf of their subjects, who felt they were ill-treated by the longer-established Boer settlers. All the situation needed was a catalyst.

In March 1899 a British subject named Tom Jackson Edgar was shot dead by a policeman in Johannesburg following a fight between Edgar and another man. The policeman subsequently escaped all charges, which led to a petition being sent to Britain signed by over 20,000 Uitlanders[22] calling for assistance. Chamberlain was strongly in favour of supporting them, arguing in Cabinet that the government should give an ultimatum to the Transvaal President, Paul Kruger, demanding equal rights for the Uitlanders or else face war. Salisbury was prepared to put pressure on Kruger but such a direct threat made him uncomfortable. To that end the Prime Minister made references in public speeches to the fact that he had opposed Gladstone's policy of detaching Transvaal once it had successfully been annexed. Shortly afterwards Kruger offered to afford residency to individuals who had lived in the country for at least seven years, hoping that this would appease the British. However, sensing that the floodgates were now open, Salisbury decided to keep the pressure up and push for more. He started actively reinforcing British forces around the region of southern Africa, claiming that he would keep doing so until Kruger gave equal rights to the Uitlanders.

In response to this, in August 1899, Kruger offered some major concessions: a five year qualification period for residency; a loosening of the restrictions on Uitlanders to vote; ten of the thirty-six parliamentary seats being allocated to representatives of the Rand (an area mostly inhabited by Uitlanders). In return Britain must respect the sovereignty of Transvaal and renounce any claims over the land.[23] Salisbury, Chamberlain and even the positively pro-war High Commissioner of Southern Africa, Alfred Milner (who was not too dissimilar to his predecessor, Bartle Frere, whose unilateral decision-making had led to the disastrous Zulu War twenty years earlier) were agreeable to settlement under these conditions. However, rather than accept the terms genially, the government sent a formal response pushing for changes to be implemented immediately and stating, rather aggressively, that should they not receive a positive reply and quickly then Britain would feel obligated to take control of affairs in Transvaal.

This did not go down well in Pretoria where Kruger responded in September by withdrawing some of the concessions made in his previous offer. It is hard to understand why Salisbury pushed so hard, risking so much, when there was so little to be gained from it. Had he accepted Kruger's August proposals unconditionally, then an incremental move towards further concessions could be said to be underway. Instead a war was now inevitable.

On 29 September the Cabinet agreed to send reinforcements to the areas surrounding Transvaal in preparation for war and to hold off sending a formal ultimatum until the troops arrived, which would probably be just over a month later. However, they were beaten to the act by Kruger, who must have known that this is what the British were about to do. On 9 October he telegrammed his demands to London: that all troops that had arrived in South Africa since June must be removed and any that were en route must not land. If the demands were not met within 48 hours then he would declare war. Kruger needed to inflict defeats on the British before reinforcements could arrive, which declaring war so soon allowed him the chance to do. Salisbury needed to win over public opinion, which being sent an ultimatum, rather than sending one himself, allowed him to do.

The rest of October saw terrible defeats for the British at the hands of the Boers and not just in Transvaal. Aside from three major battles that they had lost there before their reinforcements were able to arrive, the Orange Free State, a neighbouring independent nation also of Boer settlers, annexed a northern part of Cape Colony, formerly a British territory. Now Britain was at war with two Boer nations and victory would not be as straightforward as the Prime Minister had assumed. To add to his burdens his son, Edward, who was serving in Transvaal, found his regiment besieged by the Boers at Mafeking. Then, on 20 November, Lady Salisbury died, having been ill following a stroke during the summer. All in all the Prime Minister was at one of his lowest points ever come December. Matters were only going to get worse.

The British reinforcements led by General Sir Redvers Buller landed in Cape Town and realised early on that British forces were being besieged in various parts of South Africa, hundreds of miles apart with little in the way of communication links. Buller therefore split his forces: he personally led soldiers to relieve the town of Ladysmith in the eastern area of the territory; another group under Major General William Gatacre was to secure the central areas; and Lieutenant General Lord Methuen would lead a force to relieve the area of Kimberly in the central region.

On 9 December Gatacre's force met with a Boer one at the Stormberg Mountains, where the Boers were successful. 700

British soldiers were taken prisoner. The following day, a couple of hundred miles north Methuen was defeated at Magersfontein and therefore never made it to his destination to assist his countrymen. Then, on 15 December, Buller himself was defeated at the Battle of Colenso, before ever having chance to reach Ladysmith. Not only was he beaten, but he lost over a thousand men to the Boers' fifty during the battle. The British were being humiliated.

The Battle of Spion Kop in January 1900, which saw an entire Lancashire regiment annihilated due to worse military leadership than had even been seen in Magersfontein, Stormberg or Colenso, represented the low point of the war for Britain. Public opinion was starting to turn in favour of the war on the basis that these humiliating defeats needed retribution but morale was at its nadir as nothing seemed to go as planned. It was Buller's successful relief of Ladysmith at the end of February that turned British fortunes around. In fact, the Boers soon started to realise that they may not be victorious, having previously believed that they would be able to convince another European power to join them, so far to no avail. Consequently, in March Kruger and Martinus Steyn, President of the Orange Free State, jointly telegrammed London offering peace on the condition that their independence was recognised. They calculated that the British loss of life would lead Salisbury to find any honourable way out. However, it was exactly this loss of life that led Salisbury to reject the offer. He told them that because they had declared war, many thousands of British citizens had lost their lives and this all due to Britain having allowed the Transvaal and Orange Free State nations to have autonomy over their own affairs. The only way to end the war honourably and simultaneously ensure that Britain was never threatened again was for them to be annexed as part of the Empire. No other end was acceptable.

In mid-May Mafeking was relieved by a British force, ending a nine month siege and bringing news back to London that the Prime Minister's son was safe and well. By the summer Britain had contained the fighting to within the borders of Transvaal and by September the generals were discussing the endgame. Salisbury capitalised on the patriotic mood caused by the turnaround in military fortunes by dissolving Parliament. The result of the September election saw the Conservatives and

Unionists capture 402 seats, Liberals (now led by Campbell-Bannerman) 184 and Irish Nationalists 82.[24] A minor incident of note came with the return of two MPs for a new political party calling itself the Labour Party. However, with less than 2 per cent of the national vote this new fringe group was hardly worth considering and probably posed no real long term threat to either of the established parties.

Following the election a seventy year old Salisbury finally relinquished his grip on his beloved Foreign Office, appointing Lansdowne as the new Foreign Secretary. His abilities were waning and he was feeling his age. Balfour remained First Lord of the Treasury, with Salisbury just keeping the most important title for himself, with less of the work.

No sooner was the election won than it became clear that the Boer War was far from over. The Orange Free State invaded Cape Colony in mid-December as if to prove the point that they were not defeated yet. Further tragedy hit the nation but a month later when, on 22 January 1901, Queen Victoria died. She had been Britain's longest-reigning monarch and had presided over the largest Empire that the world had ever seen. Now it was time for the Prince of Wales to take over as King Edward VII. Relations between the Prime Minister and the incoming monarch were cool at best. Salisbury was certainly concerned that a society now entrenched in Victorian morals was about to take its lead from a royal closer in personality to the greedy and polygamous George IV, than the strict and loyal late Queen.

Meanwhile the Boer War raged on but now that Salisbury had removed himself from the Foreign Office, his influence became more one of oversight than day-to-day management. The Germans made advances towards British ministers for a formal alliance, which Lansdowne encouraged but Salisbury vetoed. The Russian Tsar complained that Britain was acting tyrannically by oppressing a small native population in South Africa. Salisbury argued that the Boers had started the war and questioned whether the Tsar would not react if, say, Sweden had invaded Russia. The rest of the session passed off without incident.

1902 was to see the coronation of the new King, which was expected, but the less expected incidents that year were just as significant. Salisbury had intended to retire immediately following the coronation, although not many people were aware of this. Events moved quickly through the spring, providing a convenient backdrop for retirement. In mid-May the Boer leadership met with Kitchener to discuss terms of surrender, which were eventually settled and signed at Vereeniging on 31 May. It was one of the worst-kept secrets of Whitehall that William Pitt the Younger was a hero to Salisbury. Now the Prime Minister had seen through the most controversial matter of his premiership and could retire without leaving a job half-done, something that Pitt failed to achieve with the French Revolutionary and Napoleonic Wars in either of his tenures of office.

King Edward VII was due to be crowned in June (although in the event this had to be postponed owing to illness) and this meant that Salisbury had just a few short weeks between seeing off the Boer War and his own planned resignation to ensure that his nephew succeeded him as Prime Minister. Although this was important to him, it was equally important that he must not be *seen* to be arranging things as such. Consequently he felt that he could not resign and have Balfour immediately kiss hands with the King without arousing suspicion that the whole thing had already been settled by the outgoing Prime Minister in advance. Many Conservatives would be happy with the Liberal Unionist Joseph Chamberlain as a coalition leader. The result was that they hatched a plot that Salisbury would resign, which he did on 11 July and then Balfour would visit senior Cabinet colleagues (notably the Liberal Unionists such as Chamberlain and Devonshire) individually to gain their support.[25] One by one they were convinced that as junior partners in the government they could not expect the leadership of the country but they would be rewarded with promotions (Devonshire would be Leader of the House of Lords following Salisbury's withdrawal). By 12 July it was clear that Uncle Bob had come through for his most able nephew, who kissed hands as Prime Minister that day.

Salisbury had been Conservative leader either on his own or in a joint capacity for twenty one years and a front bencher for thirty six years. Next to the big names of Disraeli and Peel he is often forgotten as a Victorian politician but he held the highest office in the land for longer than either of them and personally managed the transition in Britain from the Victorian age to the modern era. That said his legacy is controversial. Combining the following two facts together gives a good example of this controversy. Firstly it was mentioned earlier that he had an incredible fondness for William Pitt and would have encouraged any historical comparisons between Pitt and himself. Secondly the fact that Salisbury was Foreign Secretary for the majority of his tenure as Prime Minister means it is clear that foreign policy is the area of government that he should be judged on most strictly. In comparing his foreign policy to that of William Pitt, though, Salisbury does not come off glowingly. Pitt fought a war against someone who is now considered one of the greatest military despots in history. He entered the war reluctantly and fought only to defend Britain against actions that at the time were believed would eventually lead to an invasion. Although he would always argue that he acted in defence of Britain and protecting the rights of Uitlanders, Salisbury forced a war against the Boer republics on the basis of convenience and extending the empire. His arguments for standing up for the rights of minorities don't stand up to scrutiny as, during his time in office, he made it more difficult for immigrants to settle in Britain. So although he fought settlers' rights in South Africa, he did not apply the same principles to the homeland. If Pitt nobly stood up to a tyrant, Salisbury, it could be argued, *was* the tyrant.

Closer to home he was far more successful. War in Europe, inevitable some may say and eventually brought about in 1914, was avoided for thirteen years under Salisbury largely down to his skilful diplomacy. He avoided entering into a formal alliance with Germany even though it would have given Britain strength against her natural enemy, France, because he knew that it would eventually force Britain into a war that at the time seemed avoidable. He evaded war with Russia over China and with France over Sudan. A war in Europe, Salisbury believed, would be of benefit to nobody. Luckily for him it would never happen during his lifetime.

Arthur Balfour
(1902 – 1911)

I am quite confident that the only chance of keeping together the one party organization which can save us from socialistic radicalism is to adhere unwaveringly and with emphasis to Fiscal Reform.

Arthur Balfour, December 1903

Wise Men will always secure a Retreat; and Self Preservation is a First Principle with all Men

Daniel Defoe's *Tory*, 1692

BALFOUR'S FIRST MAJOR ACT as Prime Minister was to steer through yet another Education Bill. He had long been in favour of taking responsibility for education from school boards and transferring it to Local Education Authorities, funded by the rate payer. However, his opinion was opposed by the right wing of the Conservative Party on the one hand and the Radical wing of the Liberal Party on the other. Conservatives worried that Balfour's plans would take authority away from the Church of England, which managed most of the affected schools and would, therefore, be forced to relinquish its own influence. Liberal opposition stemmed from their feeling that rate payers funding local schools, most of which were Anglican, meant that Quakers, Baptists, Methodists and Presbyterians in England and Wales would be forced to subsidise Church of England schools, which was unfair on them.

In spite of this opposition the new Act passed through Parliament, due to come into force in April 1903. However, by finding an issue on which to unite the Liberals whilst also aggrieving a significant minority of Conservatives, Balfour was playing a dangerous game.[1]

On the international scene the new Prime Minister inherited the unenviable position that Salisbury had left. Although Britain had avoided a European war for the last two decades she was still teetering on the edge and still without allies. Balfour didn't trust the Kaiser any more than Salisbury had but the Franco-Russian alliance was still viewed as the greatest threat to stability in Europe. France was the 'old enemy' for Britain and traditionally the provocateur in Europe; Russia was a threat to Britain's interests in the East. The thinking amongst leading statesmen at this point was that it was only the balance of power that was keeping France and Russia in check: Italy, Austria and Germany were still, in theory, major powers. However, Italy looked vulnerable to collapse and Austria was no match for Russia if they ended up in a conflict, the threat of which never seemed to dissipate. That left Germany, which surely could not stave off the combined force of the *entente* on its own. If only one of these nations crumbled there would be nothing to stop France and Russia from crushing the remaining central powers from the outside. Therefore as untrustworthy as the Kaiser was and as distasteful as German colonial ambitions were, in the event of a conflict Balfour felt that Britain's only option would be to get involved on the side of the central bloc.[2]

In 1903 another attempt to appease Ireland by concession was made with the introduction of a Land Bill, intended to throw a bone both to the landed interests and to the peasant majority. Ireland had had a long history of disputes over land, with tenant farmers working the land owned by (generally) those of British descent who may or may not charge extortionate rents. The new Land Bill would provide government finance to tenants who wished to buy their land at rates that were attractive enough that they may just be taken up. It gave one more alternative to the previous two: pay extortionate rates and go hungry, or riot. The Land Bill was generally supported in the Cabinet but for the ominous exception of the Colonial Secretary, Joseph Chamberlain. His opposition to it was not of terrible concern given that it affected his department very little. However, very soon it would become clear that the differences of opinion between him, as leader of the Liberal Unionists in the House of Commons and, until the previous year one of the potential candidates to succeed Salisbury as Prime Minister, and the rest of the Cabinet were irreconcilable.

Chamberlain had recently started advancing an argument in favour of colonial preference for tariffs in order to establish greater ties with the British colonies whilst at the same time ensuring that Commonwealth produce was better protected against the likes of Germany and the United States of

America, who imposed heavy levies on foreign imports. The Chancellor of the Exchequer, Charles Ritchie, a vehement free-trader, wanted all tariffs abolished entirely. In his April budget the Chancellor announced the removal of tariffs on corn (which had been resurrected to pay for the Boer War) and Chamberlain, who had been quite public with his own opinion, was left feeling embarrassed. He spent the following weeks publicly speaking out against repeal of tariffs, claiming that other nations were taking advantage of Britain's free trade policies.[3] During the course of this Chamberlain became more explicit about what should be protected and it became clear that, in effect, he was proposing a tax on food. Aside from free-traders being concerned about the affront to their own dogma, the general public would be mortified to think about paying higher prices for food. Aside from within the Liberal Unionist faction there was no appetite for Chamberlain's proposals.

As if to drive home the message that Balfour really had lost control of his government, Chamberlain launched the Tariff Reform League while Hicks Beach and Goschen headed the Unionist Free Food League, both established in the summer of 1903. It therefore came both as a personal tragedy and yet a political relief when Lord Salisbury died at the end of August,[4] giving Balfour some reprieve while he mourned and then attended the funeral of his late uncle. However, he did not make things any better for himself when returning to lead the government. Rather than taking a decisive stance, the Prime Minister, in the cause of government unity, took that invariably destructive step of directing a compromise. He proposed retaliatory tariffs against countries that imposed them against the UK. This was of no interest to the Reformists whose ultimate aim had been greater colonial ties and, for some, a move towards a Federal Empire. On the other side the proposal was abhorrent to the free-traders who viewed any tariffs with suspicion.

On 9 September Chamberlain offered to resign, which Balfour accepted. In order to keep the balance within the Cabinet he forced the resignation of Ritchie and two of his supporters as well, meaning that his government was severely weakened but, possibly, he may personally come out looking a stronger leader than he had previously been given credit for. In October the free-trade Duke of Devonshire, leader of the

Unionists in the House of Lords and Balfour's Lord President
of the Council, resigned from the government on the grounds
that he could not support protectionist policies. Balfour went
about rebuilding his now-devastated Cabinet during the recess.
Once done his new government was now notable for only two
things. Firstly, it was considerably less authoritative than its
predecessor. Secondly, Austen Chamberlain, son of Joseph, in
a move that confounded every onlooker, entered the Cabinet as
Chancellor of the Exchequer. The Prime Minister's largest
difficulty now was more personal than professional. The Cecils
were robustly pro-free-trade, much in the manner that the late
Lord Salisbury had been. Balfour suddenly found that his
cousins, all influential in one House or the other, were set
opposed to his economic strategy.

　　　　This whole episode had been deeply harmful to
Balfour and would serve to have several long term
consequences for the Conservative Party. Firstly, the Liberals
had managed to unite their party in the cause of free trade
whereas the Conservatives and the Unionists were, as has been
shown, deeply divided. Electorally this would damage the
Tories in the short term. Secondly, and more positively, in spite
of his resignation from the Cabinet, Chamberlain's position
was certainly closer to Balfour, who was proposing retaliatory
tariffs, than to Campbell-Bannerman's Liberals who would not
hear of anything but free trade. This meant that the Unionists
led by Chamberlain were closer to a formal merger with the
Conservatives than ever before. Thirdly, notwithstanding the
likely absorption of the Unionist Party, the Conservatives
would not see their numbers increase by the amount that they
could have expected had this episode not occurred. It had been
almost inevitable for some time that the Conservatives and
Unionists would merge, this matter of free trade versus
protection simply pushed the two factions closer together.
However, what it also did was to reduce the number of
Unionists that would join when that inevitable consolidation
took place. Several of their number, such as Randolph
Churchill's son, Winston, defected to the Liberal Party, rather
than be associated with those that would impose taxes on food.[5]

　　　　So it was that going into 1904, the events of which
would shape the course of the entire twentieth century, the
government of the day was as fragile as any since Gladstone's
first government ended as a lame duck administration from
1873 onwards. The year would transform the relationships of

European states and set the stage for the conflict that would develop ten years later. Since Balfour had taken office the German Kaiser had been behaving more and more erratically, raising mistrust of him and even resulting in him being vilified in certain sections of the press.[6] Notwithstanding this, Balfour still viewed France and Russia as the real threat. In February 1904 war broke out between Russia and Japan, which put the government in somewhat of a dilemma. Britain had signed an alliance with Japan a few years earlier, the terms of which did not necessitate British intervention in this conflict unless another nation (France) got involved. However, seeing Russia defeated was desirable. On the other hand there were advantages to staying out of it, namely that Japan could weaken Russia on her own without any cost to Britain and also that remaining impartial increased Britain's standing with France, with whom the government were hoping to secure a settlement over both nations' many territorial disputes. Balfour and his Foreign Secretary, Lord Lansdowne, opted to remain out of the war, which did the trick with making the French more open to a settlement. On 8 April the two nations signed the *Entente Cordiale* in which, among other things, Britain recognised French sovereignty over Morocco while the French reciprocated with British control over Egypt. This was not an alliance, military or otherwise, but has been seen in the years since as the end to a millennium of war between the two nations.

The year was still to be dominated by foreign affairs following the signing of the *Entente*. In October a Russian fleet in the Baltic, on its way to assist in the war with Japan mistook British fishing boats near to the Dogger Bank for Japanese Torpedo boats. They sank them all. Balfour was prepared to go to war over it, only being dissuaded by Russian concessions to allow an international enquiry and to pay compensation.

Although foreign affairs absorbed much of the Prime Minister's time, the stick that would break the back of Balfour's government was Ireland. In late 1904 the Irish Reform Association had drawn up plans for devolution of power to Ireland, which they later claimed had the backing of the Irish Secretary, George Wyndham. Wyndham immediately refuted the claims but when Parliament met in 1905 the questions about his knowledge of, and involvement in, plans for devolution kept coming. Eventually it became apparent that the Irish Reform Association had written to Wyndham's undersecretary who had in turn indulged the plans. These plans had then been communicated to Wyndham who either ignored them or hadn't properly read his correspondence but, either way, the facts as they were made him look disingenuous when he claimed to have had no knowledge. Unionists were infuriated, claiming that Balfour was supporting Home Rule by the back door. In March 1905 Wyndham resigned. Many called for the government to go with him, but Balfour wanted to secure certain policies before handing over to the Liberals, which even he now saw as inevitable. In August he renewed the Anglo-Japanese alliance, one more thing off his list, in spite of suffering defeats in the House of Commons just days earlier and various Cabinet ministers asking for release.[7]

It is doubtful that he ever believed that the electorate would return to backing him, as the Conservatives and the Unionists suffered defeat time and again at by-elections during this period. However, he kept the government going right through to the autumn recess. It was 4 December before Balfour resigned the premiership, much to the jubilation of the Liberals and the nation.

Balfour was relying on Campbell-Bannerman being unable to unite the Liberals and, thereby, making his Conservatives appear more co-ordinated by comparison. However, Campbell-Bannerman was stronger than Balfour had anticipated and, surviving a plot to have him elevated to the Lords, which would have strengthened his rivals within the Liberal Party, he managed to put together a formidable government. The Liberals would now boast four current and future Prime Ministers including Campbell-Bannerman himself; H.H. Asquith as Chancellor of the Exchequer; David Lloyd George as President of the Board of Trade; and Winston Churchill as Under-Secretary at the Colonial Office. This would be an impressive line-up for any Party but, considering that within five years the Liberals would have won their very last ever general election, it makes the fact that their present administration contained three future Prime Ministers all the more incredible.

Campbell-Bannerman's first act as Prime Minister was to seek a dissolution of Parliament. He needed to achieve three aims through a general election. The first was to overturn to Conservative majority which Salisbury had carried over him at the last election in 1900. Secondly, he needed clearly to establish who was on the side of the government and who was on the side of the opposition: the defection of the Liberal Unionists from the Liberals followed by the detraction of free traders from the Liberal Unionists had blurred the lines of politics making discernible 'camps' difficult to recognise. Thirdly, he needed a mandate for the united Liberal stance on free trade, quashing both Chamberlain's position of colonial preference and Balfour's of retaliatory tariffs.

He succeeded on all three counts. Following an aggressive campaign the Liberal Party returned 400 MPs with 83 Irish Nationalists also aligned to them. The Labour Party increased its position to 30 MPs[8] and were known to be closer in ideology to the Liberals than the Conservatives. So these 513 MPs would be pitted against 132 Tories plus 25 Liberal Unionists.[9] It would be over nine decades before the Conservatives fared this badly at another general election.

To add insult to injury Balfour lost his own seat of East Manchester meaning that the leader of the Conservative Party was no longer a member of either House of Parliament. Joseph Chamberlain took over as leader of the opposition for 19 days following the opening of Parliament in February 1906 until Balfour was returned at a by-election for the City of London later in the month. During that first month of the new Parliament Balfour, Chamberlain and others sounded out the few Unionists left in Parliament to see where they stood on the issue of tariffs. It became clear to all of them very quickly that only around thirty-six out of their 157 MPs could fall in line with Balfour's retaliatory tariffs compromise. Chamberlain met with Balfour to push for a Party meeting to discuss the matter and settle on a firm policy going forward. However, in a series of discussions both men realised that if they argued their own positions then the loser would have to forfeit the leadership. If Balfour lost his only replacement was Chamberlain, who could not realistically unite the Party and was probably too old to see them into the next election. If Chamberlain lost then his supporters would undoubtedly leave the Party to campaign on their own for reform. Consequently they drew up an agreement for limited reforms on the eve of the Party meeting and presented it as a united position. It was adopted immediately and Balfour was able to stay on as leader (as soon as he won his by-election).

Balfour could have been forgiven for walking away from politics in the wake of such a devastating defeat at the general election followed by what was, in spite of how he dressed it up, clearly an adoption of policies that he did not believe in simply to appease a rival. Two things kept him going at this point. Much had been made of the Liberal landslide victory to the point that the election of 30 MPs for the Labour Party got overlooked by many, not least the Liberals. Balfour recognised the significance of this immediately and saw it as his duty to manage the opposition to the socialist 'threat' following the election. The other factor that kept him positive about his role in opposition was the in-built Conservative majority in the House of Lords. As long as both Houses had the power to veto legislation proposed in the other place, the Tories had nothing to fear from a Liberal-dominated Commons. This point would become important for Balfour's tactics in opposition. Much like Salisbury before him he decided to frustrate the government using the House of Lords, allowing through only legislation which the Unionists could accept, whilst blocking any Radical Bills.

During the past few decades whenever the Liberals won a sizeable majority Conservative leaders were able to force the government to grind to a halt by dividing them over one issue or another. Salisbury, Disraeli and Derby all used this strategy to good effect. Balfour did not even attempt it. Consequently where the Conservatives started with a minority in the House of Commons they did not attempt to overturn any Liberal legislation in that chamber, instead relying entirely upon the House of Lords to do it for them. The situation became so frustrating for the government that by 1907 Campbell-Bannerman had introduced a resolution aimed at limiting the power of the Lords, voting for which went almost entirely along Party lines (it passed the commons by 432 votes to 147)[10] but this, predictably, was also thrown out by the peers.

In April 1908 Campbell-Bannerman died and his Chancellor, Asquith, succeeded him as Prime Minister with Lloyd-George taking over at the Treasury. Balfour got along personally with Asquith a lot more than he had done with Campbell-Bannerman, but these two leaders would continue to fight out the Lords-versus-Commons issue, which was provoking the greatest constitutional crisis since the madness of King George III. The crisis started with foreign affairs. Asquith asked Balfour to sit on a sub-committee for the Committee of Imperial Defence in May 1908, which was attractive to the former Prime Minister who had always taken an interest in foreign affairs. It was an interesting time to be involved in this area as the public were becoming increasingly alarmed at increases in German military spending, not least the building of their navy which threatened Britain's Two Power Standard. Balfour campaigned passionately for increased expenditure for the military, which the government were reluctant to provide due to Lloyd-George having been working on costing a budget providing a radical social-spending programme including the provision of state pensions. The Unionists rallied behind the military-spending theme, campaigning for eight new Dreadnaught warships to be built in 1909. The nation waited to see what would come of Lloyd-George's budget in the April of that year.

In the event Lloyd-George decided to yield to Conservative calls for increased military expenditure, whilst still providing his social reforms. This would all be paid for with massive tax increases. Income tax, stamp duty, alcohol tax, tobacco taxes, estate tax, land tax, landlord tax, motor vehicle tax, petrol tax and liquor licenses were all either increased or created for the first time. Here lay the problem for Tory peers who would be hit hard by the land taxes in particular. They felt that Lloyd-George was declaring a form of class warfare and looked set to oppose the budget. Balfour fought it in the debates in the Commons but there was never any possibility of it being defeated there. In the end the inevitable clash was Balfour's doing. He knew that the Lords were discontented but they would not throw out a budget without the sanction of their Party leader. Undoubtedly motivated by his own weak position, Balfour decided that it was better for his Party to be united, which this issue did for them, than it was to play sensible politics and accept the will of the Commons. For Balfour, risking a constitutional crisis was less of an evil than allowing his Party to remain split over tariff reform. On 30 November 1909 the Lords rejected the budget and three days later Asquith dissolved Parliament, ready to fight an election on class grounds.[11]

The result of the election was not satisfactory for either of the two largest parties. The Liberals won 275 seats and were still the dominant party; Unionists (broken down into the Conservatives and Liberal Unionists) gained over one hundred seats between them, finishing with 273. However, still allied to the Liberals were the Irish Nationalists, who took 82 seats and therefore allowed the Liberals to return to government. The Labour Party increased its standing for the third election in a row by taking 40 seats.[12]

Asquith consulted with the King over creating enough Liberal peers to be able to force through their legislation, including removing the ability of the Lords to veto Commons legislation. The King refused for the time being, favouring Liberals and Conservatives solving the impasse by themselves. Asquith was forced to confess to Parliament his inability to convince the King to give him his way, much to the relief of the Conservative Party. In April the government introduced a new budget which passed through both Houses but then in May 1910 King Edward VII died, to be replaced by his son, George V. Nobody knew how the new King felt about House of Lords Reform. Asquith invited Balfour and other delegates from the Conservative Party to enter into cross-party talks in order to resolve the issue. The Liberals hoped that the Conservatives would agree to curb the power of the Lords without the need to dissolve Parliament or request that the new King create a host of new Liberal peers. The Conservatives hoped to grind out enough of a compromise as to have no actual effect on their powers. Talks began in June and went on until November. After four and a half months and more than twenty meetings they were still at an impasse. At this point the Liberals offered the Conservatives a coalition government which would reach a compromise on all matters that they disagreed on from Home Rule to House of Lords Reform. Balfour rejected this offer at the beginning of November and talks subsequently broke down.

At this point Asquith approached King George V and presented him with a detailed summary of how events had progressed over the past few years from the Lords rejecting the 'People's Budget', to the Liberals 'winning' the general election, to the Conservatives refusing to accept that the Lords' powers needed curbing. Significantly he gained the concession that he required from the King: if the Liberals could win another general election fought on this issue then he would create enough peers to outvote the Conservatives in the Lords.[13] The Liberals planned to stop the Lords from having a say over Money Bills and to reduce their power of veto over other Bills to a mere delaying power.

This battle had been coming for eighty years, it just required an amenable monarch to allow it to happen. In 1831 Lord Grey had requested that King William IV create forty-fifty new peers to allow him to pass his Reform Bill. When the King refused and Lord Grey's further attempts to pass his Bill failed, he gave William an ultimatum: create the peers or I resign. In the event he resigned. In the end William had agreed but on that occasion the Tories were sensible enough to fold their opposition rather than be forced to change their composition. Over half a century later Salisbury used the in-built Lords majority to wreck Gladstone's Reform Act of 1884, which came close to provoking the same crisis. Gladstone was not as prepared to resign over the matter as Lord Grey had been and so crisis was averted on this occasion also. Now in 1910 the country was closer than ever to seeing the Lords defeated one way or the other.

Parliament was dissolved immediately and polling took place in early December. The change was little different to the election of twelve months earlier: Liberals 272; Unionists 272; Irish Nationalists 84; Labour 42.[14] The Liberals returned to government and introduced the Parliament Act into the House of Commons. It passed through there with no issues but for the Conservatives, blissfully ignorant of the King's pledge to Asquith to create new peers, there was major divisions over whether or not to block legislation in the Upper House. Balfour argued in favour of accepting the inevitable, which once again put him at loggerheads with the Cecils, who inherited their father's intransigence and were horrified by what they saw as their cousin's weak will. Once the Bill passed the Commons in July 1911, Asquith dropped his bombshell in Parliament. He let everybody know that prior to the dissolution in December he had obtained the necessary promise from the King. The Lords were due to vote on the Bill in mid-August and their dilemma was unenviable: vote to restrict their own powers but keep their chamber intact, or else resist to the bitter end and see their House reformed anyway. If they resisted the change would come only after the elevation of far more Liberal peers, who could out-vote them in future. When it came to the vote hundreds of Lords abstained and the Bill passed by 131 to 114.[15] Parliament would never be the same again.

Following such a defeat, even though there was no possibility of a successful outcome, Balfour's days were numbered. The Conservative press called for him to go, the Right wing of the Party were dismayed with him and he had had enough of the inevitability and consistency of defeat. He took a break once the recess was called but at the beginning of November he resigned as leader of the Conservative Party. He had led the Party outright for nine years and in the House of Commons for twenty. Although during his career he had done a great deal to shape British politics, (The Fourth Party had provided strong opposition to Gladstone and had been instrumental in preventing Northcote from taking the Tory leadership) his time as Prime Minister and leader of the opposition were marred by his inability to unite his Party and his weakness as a leader. His predecessor had managed to keep the Conservatives together, bring some Liberals into the fold and keep both factions satisfied and obedient. Balfour inherited what was in all but name a united Unionist Party and managed to fragment it into bickering factions. Finally he can be judged on the passing of the Parliament Act. Today we see this piece of legislation as essential to the workings of the British legislature, ensuring the supremacy of the House of Commons and, by extension, the will of the people. But in 1911 it was a disaster for the Conservative Party and Balfour watched its passage with anaemic opposition.

The transition from the nineteenth- to the twentieth century provides a convenient pivot on which Balfour's career can be summarised. He is remembered as an important figure in late-Victorian politics, but a lacklustre Prime Minister in the context of twentieth century politics.

Andrew Bonar Law
(1911 – 1923)

We are abound to do what we think is right in the national interest
without regard even to the interests of our Party. Whether I am right
or wrong that is what I am doing now.

Andrew Bonar Law, 7 July 1916

Union and Integrity will do great Matters: you Whigs cannot pretend
to this, for you are not all of you in the Same mind

Daniel Defoe's *Tory*, 1692

ONCE THE LEADERSHIP of the Unionist faction became
vacant (the opposition, made up of Conservatives and Liberal
Unionists required a leader for all Members) there were two
obvious candidates. The first was Austen Chamberlain, son of
Joseph, Balfour's last Chancellor of the Exchequer and a
Liberal Unionist. His credentials, experience and support
amongst both Liberal Unionists and any other member of the
opposition in favour of tariff reform made him arguably the
front-runner.[1] His fault was the same as that of his father in
1902: he was a member of the smaller of the two unionist
parties.

The second candidate was Walter Long, a
Conservative MP and Balfour's former Irish Secretary. Long
was an English landowner, a vocal champion of the Unionist
cause (including opposition to Home Rule) and former
Oxonian, the sort of character that the Tories would expect to
be their leader. His greatest flaw was that he had a tendency to
compliment his opponents during debates, which often stuck in
the minds of observers more than his criticisms.[2] Bonar Law
only threw his hat into the ring at a relatively late stage,
although he can be forgiven this on the basis that it was
ambiguous at best how the contest would be decided.
Historically, a Tory Prime Minister moving from government
into opposition retained the overall leadership. If they then left
their post during opposition (as happened when Beaconsfield

died in 1881) then a leader would be found for the Lords and one for the Commons. One may have overall charge of the Party but this was not essential as it could be settled when called to form a government. However, the passing of the Parliament Act now meant that the Commons was in law what it had been in practice for a long time – the superior House. This meant that the leader of the Commons was superior to the leader of the Lords and, therefore, the Party would be naming one individual that they expected to be the next Prime Minister. Therefore a process was required.

It was decided that Members of the House of Commons should settle upon their own leader. After some initial canvassing of the 272 unionist MPs it was discovered that Bonar Law had support from around 40, Chamberlain and Long having roughly 115 each. Both Chamberlain and Long feared the effects of dividing the Party so absolutely with a deadlocked leadership contest, the scars of the Balfour years still being so fresh. On 9 November they each agreed to withdraw as long as the other did, thereby avoiding any conflict. The only remaining candidate took the leadership by default: Bonar Law was now the leader of the opposition.

The fact that Conservatives and Liberal Unionists had jointly elected him meant that now was a better time than ever before to highlight the redundant and impractical nature of having two parties. So, between February and May 1912, the two parties became united as the Conservative and Unionist Party. For the time being they would be known as Unionists but after ten years they would revert to referring to themselves as Conservatives. In fact, in the years since then the Party has almost always referred to itself simply as the 'Conservative Party', with the glaring exception of any documentation used in relation to the 2014 referendum for Scottish Independence, in which they invariably made use of the term 'Unionist' as though it were an everyday occurrence.

As a leader Bonar Law soon became renowned for adopting a confrontational style. Debate in the House of Commons, though always highly charged, had traditionally been enshrouded in a gentleman-like quality. Now Bonar Law attacked the integrity of individual ministers without reservation. By all accounts he was not aggressive by nature, no doubt feeling compelled to act so in the name of Party unity after watching Balfour fail for not being tough enough. This is not to say that he would attack the government on every issue indiscriminately. If he felt that no political capital could be gained from entering the fight then he would not bother. For example the campaign for female suffrage was growing during this period but Bonar Law was satisfied to keep away from it, allowing the government to take responsibility for not introducing it from its opponents, whilst not actually supporting it himself thereby keeping opponents of universal suffrage from turning on the Unionists. Likewise with social reforms; although some measures may have appealed to him he was aware that the Conservatives would never be seen as the Party of reform when contrasted to the Liberal Party and, therefore, he may as well not raise the issue in the first place.[3]

What did matter to the Party was tariff reform and Home Rule. On the former issue Bonar Law immediately set the position for colonial preference as being the Party line, perhaps not surprisingly for a politician who was Canadian-born. He was not prepared to try to strike compromises at the expense of Party unity as Balfour had done. When it came to Home Rule there was really only one option: the Unionist movement was defined by its opposition to any devolution of power to Dublin. These two issues would dominate the political agenda in 1912 with the government introducing another Home Rule Bill in April (now a real threat on the basis that the Lords could no longer veto it) and the Unionists refining their position on tariff reform (more specifically that they would not be obligated to hold a referendum on the matter if elected to government) throughout the year.

In the campaign for Ireland the Unionists now looked set to lose. The Liberals had a majority in the Commons and they were overwhelmingly pro-Home Rule. Bonar Law did not allow defeatism to deter him from a hard-fought campaign, though. If Home Rule could not be beaten, he could at least limit its scope. He argued passionately that it was the role of all Britons to protect the interests of Ulstermen, that Ulster would not leave the Union voluntarily and, therefore, that Britain would have to coerce an unwilling people into secession if Home Rule was to be accepted. Finally he argued that the same arguments used in favour of Home Rule for Ireland – that although the United Kingdom was one country if a minority do not wish to be a part of it then they should not be forced to be –

should be applied to Ulster in an Irish republic: if they wanted to remain loyal to the Union then they should be allowed to.

In spite of Unionist opposition the Bill made its way through its first and second readings in the Commons. There was nothing that the Unionists could do in the face of the combined Liberal/Irish Nationalist majority. It was at committee stage after the second reading that they finally achieved a small concession: A Liberal MP introduced an amendment allowing the counties of Down, Armagh, Londonderry and Antrim to remain in the Union should the rest of Ireland be granted independence. Bonar Law was still opposed to Home Rule whatever the amendments, but was prepared to support this one rather than see the Bill pass without it. The amendment was defeated, the Liberal majority being just too large.

Bonar Law's combative style in the Commons, combined with the emotive depth of feelings on these issues, provided for some spectacular scenes in the House of Commons during the legislative session. During a debate on Home Rule in the November Bonar Law had managed to get both sides so riled that, at the end of it Winston Churchill stood and waved his handkerchief at the opposition as a taunt. In response Ronald McNeill, Unionist MP for St. Augustine's, threw the speakers copy of the *Standing Orders of the House* at Churchill, hitting him in the head.[4]

By the end of the year Bonar Law was being hounded by Unionist free-traders, rallied by Edward Stanley, 17th Earl of Derby and grandson of the former Prime Minister, the 14th Earl. He combatted this threat by stating in no uncertain terms that if the majority of the Party were in favour of a referendum on tariff reform then this was the path that the Party must take, but given his public pronouncements to the contrary he would have no choice but to step down if this went ahead. 231 Unionist MPs – who on the whole cared more about preserving Party unity so as to combat Home Rule than they did about tariff reform – signed a pledge of allegiance to Bonar Law in January 1913.[5]

The new year saw further political battles over Home Rule and Ulster. The Lords rejected the Home Rule Bill in January and, when it was reintroduced later in the session they rejected it again in the August. However, owing to the Parliament Act if they were to reject it a third time then the government could force it into law anyway, without ratification by the Upper House. Notwithstanding what was looking increasingly set to be an historic victory for the government, there were strong reasons for both sides to enter into a compromise. For the Unionists they knew that they were all but defeated: nothing could stop the Bill from becoming law, their only chance at leaving the battlefield with some semblance of dignity was to find a way of protecting the Protestant/Unionist majority in Ulster. For the government there were two concerns. The more minor one was that the King was uncomfortable with the measures proposed given that the government would not call an election on the issue and therefore strength of feeling was untested. He felt further that it may lead to violence between Nationalists and Unionists within Ireland and also that Ulster should be protected.[6] The bigger problem for the government was Ulster itself. If they passed a Bill giving Home Rule to Ireland, what would they do about the majority in Ulster who remained staunchly loyal to the Union? Would they really force people to live in a country that they didn't want to (or else leave their homes)? What if they refused to be governed by Ireland and violence broke out, would the British government then send in the army to make them capitulate? Any outcome was not desirable and, therefore, a compromise was attractive even if they could pass sweeping measures without the need for negotiation.

In mid-October 1913 Bonar Law met with Asquith so discuss their differences. During the meeting the Tory leader impressed upon his Liberal adversary how important it was for him to seek a dissolution and how he wouldn't stop pushing the Prime Minister until he achieved it. When the pair met again in October they provisionally agreed on excluding Ulster from Home Rule on the proviso that a referendum was held there at some point in the future on the issue of joining a united Ireland.

Then Asquith called a third meeting in December in which he tried to convince Bonar Law that they should agree on a united Ireland with certain devolved powers for Ulster within it. Bonar Law was horrified, having believed the deal almost secured a month earlier. Apparently Asquith had had trouble convincing his Cabinet of the merits of their agreement.

Bonar Law was well aware that if nothing changed Home Rule would become law by the end of the 1914 legislative session but he could not accept such insulting terms. In 1914, therefore, he resolved himself to push harder than ever to force an election for the Unionist cause.

Parliament opened in the February and the government immediately moved a Home Rule Bill. When it came to the second reading in the Commons in March Asquith outlined a compromise proposal that he intended to introduce alongside the Bill. The idea of proposing a compromise was to win public sympathy for the government but the proposal itself was worse even than his devolved-Ulster-within-Ireland idea of the previous December. This time Asquith announced that Ulster would be given a six year temporary exclusion from the Home Rule Bill at the end of which they would join a united Ireland. This was effectively the same consequence as the initial Home Rule Bills but with a slight delay and was therefore wholly unacceptable to the Unionists. But would the public appreciate this gesture from Asquith? Bonar Law responded by publicly suggesting that the government should hold a national referendum on the issue of Home Rule and promising that, should the government carry the support of the nation, his Unionists would no longer stand in the way of Home Rule.[7] He knew that Asquith could not accept this challenge, but by making such a bold pledge he had pulled the rug of reasonableness from under the feet of the Prime Minister.

Throughout the spring Bonar Law relentlessly kept up the pressure on the government but it was not enough. On 26 May the Home Rule Bill passed its third reading in the Commons and, now unable to be amended or blocked by the Lords, simply needed Royal Assent. True to his word, though, Asquith introduced an Amending Bill in June giving six Ulster counties an exemption for a period of six years after which they would revert to Irish rule. Bonar Law's tactics necessarily changed. The Unionists in the Lords were instructed to amend the Bill giving all nine Ulster counties exemption from Home Rule indefinitely. This would never be acceptable to the Liberals but if they could delay the legislation until after the next election then the Unionists had a fighting chance of taking control of both Houses of Parliament and putting forth whatever proposals they wished. Asquith was in a bind. He knew that he was unlikely to remain in office after the next election and therefore needed the legislation to pass immediately. However, he could not ask for Royal Assent for his Home Rule Bill without a compromise Amending Bill for the same reasons that he was concerned about in 1913. Namely that ordering the army to evict loyalists from Ulster could be seen as declaring a civil war, in which case there was no guarantee that the army would obey. Not ordering the army to do this would mean that his Act was unenforceable and therefore redundant. His only option was to re-enter negotiations with Bonar Law.

However, the question of Home Rule, the biggest issue facing Parliament for a generation was soon to be put on the backburner. The eyes of Westminster turned rapidly away from Ireland and towards Europe when, on 28 June 1914 Franz Ferdinand, the Archduke of Austria-Hungary was assassinated by a Serbian nationalist frustrated at Austrian subjugation of Bosnian Serbs. Suddenly the delicate balance of Europe, maintained for decades in spite of empire-building, territorial disputes, royal rivalries and ministerial animosities, was now shattered by a 19 year old with a gun.

The Austrian government felt that they had no choice but to declare war on Serbia as retribution for the death of their Prince, which they did on 28 July. Russia felt obligated to defend Serbia if for no other reason than to keep Austrian influence in the Balkans at bay – exactly the same mentality that drove their demands during the Congress of Berlin nearly forty years earlier. They began mobilisation the following day. Germany had a military alliance with Austria-Hungary, requiring them to resort to taking up arms if their allies were at war with more than one nation, meaning that Germany had to declare war on Russia. They immediately sent a demand to Paris insisting that France remained neutral which, owing to the Franco-Russian entente they were not likely to do. However, it was the Germans who declared war on the French a few days later, rather than the other way around.

The question facing the British government now was how would they act? For decades different Prime Ministers had come down on different sides of the France or Germany question. What they all agreed on was that France was the old enemy and a greater threat to the colonies but the Kaiser could not be trusted. The *Entente Cordiale* of 1904 had eliminated most of the French colonial threat by agreement, whereas in the years since Germany had been acting increasingly belligerent, making the Kaiser even more vilified in the eyes of the British public. He had sent warships to Morocco, provoking the

French, and tried to build a German Empire, a threat to British interests. Throughout the crisis of July it was not certain that Britain would join the war, but if it did then it would be against the Germans. It was the German invasion of Belgium, required in order to access France, which sealed the deal. Under an 1839 treaty Britain was obligated to act militarily in order to protect the sovereignty of Belgium and so, on 4 August, Britain entered the Great War and the Kaiser found himself at war with two nations ruled by his cousins.

Bonar Law promised Asquith that during the campaign there would be no partisan politicking, but one nation. In other words the Prime Minister could rely on support from the opposition. Taking complete advantage of his opponents' patriotism, Asquith sent the Home Rule Bill for Royal Assent, which it had to have by law, but with a delay on enforcement until after the war. The Unionists were horrified by this underhanded tactic but Bonar Law, in spite of his anger, refused to be drawn into politics while the country faced a war.

The war started badly, with Britain suffering embarrassments at sea and difficulties on land, the army being under-equipped and having not enough soldiers to fulfil their duties. Although Bonar Law was putting nation before Party by not attacking the government during this time, there is an argument that the political truce actually shielded the public from the truth about the mismanagement of the war effort.[8] The only way to prevent the government from taking advantage of their political armistice as well as to try to ensure that the management of the war improved, was to enter into coalition with the Liberals. Asquith was not open to the idea of coalition but was worn down over the period of ten months by Winston Churchill, *inter alios*. Ironically given his importance in bringing it about, Churchill would be the greatest casualty of coalition.[9] As First Lord of the Admiralty he was blamed for Britain's terrible naval record during the first months of the war, so when the Unionists were invited into government and the necessary reshuffle undertaken, he lost his position but was mollified with the sinecure Chancellorship of the Duchy of Lancaster.

So in May 1915 eight Unionists entered the Cabinet including Bonar Law (coming in as Colonial Secretary), Balfour, Lansdowne and Austen Chamberlain. Difficulties arose for the new Cabinet during the year with a split over what to do about the Dardanelles Strait, which Britain had protected from Russian interference on behalf of Turkey for generations. It was still an important strategic point for protecting maritime movement from the Mediterranean to India but now the Russians were Britain's allies in the war and Turkey were fighting them over control. Britain taking arms on behalf of Russia in the Straits sat uncomfortably with many Tories, including Bonar Law. The episode led to Britain fighting in Straits, as proposed by Churchill back when he was First Lord, but then abandoning their position when it was realised that it was unwinnable, leading Churchill to resign from the Cabinet completely by the end of the year.

Further difficulties that same year were met over the issue of conscription, which had not yet been implemented in Britain. By mid-1915 it was clear that vast numbers of men were needed on the Western Front but that volunteer recruits were not enough to satisfy the demand. Nobody carried the political will or capital to carry such a drastic measure into law, though. In the end it fell to Kitchener, now Lord Kitchener of Khartoum and Minister for War in the coalition Cabinet, to force the hand of the government by demanding more soldiers than could possibly be obtained by any other means. After much procrastination in December 1915 the Cabinet agreed for a National Service Bill (or what has become known as the 'Bachelors Bill'), intended to force subscription on all unmarried men between the ages of 18-41.[10]

Kitchener's decisive push for conscription came just in time, as within five months of the Bill being passed, in June 1916, he would be dead. A ship he was aboard was sunk by a German mine. Lloyd George succeeded him as Minister for War, now the most important position in the Cabinet after the Prime Minister. Before taking this position, however, Lloyd George had started, and so was allowed to complete, negotiations with Irish Nationalists. On Easter Monday, 24 April, a group of Nationalists in Dublin had declared a Home government and raised their flag in the capital. Riots ensued and many people died. Lloyd George started discussions with both sides, was then named Secretary for War following Kitchener's death on 6 June and a few days later put forward proposals for the immediate implementation of Home Rule with permanent exclusion for six Ulster counties. Bonar Law accepted that this was as good as the agreement that he had reached with Asquith in 1913 but many Unionists were outraged, feeling that Lloyd George had reneged on the agreement not to act until the war had ended (by which time an election followed by a Unionist majority could stop it anyway). Further to this, Lloyd George had acted disingenuously by convincing the Nationalists as well as the Unionists that he had the full backing of the Cabinet for his proposals. When it emerged that he didn't have this, Asquith had to throw his support to Lloyd George rather than admit that he had just promoted an untrustworthy man to the position of Minister for War. Bonar Law, aware that he was unlikely to secure more favourable terms at any point in the future, publicly supported the plan. The House of Lords did not and defeated the proposals in the July, forcing the government to abandon them and revert to Westminster Rule for the remainder of the war.

The government's fortunes did not improve throughout the year. A plan for an offensive against the German army, put forward by Field Marshall Sir Douglas Haig, was approved by the War Cabinet and commenced on 1 July. Haig was convinced that the German army was weak and susceptible to being broken if enough men were thrown towards it. He was wrong. On the first day of the Battle of the Somme British forces suffered 57,000 casualties: the worst day in British military history. Undeterred, Haig continued with the plan, sending nearly half a million British soldiers to be killed or wounded between July and November.[11] For the first time an ignorant British public, now receiving consolation letters about the deaths of their loved ones, began to realise that the war was not the success story that the government had been portraying.

Dissatisfied with how the war was being managed, Bonar Law visited the Prime Minister in the November and insisted that he establish a permanent War Council made up of senior ministers to take executive decisions and manage overall strategy. Asquith was uninterested but, despite believing himself irreplaceable, he was unaware that his coolness towards Lloyd George and outright frostiness towards Bonar Law in general now meant that inaction on his part was not an option. Bonar Law's advice may have come across as a suggestion but in fact it was an ultimatum. To make things clearer, by the end of the month Lloyd George, Bonar Law and a Unionist backbench leader by the name of Sir Edward Carson, together drew up a document to implement a War Council, ready for Asquith's signature. Bonar Law had the pleasure of presenting it to the Prime Minister and within a few days received his rejection.

Lloyd George then met Asquith on 1 December to impress upon him the need for restructuring the way the war was being managed but got a similar response to Bonar Law. Over the following days Asquith, Lloyd George and Bonar Law all had various meetings with each other to try to break the deadlock. In the end Asquith was immovable and so, on 5 December, Lloyd George resigned. Bonar Law now had the role of Warwick, the 'setter-up and plucker-down of kings'. Whichever man he threw his support behind would almost certainly be Prime Minister from this point forward. In the event he backed Lloyd George. Asquith spent the rest of the day trying to muster support from senior members of both major political parties, to no avail. Ultimately he had no option but to resign.

The King sent for Bonar Law that evening and asked him to form a government. The chances were slim but the latter promised to try before giving an answer. He immediately sought the assistance of Lloyd George, who promised to serve under him, and of Asquith, who did not. All three men as well as Balfour and Arthur Henderson, leader of the Labour Party, met at Buckingham Palace the following day. Asquith still refused to serve under anybody else and so they were mostly agreed that Lloyd George had the best chance of forming a stable government without the need for an election, which was undesirable at wartime. The men then all went about forming a government together, with the exception of Asquith. Bonar Law came in as Chancellor of the Exchequer and a member of the new War Cabinet, Henderson entered the War Cabinet without portfolio, and Balfour would be in the general Cabinet as Foreign Secretary.[12]

Bonar Law considered that life inside Lloyd George's government would be a more pleasant experience than life inside Asquith's – which it was – but probably did not consider that the year ahead would be more difficult for him than any year left behind – which it also was. Both his elder two sons had joined the army at the first opportunity (James at the outbreak of war in 1914 and Charlie when he turned eighteen in 1915) and in April 1917 his second son, Charlie, was killed at the battle of Gaza. In the September James, an aircraft pilot, was shot down in France and his body never recovered. These notifications understandably hit Bonar Law hard and he reacted by immersing himself in his work.[13]

On nowhere near the same scale, but adding to Bonar Law's depressed mood nonetheless, Winston Churchill, who had left Parliament for active military service having resigned from the Cabinet in 1915, was now back at Westminster, rabble-rousing as usual and Lloyd George wanted to bring him into the government. Bonar Law could think of nothing worse. In July 1917 Lloyd George took the decision to bring Churchill in unilaterally, knowing that it would anger Bonar Law and in spite of a petition signed by 300 Unionists MPs and Lords that it would be seen as an insult to the military. Since the election of 1910, thanks to regular by-election victories, the Unionists were now the largest single Party in Westminster. Bonar Law must have considered that he could remove Lloyd George if he wanted to, but for his own reasons he stood loyally by him.

As events in the war unfolded and the public became increasingly aware of the truth of what their soldiers were suffering the government came under greater strain throughout the last six months of the year and into 1918. This was intensified by the Russian Revolution and subsequent withdrawal from the war. In the spring of 1918 the Kaiser, having been able to reinforce his troops on the Western Front with soldiers that had previously been fighting on the Eastern Front, launched his last offensive. For months British soldiers came under heavy attack from their German foes, retreating for miles and sustaining heavy casualties. Manpower on the front line was desperate and the government considered introducing conscription to Ireland for the first time to facilitate the demand, with a Home Rule Bill introduced simultaneously to make the pill that little less bitter to swallow. This would never be acceptable to the Irish or the Westminster Unionists and so the idea was swiftly dropped. Ultimately the German gamble failed. In spite of making heavy in-roads into the British-protected French territories, their attacks were unsustainable. The British counter-insurgency, commencing on 8 August, would spell the end of the German resistance. One by one the Central Powers bowed out of the war and, on 9 November, the Kaiser was overthrown from Germany, which was subsequently declared a republic. The Great War officially ended on 11 November 1918.

Once the war was over the House of Commons, which had been elected eight years earlier, could not stave off a general election for another moment. Under the rules of the Parliament Act 1911 parliamentary terms now had a five year maximum limit, although this had been extended with the consent of all parties for the war. Going into the election Bonar Law was confident of success for the Unionists but he also enjoyed his working relationship with Lloyd George and felt that the Prime Minister was a good leader for the country. More to the point, he knew that Lloyd George working in government with Unionists was far better for his Party than him working closely with the Left wing of the Liberal Party. He also felt that by courting the Prime Minister he may be able to steer the Liberals towards his Party and away from alliance with the Labour Party, who he saw as a threat to the British way of life. So it may have been in his mind long before the election that a further coalition with Lloyd George was necessary, otherwise his actions following the election, if looked at purely from the point of view of the numbers involved, are completely inexplicable. In the autumn Bonar Law and Lloyd George agreed not to attack each other during the campaign and to see if they could rebuild a government of a similar calibre afterwards in order to see through the rebuilding of the nation following the war. In November Parliament was dissolved and the election held in December. The government had passed a Representation of the People Act in 1918 which gave the vote to women for the first time (although only those over 31 years of age) meaning that turnout at this election was greater than at any other time in history. The results are difficult to understand.

There were 358 Conservatives and Unionists returned, enough for a majority by themselves, against 161 Liberals.[14] However, this was not the true picture. Because most Unionists and most Liberals had officially campaigned for the return of the War government, but some 'Conservatives' and some Liberals had not, the parties actually split between government and opposition. So what happened was 335 Unionists, 133 Liberals and 10 Labour MPs joined the government. The rest were made up of 73 MPs from Sinn Fein, who refused to take their seats and 23 Conservatives who despised Lloyd George but hated the opposition Liberals more.[15] The official opposition was made up of 28 Liberals led by Asquith and 63

Labourites led by William Adamson. With only 91 MPs in this ragtag coalition of opposition parties, Labour for the first time in history led the opposition, against 478 Members for the government.[16]

In spite of his Party clearly being the junior partner in the government Lloyd George stayed on as Prime Minister with Bonar Law's blessing. The Unionist leader became Lord Privy Seal, allowing Austen Chamberlain to take his old post of Chancellor of the Exchequer. The senior ministers got down to the business of negotiating peace terms with the Germans, which was eventually signed at Versailles on 28 June 1919.

Now that the war was officially over, the government had no choice but to turn their attention to home affairs and once again to the dreaded Irish Question. To add to the strain the government would have to focus on what was becoming an economic depression in Britain. The rise of the Labour Party over the previous two decades had been both formidable and worrying as the spectre of socialism started to hang more prominently over British politics. With economic troubles deepening, the possibility of a national strike and the demand for the nationalisation of industry (an ideal written into the Labour Party constitution in their infamous Clause IV) became the first concern of both the government and the Unionist Party. A rail strike at the end of 1919 only served to crystallise this fear of the working class labour movement.

Labour was not the only threat posed from the results of the previous election. Sinn Fein made the Irish Nationalists look decidedly moderate by comparison and they had practically obliterated them at the election. This strong return for Sinn Fein, as well as the founding of the Irish Republican Army in 1919, meant that few in Westminster now really believed that Home Rule was avoidable. The government came together in a desperate bid to salvage what was getting close to a revolution in Ireland by introducing and (a testament to how troubled the situation was) passing through both Houses a Government of Ireland Act in 1920. The Act split Ireland into two: the six north-eastern counties of Ulster made up Northern Ireland which was to remain a full part of the UK. The rest of the country would be called Southern Ireland, still a part of the UK but with full autonomy of government from Dublin. The Act was completely unsuccessful in achieving its aims of quelling the rebellion in the South and the IRA kept fighting British forces.

By the beginning of 1921 the pressures of office, and undoubtedly of working through the deaths of his two sons for the good of the nation, took their toll on Bonar Law and he took leave from the spring into the summer in France to recover from what was close to becoming a breakdown.[17] He had to resign his post in the government, allowing Austen Chamberlain to succeed him as Lord Privy Seal and Leader of the House of Commons.

Following the failure of his 1920 Irish settlement, and now with Bonar Law and his insistent championing of the Ulster Unionists temporarily out of the picture, Lloyd George attempted to negotiate a settlement with the Irish republicans. Although the Prime Minister was able to gain agreement from them on having a sovereign Dublin Parliament in control of the entire island of Ireland but as an imperial dominion with George V as King, the Ulstermen would not accept the proposals. Bonar Law, upon hearing of the plans, readied himself to split the government and oppose Lloyd George. Unionists started to plot the overthrow of the Prime Minister with Bonar Law returning to take the position for himself. It was this, more than anything else, which led Lloyd George to change his stance in the negotiations. By December 1921 Lloyd George's government, supported by the Unionist majority in Parliament, introduced an Act of Parliament creating an Irish Free State for the entire island of Ireland but allowing Ulster to revert to the UK if it wished by general consensus, which it almost immediately did. The Lloyd George administration – a Unionist/Conservative government headed by a Liberal premier – had just achieved what was thought to be an unachievable victory going into what was to be an historic year for the Conservative Party.

Lloyd George, hoping to capitalise on the mood of the nation started to talk of fusing the parties of government into one, allowing Asquith's small band of loyal Liberals along with the Labour Party to form the opposition. He then proposed to hold a snap general election which they would fight as one party. There was a lot of sense in his proposals: now that Ireland was settled there was little that Unionists and Coalition Liberals disagreed over. Even the name 'Unionist' was now redundant and so most reverted to calling themselves Conservatives. His one difficulty was Bonar Law. Bonar Law had always been supportive of the Prime Minister but now that he was out of the government he was an obvious rallying-figure for any Conservative who was unhappy about the thoughts of serving under Lloyd George.

The Prime Minister made the mistake of talking openly about an early election during December 1921 and so when it became clear that there was little support for his proposals, early in 1922, he had to abandon the plan. What he had not appreciated was just how little the Tory side of the coalition enjoyed the relationship compared to the Liberals that he surrounded himself with. This was his first clue. Lloyd George then fell ill in March and left London. Fearing that opinion was slipping away from the coalition, Bonar Law's old friend Edward Goulding hosted a meeting of Conservative MPs to show support for the government. Embarrassingly the MPs largely turned on the coalition during the meeting and it was swiftly abandoned.[18]

Then in the spring Ireland turned up more trouble. On 22 June Field Marshall Sir Henry Wilson, now an MP, was assassinated by Irish republicans outside his home in London. Conservatives were horrified as Ireland then descended into violence. Over the following week pro- and anti-treaty Irishmen fought each other with arms, the country effectively becoming embroiled in a civil war. Many blamed the Irish settlement signed by Lloyd George. However, the internal affairs of Ireland were no longer of British concern so all the government could do was watch helplessly.

By July the Conservatives were actively agitating for the removal of Lloyd George and more Cabinet positions for their Party members. Parliament went into summer recess through August and in September Lloyd George called his Cabinet together to discuss the possibility of an early election, which the coalition parties would fight on the same side. Austen Chamberlain, now the most senior Conservative in the government, fully agreed. He was completely out of touch with the rank and file of his Party. It was October before the cracks in the coalition started to show signs of developing into a complete earthquake, when Stanley Baldwin resigned from the government over the possibility of having to contest an election as a Coalition Conservative instead of an independent Conservative. In the middle of the month Baldwin visited Bonar Law to convince him to usurp the Prime Minister. Bonar Law was reluctant. He was concerned for the welfare and independence of the Conservative Party and he was clearly opposed to Lloyd George on several issues now, but he was starting to feel older than his 64 years and was unsure that he could see through a full term in office.[19] Baldwin left the meeting and started to organise a discussion of junior ministers for Monday 16 October. The rallying process had begun. The Party were already well aware that Chamberlain had called a meeting of parliamentarians at the Carlton Club for 19 October. During that meeting it was widely expected that Chamberlain would push for a snap general election to be fought as a coalition with the Liberals under Lloyd George. Baldwin's representations were not the only ones made to Bonar Law during this time, with Derby and Salisbury both pushing for him at least to attend the Carlton Club meeting, knowing that his presence would act as a beacon to the rest of the Party who were desperate to turn on Lloyd George which, presently, meant the removal of Chamberlain.

On 19 October Chamberlain did indeed make a long speech aimed at securing support for an election fought under Lloyd George's leadership. Baldwin followed with a spirited speech in which he brutally attacked both the coalition government generally and Lloyd George personally.[20] His peroration was met with rapturous applause and was followed by a motion put forward to fight the election independently of the Liberals and, more importantly, with their own leader. Balfour spoke against the motion but when Bonar Law rose and spoke in favour, the fate of the rest of the senior leadership – Chamberlain and Balfour included – was sealed.

Lloyd George, hearing of the result, went straight to the King to resign the premiership and recommend that Bonar Law be sent for. In an attempt to reunite the Party in time for the upcoming battle, Bonar Law organised a leadership election so that all Conservatives could say that they had elected whoever led them from that point onwards. An official Party ballot was scheduled for 23 October, which Bonar Law won unanimously (as the only candidate) and subsequently became Prime Minister. It had taken eleven years of leadership for him to gain office. Coming into the new Cabinet would be Baldwin (Chancellor of the Exchequer), Curzon (Foreign Secretary), Salisbury (Lord President of the Council) and Derby (Secretary of State for War). There was no doubt that this was a Tory government.

On 26 October Parliament was dissolved and the election campaign got underway. When the results came in the Conservatives could feel vindicated in the action they took at the Carlton Club. They returned 345 MPs, with Labour now the largest opposition party, retuning 142 Members. Lloyd George's Liberals won 62 seats and Asquith's won 54. Labour were now the official Party of opposition, the Liberal lights of the 18th century Whig domination, Melbourne and Russell, Palmerston and Gladstone having faded into obscurity, never to burn brightly again.

The new Parliament met at the end of November so that it could ratify the 1921 Treaty creating the Irish Free State, which passed comfortably and, three weeks later, they prorogued until the new year. During the recess the Cabinet had to negotiate repayment of Britain's war debt with the USA. The Americans were demanding a repayment plan starting immediately with heavy interest rates. Other European nations owed Britain similar debts following the war. However, not wanting to cripple their allies, the British government had allowed France and Russia time to rebuild their economies following the war before asking them to repay. Bonar Law expected the same treatment from the Americans. He felt that until France and Russia were in a position to start making repayments, Britain shouldn't be expected to either. He felt further justified in his stance due to the fact that the USA had joined the war in early 1917 but hadn't started fighting until a year later, during which time Britain spent money that it needn't (by borrowing from the U.S.) and lost countless lives that it need not have. The Cabinet were decidedly against him on this, believing that not to pay a debt required by a creditor was dishonourable. Eventually the Prime Minister had to give in to his colleagues.

By 1923 Bonar Law was dying of throat cancer, although it was undiagnosed at this point. What was clear was that he was frail, speaking quietly and looking tired. When the parliamentary session began in February the government proposed very little in the King's Speech, the Prime Minister not being up to much of a fight. He had two weeks leave in March and then, when returning in April, found that he couldn't make himself heard in the House of Commons, his voice being too weak. Baldwin took over some of his speaking duties. By the end of the month he heeded his doctor's warnings to take a break, travelling in early May to the Mediterranean. Eight days later, having made his way to Paris, Bonar Law was in a great deal of discomfort and looker more unwell than ever. It was here that he realised that his time as Prime Minister was at an end. He returned to Britain on 19 May and despatched a resignation letter to the King the next day, refraining from naming a successor.

Bonar Law had taken his Party from political disaster following the successive election defeats under Balfour, through the war years and into majority government. He had seen through the settlement of the Irish Question, which had split the Liberal Party thirty years earlier and had caused so much pain to Unionists ever since. He kept the government of Britain propped up during the worst conflict ever known to the history of the planet by pledging his support to the Prime Ministers of the day. Finally he brought down Lloyd George, so despised by Conservatives at the time and gave the Party their most celebrated political year in 1922.

When looking back over the list of twentieth century Prime Ministers Bonar Law is (understandably given that he was only in the job for six months) often forgotten. When looking back on the leaders of the Conservative Party during the same period Bonar Law is not only one of the longest enduring, not only present during some of the most dramatic years (First World War, removal of Ireland from the Union, the famous victory of 1922) but also one of the most successful. When others were despised by Unionists or hated by Home Rulers, he was respected by both. When some were distrusted by Independent Conservatives while others were seen as a nuisance to coalitionists, he was able to lead both. He provided stability and strong leadership to a Party that was determined to fight itself and looked set to implode in 1908-11 over Balfour and Home Rule and again in 1916-22 over the coalition. Once Bonar Law secured office for the Conservatives in the election of 1922 the Party would go on to govern Britain for 47 of the remaining 78 years that century, making it their most successful century ever. The ability of a leader to take their Party from the brink of disaster to being electable once more is no minor achievement and this is what Bonar Law gave to the Conservative Party.

The 1922 Committee

THERE ARE MANY MYTHS surrounding the formation of the 1922 Committee of Conservative backbench MPs, known as the 1922 or even the '22 for short. The two most common fallacies relating to the birth of this group are that it is 'the 1922 Committee, which takes its name from the year it was formed'. However, the fact that it was formed on 18 April 1923 clearly shows this widely-held notion to be false. The second false notion is that it takes its name from that famous Carlton Club meeting back in October 1922 when Conservatives came together to vote against supporting the government and forcing Lloyd George's downfall. Such a celebrated event should be honoured forever with a committee named after it. Alas, no.

The beginnings of the '22 are much less glorious but as an organisation it has since grown into one of the most influential in Westminster. In essence, it is not much more than a sounding board for backbench opinion. The front bench of the Conservative Party (whose members cannot be members of the 1922 Committee) still formulate the policies, but much like they take soundings from the grassroots through the Party conference or from local associations, they can take soundings from their backbenchers through the '22. However, in reality it is much more than this. A Prime Minister cannot hold office if he or she cannot win an election, but a *Conservative* leader and, indeed, Prime Minister cannot remain in power without the backing of the 1922 Committee. To go into detail of the history of the Committee's success in removing Party leaders would be to get ahead ourselves. For now, let us consider the beginnings of this influential body.

Imagine becoming a newly elected MP. Following a campaign in which candidates have sold themselves to the electorate, they are returned to a Parliament with a 700 year history. In the House of Commons chamber sit the most influential people in the country and therein have sat the most influential people in the entire history of the country. A new Member famously has to make a maiden speech that can be at any time on any topic but will forever be remembered as their first. What to include? Should it be serious or funny, long or short? What should a new Member be doing to fill their time?

There are various committees but how to go about getting on them? A first time MP in Westminster will undoubtedly find themselves in a cliquey environment, with the old hats not wanting to associate with newcomers; front benchers not having time for less influential Members. The chamber of the House of Commons is a place in which a few hundred people out of a population of millions come together for the common good, an experience that few ever know and, therefore, should be a nurturing place where the lucky few support each other. It can also be one of the most intimidating places on earth. One wrong word and half the chamber will berate you while the other half are prepared to deny that they have ever met you. The hallways of the palace of Westminster, deliberately gothic in style since the great fire of 1834 and the subsequent restoration, are, therefore, more intimidating than welcoming. There is no training academy for newly elected MPs and so the whole process can be rather daunting.

After the 1922 election 345 Conservatives were returned, many of whom had been elected for the first time. Some of these individuals turned to each other for support during this uncertain period. On 18 April 1923 a small group of these newly elected MPs met in Committee Room 8 of the House of Commons[1] to discuss mutual co-operation, whilst agreeing that in doing so they must assist the government and Party to manage the country on conservative principles. On 23 April the Executive was elected and the Conservative Private Members (1922) Committee officially came to life. It was so called because it was exclusively for Conservative Party MPs and had been formed by those that had first been elected in the 1922 general election.

How useful such an establishment would be to newly elected Members of Parliament can be argued from both sides using examples of Tory leaders in the century before the founding of the '22. If we discount Lords, not just on the basis that they cannot be members of the 1922 Committee but because their induction into Parliament is a world apart from that of Members of the Commons. Looking at the great Tory Lords leaders of the nineteenth century, Liverpool, Derby and Salisbury all knew from a very young age that their destinies were to become parliamentarians. Whether they expected to become Prime Minister is almost irrelevant. They were groomed from childhood for a career in governing the country, like their fathers before them. Even Wellington (whose father was a Lord but who, as the second son, was not necessarily going to enter the Upper Chamber) had become a Marquess on the battlefield and a Duke after Waterloo. When he entered the House of Lords as a career politician he already had an aura of leadership about him that made his peers come flocking to him. No, for the purpose of gaining a feel for what it is to be a newly elected parliamentarian, Lords can be ignored. Looking at the fate of the great Commons leaders in the same party – Pitt, Peel, Disraeli – and there are varying arguments for how their early careers could have been different had they had a committee to assist them in finding their feet. Pitt, much like the Lords mentioned above, had been groomed for parliamentary life from an early age. His father had been Prime Minister and he had personally attended the House of Lords when his father, as Earl of Chatham, made speeches about the American War of Independence. He felt destined to be Prime Minister and so a '22 equivalent would not have been necessary for him.

Peel and Disraeli, though, are two opposing ends of the spectrum when it comes to the experiences of new Commons Members. One found the experience all too easy, the other far more difficult than it needed to be.

Robert Peel entered the House of Commons in 1809. William Pitt had died in 1806 and his ministry had been succeeded by the (largely Whig) Ministry of All The Talents, which survived until 1807. The Duke of Portland headed a Tory ministry then until October 1809, when Spencer Perceval took over. Entering Parliament as a young 22 year old, the scene that Robert Peel was faced with was as follows: The man that had led the Tories for over twenty years had died only a few years earlier, meaning that the Party had lost direction. The Grenvillites had defected to the opposition benches. The new Tory government headed by Perceval no longer had the full backing of the Duke of Portland's followers, as their leader had retired to his deathbed. The Tory political giants of the day had blown themselves up, with Castlereagh and Canning fighting each other in a duel and in doing so harming their own reputations to the point where the highest offices would have to be filled by others. In the desperation to fill senior and junior Cabinet vacancies (Perceval having to retain the Chancellorship of the Exchequer himself) the Tories found that they used up much of their support just in forming the Cabinet.

In order to move and second the reply to the King's Speech at the beginning of the 1810 session, Perceval selected Robert Peel as one of the two required names: he was completely untried but there were few other options. This would be his maiden address to the House.[2] Although it was a gamble for Perceval using such a fresh-faced Member, for Peel, with the effective endorsement of the Prime Minister, his maiden speech could be nothing but a success. Consequently his political genesis was a triumph without the need for a committee dedicated to helping him. That said, his story is an exceptional one and, in reality, the support of the Prime Minister and the Cabinet is even more encouraging than the support of a committee of one's direct colleagues. Therefore Peel did have a 1922 equivalent.

Contrast his experience with that of Benjamin Disraeli. The descendant of Jews, Disraeli had been discriminated against all his life. When he went on to support Lionel de Rothschild's bid to become an MP in spite of his practicing Judaism, Disraeli was described by his nemesis Gladstone as courageous for it. A lifetime of discrimination will teach a person to be thick-skinned, but no thickness of skin could have repelled the embarrassment that Disraeli would undoubtedly have felt after making his own maiden speech. He was already tenacious – he was a new Member of Parliament in 1837 after his fifth attempt to get elected – but the House can be a cruel place and on the occasion of his maiden speech it was at its cruellest. Had there been a supportive community available to dispense advice to newcomers – a 1922 Committee, for example – then Disraeli probably would have done everything differently (or perhaps he wouldn't, given what we know about him). One piece of advice that they may have given would be not to challenge the most aggressive debaters until you have become a veteran of the House yourself. Another may be not to speak on a topic for which you are unprepared. A third may be that to get on to begin with it may be worth flattering your colleagues and the House.

Instead, Disraeli broke all three of these rules. His sarcastic speech, challenging one of the most dominant and aggressive speakers of the time, Daniel O'Connell, on the issue of Irish election returns, which he knew little of, was drowned out by boos and hisses. There was a history to this particular diatribe. In 1835, when Disraeli was contesting his fourth (ultimately unsuccessful) election he had made a speech claiming that Ireland could not be given independence without the United Kingdom descending into civil war. Daniel O'Connell, the Irish nationalist and first Catholic elected to Westminster, responded by publicly stating that Disraeli was 'the worst possible type of Jew'.[3] This sort of racism wasn't unusual but it enraged Disraeli. As soon as he lost the election he vented his fury by trying to lure O'Connell and even his son into a duel. Neither of them took the bait, which only further infuriated Disraeli.

Now in 1837, as a newly elected Member of Parliament, he found a way to attack his enemy on the very issue which O'Connell cared most about: Ireland. The problem was that even the most experienced political debaters generally avoided conflict with O'Connell because his invectives were so scathing. As a novice, Disraeli had no chance. What he failed to appreciate was that O'Connell was well aware of his presence and had already forewarned his followers that should Disraeli speak, they should make life as uncomfortable as possible for him. Their hissing was joined by the majority of the House once they had heard enough of his sarcasm. In future years Disraeli's ironic diatribes would have all sides of the House in stitches, as a young and apparently arrogant man it came across merely as disrespectful. When it became clear that he could barely be heard above the jeering, Disraeli ended by angrily declaring 'I will sit down now, but the time will come when you will hear me!'[4] He was right about that, at least.

The point of all this is that Peel had a strong support network, if only owing to circumstance, that allowed his career to flourish early on. Disraeli didn't and consequently humiliated himself in the most public of arenas. Since the inception of the '22, every Conservative elected to Parliament has automatically become a member and so they have been that little bit less alone. The constitution of the Committee has slowly evolved as well. Famously the executive now has the ability to call a want of confidence vote in the leader of the Conservative Party should 25 per cent of MPs write to the Chairman of the '22 expressing their dissatisfaction with the leadership. This has led to the downfall of at least one leader since the Committee's inception.

However, despite media portrayals of the Committee as a conspiratorial network of MPs always looking to advance an agenda often at odds with that of the Party leadership, the '22 was established simply to make the transition into parliamentary life a little more comfortable for newly elected MPs. In the first meeting they did establish the principle of supporting their own leadership (on the condition that they maintained conservative principles).

Stanley Baldwin
(1923 – 1937)

What I want, Sir, is what you told me you wanted: to go with dignity,
not dividing the country, and to make things as smooth as possible
for your successor.

Stanley Baldwin to King Edward VIII, 2 December 1936

Bringing in these Gentlemen you call the King's
Enemies…reconciling them to the King and his Government, to
make the Foundation of it broader and deeper

Daniel Defoe's *Tory*, 1692

ONCE BONAR LAW HAD RESIGNED there were four
potential candidates for his job. The first was his Chancellor of
the Exchequer, Stanley Baldwin. The second was his Foreign
Secretary, Lord Curzon. The third was the Earl of Derby. The
last being Austen Chamberlain. Chamberlain desperately
coveted the role but was distrusted now by almost the entire
Party and, therefore, was an unlikely option. Derby was liked
throughout the Conservative ranks but immediately discounted
himself from the contest and announced that he would refuse to
serve under Curzon. In the event, though, much like with
Salisbury and Northcote forty years earlier, the decision fell to
the monarch, rather than to the Party. Whether the King would
choose Baldwin or Curzon was unknown to anyone including,
apparently, the monarch himself, at least initially.[1] Both men
were capable, both men were respected and both could clearly
lead the present government. It may only have been the
Parliament Act, which forever weakened the House of Lords
and its members, which swayed the decision. Baldwin was
chosen and the Party accepted it.

     Cabinet selection would not be any more comfortable
for Baldwin than it had for any of his predecessors. It should
have been easier because he had inherited his entire Cabinet (to
the last individual: initially he kept for himself the role that he
had held under Bonar Law as Chancellor of the Exchequer,

while he decided what to do with it). He had to consider how to placate the coalition Unionists that had been displaced only a year before whilst also mulling over the possibility of bringing in some Liberals to give the Party greater strength. Both of these ambitions were overly optimistic. The half of the Liberals that had been receptive to the coalition had not forgotten that Baldwin had resigned from it and pro-actively prompted Bonar Law to bring about its downfall. The coalition Unionists found their lead in Austen Chamberlain, who had been Baldwin's senior at the Treasury during the wartime coalition. Chamberlain, too, remembered only too well Baldwin's betrayal of the year before. That said there is an argument to be had that he would have accepted the Chancellorship, had it been on offer, as a potential stepping stone to his future leadership aspirations. It was not on offer, though.[1] What was on offer for Chamberlain was the US embassy, which he saw as nothing short of an insult. If that wasn't bad enough, injury was added to it when the new Prime Minister handed the Exchequer to Austen's younger brother Neville Chamberlain in the August. Baldwin then went away for the summer recess.

It was abroad, alone, that Baldwin took the decision that would affect much of his future economic policy and would unalterably change the political fortunes of the Conservative Party.[3] While away he spent much of his time considering unemployment and how it was unprecedentedly high (presently 2 million people were out of work). He also considered the incredible rise of the Labour Party. Baldwin did not like chaos. By disposition he was well equipped to handle one crisis, one problem, one task at a time but if any more was going on then it made him deeply uncomfortable. Throughout the entire history of Britain there had been two political parties and in that sense politics had been straightforward. Now there were three and although the Liberals would spend the next forty years declining into negligible figures, right now they were roughly equal in number to Labour. Either of these political parties could become the largest after the next election and if either played their cards right then it may even be the Conservatives who were forced into third place.

While thinking over all these things Baldwin couldn't escape the conclusion that Labour's meteoric rise was inextricably linked to the economic difficulties that he now presided over. If he mismanaged the unemployment situation then Labour may become even more Leftist than they already were. He found socialism abhorrent in whatever guise it presented itself. Thankfully Labour, albeit they professed a desire to see state control of industry, weren't quite as bad as the Bolsheviks that had taken control of Russia only a few years earlier. As recently as 1922 this latter group had formed the Union of Soviet Socialist Republics (USSR). That said, it wasn't hard to imagine this Labour movement going that way. Then there was the Liberals. Baldwin became convinced that in order to try to win back voters from Labour, Lloyd George would return from the summer recess with a pledge to introduce some levels of protection for domestic goods, which would in turn boost employment and bring the working classes flooding back to him. It is unclear whether this was Lloyd George's intention but Baldwin certainly thought it was and, the more he thought about it, the more protection looked like the silver bullet that would remove all his problems: reducing unemployment; neutralising the threat of Labour; removing the Liberals' only chance of regaining lost ground. Protection would have to be a Conservative policy and he would have to announce it before Lloyd George got in there first.

The only problem was that the previous year Bonar Law had promised that the government would not drastically change its economic policy without first consulting the country. Once Baldwin's mind was made up, there was no going back. So he returned to Britain at the end of the summer, informed his Cabinet of his decision in early October and by mid-November had informed King George that there must be yet another general election. The King subsequently dissolved Parliament for an election on 6 December.

Lloyd George, in response to the Conservative *volte face* on protection, declared himself an ardent free trader, meaning that he outflanked Baldwin on the other side. The result of the election was incredibly disappointing for the Conservatives. They were still the largest party but came far short of a majority, losing nearly one hundred MPs altogether. They ended up with 257 seats to Labour's 191 and the Liberals' 158.[4] Baldwin was humiliated. He had been rejected by the nation as well as the object of much anger within his own party, where he had thrown away a clear majority after just one year of the parliamentary term. He decided to remain in office during the Christmas recess in order to meet Parliament in the new year and see how the land lay. Throughout Christmas he comforted himself with the fact that, although he would almost certainly be defeated in the first vote in the new House of Commons, Lloyd George's position on free trade had made his co-operation with Labour impossible, meaning that a coalition of his opponents was unlikely. The only possibility was a minority Labour government, which would be smaller in number even than his Conservative Party in opposition.

On 21 January, when Parliament met again Baldwin was, as expected, defeated in a vote on the King's Speech. He resigned the next day and Ramsay MacDonald, leader of the Labour Party, took office as their first ever Prime Minister.

Now in opposition, Baldwin quickly corrected the errors he had made while in Downing Street. He retreated on tariff reform and brought Austen Chamberlain back into front line politics (at this point with no official title but he would eventually come to supplant Curzon as Foreign Secretary when the Conservatives returned to government).

Owing to the fact that the government held fewer than one in three parliamentary seats there was not much in the way of legislation throughout the 1924 session. Parliament prorogued for the summer and reconvened on 30 September with the possibility of a third election in as many years hanging over MPs. In the end the opposition parties forced the issue with a motion to censure the government. The motion was over their forcing the Director of Public Prosecutions to drop a prosecution for sedition against a writer who had tried to incite soldiers never to turn their weapons against fellow working class people, regardless of whether they were at war with them or not. The Liberals attached an amendment to the motion calling for an enquiry and it was on this that both opposition parties voted and defeated the government. MacDonald immediately called for a dissolution.

The election of October 1924 was incredible for a Conservative Party that had fared poorly at the polls only ten months earlier. They returned 419 MPs to Labour's 151. The Liberals returned only 40,[5] their decline now well and truly established.

This time Baldwin was able to take control of his own Cabinet, rather than inheriting one from his predecessor. He wasn't afraid to make waves. Curzon, who had come so close to becoming leader of the Party himself only eighteen months earlier, now found himself Leader of the House of Lords, but without any other prominent office. His previous role of Foreign Secretary went to Austen Chamberlain in exchange for the loyalty of all the coalition Unionists (who now found their cause of fusion with the Liberals pointless due to the mauling of that party in the election). Neville Chamberlain was moved from the Exchequer to become Minister for Health, by his own choice. Now the second most senior position in government was available and Baldwin would offer it to the most controversial of choices. Winston Churchill had left the Conservative Party in 1904 to join the Liberals. He had since been seen as an eccentric and a difficulty for every Liberal administration since. In 1922 he had lost his seat in Dundee during the Conservative victory of that year, then in 1923 he unsuccessfully contested Leicester, still as a Liberal on the basis that he was a free trader and Baldwin's sudden lurch to protectionism was abhorrent to him. Then in the 1924 election he stood as a 'Constitutionalist' gaining his seat but immediately dropping the term, which meant very little. Now he was in Parliament once more and the Prime Minister of the United Kingdom was asking Churchill to become Chancellor of the Exchequer.[6] He could hardly refuse. His reunification with the Conservative Party was complete.

      Now with a majority and a Cabinet of his own Baldwin could get on with the business of governing. Arguably the single most defining event of his premiership was the conflict with the coal miners which led to the 1926 General Strike. It cannot be overstated how important coal was at this point to the British economy. The industry employed over a million men,[7] the vast majority of whom worked in pits mining for the coal. It fuelled houses and business, most bulk transport and was depended upon for the maintenance of the crumbling empire. Prior to the First World War Britain had been a major exporter of coal which had brought in direct income as well as the support it lent to other industries. Since that point other nations such as the US and Germany had become more competitive by employing newer mining techniques such as machinery for digging, while Britain still relied on the Victorian methods of human extraction. During the War the method had remained unchallenged as the needs were so great that the industry could afford to be over-manned while still turning a profit due to a lack of competition from elsewhere (Britain was hardly going to import coal from Germany at this point). The artificially high prices generated from the fact that the government would purchase whatever was produced in order to support the war effort. Since then, though, the outdated practices of British mining were suffering in a global marketplace. Rather than modernising, the response of pit owners to falling profits was to reduce the wages of the miners, so that their margins remained intact. Clearly this was not sustainable.

There was a further problem with miners being discontented. Because of the size of their industry they held an incredible sway over the other sectors involved in the Trades Union Congress (TUC). If the miners were unhappy, everyone was unhappy and a General Strike was likely. In mid-1925 tensions had reached their peak when pit owners proposed a further reduction in miners' wages and the Triple Alliance of miners, transport workers and railwaymen all looked set to stick together during the dispute. In the negotiations that followed Baldwin eventually agreed for the government to subsidise the miners' wages (for a period of nine months) rather than face a General Strike. Evidently he felt that the country was not ready to face such a prospect in 1925.[8] During the nine month respite that he had bought for the country Baldwin appointed Sir Herbert Samuel to head a Commission looking into the matter.

The Samuel Commission released its findings on 11 March 1926 and it pleased nobody. It recommended investments in new technologies which pit owners were reluctant to pay for, as well as welfare benefits for miners such as improved holidays and housing, again to the annoyance of the owners. Further, it recommended pay reductions for miners which the unions simply could not accept. Throughout April Baldwin negotiated with the TUC and with the mine owners for some form of compromise but, balancing their needs with the will of a Cabinet that felt any concessions to the miners would be viewed in the country as the government buckling under threat of a strike and the task was next to impossible. By the beginning of May talks had broken down and the General Strike began on the 4th.[9]

Baldwin saw his principal task as being to ensure that the Strike did not cause panic in the country. His calm demeanour was perfectly made for such a task and on the whole the Cabinet would not pose a problem in following his lead, with one glaring exception. Churchill, ever the firebrand, would have to be muzzled for allowing him to speak out would be tantamount to inciting riots. Consequently Baldwin kept a tight leash on his Chancellor during the eight days of the Strike.

As far as Baldwin was concerned a coal strike could be negotiated away. He believed that the miners had genuine grievances which was why he was so prepared to spend April trying to secure an agreement between them and the pit owners. A *General* Strike, though, was not something which he could negotiate over. This was a different circumstance altogether with members of different industries all grouping together not to secure a deal by negotiation but to force an agenda through legalised terrorism. A General Strike was an attack on the British Constitution and only once he had defeated the TUC would he be prepared to listen to the concerns of the miners and thrash out an acceptable settlement.

On 12 May the TUC announced that they were calling off the General Strike, meaning that transport workers and railwaymen would be returning to work, but the coal miners remained at home. Now Baldwin could start to discuss a settlement with them. This was easier said than done and by the end of May he had lost patience with the whole process. Throughout June and July negotiations floundered due to recalcitrance on both sides and an exhaustion in the Prime Minister who was overseeing the discussions. In August Baldwin left the country for a break in Aix-les-Bains, France, leaving Churchill in charge of the coal dispute. Once he returned in the September the Cabinet had become opposed to making any significant push for a settlement on the basis that they believed the miners to be close to starvation and so they would have to return to work soon anyway.[10] They were right. In November the strike collapsed and the country returned to business as usual. Better than usual, in fact. Due to the government's unwillingness to crumble to Union demands the country would be much less affected by strikes in the years following 1926 than it had in the years leading up to it. That said, Baldwin's handling of the situation was a mixed affair. He had been right to separate the General Strike from the miners' qualms (defeating the one while addressing the other). He did indeed defeat the General Strike and demonstrate once and for all that the state was supreme and that revolution would never establish itself in Britain. On the other hand, despite his determination to do so, he never actually gained a settlement on behalf of the miners once the General Strike had ended. Instead he burnt out relatively quickly and had to let the process run its course.

This was the defining event of a difficult five year administration. 1927 and 1928 brought little in the way of meaningful politics. The government coasted along with a majority in the House of Commons and a lacklustre opposition but looking to the outside like a spent force. The very fact that the opposition provided no major criticism meant that the government did not have to raise its game to counter them. Baldwin should probably have moved his Cabinet around long before the general election of 1929 but for reasons best known to himself he did not. It was only Neville Chamberlain, the astute and meticulous Minister for Health that retained any form of credibility towards the end of the parliamentary term. Austen Chamberlain had become a name groaned at by large sections of society, seen as an outdated politician who, as Foreign Secretary had been too distant with the United States and too cosy with France. Winston Churchill had many political enemies but had managed even to alienate some of his friends once he had taken over Baldwin's strike negotiations in 1926. Determined to make some headway, Churchill had taken a much more robust stance than his Prime Minister had, which had left many to conclude that he had leadership ambitions of his own and he would do better to control them. As Chancellor of the Exchequer his most recent budgets had contained little substance, which irritated some, but with some eye-catching initiatives, which irritated the rest.

The rest of the Cabinet were in no healthier position. Lord Balfour, as Arthur Balfour had been since 1922, was now Lord President of the Council but was 80 years old by the time of the election. Lord Salisbury as Lord Privy Seal and leader of the House of Lords was in his late sixties, as was Sir William Joynson-Hicks, the Home Secretary. All in all the Cabinet looked like it had seen better days by 1929 but for the lack of assaults against ministers in either House, Baldwin had no idea of this image problem. During this same time he was convinced that he was coasting towards electoral success.[11]

Owing to the five year term limits the election could not be put off any later than 1929. In the event the Cabinet settled on a May election if for no other reason than that Baldwin could enjoy his annual summer retreat to Aix-les-Bains afterwards. The campaign message was 'Safety First' which, although was intended to counter the socialist argument that everything needed changing immediately, simply came across as out of touch in a country where unemployment was near a record high. On polling day, 30 May, Baldwin and Churchill spent the evening together at 10 Downing Street watching the results come in: Conservatives 261 seats; Labour 287; Liberals 59.[12] On 4 June Baldwin resigned, handing the premiership over to Ramsay MacDonald. Labour had not won a clear majority but they had certainly won more seats than the Conservatives.

His period in opposition would not be as smooth a ride as he had allowed himself to have for his last few years in government. It started in October 1929 when Lord Irwin, the Viceroy of India appointed by Baldwin when in government, declared his backing for India being given dominion status. Baldwin supported this notion but the idea was anathema to many within Britain who felt that any form of self-government would lead eventually to independence. Effectively this was the same argument that had been used against Irish Home rule in the preceding decades. Baldwin's problem with his position was that he could not carry the Shadow Cabinet with him. Notably, Churchill and Austen Chamberlain were highly critical of Irwin's remarks.

If India wasn't enough, various factions within the Conservative Party, seeing a period of opposition as a chance for renewal, started agitating once again for tariff reform. Baldwin had been burned by this issue before, losing the 1923 election after promising to implement some mild forms of protection. Early in 1930 he told the Conservatives that he was a supporter of free trade but that there should be a conference of nations within the Empire to decide upon how trade relations would work in the long term. If the result of such a conference was the imposition of food taxes, then so be it but even then he would put this to a national referendum.[13] This was a rather uninspiring policy: stating his own position but acknowledging his readiness to reverse it should it be necessary. Rather than showing strong leadership, which the Party was desperate for, he was running the risk of treading the compromise ground that Balfour had to his own detriment two decades earlier. It wasn't just on this matter that Baldwin's leadership seemed lacking. The Party faithful were becoming increasingly dismayed with his apparent lack of willingness to attack the government on any issue.[14]

As 1930 went on discontent grew. Baldwin was all too aware that there was no consensus within his Party on any of the dominant issues (India, tariffs, even who should be leader). Eventually tensions grew and when Baldwin returned from his summer in Aix there was no means left to settle the matter other than to have a meeting of all Party members (MPs and Lords). The meeting at Caxton Hall on 30 October was designed with one issue in mind: the future of the leadership of the Conservative Party. Baldwin attended in calm spirits and made only a brief address to the gathering before leaving, allowing his fate to be decided in his absence. In the event he was supported by a majority of 462-116.[15]

The difficulties should have ended there but once his leadership was secured he needed to sort his Party's split over tariffs and India. Just six weeks after the 30 October meeting, in mid-December, Churchill began an anti-dominion campaign in relation to India, delivering what can only be described as angry tirades against what he saw as a heinous proposal. By January 1831, realising that his position over India was incompatible with that of Baldwin, he resigned from the Shadow Cabinet.

The only good news for the Conservatives at this time was that Labour was faring even worse than they were. 1929 had seen the Wall Street Crash and a global economic downturn. Consequently unemployment had risen sharply throughout 1930 and, although the leader of the opposition did not wish to attack the government directly, the public saw nobody else to blame. The Labour Party had no answer to the unemployment problem and so, in spite of having a disunited Party, the Conservatives won some by-elections in early 1931. This was the backdrop to the summer of 1931, in which the entire direction of 1930s politics would be determined.

In early summer Germany began defaulting on its reparations payments which only added to the difficulties faced by the Treasury as the country struggled through the depression. Baldwin went to Aix on 8 August but was summoned back on the 12th for a meeting of senior political leaders and the Governor of the Bank of England. He did return but only for long enough to delegate to Neville Chamberlain the responsibility of negotiating on his behalf, before he returned to Aix 24 hours later. This may have been one of the biggest mistakes of his political career, which allowed Chamberlain to negotiate away what could have been a decade of Conservative dominance for subordination to a smaller Labour Party in a National Government.

A meeting was scheduled between MacDonald and Chamberlain as well as other senior officials for both parties on 18 August. By the 19th MacDonald was split with the majority of his Cabinet and his Party over what to do about government expenditure (the Prime Minister wanting it cut in order to reduce the deficit, the majority of the Labour Party wanting it maintained in the form of unemployment benefits). On 20 August Chamberlain wrote to Baldwin requesting his return, on the 21st Chamberlain and MacDonald discussed a coalition between all the main parties, including the Liberals, and on the 22nd Baldwin arrived in London. The Conservative leader was deeply reluctant to form another coalition government having risked his entire career in 1922 in order to bring down a previous one. However, Chamberlain impressed upon him that there was no alternative and in a meeting with the King a few days later Baldwin found the sovereign equally keen on the idea. He was backed into a corner.

On 24 August MacDonald's Cabinet resigned and he formed a National Government with a Cabinet of ten ministers made up of four Labour members (MacDonald as PM; Lord Sankey as Lord Chancellor; Philip Snowden as Chancellor of the Exchequer; and J.H. Thomas at the Dominions & Colonial Office), four Conservative Members (Baldwin as Lord President and, significantly only third most senior position in the Cabinet behind MacDonald and Sankey; Sir Samuel Hoare as India Secretary; Sir Philip Cunliffe-Lister as President of the Board of Trade; and Neville Chamberlain returning as Health Secretary) and two Liberals (Sir Herbert Samuel as Home Secretary and Lord Reading as Foreign Secretary). The Labour ministers who were in the House of Commons (MacDonald, Snowden and Thomas) were all quickly expelled from the Labour Party and had to form their own group, known as the National Labour Party.

The problem with having a government consisting of three different political parties is that little can be settled upon. How to deal with the economic crisis? Or protection? Or unemployment? Or spending cuts? There was no consensus and, after two months the only thing that could be agreed on was that a general election should be called and that the three parties should contest it as one National Government. They would be up against opposition in the form of the Labour Party led by Arthur Henderson and some non-nationalist Liberals led by David Lloyd George, who advocated the Liberal Party removing its support for the National Government. The result was historic for two reasons: firstly it saw more Conservative MPs returned to the House of Commons than any other election in history; and secondly no other Party reached triple figures in terms of the number of MPs returned.[16]

The government returned the following numbers: Conservatives, 470; Liberals, 68; National Labour, 13. The opposition consisted of 46 Labour MPs and just 4 Lloyd George (Independent) Liberals. The Conservatives had a majority to themselves but they were still prepared to go on under MacDonald who led a faction of just 13 MPs, the fourth in terms of size. Thus the top positions in government remained the same except that Neville Chamberlain was promoted to Chancellor of the Exchequer.

Now the government had to find a way to keep these three political parties together, when their individual leaders could scarcely keep their own followers in line. When it came to free trade versus protection the answer was simple. It was the same one that Lord Liverpool had come to 120 years earlier over the issue of emancipation: everybody can vote with their conscience. There would be no whipping of a particular government position and if senior members of the Cabinet decided to propose a Bill going in one direction (as they did with an Import Duties Bill in March 1932) then the more junior members could feel free to oppose it. In terms of keeping the government together this worked well. The Import Duties Bill was passed and with it came a sweeping general tariff, but the free traders remained in the Cabinet having exerted their opposition during House of Commons divisions.

In that same year German reparations were done away with, giving that nation the chance to come out of an economic mess worse than any other, and nothing to do with the Great Depression. Certain sections of German society started to call for rearmament as a means of creating employment, increasing security and, not insignificantly, generating a sense of national pride. This would have been a breach of German obligations under the Treaty of Versailles but, really, who was going to police *that*? The rest of the world had its own problems. Most European nations were engaged in discussions around general disarmament but the move towards consensus was slow and the end still far out of sight.

        In January 1933 Adolf Hitler became Chancellor of Germany, by August he was hinting to other leaders that he had expansionist ambitions in order to gauge their reactions and by October he had withdrawn Germany from the European Disarmament Conference.[17] This was significant for most other nations: the USSR and France both started discussing the possibility of war; Italy and the Baltic nations all realised that one way or the other they would be sucked in if the major powers took to arms. Only in Britain was this not a consideration. This may seem strange looking back, knowing what we do about what would become the Second World War, but for an explanation we need look no further than the top three men in government. The Prime Minister, Ramsay MacDonald, was Labour through and through. He had been expelled from their Party because he had agreed to coalition but he still adhered to their principles. Since the 1920s the Labour Party had been a strictly pacifist organisation. This was a matter of policy for more reasons than a mere distaste for war. Labour was a working class movement and they saw their loyalty to the working classes as transcending national boundaries. Solidarity among workers meant solidarity with those in the Soviet Union, Germany, France, Italy, Spain and anywhere else in the world. For the Labour Party war meant rich men deciding policy while poor men fought and died, which was completely at odds with their ethos of promoting the welfare of working men. Therefore any form of conflict was abhorrent to MacDonald.

        Baldwin, the leader of the largest party in the government, was similarly opposed to war but not for the same reasons as MacDonald. That is not to say that Baldwin felt no affiliation with the working classes – he had been a businessman before entering into politics and had had many dealings with workers and unionists throughout his time. His opposition to war was nothing to do with ideology but driven by a belief that the process was pointless. Always considering the business case for any course of action he had watched Britain go to war in 1914 and come out victorious on the battlefield but at what cost? The country lost over a decade of economic growth after the war finished, millions of men died and the country gained no territory or any other prize for that matter from having partaken in it. When faced with a general strike in 1925 he worked hard to negotiate with the miners, exhausting all options before taking them on in 1926. No, for Baldwin conflict should only ever be a last resort.

Then there was the Chancellor of the Exchequer, Neville Chamberlain. He was in an unusual position in that he was in control of the country's finances, senior to Baldwin in the Cabinet but junior to him within the Conservative Party. That said, Baldwin delegated much of the management of the Conservative Party to Chamberlain which gave him a lot more influence than his official position alone did. In terms of his disposition Chamberlain was averse to war. He had not had much chance to demonstrate this but certainly would do in the coming years, which is what allows an historian to make such a conclusion about him. For the time being it is fair to say that any discussions in the Cabinet would involve him and his opinion would be given a great deal of weight.

So MacDonald, Baldwin and Chamberlain were all, for different reasons, pacific meaning that when Germany withdrew from discussions of disarmament and started to build up its military the British government did not react. From the back benches Winston Churchill unashamedly criticised the government for its lack of military preparedness. In doing so he knew that he was stirring up trouble: the nation was in a pacifist mood as were the senior men in government. But the government was in power with a massive majority of MPs, six in seven of whom were Tories. Unlike Labour the Tories did not support pacifism at all costs. Tories believed in Britain. Tories believed in King and Country. Tories were imperialists. By making speeches on the record criticising the government for not defending the realm and, thereby, implying that they are less patriotic than he was, Churchill came across only as mildly eccentric. Deep down his words struck a chord with those Tories that felt the same but couldn't quite bring themselves to say it. For now Churchill was marginalised, merely an embarrassment to Baldwin who had brought him back into the Conservative Party; a thorn in the side of yet another leader as he had been to Balfour when he left initially and to Asquith and Lloyd George when he was a Liberal. However, when the time came for war anybody searching through Hansard records of the 1930s will find only one person that had advocated throughout and on a regular basis that Britain needed to change its stance on military expenditure.

Throughout 1934 military expenditure dominated the political agenda as the Conservative Party lost some early by-elections to Labour candidates, which was widely interpreted as being due to Labour's pacifism. Meanwhile Churchill kept putting pressure on the government not just to spend more but to declare what it was spending and what the relevant military figures were: how many aeroplanes did Britain have? How many submarines? At what rate was the British military growing relative to that of Germany's? Increasingly, Baldwin was expected to answer these awkward questions (difficult because the answers could not inspire any confidence in the event of war. In 1934 Britain's air force was smaller than a third of the Soviet Union's[18]). MacDonald's health was failing him, he was becoming more and more forgetful, even losing his way during speeches to the House. On 16 May 1935, once it had dawned on him what had been apparent to most of his colleagues for a long time, he notified the King of his intention to resign.

On 7 June 1935 Baldwin succeeded MacDonald as Prime Minister. He kept Chamberlain as his Chancellor of the Exchequer and brought in Sir Samuel Hoare as Foreign Secretary. The parliamentary term had a little over a year left to run and in spite of the huge majority of Conservatives within it Baldwin was still technically inheriting the National Government. Therefore it made sense to hold a general election in order that the leadership and Party lines be clearly defined. He took the summer recess as a chance to avoid the question but in October requested that Parliament be dissolved for a November election.

Supporters of the government won 428 seats in the election, compared with around 154 for Labour, led by Clement Attlee, and 21 for the Liberals. The Conservatives were returned with a reduced, yet still substantial, majority. The first task of the post-election government was to deal with Italian foreign policy. During 1935 Italian Prime Minister Benito Mussolini had ordered the invasion of Ethiopia which had caused an outcry from the international community and the imposition of economic sanctions on Italy by the League of Nations, largely pushed for by Britain and France.

In December Hoare travelled to France to negotiate how to proceed on the Italo-Abyssinian conflict with the French Prime Minister, Pierre Laval. He went there with no mandate to negotiate anything specific but then this was not uncommon. Baldwin often gave his Foreign Secretaries carte blanche to do as they pleased. The result was the Hoare-Laval Pact, which was agreed by both men and was effectively a blueprint for how to act once the conflict was over. The French press immediately reported that they had agreed to appease Italy, which was detested by the public in both countries. Their British counterparts soon took up the story and the campaign for a reversal of policy was well established long before Hoare had even left France. Baldwin looked set to be humiliated (the public, not knowing or caring that he took little interest in foreign policy would have blamed him for the overall policy) but Hoare fell on his own sword by resigning as soon as he returned to the UK in mid-December. In terms of the French backlash, it was too much for Laval to survive. He resigned as Prime Minister in January 1936.

Further difficulties presented themselves in the new year when, on 20 January, King George V died. A transition from one monarch to the next is never something that a Prime Minister relishes but in this case it made Baldwin positively uncomfortable. He was not convinced that King Edward VIII was suitable for the role of leading the nation and even less convinced that he would last on the throne for the rest of his life.[19] If he was right, then this would throw up all sorts of constitutional difficulties that Baldwin had neither the energy nor the desire to tackle. The new King was irresponsible, selfish and, it was widely known, in a relationship with an American socialite named Wallis Simpson, who was once divorced and now married to her second husband. It was unthinkable that a King could *marry* a double-divorcee, should she leave her second husband, and in most circumstances the relationship would be left as an affair. But Baldwin did not believe that the new King was responsible enough not to marry her, the only question was when it would happen and what action to take when it did.

Events came to a head in October when news broke of Mrs Simpson's impending divorce from her husband, which meant that her affair with the King would become not just common knowledge among those in power, but public knowledge, which was a far more dangerous concept. That autumn Stanley Baldwin faced the very realistic prospect of the collapse of the British monarchy.

On 20 October Baldwin had what must have been the most difficult meeting of his career. He went to see the King for a private talk in which he told his monarch that the situation could not go on as it was. The Prime Minister suggested that Mrs Simpson go away for some months and that she put off the divorce, to which the King replied that this was her business. Baldwin did not enquire as to whether King Edward had any intention of marrying Mrs Simpson but he had delivered the message that he had intended and that was enough for now.

Shortly afterwards the Cabinet, led by Neville Chamberlain, presented Baldwin with a draft ultimatum that they expected him to deliver to the King, insisting that he terminate his relationship with Mrs Simpson. Baldwin chose not to use it but this was possibly the first time that he realised that the Cabinet were prepared to force abdication on the King, rather than allow public opinion to do it (or worse, allow public opinion to turn against the monarchy altogether). The Prime Minister had a further meeting with King Edward on 16 November in which the monarch informed him of his intention to marry Wallis Simpson. Baldwin refrained from suggesting that the government would force him to go, again falling back on the public in advising the King that they would not accept it. The King allegedly made it clear during this meeting that he would abdicate rather than give her up, thereby confirming Baldwin's worst fears.

At a further meeting on 25 November they agreed to look into the possibility of a morganatic marriage but nothing else was settled upon. Baldwin was against the idea but resolved to consult with others before dismissing it.

Throughout the next week Baldwin took soundings from the Cabinet, from Attlee as leader of the Labour Party and from the heads of the Imperial Dominion States. The view was unanimous: a marriage of any sort, morganatic or otherwise, would be incompatible with the King remaining on the throne.

On 2 December Baldwin again met the King and advised him that the morganatic plan was impossible. The King is recorded to have challenged Baldwin directly with the words 'You want me to go, don't you?' to which Baldwin replied that he wanted any transition to be as smooth as possible.[20] The following day, in the House of Commons, Attlee asked Baldwin whether any decision had been taken, to which he replied that it had not. Churchill then rose to demand that nothing be done on the issue without a statement first being made to Parliament. Baldwin avoided directly answering the question but Churchill was proving increasingly difficult to handle. Most of the press were opposed to the King having anything to do with Wallis Simpson but three papers in particular (the *Daily Mail*, *Daily Express* and *News Chronicle*) were supportive of the King's rights to do as he pleased in this matter. Churchill, utilising his contacts within these papers, was agitating in favour of the King and looked set to break with the Conservatives in order to form a King's Party in Westminster. If done, this would have been his seventh change in Party identity during his political career (between Unionist, Liberal, Coalition Liberal, Liberal again, Constitutionalist and Conservative).

On 3 December Baldwin had a brief audience with Edward in which the King asked if he might meet with Winston Churchill, as one friend to another. Baldwin was caught off guard and agreed but realised immediately that it was a mistake. Churchill later wrote to Baldwin that the King was not fit to make a decision on the subject at the moment and so the whole thing should be delayed, but the Prime Minister was not going to accept any procrastinations at this late hour. He paid a visit to the King the following day, Friday 4 December, to push him for an answer: abdication or separation. The King had the weekend to consider it.

On Monday 7 December, in the House of Commons, Baldwin defended the position of the government to press the King for a decision. He came under heavy criticism from Churchill but the mood of the chamber had changed. Whereas only a week previously Churchill had received cheers for his defence of King Edward, now he found support lacking. Over the next few days the King told his ministers of his intention to abdicate and their job became steering through the transition from him to his younger brother with the minimum of disturbance.

King Edward VIII abdicated on 11 December 1936, handing power over to his younger brother Albert, who became known as King George VI. Into 1937 and Baldwin started to plan his retirement. He would not be forced from office by the electorate or an ambitious colleague but would pick a date of his choosing and enjoy his retirement. During the first few months of the year he transferred more and more of his responsibilities to Neville Chamberlain. He decided to stay long enough to witness the coronation of the new King in May, but no longer. On 28 May 1937 Stanley Baldwin resigned the premiership and his seat in the House of Commons, being elevated to the Lords as Lord Baldwin.

He had led the Conservatives through recession and depression, through strikes and abdication, through the rise of Nazism and disarmament, and through no fewer than five general elections. In terms of successes, the election results are easy to quantify (won two as Conservatives, won a majority in another one in the National Government, lost two) but the other factors less so. Historians generally commend the way that he handled the miner's strike but the depression is often seen as having been worsened by his mid-1920s economic policy (driven by his then-Chancellor, Churchill) to return Britain to the gold standard.

He is often credited with dealing with the abdication crisis in a much more calm manner than many of his contemporaries could have managed but his failure to confront German rearmament, particularly in the context of what we now know followed his premiership, is often a source of criticism.

There were many contenders for the leadership during his fourteen years at the top. Not least of these were the Chamberlains: Austen in the early days, firmly of the belief that he was the better man and had been passed over unfairly; and Neville in the later days, loyal to Baldwin on the whole but undoubtedly frustrated towards the end that his leader had not made way for him sooner. Then of course there was Churchill. With his father's blood running through his veins he was no sensible politician. He was prepared to attack his own Party's leadership, regardless of how it would affect his own ambitions. Typically paranoid, to him everything was a conspiracy whether it was the miners conspiring to have their own Bolshevik-style revolution, the Nazis conspiring to take over Europe or Baldwin conspiring to remove the King, he would lend a voice of opposition to them all. When he was right, he was right. For the rest of the time he simply made life difficult.

Baldwin handled most of his rivals with skill. Initially he took the wind out of Austen Chamberlain's political sails by offering him junior positions in the Cabinet, even below that of his younger brother. Towards the end of Austen Chamberlain's life he had actually converted to backbench support for Baldwin. With Neville Chamberlain Baldwin knew his man. He was loyal for the most part but in any case lacked the courage for a leadership battle. As long as there were vague promises of a cordial handover at some point in the future the younger Chamberlain would be kept in line. With Churchill he managed to neutralise the threat by bringing him into the Cabinet as his Chancellor of the Exchequer, which kept him from doing harm for around six years. Only when he removed himself from the Shadow Cabinet over the matter of India's status did Baldwin have to suffer his backbench agitations, but by that point his majority in the Commons was so substantial that, annoying though Churchill was, he was never a threat per se.

So was Baldwin a success or a failure? Of all the leaders of the Tories and Conservatives he is arguably the hardest to categorise in this manner. War historians would argue that the 1930s represented a decade in which Britain could have prepared for war, but didn't and this was down to Stanley Baldwin. Thatcherite economic historians would point to the General Strike as the moment when trade unionism in Britain first realised its limitations and without Baldwin's resolve Britain's drift towards socialism would have been accelerated, transforming the country from the one we know today. Even his election results do not help us as he lost as many as he won outright.

What can be said for Baldwin is this: all the evidence suggests that in every situation he did what he though was right. Churchill once argued, shortly after Baldwin's death, that he put Party before Country, alluding to a speech Baldwin gave justifying his stance against rearmament in the early 1930s in which he stated that the electorate were against it. In this context he was saying that because the country were against it a government could not do it, meaning that his considerations were of the opinions of the people, rather than the opinions of ministers. In retrospect we know that the 1930s could have been handled better and in this sense he cannot be said to have been successful. But equally it cannot seriously be argued that this was due to either malice or politicking. He did what he thought was right, even when it wasn't.

Neville Chamberlain
(1937 — 1940)

This is the second time in our history that there has come back from Germany to Downing Street peace with honour. I believe it is peace for our time.

Neville Chamberlain, 27 September 1938

I would sooner Forgive a Man that dislik'd my Title, than one who dislik'd my Conduct

Daniel Defoe's *Tory*, 1692

WHEN NEVILLE CHAMBERLAIN TOOK OVER as Prime Minister in May 1937 there was no major outcry from his detractors in the Conservative Party. There was no sustained opposition or even a token contest, simply a smooth transfer of power from one Prime Minister to his accepted successor.[1] Of all those that had served in the Cabinets of Baldwin during the previous fourteen years there were none that were as highly regarded as Chamberlain, who had excelled as Minister for Health and had performed competently during his time as Chancellor of the Exchequer. Furthermore, most of his senior Conservative colleagues were extremely old and tired. Chamberlain himself, at the age of 68, was no spring chicken, but brought so much vigour to his daily toil that he gave the impression of a much younger man.

The only person who would have considered taking the leadership from him was Churchill but he lacked any substantial following and therefore was not a serious contender. In the event it was Churchill who seconded Chamberlain's nomination for the leadership,[2] thereby giving his blessing to what was in any event a *fait accompli*. Chamberlain immediately started to shape his Cabinet. Anthony Eden was to remain as Foreign Secretary (having been appointed by Baldwin two years earlier), Sir Samuel Hoare was to be brought back into the Cabinet as Home Secretary and Sir John Simon took Chamberlain's old post of Chancellor of the Exchequer.

In spite of Chamberlain's successes in domestic politics in the twenty years prior to his leading the country, it was foreign affairs which would dominate the political agenda during his premiership and, therefore, foreign affairs on which he is judged today both as Prime Minister and as leader of the Conservative Party. Many historians have claimed that this is an unfair way to remember his contribution,[3] given that these last three years of a political career spanning decades are only a small proportion of his overall work. That said, these were the three years that he was leader and we must stick to the facts in assessing them.

The Foreign Office was the one major office of state for which Chamberlain had allowed continuity from the days of Baldwin. He had kept Anthony Eden in his old role, which was hardly a surprise given that Eden was first of all a relatively young man in an otherwise ageing Cabinet and that he and Chamberlain had been on very good terms over the past few years.[4] For the nine months which followed, though, their relationship would become increasingly strained. The new Prime Minister was eager to demonstrate that his foreign policy would be different to that of his predecessor and so was far more willing to take matters into his own hands (Baldwin had been of the firm belief that foreign policy was for foreign ministers and had little, if any, active involvement).

The difficulties began almost immediately as Eden proposed continuing with rearmament, which had finally begun towards the end of Baldwin's premiership but at a very slow pace. He had no time for the 'dictator powers' of Germany and Italy, believing that both Hitler and Mussolini were despicable characters that Britain should approach with caution. He planned to keep Germany guessing as to British foreign policy while taking the time to develop a military strength that gave the country options. On the other hand Chamberlain was of the mind that Germany and Italy were significant powers in Europe and that Britain should find a way to co-exist with them. For Chamberlain, the previous foreign policy was unnecessarily provocative and instead Hitler and Mussolini should be engaged constructively.

At the same time the Spanish Civil War raged on, having begun in 1936, with Germany and Italy committing troops to support the Republican group led by General Franco, while the USSR was actively backing the other side, the Nationalists. Consequently tensions on the continent were already high and the possibility of an all-out war more than a small possibility.

Throughout the summer of 1937 the two men's ideals clearly diverged, but they rarely clashed. Instead Chamberlain would by-pass Eden and make decisions without him so as to avoid the confrontation. In July the Italians accused Britain of acting belligerently and claimed that they would have to accelerate their own armaments production in response. Eden believed that Mussolini was trying to push Britain into a corner and pointed to evidence that, following their conquest of Ethiopia in 1935, Mussolini was now positioning 60,000 troops in Libya, which could attack any number of British forces in Egypt, Sudan or the Mediterranean. Chamberlain was sympathetic to Mussolini's claim that his sabre-rattling was entirely in response to Eden's calls for increased military expenditure, which he was threatened by. Then, in August and September, British merchant ships were repeatedly attacked in the Mediterranean by Italian submarines, which at the time Mussolini denied and Britain could not prove. The Italians kept accusing Britain of provocation while attacking British ships. For the Prime Minister the only answer was to continue to engage Mussolini and try to reason with him.

By November Chamberlain and Eden were clashing over military expenditure. The Foreign Secretary was insistent that without a strong military, negotiation was futile anyway as the country would never be taken seriously but the Prime Minister, possibly as a hangover from his days at the Treasury, was uncomfortable with the financial implications.[5] Then in the middle of the month Lord Halifax, who was Lord President of the Council and absolutely nothing to do with the Foreign Office, was invited to Germany by Herman Göring, their Minister of State, ostensibly for a hunting trip. However, Chamberlain had sanctioned Halifax to enter into talks with Hitler about Germany's ongoing claims to Czechoslovakia and Poland. Eden, quite understandably, felt undermined and humiliated by this development, paying a visit to the Prime Minister on 16 November during which the two argued. In the end Halifax went to Germany and spoke with Hitler. Only when he returned did the Foreign Secretary become aware that

Chamberlain and Halifax had settled upon their own course of policy without him. Whereas Eden had told Halifax to be firm and stand by the principle that the nations surrounding Germany should not be compromised in any way, what actually happened was that Halifax told Hitler that Britain accepted Germany's case for taking some of the land from these countries, but that it must be done peacefully.

Then, in January 1938, the US President, Franklin D. Roosevelt, sent a telegram to Chamberlain stating that he was shocked at the deteriorating situation in Europe and that he wanted to make a public address stating that the smaller nations were at threat from the dictator nations because there was not enough opposition to them. However, the President needed to know that he would have British support if he made such a declaration. Chamberlain replied that he could not approve. He wanted to acknowledge Italy's sovereignty in Ethiopia in order to bring Mussolini onside and he wanted to maintain cordial negotiations with Germany.[6] Roosevelt threatened these ambitions with his rhetoric. Chamberlain did not consult Eden before replying. The Foreign Secretary was horrified when he found out and spent the next few days and weeks trying to change the Prime Minister's mind. However, Chamberlain was more frequently taking decisions without including Eden and, on 20 February, Eden resigned. He was replaced, almost predictably, by Halifax.

Chamberlain no longer had the bind that was Eden preventing him from conducting the policy that he vehemently believed was the only one which could avoid war. He was going to negotiate with the dictators of Europe and then history would remember him as a hero: the man who single-handedly avoided another Great War such as the one that Britain was sucked into in 1914. At this point there was great support in the country for appeasement and there were very few who foresaw the lengths that the government would have to go to in order to give it a chance of success.

During the summer Hitler had made it clear that he viewed Czechoslovakia as an illegitimate state. It had been created following the Great War from land that had belonged mainly to Austria-Hungary. On the west side of the country there were over 3 million Germans living in an area known as the Sudetenland, which Hitler wanted to annex and bring under

German control. At this time Hitler was encouraging German leaders in the Sudetenland to stir up trouble so that he could use the outbreak of disorder as a *casus belli*. At the beginning of September the Czech government, realising that they would get no military support from Britain or France, offered to negotiate with Germany over the Sudetenland. However, on 12 September Hitler publicly denounced Czechoslovakia and claimed that they ill-treated their German minority.

On 15 September Chamberlain flew to Berchtesgaden to meet with Hitler during which the Führer demanded that the Sudetenland be ceded to Germany or else war was unavoidable. Chamberlain returned to the UK and discussed the matter in Cabinet, after which he felt compelled to sell the proposal to France and Czechoslovakia, reluctantly gaining their agreement.[7] He then returned to Germany for a second meeting with Hitler in order to finalise the accord. However, the Führer was prepared to push his luck further. When Chamberlain arrived for their meeting in Bad Godesberg on 22 September Hitler insisted that German troops must be moved into the Sudetenland immediately, giving no opportunity for a prolonged transfer of power. The only concession Chamberlain could gain was that the Germans would not act until 1 October.[8]

The Prime Minister returned home and informed his Cabinet of Hitler's demands and of his belief that Britain should accept them. This time he found that there was a vocal opposition to his appeasement. Ministers had started to question where it would end if Hitler kept making demands that were never challenged. Should the Cabinet not support continued appeasement, war was the only outcome remaining. On 28 September Chamberlain made a detailed statement to the House of Commons informing them of the events of that month. As he was drawing to its conclusion he was passed a note from Sir John Simon informing him that, thanks to an intervention from Mussolini, Hitler had agreed to a four-way conference to settle the matter (the four powers involved being Britain, France, Germany and Italy, but not Czechoslovakia), which was to be held in Munich the following day. He announced his acceptance of the invitation and no more discussion followed as Chamberlain left to prepare for his trip.[9]

In the early hours of 30 September the Munich Agreement was signed by all four nations. Chamberlain returned to Britain later that day and announced to the gathering crowds that his diplomacy meant 'peace for our time'. It seems that the nation was happy that war had been avoided and Chamberlain felt satisfied with his work but it is hard to understand what he felt that he had achieved. The Munich Agreement was similar to the Godesberg agreement in that the Sudetenland would be ceded to the Germans, but Czechoslovakia was given until 10 October to evacuate any non-German from the area. For all the diplomacy and for all the rhetoric of a successful mission, all that had been achieved was a ten day extension to the deadline.

Parliamentary discussion of the settlement was set for 3-6 October and most in the Commons seemed to accept the Agreement. It consequently passing the division on the 6th. The most outspoken critic was Churchill, who claimed that the Munich Agreement represented a 'total and unmitigated defeat'[10] and that the Czech government could have negotiated a better settlement themselves a month earlier had Britain not gotten involved and handed Germany everything that it had demanded. His peroration made no difference to the outcome of the vote, which was one of overwhelming support for the government's position. Chamberlain's promises of peace for Europe seemed tentatively to hold over the coming months, with Germany not over-spilling its borders again in 1938. What was happening within its borders, though, was a different matter altogether. The night of 9-10 November bore witness to *Kristallnacht*, in which Jewish properties across Germany (and Austria, which had been under Nazi control since the previous February) were destroyed by SA Militants while the authorities watched. Scores of Jews were killed and hundreds of thousands imprisoned in concentration camps.

By this time Chamberlain and Churchill were both attacking each other's 'judgment'[11] and thereby raising the stakes higher. The public nature of their disagreement meant that one of them would end up looking foolish before long and, both being well into their sixties, whoever came out the loser would end their career on that nadir. It was March 1939 before the impasse seemed to sway, although even then it wasn't immediately apparent to all parties that it had been broken. On 15 March German forces breached Czechoslovak territory which had been guaranteed by the agreements of the previous year. Hitler's forces reached Prague with little in the way of resistance and Churchill claimed to have been vindicated for all his warnings over the past six years. Chamberlain, however, was unwilling at first to accept that appeasement had failed. He spoke to the House of Commons that same day in defence of his policies but on this occasion he found that he was not well received.[12]

On 7 April Mussolini attacked Albania and it was at this time that Chamberlain realised that his tactics had to change. He still wished to avoid war, but he replaced appeasement with deterrent, offering guarantees to protect the independence of Poland (from Germany) and Turkey and Greece (from Italy). At this time Churchill impressed upon the Prime Minister his own desire to return to government but this was denied him. Months later, on 23 August, news broke that Germany and the Soviet Union had signed the Nazi-Soviet Pact. Unlike in 1914, the German army would not be fighting on two fronts if they went to war with Britain and France. The consequences were unthinkable and at home Chamberlain was blamed. Churchill had been warning for years that Britain should sign a military alliance with the Soviets, why had Chamberlain refused? Churchill had been announcing for years that Hitler's expansionist ambitions would never be satisfied, why had Chamberlain not harkened? If Britain had acted militarily in defence of Czechoslovakia then there would be one more anti-German army standing today. What the country, and indeed the Cabinet, did not seem to acknowledge was that the majority had given their whole hearted support to Chamberlain's appeasement strategy. Years later, when recording their own recollections, the Cabinet ministers of 1936-39 largely remembered having misgivings about appeasement[13] but this is not what the evidence from the time suggests.

Now it looked inevitable that Churchill, that modern day prophet, would have to return to government owing to popular opinion, regardless of how Chamberlain felt about it personally. On 1 September Germany invaded Poland, meaning that both appeasement and deterrence had failed. The government declared war on Germany on 3 September 1939. Chamberlain was aware that he needed to broaden his ministry – in the event of war he could no longer sustain backbench attacks from detractors within his own Party. On the day of the declaration of war he summoned both Churchill and Eden to see him. The former was offered the Admiralty and a seat in the War Cabinet, the latter was offered the Dominions but excluded from the War Cabinet.[14]

The first few months of the war are now known as the Phoney War because no major offensives were initiated by either side. Chamberlain had no desire to commit ground troops to the continent. He had been devastated by the inevitability of the war. He didn't see himself as a war leader and had staked his reputation on peace. In this sense the parallels with Henry Addington in 1803 are incredible. Both were hailed by the nation as men who brought about an unlikely peace; both tried to avoid war at any cost; when war became inevitable both men declared war in spite of their clear distaste; once both the Napoleonic War and the Second World War had started, both leaders procrastinated rather than engaging in conflict, wanting of course to win their respective wars but desiring even more not to lose them. The final parallel is the one that devastated each of them: both Addington and Chamberlain were inflicted with another, extremely popular, leader lurking in the shadows. Men who had formerly criticised their foreign policy and who had advocated taking a tougher line with dictators, whether Napoleon or Hitler.

September 1939 until April 1940 saw very little military action but that would all change and with it Chamberlain's premiership came crashing down around him. The irony was that the failures for which he would be forced to resign were actually based on decisions that he had taken at the urging of his successor.

At this time Germany imported a large quantity of iron ore from Scandinavia which usually started life in Sweden but was exported via the Norwegian port of Narvik. In early 1940 Churchill pushed the argument in the War Cabinet that a naval blockade of Narvik would swiftly crush the German war effort. Chamberlain responded by further procrastination – he wanted to keep the proposal open as an option without actually committing to it immediately. It was spring before Chamberlain got on board with the plan and eventually it was agreed to plant floating mines around Narvik, which was to commence on 8 April. However, a few days before this

Germany launched an invasion of Norway and took control of all ports. A British blockade of one was now largely irrelevant. It went ahead anyway with British cruisers patrolling the sea but because of the German invasion opinion became that for the operation to succeed British troops would have to land in Norway. Although several landings took place they were always followed soon afterwards by the evacuation of those same troops.[15] Germany did lose some ships but Britain did also. All in all the Norwegian Campaign, the first major military engagement of the war, was viewed as a failure.

The debates in the Commons which followed the first month of the campaign covered 7 and 8 May. Chamberlain rose to speak on the first day but the House was in no mood to hear him. Attlee, as leader of the opposition, got a more positive response than the Prime Minister in spite of the large Conservative majority. Then Labour Members criticised the government's conduct of the war, working themselves up into causing a division, when they had entered the debate committed to promoting unity. Before the fatal division Lloyd George rose and told the House that Hitler had always bested Chamberlain and that as a result the Prime Minister could not continue.

Chamberlain made a speech towards the end of the second day imploring Members to support the government but looking defeated in doing so. At the end of the second night Churchill rose and gave a commanding speech condemning the detractors who would not support Chamberlain now, noting that those same people had supported him during the appeasement years. After his speech the House divided to vote. The result was that in spite of a Conservative majority of 213 the government only carried the debate by 81 votes.[16]

Chamberlain knew that he couldn't go on. He had won a majority and a substantial one at that but with the numbers that the Conservatives had in the House of Commons he should have done better. He had been attacked by Lloyd George's Liberals and Attlee's Labour at a time when all parties should have been united. At a meeting with Churchill and Halifax the next day Chamberlain tried to get Halifax to take the premiership. As a peer Halifax refused believing that, particularly in times of war, a Prime Minister needed to sit in the Commons. Churchill it was.

However, although Churchill would be popular with the country, he would not be the first choice of many MPs. The Conservative Party still largely didn't trust him and Eden was arguably more popular within their ranks. Therefore two unconventional things happened: firstly Chamberlain remained as leader of the Conservative Party while another Conservative became Prime Minister; secondly Churchill had to court the support of Attlee's Labour in order to ensure that he could guarantee himself a majority in Parliament at any point in the future. Attlee therefore entered the government's front bench and Chamberlain stayed on as Lord President of the Council, the other major change at the top of the government being Sir Kingsley Wood replacing Sir John Simon at the Exchequer.

On the day that Chamberlain resigned the premiership Germany invaded France. Six weeks later the French had capitulated and signed an armistice with the Germans surrendering their land to the Axis powers of Germany and Italy. The events were summed up by Churchill in a Commons speech on 16 June in which he announced that the 'Battle of France is over…the Battle of Britain is about to begin'. That summer would indeed see what history now knows as the Battle of Britain in which the German Luftwaffe tried to exert aerial dominance over the Royal Air Force in order to clear the way for an invasion. The RAF tactics were to engage oncoming German bombers with their gun planes. The Battle went on throughout the summer and early autumn of 1940 and the inability of the Luftwaffe to overwhelm the RAF or inflict any significant damage to British naval ports is largely viewed as the reason why no invasion of Britain ever occurred. For Chamberlainite historians the success of Britain in staving off the German threat was vindication for his policy of not engaging Germany during the crises of 1937-8 as this had given Britain time to build its forces. By 1940 Fighter Command had a presence almost ten times its 1938 strength.[17]

For Chamberlain the victory of the Battle of Britain would be the last he would witness. Feeling ill during the summer he underwent an operation for stomach cancer and then stayed in Hampshire recuperating throughout August. However, he still felt ill and weak into the autumn and so he resigned from the government on 1 October. On 9 November he died of his cancer.

As leader of the Conservative Party Chamberlain never faced the electorate but his popularity had seen highs and lows. For the most part, in spite of the revisionist versions of those events written in the years which followed, the country greatly supported his policy of appeasement. Having witnessed a war with Germany once in their lifetimes the majority of the public had no appetite for another one. However, Chamberlain's misjudgement of the characters both of Hitler and Mussolini were a deep source of embarrassment for him and led to the policy on which he has been (negatively) remembered by history. The fact that he tried to avoid war is undoubtedly honourable. The fact that war was inevitable and, therefore, his appeasement of the dictator states throughout the years 1937-9 simply meant the loss of Ethiopia, Albania and Czechoslovakia which, if not avoidable, could have put up more resistance had they anticipated British and French support.

The fact that Churchill had been arguing for a tougher stance to be taken against Hitler and that Churchill went on to succeed Chamberlain as Prime Minister means that history has judged Chamberlain especially harshly. Had anybody else taken over in 1940, his policy of appeasement would still have been seen as a failure but possibly a little less marked than it is. However, the fact that Churchill was in Number 10 when the allies won the war means that he was, by his mere presence, saying 'I told you so' to all of his critics from the 1930s.

That is not to say that Chamberlain's leadership was a success, it wasn't. Had appeasement worked history would have remembered him as a hero, but it didn't so it doesn't. Much like Henry Addington nearly a century-and-a-half earlier Chamberlain learned the hard way that dictators cannot be appeased, they understand only military might. Thus Chamberlain is remembered as an able administrator but a failure as a statesman.

Winston Churchill
(1940 — 1955)

In the long years to come not only will the people of this island but
of the world, wherever the bird of freedom chirps in human hearts,
look back to what we've done and they will say 'do not despair'…

Winston Churchill, 8 May 1945

To be the Deliverer of Europe, was a greater Character than to be
Conqueror of it

Daniel Defoe's *Whig*, 1692

WITH THE DEATH of Neville Chamberlain in November
1940 Winston Churchill inherited the leadership of the
Conservative Party. This was merely a formality as he was
already the most senior member of the Party in Parliament and
therefore had to become the leader, particularly when stability
was of such vital importance. His duties as Party leader were
hardly arduous, given that there was no structured opposition at
Westminster, Attlee now being a minister in the new Wartime
National Government. Churchill, therefore, could get on with
the job of governing the country and managing the war effort
without the distraction of Party politics.

That same month he began to compose a letter, only
sent in December, to President Roosevelt of the United States
in which Churchill argued that German military vessels in the
Atlantic were destroying British merchant ships at a rate that
would cripple the British war effort before long. The United
Kingdom could afford these ships protection close to home but
the Royal Navy could not guard them all the way to America as
they were needed to protect the Channel. Without assistance
the Nazis would soon win the war and America should be
obligated to assist because it was only trading with the US that
was bringing British ships into the Atlantic in the first place.
Roosevelt's response in 1941 was to use the US navy to protect
trading ships from the American coast until they got roughly
two-thirds of the way across the Atlantic.[1] This had been no
easy task given that Roosevelt had been elected President for a

third term in 1940 by pledging not to send American troops into another European War. The Prime Minister would have to work very hard, and indeed rely upon other factors, to ensure that the President changed his mind. The year 1940 ended with Eden replacing Halifax at the Foreign Office, Churchill spending Christmas in Chequers and, on 30 December, substantial areas of London being destroyed in an overnight Blitz attack.

The new year started badly in terms of Britain's fortunes in war. The Luftwaffe began targeting ports with the intention of disrupting trade. Liverpool, Manchester, Glasgow and Plymouth all suffered terribly.[2] In April Germany invaded Yugoslavia and Greece, both of which fell within a matter of days, further hurting British morale. However, the year would prove to be a turning point in the war.

In 1939 the Soviet Union had signed an accord with Germany in which both sides agreed to split the spoils of eastern Europe but that neither would attack the other. Almost immediately afterwards Germany had invaded Poland from the west and the USSR had invaded from the east, both sides stopping short of their agreed line of division. Throughout the early months of 1941 Hitler had started to fortify his positions on the eastern side of his territories and as early as April Churchill had written to the leader of the Soviet Union, Joseph Stalin, to warn him that Hitler would turn on him. Stalin was convinced that Hitler would not break their pact, at least until Britain was defeated.

On 22 June German forces launched an invasion of the Soviet Union. Churchill became aware soon after and, in spite of his lifelong crusade against the dangers of socialism, he committed every minute from that point onwards to assuring Stalin of his support. Every significant observer – Churchill and Hitler among them – fully expected the Soviet army to be defeated easily by the Germans. For Churchill this did not matter, the fact that the Germans would have another front to manage was a positive sign. However, the Red Army fared better than expected and managed to hold the Germans off through the summer and autumn. At this point Hitler's army would have to suffer a harsh Russian winter, which it was completely unprepared for.

In August Churchill met with Roosevelt in Newfoundland. For the Prime Minister the occasion was a chance to build relations that might one day bring America into the war. In the short term it may at least result in the United States issuing a warning to Japan not to act on any ambitions she may have to take control of British territories in the Far East, which had become a genuine concern over the preceding months. For the President the meeting was a diplomatic gesture and nothing more. There would be no lectures delivered to the Japanese (why risk making a statement which he may be forced to act upon when only a year previously he had won an historic third term as President by promising to avoid war?) and he had no intention of supporting, militarily at least, the British war effort. The meeting was pleasant enough but wholly unproductive.

In terms of the Japanese, Churchill's suspicions had been well founded. They had imperial ambitions in south-east Asia and throughout 1941 had become convinced that, in spite of Roosevelt's unwillingness to make a public declaration, if they attacked British territories in the region the United States would interfere. They therefore developed a strategy to prevent American interference by disrupting the US naval fleet in the Pacific. On 7 December Japan launched an unannounced air strike on the US naval base at Pearl Harbor, Hawaii, which resulted in the US declaring war on Japan. Churchill got extremely excited by the development and arranged a visit to the United States for the following week. Eden was horrified, pointing out the he was about to leave for the Soviet Union to speak with Stalin and so, with the Prime Minister and Foreign Secretary out of the country at the same time, who would be conducting the war?[3] Had Churchill even considered it?

Things started to move quickly from that point. On 11 December Germany and Italy both declared war on the United States in order to demonstrate their solidarity with Japan. This sealed their fates: America would be entering the war in Europe. So Churchill headed west to meet with Roosevelt while Eden travelled east to see Stalin. One of these meetings would be far more productive than the other. In the Soviet Union the Foreign Secretary found that Stalin had already drawn up some proposals which he expected Eden to accept on behalf of Britain. His plan was for an agreement now on a post-war settlement, should the allies be successful. In this plan the West would recognise the USSR's current frontiers including their absorption of Romania and eastern Poland. Britain had entered the war against Germany due to their invasion of Poland from the west so Eden could not recognise the Soviet's claims to territories in eastern Europe.[4] After a few days of talks Eden undertook to take the proposals to Churchill despite knowing that the answer would still be no.

On the other side of the Atlantic Roosevelt and Churchill were busy establishing the United Nations and, to Churchill's delight, he found that the US command was adopting a 'Germany First' strategy for the war.[5] The Prime Minister had been concerned that America – understandably given the events that had brought them into the war in the first place – would be focused on the conflict with Japan and rather indifferent to their German foes. On the contrary, US military strategists had determined that in order to defeat the Axis powers Germany must be routed first, after which the other nations would soon capitulate.

However, if anybody had any expectations that the war would be a smooth operation from that point onwards they would be sorely disappointed. The early months of 1942 were nothing short of a disaster. On Christmas Day 1941 Japan conquered Hong Kong when the Governor surrendered after eighteen days of fighting. In February 1942 British forces in Singapore were overwhelmed by a Japanese offensive. By this point it seemed that Japan was going to march through South-East Asia with Britain powerless to put up any reasonable form of resistance. During the Japanese conquest of Singapore three German naval ships escaped a Royal navy blockade in the north Atlantic and then, with a chutzpah not seen on the sea since the time of Nelson, proceeded through the English Channel back to German ports.[6] This humiliation hit British morale hard.

In April an American delegation arrived in Britain to suggest that a joint Anglo-American operation should be launched sending ground troops into northern France. The idea was to provide a Western Front for battle in order to relieve the Soviets on the Eastern Front. Churchill was agreeable to this idea but the timetable pushed for by the Americans (spring 1943 at the latest, possibly even autumn of 1942)[7] would undoubtedly have left the allies at a disadvantage. As if to demonstrate just how difficult it would be to land troops on a heavily fortified coast Britain organised the Dieppe Raid for 19 August 1942.

6,000 troops, predominantly Canadian, landed at Dieppe, Northern France, at 5 a.m., 19 August. Within six hours they were retreating. 1,000 were dead and a further 2,000 captured.

Before this doomed raid, though, Churchill would have to face down a no confidence vote in the House of Commons, focused on the direction of the war. The motion was moved by Sir John Wardlaw-Milne, a Conservative MP and the debate scheduled for 1 and 2 July. Churchill did not speak until the second day and he recorded an overwhelming victory (477 to 25) but the fact that the debate had occurred at all was damaging. During it Aneurin Bevan, whom history would remember for the Bevan report and subsequent establishment of the National Health Service, commented that Churchill was excellent at winning debates while losing battles.[8] Given the backdrop of the military defeats earlier in the year the point was not lost.

Meanwhile the Allied powers could not agree on a co-ordinated strategy for the war effort. The Soviets were committed to fighting on their own front and so kept up the pressure for a second front in Europe to relieve their troops. The Americans, who had been in favour of Operation Sledgehammer – a plan to land troops in Europe to open up the second front – right up until the Dieppe fiasco (some even being in favour afterwards) were won round by Churchill's argument that any European landings at this point would end in disaster. He instead pushed for Operation Torch, which would be a concerted effort to take North Africa from the Nazis and push them back into Europe before retaking the home continent via the Mediterranean. At the end of October British and German forces engaged at el-Alamein, northern Egypt, which resulted in over two weeks of conflict that eventually saw Britain victorious. The end of the Battle of el-Alamein coincided with the beginning of Operation Torch, which was allowed to operate a lot more smoothly as a result of the Germans being stalled in Egypt. Now the tide of the war began to turn. A week after its commencement Operation Torch had resulted in the Allies taking control of French Algeria. The Battle of Stalingrad, which had begun in August 1942 ended in February 1943 with a decisive Soviet victory in defending their city. Consequently, by the beginning of 1943 the Allied position was a lot more positive than it had been even six months earlier.

In the first week of July the Germans assaulted the Eastern Front for what would be the last time and Britain and the US captured Sicily from the Italians. King Victor

Emmanuel III of Italy now decided that Benito Mussolini's position was untenable and, on 25 July, had him dismissed and arrested. Marshal Pietro Badoglio replaced Mussolini and at once entered into negotiations with the Allies. The momentum had now shifted decisively away from the Axis powers.

Now Churchill, Stalin and Roosevelt began to give serious consideration to an Allied invasion of Western Europe, the plans codenamed Operation Overlord. There were disagreements about who would be the Supreme Commander for Overlord, with Churchill eventually conceding that it should be an American, given that once the Operation reached its climax there would be more US troops involved than British ones. Dwight Eisenhower, the US General, was eventually named in December. Once Operation Torch had been completed in the spring of 1943 and Northern Africa secured, the Allies started to consider the late spring-early summer of 1944 as a possible date for Overlord. Indeed during the first few months of 1944 the Allies launched assaults on Italy, which had been invaded by the Nazis immediately after Italian withdrawal from the war, which progressed steadily northward and encouraged further speculation about landings in northern France to create a pincer movement against the Germans.

For three years Churchill had stalled putting British boots on the ground in France, withstanding intense pressure from Stalin and even an enthusiasm for the idea from Roosevelt, on the basis that he felt it would be futile and many would be killed in vain. Now the reasons for deferring were becoming fewer and farther between. In the end Overlord was set for 6 June, which became known in Allied circles as D-Day. The invasion of Europe by Allied forces commenced in the early morning of that day with around 1,200 planes bombing the coast of Normandy to pave the way for around 5,000 ships carrying foot soldiers to the shores. The beaches were captured almost immediately but then came a period of impasse which evoked fears of another trench war as had happened in 1914-18. By the end of July, though, the Allies broke through and began a steady march southwards, capturing Paris on 24 August.[9]

The rest of 1944 saw international conferences in which the post-war-world was divided between the victorious nations, albeit rather prematurely. Churchill agreed that the USSR could be given a free hand in the Balkans in exchange for British control of Greece. Roosevelt remained aloof from much of the discussions towards the end of the year, instead fighting a Presidential election and then preparing for his historic fourth inauguration in January 1945. (Curiously FDR is remembered favourably by many Americans yet one of the first acts of his successor, Harry S. Truman, was to introduce the 22nd Amendment to the US Constitution imposing a two-term maximum limit on Presidential tenures, so that Roosevelt's long Presidency could never be repeated).

Once the Germans had been pushed back as far as northern Italy from the south and near to their own frontiers from the French side the war began to look as though only one outcome was possible. This fully justified the Allies' redrawing of European maps in anticipation of a settlement. However, it was not all plain sailing. In mid-December 1944 Hitler launched a westward counter-offensive, intended to move their frontiers back into France and, significantly, to recapture the Belgian port of Antwerp, which was of strategic importance. The conflict later became known as the Battle of the Bulge and the Germans advanced rather successfully for the two weeks leading up to Christmas 1944 at which time they were halted. They would never again get further west than they did at that point.

During Christmas Churchill visited Athens to oversee the plans for a post-war British controlled Greece. Communist guerrillas in the country had been making revolutionary noises and a Communist Greece was an abomination as far as Churchill was concerned. He was only able to tolerate Stalin on the basis that Hitler was worse.

In the new year Churchill could almost see the peaceful light at the end of the tunnel of war. In February he took the decision to intensify air attacks on German cities, hoping to bring the war to a quick end. The decision was controversial because civilians were being killed rather than soldiers. That said in Churchill's mind he was trying to save British lives by forcing the war to its conclusion without soldiers having to go into direct conflict. In the middle of February the German city of Dresden was almost entirely destroyed in two days of intensive assaults from both the RAF and USAF.[10]

Before this, though, came the Yalta Conference. On the surface this was just another gathering between the three Allied leaders and their Foreign Secretaries. In the event it served to determine, once and for all, issues which had been skirted around throughout the duration of the war, namely what would happen to Poland once the conflict came to an end. Stalin was determined that he should be allowed to keep the ground that his country had taken in 1939 and that the Poles could be compensated by taking land from eastern Germany. Since taking over as Prime Minister in 1940 Churchill had been saying that this was not acceptable given that Britain had declared war on Germany on the basis that they had violated Poland's neutrality. He had hoped for Roosevelt's support in getting Stalin to back down but the President was decidedly weak at the conference, which disappointed everybody in the British contingent.[11] His health was starting to fail him and his powers of concentration were not up to the task of managing an international summit of this magnitude. Alone arguing against Stalin, Churchill knew that war with Russia over Poland was impossible. Furthermore, he knew that Stalin was aware that Britain could not commit to this. The Soviets would be moving into eastern Europe.

On 12 April President Roosevelt died, meaning that the remainder of the war would be overseen by his successor, Harry S. Truman. The following weeks saw the collapse of the German resistance, although the push came from the power in the East, rather than the West. While British and American forces were held up in Italy and western Germany, the Red Army of the Soviet Union took Vienna, Prague and Berlin by the end of April. On 30 April Adolf Hitler committed suicide and on 7 May the Germans surrendered, bringing to an end the war in Europe.[12] For Churchill, this just meant that the battleground had shifted from Europe to Britain, as now the political calm generated by the coalition government over which he presided was to be replaced by the norm of partisan politics at home. This was best symbolised by that most partisan of events, a general election. Churchill offered Attlee to remain in the government until after the defeat of Japan, the war with which was still ongoing. However, by the end of May the Labour Party had declined this offer, bringing to an end the great wartime coalition government.

The Conservatives, although disappointed that Labour had withdrawn so soon, actually believed that this favoured them electorally as Churchill would give them a great deal of popularity with the memories of VE Day still fresh in the minds of many. Churchill, to the British public, embodied the national victory: he had not only been the man whom had foreseen the evil of Hitler, not only been the leader throughout the thick and thin of the war, but he had been the most visible politician on VE Day, making various speeches throughout the day which reflected the national mood of relief and celebration and giving his famous 'V for Victory' salute.

Parliament was dissolved for a July election and right up until the count Churchill held out hope for a victory. While Labour campaigned on a platform of social reform and the introduction of a National Health Service, Churchill relied on his reputation as a successful war leader to get him re-elected during times of peace. The defeat was crushing. The Conservatives were reduced to 197 seats (although there were 15 National Liberals in alliance with them), with Labour taking 393 seats and the Liberals only 12.[13] On 26 July Churchill met with the King to resign as Prime Minister, making way for his former Deputy Prime Minister, Clement Attlee. There is no evidence that there was any serious suggestion of replacing Churchill as leader of the Party at this point, although Eden may well have felt (with some justification) that his time had long since come.

Churchill attended the State Opening of Parliament in August, gave a benevolent oration at the debate on the King's Speech and then retired abroad for the rest of the summer to relax. The war with Japan had come to an abrupt end when President Truman ordered the dropping of an atomic bomb over the city of Hiroshima on 6 August and then Nagasaki on the 9th. The Japanese surrender was formalised within a week of the second bomb meaning that Britain could now focus on rebuilding. The Conservative Party would also have to consider rebuilding as they had been shattered in an election in spite of Churchill's popularity. It seems that the British public were sold on Attlee's vision of a fairer Britain with social security for people of all ages and free healthcare for all, whereas the Conservatives represented a return to the domestic instability of the 1920s and 30s, which had seen recession, depression and the General Strike. The problem for the Conservatives was that Churchill was not overly interested. Throughout the war he had been obsessed with managing the strategy but had given little consideration to domestic policy, instead leaving this to Attlee. Now he wasn't overly bothered about organising policy or giving a structured opposition to the government. When

Labour were eventually defeated at the polls it was more a matter of them burning themselves out than of Churchill offering an attractive alternative. It could be argued that Churchill could hardly be blamed: he had faced off the Battle of Britain and given the nation the most important victory in its history. What else could compare with that? The fact is that Churchill was more interested in glory than he was in the mundane management of the nation. Throughout his entire career he had been excited by the big events (leading the admiralty during the Great War, facing down the Trades Unions in the General Strike, leading the country during the Second World War) but had become bored during more tranquil times. On these occasions he could only entertain himself by taking on his own Party (he quit Parliament when demoted by Asquith, he resigned from Baldwin's front bench when they were in opposition, he attacked his own government for their international policy in the 1930s to keep himself interested). Now he was happy to leave Party administration to Eden and others and he would only become involved again if it meant a triumphant return to Number 10.

In early 1946 Churchill visited the Unites States and whilst there made one of his most prophetic speeches, in which he stated that the United Nations allies should no longer pretend that they are all equally close to each other. He claimed, in reference to the Soviet Union, that 'from Stettin in the Baltic to Trieste in the Adriatic, an iron curtain has descended across the continent. Behind that line lie all the capitals of the ancient states of Central and Eastern Europe: Warsaw, Berlin, Prague, Vienna, Budapest, Belgrade, Bucharest and Sofia. All these famous cities and the populations around them lie in what I must call the Soviet sphere.' His whole period in opposition would be memorable for incidents like this: Churchill playing the world statesman while domestic politics was left behind at home, for men such as Eden, Rab Butler and Harold Macmillan to manage.

Not surprisingly, therefore, the Conservative Party did not fair particularly well in opposition. Macmillan, having lost his seat in the Labour landslide victory of July 1945, won a by-election in the late autumn of that year to return to the Commons.[14] However, that was the last victory the Conservatives won during that parliamentary term. Between the end of 1945 and 1950 they lost every by-election that they contested.[15]

One benefit of Churchill's foreign endeavours was that he was determined to bring security to the world following the war and his prestige allowed him influence in the far corners of the globe. NATO would be established in 1949 following US acceptance of his 'Iron Curtain' warning. Furthermore, he pushed for a Council of Europe to debate matters of conflict rather than resorting to arms as had happened in 1914 and 1939. This was established in Strasbourg, again in 1949 and would eventually evolve into what we now call the European Union.

One area in which Churchill had clashed with the government was over Home Rule for India. Very early on in their term the Labour government made up its mind that India needed to be given independence and with their majority there was nothing that the opposition could do about it. The idea was abhorrent to Churchill, who not only believed that India was one of the most important pieces of the Empire, but had personally fought so hard for it several times throughout his life. In the late 1890s he had been stationed in Bombay as a cavalryman in the British army. During Baldwin's flirtations with the idea of giving India dominion status in the late 1920s-early 1930s he had fought hard against his leader, harming his own career in the process. Now he was powerless to stop the transition and, even worse, the government split India into two nations: one for Hindus and one for Muslims, the latter subsequently renamed Pakistan.

This aside, the five years of Conservative opposition until 1950 were lacklustre. Churchill seemed to expect that it was a matter of waiting his turn and that re-election was not necessarily something that had to be worked for. Come 1950 an election was due and now the traditional dirt throwing that accompanies Party politics began. Polling day was set for 23 February[16] and so the Parliament that broke up for Christmas in 1949 never again met before being dissolved in January 1950. The Party had little reason to feel confident in 1950, given that they had not provided much in the way of opposition for half a decade, but they were. Many of the faces that would shape the next thirty years of politics were returned to Parliament during that election, including Churchill, Eden, Macmillan, Edward Heath, Enoch Powell, Reginald Maudling and Angus Maude, which may have accounted for the optimism – a combination of naivety, brought about by a lack of experience, and self-assuredness, brought about by those people being who they were.

In the sense that the Party was able to claw itself back from the nadir of 1945 they had every right to feel positive about the result. However, they were still denied victory. The results were that Labour still held an overall majority (just) with 315 seats. The Conservatives took 298 and the Liberals just nine.[17] Churchill now found himself in a quandary. He had led the Conservatives in opposition presumably because he felt that he could become Prime Minister again following another election. However, with a five year parliamentary term in front of him he had to consider how realistic his chances were of returning to Downing Street. In the spring of 1950 he was already seventy-five years old. If the Parliament should run to a full term he would be eighty at the next election. If he planned to contest that plebiscite as Leader of the Conservative Party, he could potentially be eighty-five years old before his next term as Prime Minister came to an end. He must also have known that others were considering the same thing and Eden, loyal though he was, must have been an attractive prospect to a Party that was becoming frustrated with life in opposition.

Churchill consoled himself that because of the slenderness of Labour's majority another election would have to be called within a few months, meaning that he had a chance of seeing out his next term whilst still in his seventies. He probably remembered how his father was one of Gladstone's staunchest opponents while the Grand Old Man was well into his eighties but that nobody within his own party had dared to challenge him because of his stature. If his plan was to succeed, though, he would need to provide some genuine opposition. Another term like the last and the government could coast through in spite of its fragile majority because there was nobody to bring them down. If the government must fall – and Churchill's only hope of becoming Prime Minister again relied on it falling soon – then he would have to attack relentlessly over the coming months.

In June the Korean War broke out when North Korea, supported by the USSR and China, invaded South Korea. The USA got involved and asked for British support, which it received. Churchill was fully in favour of supporting the American military campaign but this did not sit well with his new policy of out-and-out opposition. Consequently he attacked the government for its lack of military preparedness and for mismanagement of the armed forces. Given who the speaker was, the allegations carried a lot of weight. The end of the session in August could not come quickly enough for Attlee, who was tired after nearly six years in government and one year of sustained attacks from Churchill. His ministers were also tired and many of them would not survive in politics for another full year.[18]

When 1951 came around Churchill intensified his attacks. Now, more desperate than ever to force an early election, he challenged every government motion, inciting his followers to do the same and to make long, drawn out speeches in the process. The strategy was brilliant. Losing a vote is devastating to a government, who must at all times demonstrate that they have the confidence of the House. The same pressure does not apply to the opposition, who could therefore afford to challenge anything and everything. Consequently, in order to maintain their dignity the Labour Party was ordering its members to turn out to all divisions in order to vote, just to keep the ship afloat. The problem with this was that the Conservatives in general, and Churchill in particular, made lengthy perorations at every turn, dragging debates often into the early hours of the morning and occasionally past daybreak the following day. Roy Jenkins recorded that the 1951 session was 'the most burdensome summer of all my thirty-four years in the House of Commons.'[19]

The tactic worked. By the middle of the year Aneurin Bevan, who had started the year as the successful Minister for Health who had created the NHS, resigned from the government before Easter; Ernest Bevin began the year as Foreign Secretary but by April was dead; Attlee himself had to take a month off with an ulcer, possibly caused by stress. As soon as the session was over Churchill went off to holiday in Europe while Attlee took the time to rest before asking the King to dissolve Parliament, unable to face another Opening. The election date was set for 25 October, which Churchill knew would be his last opportunity to return to Number 10.

The Conservatives fought a moderate campaign, arguing for reconciliation rather than division along party lines. Labour looked as tired as they had seemed during the session, and the result reflected this: 321 Conservatives; 295 Labour MPs; six Liberals.[20] Churchill was Prime Minister once again.

In forming his cabinet he brought Eden back to the Foreign Office, Rab Butler in as Chancellor of the Exchequer and Harold Macmillan as Housing Minister. Although he was back in power speculation was already rife, owing to his age, about when Churchill would be retiring. The Prime Minister was well aware of this and in order to combat it he set about using delaying tactics: any opportunity to suggest that it was not quite time to go was seized upon. The first being a change in monarchy, the transition for which needed continuity of management, he would argue.

On 6 February 1952 King George VI died. He had been ill for some time with various ailments including lung cancer. Although Churchill had argued strongly in the late 1930s for the retention of King Edward VIII as monarch, as a true Tory he was staunchly loyal to whoever was on the throne. When King George took over in 1938 he was no exception, but there is little to suggest that their working relationship – so important during the years of the war in which the King supported his Prime Minister throughout – was not based on genuine mutual affection, as opposed to a forced loyalty. Consequently Churchill was genuinely affected when the King passed away. That notwithstanding he used the event as an opportunity both to postpone discussion of his retirement until after the coronation of Queen Elizabeth II (scheduled for sixteen months later) and to impress the new Queen. In relation to this last point, he knew that her reign was likely to be a long one and therefore wanted to ensure that his period with her would be memorable as against the countless premiers to follow him.

For the most part 1952-53 was otherwise a quiet time for Churchill. His Party had for the most part accepted that he should remain for the monarchical transition, the Labour Party was too busy recovering to offer any substantial form of opposition and there were no real issues of contention that arose over which he could be challenged by the public. He knew that his real test would come in mid-1953 when the coronation was done with and he would have to find another strategy to defer the question of his retirement.[21]

That is exactly what happened. In March 1953 Stalin died, which Churchill interpreted as a sign that improved relations with the USSR may be on the horizon. However, others noted that of the great wartime leaders (Roosevelt,

Stalin, Churchill) two were dead, their time had clearly come
and gone, so Churchill's number must also soon be up. Then, at
the end of June, almost as if to prove the point of the doubters,
Churchill suffered a stroke which left him temporarily unable
to fulfil his duties. Luckily for him Eden, as the only viable
alternative as a leader, was also incapacitated having had, and
requiring further, operations on his gall bladder. It has been
argued strongly by more than one historian that, had Eden been
healthy in 1953, the premiership would have been his then.[22] The
Foreign Secretary would undergo three operations that year
and be removed from politics for much of it. Throughout the
summer Butler led the government in the absence of its two
senior members. We now know, given what was to come in the
following decade, that Butler had Prime Ministerial
aspirations, trying (and failing) on two occasions to obtain the
Conservative Party Leadership. 1953 was not such an occasion.
With nobody to oppose him this would have been his strongest
opportunity to take power but he didn't attempt to *carpe* that
particular *diem.*

        By autumn Churchill had made a full recovery, just in
time to discover that he had been awarded the Nobel Prize for
Literature. In December there was a summit between French
Prime Minister Laniel, US President Eisenhower and
Churchill, held in Bermuda. During the meeting Eisenhower
declared that he would use nuclear weapons against China or
North Korea if either breached their frontiers in the Korean
War, much to the horror of Eden, who was also present. By all
accounts Eisenhower, possibly not unsurprisingly for a former
general, came across as a belligerent warmonger.[23]

        Into 1954 and the pressure for Churchill to go
intensified. The press appeared to assume it was inevitable, his
Cabinet had begun to notice that his mental powers were not
what they once were, and Eden was back to full strength,
looking more like a leader-in-waiting than a loyal and
subordinate Foreign Minister. As the winter transformed into
spring it seemed that the only option was for a retirement at the
end of the parliamentary session that summer. However, the
Prime Minister had visions of himself securing world peace by
striking an agreement between Eisenhower and Stalin's
successor as Soviet leader, Georgy Malenkov. Clearly, one
Nobel Prize was not enough.

        With yet another international triumph at his mind's
fore Churchill flew to the United States at the end of June where

he managed to get Eisenhower to agree to meet with Malenkov in principle. Phase one was complete. Aboard the ship on the way home Churchill sent a telegram, against Eden's advice, to the Kremlin proposing a summit and stating that Eisenhower desired it. This is the point at which his plans came tumbling down around him. Firstly, the Cabinet rebelled in their next meeting once Churchill returned to Britain, some claiming that they could not support a summit and others affronted that they had not been consulted. Eden sided with the dissenters on the basis that he had warned Churchill about the need for collective responsibility before the Prime Minister had sent his telegram.

Next, Eisenhower messaged London reprimanding Churchill for making an approach to the Soviets without first allowing him to proof the language of the text. Lastly came the Soviet response. It was positive in that they wanted a meeting but they required terms to be met that rendered the summit pointless, at least insofar as Churchill personally securing world peace was concerned.

Even with all of this going against him Churchill could not be persuaded to retire immediately. Eden was waiting in the wings but not strong enough to strike the *coup de grâce*. In fact their relationship at this point was very much like that of Blair and Brown fifty years later: there was the master who had brought glory to a discredited Party; the loyal colleague who had been promised an inheritance that never seemed to materialise; the one irritated by the impatience of the other while the other was frustrated by the determination of the one to remain; finally neither could eliminate the other as a rival without destroying their own electoral prospects in the process as it would surely split the Party and create an ugly public spectacle.

Churchill saw out the year at Chequers, having had a difficult final Cabinet at the end of December in which his ministers had made it clear that they expected a firm decision from him as to when he would retire – no more vague suggestions and delaying tactics. When he next met with senior ministers in early January 1955 Churchill told them that Easter was the time.

There were several occasions between January and April when he faltered and considered reneging on this agreement. In the end, though, there was no dignified way to do it and, on 5 April, he duly attended the palace to resign.

Churchill had led the Conservative Party for fourteen-and-a-half years, through war and peace, and had retired as an octogenarian Prime Minister. In terms of political success he lost as many elections as he won during his leadership (one apiece) and undoubtedly the most successful of his two stints as Prime Minister was his first, for which he was unelected. That said following his election victory of 1951 the Conservatives would enjoy thirteen years of uninterrupted power.

Although Churchill led the Party for ten years following the end of the Second World War, he is remembered for his achievements as a wartime leader and not because of anything that followed. However, it was an incredible achievement and consistently in the decades that have followed Churchill has been voted by the people of the United Kingdom as being one of history's greatest Britons. During his time as Leader of the Conservative Party he prophetically nurtured relations with US President Roosevelt, correctly identifying the Anglo-American relationship as one which would win the war; he led British strategy during the war which saw his country victorious; he then became bored and lacklustre in opposition before ambling through his second term as Prime Minister, struggling with age and opposition from within his Party. Consequently as Leader of the Conservative Party his success was mixed, notwithstanding the fact that he is, quite rightly, remembered as a national hero.

Post-War Conservative Failures
(1945 – 1979)

THROUGHOUT ITS HISTORY the Conservative Party and its predecessor, the Tory Party, was ill at ease with itself. Its members struggled with their sense of identity. After all, what exactly *was* their identity? The Tories had been born out of Whigs and the Conservatives born out of a need to disassociate themselves from the Ultra Tories. Stated in the introduction was the point that the Tories had evolved their constitution over time in order to appeal to a changing electorate. However, with this constant change came a crisis of identity. In *Coningsby* Disraeli wrote that the Tories' 'policy was a mere pandering to public ignorance'.[1] When he went on to say that a Conservative government was 'Tory men and Whig measures'[2] what he meant was that the role of the Party seemed to be to conserve whatever it inherited. The Tories/Conservatives loved their country, they loved its traditions and its institutions. Whatever political party they were up against seemed to want to change all that and so must be opposed, whatever the cost. Then when changes were made by a Whig/Liberal/Labour government the next generation of Tories to come into power, rather than trying to reverse the trend, simply accepted it and defended the new status quo against further change.

Throughout the history of nineteenth century conservatism there was something of a defeatist attitude about the Conservative Party. They seemed to accept that radicalism would eventually win the day and their role was to hold it off for as long as possible. Hopefully nothing drastic would happen on their watch and they could pass the torch on to the next leader who came along to do the same.

Once the Second World War had been concluded Churchill needed another campaign to wage and he duly chose socialism as his new enemy. Whether he was warning of the evils of Stalinism abroad or in opposition to Attlee and Bevan at home, he was vehemently opposed to the socialist creed. Under him the Conservatives were against something specific, rather than just opposed to change in general. However, their attitude towards the campaign was incredibly similar to that of their nineteenth century forebears: socialist changes were inevitable, the best that can be hoped for is that they can be delayed. Margaret Thatcher noted that 'Almost every post-war Tory victory had been won on slogans such as 'Britain Strong and Free' or 'Set the People Free'. But in the fine print of policy, and especially in government, the Tory Party merely pitched camp in the long march to the left. It never tried seriously to reverse it.' The reason for this was that, although they believed in individual liberty and they desired personal freedoms, they also accepted, possibly subconsciously, that socialism was inevitable and that Britain was moving inexorably towards a planned economy and they were simply there to give their contemporaries a little longer without it.

This sense of defeatism stemmed from a lack of collective confidence. This is different from self-confidence, as there was no lack of that: Eden had been groomed for office for two decades before becoming Prime Minister; Macmillan had led men during the Great War and had led ministers since then; Douglas-Home had been raised by an Earl and took with him all the self-assuredness that an upper-class upbringing instils in a young man; Heath had been convinced by his mother from a young age that he was the centre of the universe and never seemed to have forgotten it. However, there was a collective lack of confidence in conservatism as a doctrine. Their purpose had initially been to oppose change because they were traditionalists, now it was to oppose socialism because they were libertarian, but that was the extent of their collective identity. In other words, whereas it was easy for Labour to understand *why* their Party pursued certain policies (they had a written Party constitution which set out their ideals) the Conservatives were not entirely certain *why* they supported or opposed what they did. With a change of leader could come a change in direction, which bred uncertainty and, consequently, led to their defeatist nature.

By the 1980s a new form of conservatism had emerged. It was committed to free markets, to small government and reduced state interference, to free trade, to free enterprise and privatisation of business wherever possible. Not everybody agreed with the doctrine (in fact it created a dislike of the Tories that had never before existed) but at least they had a doctrine of their own. The Conservatives had a set of values, just like the Labour Party did and this brought about a sense of Party pride, to go with the resentment generated in their opponents, which had also not existed before. Eventually this new conservatism not only reversed the socialist trends set in the period from 1945-79, curbing the power of trades unions, privatising formerly nationalised industries and creating a competitive economy, but they made the Labour Party unelectable to the point where they had to reform their constitution in order to survive politically. Significantly, Clause IV of their constitution, which committed the Party to public ownership of industry, was abandoned when Tony Blair became leader of the Labour Party. He saw this as one of his crowning achievements.[4]

Each of the leaders who took the Conservative Party forward between Churchill's resignation in 1955 and Thatcher's nomination as leader in 1975 had their own successes and limitations. However, all of them noted that the economy was struggling and that their principle task was to rescue it, all of them were sceptical of socialism as a doctrine, yet none of them challenged it head-on and none of them had any real success in limiting its effects.

Anthony Eden
(1955 – 1957)

Israel and Egypt are locked in conflict in that area. The first and urgent task is to separate those combatants and to stabilise the position. That is our purpose.

Anthony Eden, 1 November 1956

A whole Party ought not to share the Miscarriages of some few particular Men

Daniel Defoe's *Tory*, 1692

EDEN KISSED HANDS on 6 April 1955 and decided to retain most of Churchill's Cabinet. Harold Macmillan replaced him as Foreign Secretary but aside from that Rab Butler remained as Chancellor of the Exchequer and Robert Gascoyne-Cecil, 5th Marquess of Salisbury and grandson of the Victorian Prime Minister, was retained as Lord President of the Council. Of minor importance at the time, but significant due to later developments, the Earl of Home entered the Cabinet in the junior position of Minister for Commonwealth Relations.[1]

Nine days later the new Prime Minister announced that Parliament would be dissolved the following month for a general election on 26 May.[2] The election – a brave decision for a Prime Minister who risked being remembered as the shortest-lived of all time – resulted in a triumph for Eden. The Conservatives increased their share of seats to 345, with Labour winning 277 and the Liberals 6.[3] If his electoral success had led Eden to expect a leisurely honeymoon period he was to be sorely disappointed. Within days it was all hands on deck as a State of Emergency was declared following a locomotive drivers' strike on 29 May, which intensified an already difficult situation with dock workers having walked out weeks earlier. By mid-June Eden had managed to get the workers' unions and the TUC into negotiations which proved successful insofar as they ended the strikes. Union leaders at this time are generally believed to have been less militant than their successors,[4] however, Eden was still prepared to give up a lot in negotiations in order to get a settlement.

Then in July he was to attend a Heads of Government summit in Geneva from the 18th – 23rd, which the Presidents of France and the United States as well as the leader of the Soviet Union would also be attending. Eden had seen too much of international politics over the past two decades to have had any real hopes of achieving an agreement over mutual disarmament and, consequently, he cannot have been as disappointed as he might have been when nothing was settled in Geneva.

For the rest of the year the Prime Minister was plagued with difficulties both at home and abroad. In foreign affairs Cyprus, currently under British control, was pushing for unification with Greece. This was unacceptable to Britain on the basis that Cyprus was strategically important: the Middle East was becoming increasingly unstable, the creation of the Israeli state following the Second World War had led to conflict between the Arabs and the Israelis. Britain had many interests in the region, not least in terms of oil supply and the Suez Canal, so a military base in the South Mediterranean (that is, Cyprus) was advantageous. Ostensibly Eden cited concerns for the Turkish minority in Cyprus as the reason for denying the people their right to self-determination.

At home the economy was undergoing a natural slowdown in growth. The cyclical nature of economics is such that growth could not continue as it had done in the early 1950s indefinitely and there was little Eden could do to prevent it. However, as the Prime Minister he was inevitably associated with the declining living standards that followed.

To make matters worse politically, Attlee stepped down as Leader of the Labour Party in December. Well into his seventies, Attlee was in this sense at least at an electoral disadvantage to Eden, who was yet to turn sixty. He was replaced by Hugh Gaitskell, a forty-nine year old MP of moderate standing – far more appealing than the hard Left of the Party, who had become an electoral liability (at a later time Gaitskell would even take the radical step, albeit unsuccessfully, of proposing the abolition of the controversial Clause IV).

Despondent at how his first calendar year was ending and hoping for something better from 1956, Eden reshuffled his

Cabinet at the end of December. Macmillan, who had clashed with the Prime Minister several times over Middle East policy, was moved to the Treasury, where it was believed he would be less of a nuisance. Butler was made Lord Privy Seal and Leader of the House of Commons, while Selwyn Lloyd replaced Macmillan at the Foreign Office.

In January 1956 Eden visited Washington for a summit meeting to discuss, *inter alia*, the situation in the Middle East. During 1955 Israel had conducted air strikes against Palestinians living in Gaza. Gamal Abdel Nasser, Prime Minister of Egypt, had wanted to retaliate and had requested that the United States supply Egypt with the arms to do it. When the US refused Egypt acquired the necessary equipment from Czechoslovakia. The concern by the turn of the year was that Egypt was entering the Soviet sphere of influence, rather than remaining within the sphere of the West.

Now Nasser wished to build a dam, known as the Aswan High Dam, in the river Nile in order to prevent flooding when the tide was high. Eden was concerned that Nasser would turn to the Soviets for finance for the project, as he had done with arms, unless the West provided it. Allowing the USSR to finance a dam in the Nile was not just to risk them having influence in Egypt, it gave them a vested interest in Egyptian waterways, which the Prime Minister saw as a threat to British interests on the Suez Canal. He intended to raise the matter in Washington. Eisenhower was sceptical about the chances of the Soviet Union financing the dam, but Eden was forceful and the pair agreed to explore a joint Western proposal.

Eden's return to Britain was not a happy one. Almost immediately he found himself at loggerheads with Macmillan, who was apparently able to make mischief wherever he was stationed. Macmillan confronted the Prime Minister about inflationary pressures in the economy and suggested that subsidies on bread and milk should be removed or reduced. Eden had previously made public declarations pledging to keep food subsidies in place and so refused Macmillan's request. However, the Chancellor threatened to resign if he didn't get his way and so the Prime Minister was faced with a dilemma: should he let Macmillan go potentially to create trouble for him from outside the Cabinet, or should he give in to him, awarding him a victory as well as costing himself capital with the electorate.? In the event he chose the latter course.

The only success that Eden could claim in the early months of 1956 was a visit to Britain by the Soviet leader Nikita Khrushchev in the April. The visit did not go particularly well for the Prime Minister but the fact that a Soviet leader had attended Britain at all could be interpreted as a step forward.

Throughout this time Eden's government was negotiating with Eisenhower's administration over the conditions that should be attached to Western financing of the Aswan High Dam, including preventing Egyptian trade with the USSR and keeping Western influence in the region. By mid-July Nasser had accepting all caveats imposed on his country but by this time American enthusiasm for the project – never warm in the first place – had cooled considerably. On the 19th the US administration, influenced by a belief in Congress that no support should be given to a nation intent on destroying Israel, issued a public communiqué declaring its withdrawal from the project.[5]

One week later – on 26 July – Nasser announced that he was nationalising the Suez Canal. The end had begun for Eden. The following day, 27 July, Eden's thoughts were entirely focused towards military action to re-secure the Canal. It is difficult to understand today why the Egyptian Prime Minister nationalising an Egyptian Dam was so controversial. However, there were at least two international treaties signed by Egypt which guaranteed French and British autonomy over the Canal. Most oil imported to Britain came via Suez so, even though access to India was no longer a factor post-independence, the Canal was still vital for the British economy. Eden knew that he needed American support to launch a military campaign and must have felt that Eisenhower would be willing to back him at this stage. Consequently, throughout August Britain and France discussed military options while trying to persuade the Americans to put diplomatic pressure on Nasser to back down. However, the Egyptian leader, if ever he considered capitulating, which is unlikely, was emboldened by an announcement by Eisenhower on 4 September that he was committed to a peaceful solution and nothing more.

Eden, having been outspoken on the need to reverse Nasser's nationalisation of the Canal and also being leader of the more imperialist of the major UK political parties, looked set to come out very embarrassed if the US did not back him in the use of force. The French were in favour of launching an assault anyway but Eden wanted American support. So when the United States suggested yet another summit in September, Eden agreed, hoping that Nasser would either desist in the meantime or else deliver a further *casus belli.* The French were more realistic, well aware that neither was likely to happen and that another discussion simply delayed the inevitable and made it look less necessary in the process.

The meeting of the Suez Canal Users' Association (SCUA) took place in London from 19-22 September. During the summit the American delegation seemed to advocate Eden's worst fears: proposals should be put to Nasser, if he rejected them he should be criticised but no enforcement should take place. Within hours of the end of the conference Britain and France had referred the case to the United Nations Security Council. It was scheduled to be heard on 5 October. It is hard to understand what they hoped to achieve from putting their case to the UNSC. After all, the Soviet Union was a permanent member of the Security Council meaning that any Western request for support for the use of force would be vetoed. Likewise any similar requests from the Warsaw Pact nations would be vetoed by the Western powers. The UNSC was a redundant vehicle at this time.

Further complicating matters for Eden was Macmillan. The Chancellor was clearly emerging as a darling of the Tory Right and he made it clear in a Cabinet meeting at the beginning of October that should Eden try to negotiate a settlement with Nasser, rather than delivering a show of strength, he would resign. What was more, he informed the Prime Minister that his followers felt the same way. The Prime Minister, therefore, had only three options. Firstly he could back down to Nasser, look weak to the public and undoubtedly face calls for his resignation, which he was unlikely to overcome. Secondly he could negotiate with Nasser, lose Macmillan and that entire wing of his Party, which he needed. Thirdly he could resort to arms but in doing so he would alienate the moderates in the Conservative Party who felt that peace was worth any price. It would also have the effect of strengthening the opposition who were united behind appeasement as well as angering the Americans, who had been Britain's staunchest allies for fifteen years.

It was an impossible decision only made possible by a French proposal of 14 October. The French were in favour of military force but needed Eden onside, not least because Britain had an air force that France could not hope to match. Consequently they concocted a pretext for invasion. The French plan was that Israel would first attack Egypt and then move troops towards the Suez Canal. Britain and France would then send troops to the Canal to keep the warring parties separate and therefore the invasion would be a peacekeeping mission rather than an act of aggression. Eden and Lloyd flew to Paris on 16 October to discuss the plan with their French counterparts and came away resolved to sell the idea to the Cabinet. It was put to their colleagues whether, should Israel invade Egypt, Britain should defend Egypt. They declared that Britain should not. The question was then put to them whether, if an Israeli invasion threatened the Suez Canal, Britain should intervene. There was some dissent but the overall atmosphere was positive. Rab Butler proved to be the notable exception.[6]

At this point Eden would forever be able to deny foreknowledge of a plot to remove Nasser's control of the Canal. This deniability disintegrated on 21 October when the French Cabinet informed him that Israel was unwilling to invade Egypt without active support from Britain first. Lloyd was despatched to Paris to meet an Israeli delegation where he was informed that Israel required Britain to eliminate the Egyptian air force prior to an invasion, otherwise Egypt would flatten Israel from the air before their troops got anywhere near the Suez Canal. On 25 October Eden agreed to a new plan: Israel would invade Egypt on 29 October and head straight for the Canal, aiming to be there by 30 October. Britain and France would immediately call for a ceasefire and for a withdrawal from both sides to a zone of ten miles either side of the Canal. They would then call for both Egypt and Israel to accept Anglo-French occupation of that zone and if either side disagreed (which the Israelis would not) force would be used to ensure compliance.[7]

So on 29 October the Israelis attacked Egypt. The following day Eden told Parliament that Israel and Egypt had both been given an ultimatum by Her Majesty's Government: fall back to ten miles from the Canal within twelve hours and agree to Anglo-French occupation of certain strategic points. Eisenhower's reaction was to move in the UNSC that no outside force should be used. For once the USA and the USSR were united but Britain and France both used the veto.

Nasser rejected the British ultimatum and, on the night of 31 October, the RAF bombed Egyptian airfields. On 2 November the French Foreign Minister Christian Pineau disclosed to the Americans the whole saga of collusion between Britain, France and Israel, completely discrediting Eden who had promised to have had no foreknowledge whatever of Israel's intentions to invade.[8]

On 4 November Eden ordered an airborne invasion of Egypt for the following day (an amphibious assault team was due to arrive on the 6th) but when he informed the Cabinet he was met with dissent. Butler, sceptical about the entire operation from the start, pointed out that Israel at this point had publicly agreed to a ceasefire so their entire reason for putting troops on the ground had been removed. The landing went ahead anyway but within twenty-four hours Eden came to realise that he had completely lost the support of his Cabinet.[9] On the evening of 6 November he announced to the House of Commons that a ceasefire between Israel and Egypt had been confirmed and, consequently, British troops were being ordered to withdraw.

In the days which followed Eisenhower demanded that Britain withdraw unconditionally from Egypt, not partake in the United Nations Emergency Force (UNEF) which was to be placed on the ground to keep the peace, and not to be involved in international negotiations over the future of the Canal. If Britain refused these demands the United States would put such economic sanctions in place as to cripple the economy. The Prime Minister had no choice but to accept the ultimatum, as humiliating as it was.

On 24 November Britain and France were censured in the United Nations General Assembly. Meanwhile Eden was in Jamaica, citing ill health as a reason for an extended holiday.[10] When he returned in mid-December Butler and Salisbury informed him that he probably could not survive for long. Shortly afterwards it dawned on Eden that he had lost the support of the Conservative Party. On 9 January 1957 the Prime Minister tendered his resignation to the Queen, effective the following day, at which point he would also relinquish the Party leadership.

Eden's tenure as leader had been nothing short of a disaster. In under two years in office he had gone from an electoral victory to isolating himself within his Cabinet, his Cabinet from the country and his country from its international allies. Defeat over Suez would have been embarrassing for any leader and at any stage of the crisis (whether it was rolling over following the nationalisation of the Canal or actually taking up arms and being defeated). However, having been found to have been dishonest over the reason for going to war in Egypt his position went from embarrassing to irrecoverable, his credibility forever tarnished.

Eden is consistently ranked as one of the worst, if not the worst Prime Minister of the twentieth century. It is not difficult to understand why. He brought an embarrassment upon the nation that it would take years to shake off, probably accentuated by the fact that he was forced, ultimately, to bend to the will of the American President. Up until this point in history imperialists had been able to convince themselves that the United Kingdom was still a dominant force in world affairs and that the Empire, albeit reduced in size, was still alive and well. The fact that the threat of economic sanctions by the US was enough to make the Prime Minister of the United Kingdom throw in the towel only illustrated the point that next to the USA and the USSR Britain was a second-rate world power.

In 1812 Lord Liverpool had taken the country to war with the US for less and had come away with an acceptable result. In 1956 there would be no such repeat. The British Empire was well and truly a spent force. Anybody who wasn't yet aware of that fact was brought into reality by the premiership of Anthony Eden.

Harold Macmillan
(1957 − 1963)

Let's be frank about it; most of our people have never had it so good.

Harold Macmillan, 20 July 1957

The King will chuse any one Party, I think we are the most numerous and considerable

Daniel Defoe's *Tory*, 1692

WHEN EDEN RESIGNED, he held a Cabinet to inform his colleagues of his decision. He was eager for a smooth transfer of power from him to his successor, apparently aware that he had caused enough damage and that the Party could possibly crumble under the factionalism necessitated by an open leadership contest. After the Cabinet Eden, Macmillan and Butler all left while Salisbury, under instruction from the outgoing Prime Minister, held one-to-one meetings with each of the other Cabinet members. Inflicted with a slight speech impediment, Salisbury allegedly asked ministers individually the rather blunt question: 'Well, which is it to be, Hawold or Wab?'[1]

All but two spoke in favour of Macmillan, in spite of the fact that he had personally pushed for military action in Egypt and Butler had been the strongest critic within the administration. Most ministers, though, felt that their supporters did not apportion blame on Macmillan and, in fact, fully supported him. In their eyes the big mistake had not been military action but the collusion to create a false *casus belli*. For that Macmillan was seen as blameless.[2] On the other hand Butler had been against the war, which was viewed as disloyal. So it was settled. Macmillan kissed hands on 10 January and went about forming a government. He allegedly told the Queen that he didn't believe his administration could last for more than six weeks.[3]

As always the task of appointing ministers was political but particularly so in this instance. MPs and the public were well aware that Macmillan had supported military intervention in Egypt. They were also aware that Britain had foreknowledge of the Israeli plan to invade. What they did not know was the extent of the collusion and that Macmillan (at that time Chancellor of the Exchequer and not in any way obviously associated with the whole affair) not only knew about it, helped perpetuate it, but also pushed Eden into it more than any other minister. If this leaked then he was done for. The only people who knew for certain what had happened were those in Eden's Cabinet and, therefore, Macmillan could not sack many of them.

Therefore Selwyn Lloyd remained as Foreign Secretary. Salisbury, generally loyal to whoever led the Conservative Party but, being a Lord, could not be controlled by the threat of losing a parliamentary seat, was retained as Lord President of the Council and Leader of the House of Lords. Rab Butler, who had good cause to talk because not only had he been defeated by Macmillan for the leadership but he knew that if the truth leaked the world would see that he had opposed collusion, was awarded the Home Office in exchange for his loyalty.[4] The rest of the Cabinet formation came easily enough. Lord Home remained at the Commonwealth Office, Edward 'Ted' Heath was returned as Chief Whip, where he had been installed by Eden towards the beginning of what would be an extremely long parliamentary career and Peter Thorneycroft replaced Macmillan as Chancellor of the Exchequer.

Macmillan's first task was to rebuild Britain's reputation on the international stage. The relationships that Churchill had carefully fostered with the US and France over fifteen years had been shattered over the previous months but the new Prime Minister was determined to win them back. With this aim in mind he met Eisenhower in Bermuda from 21-24 March. However, discussions were not entirely amicable. Macmillan made it clear that Britain had felt let down by the US over Egypt and that he expected at least some diplomatic pressure from the Americans with the aim of ousting Nasser.[5] Eisenhower defended himself by saying that he had made his position clear from the outset, so had let nobody down and that he had no intention of making any attempt to oust anybody.

Macmillan then returned to the UK and incorrectly determined that his problems were only just beginning. Within a month Lord Salisbury had resigned from the government over his belief that Macmillan was acting too leniently towards Cypriot separatists (who were still agitating for unification with Greece) and, in particular, towards their leader Archbishop Makarios. Although this seemed to Macmillan to be a significant resignation at the time of its occurrence, it had little impact on the Cabinet, on the Conservative Party or in making interesting stories for the press. Consequently it was a storm in a teacup for Macmillan's premiership. In fact, the resignation served to Macmillan's benefit just a month later. Given that Eisenhower had refused to help bring Nasser down (which Macmillan had still hoped might happen right up until the end of April) and Nasser himself had declared that Britain and France could have no future in the administration of the Suez Canal, the government had no choice but to accept this declaration. However, as one of the staunchest proponents of action over Suez only a few months earlier, the Prime Minister would have difficulty selling these embarrassing terms to Parliament.

The debate over Suez was scheduled for 15-16 May but Macmillan was despondent in the days prior for several reasons. Firstly, he did not hold with conviction that Britain should be forced to accept the terms laid out. Also he knew that the Labour Party were angling for his immediate downfall as the toppling of two governments within six months would surely lead to their installation in office. Finally, Salisbury had decided to try to whip votes against him. He was able to appease some of the waverers in the Conservative ranks by announcing that Britain had successfully tested its first Hydrogen-Bomb in the Pacific Ocean. This demonstrated that he would be able to be taken seriously in international conferences in future, regardless of how the vote went. He also mollified his backbenchers by withdrawing oil rations (which improved peoples' standards of living meaning that a collapse of the government wasn't necessarily desirable). In the event he carried the vote, which can largely be attributed firstly to the fact that Salisbury had resigned in the April, meaning that when he attempted to whip people in opposition he was not a Cabinet minister breaking ranks but an out-of-office peer getting a little too involved in House of Commons politics, and secondly due to some effective whipping from Ted Heath for the government. The Tories could finally bury Suez and move on.

Ironically, then, providing a positive outcome for Macmillan was the biggest consequence of Salisbury's resignation.

The government seemed to have turned a corner. Macmillan had survived his six weeks prediction and the most difficult of issues had been put to bed. The only significant obstacle left to overcome was an issue that reared its head in the August and was filled with more irony than many ministers ever encounter. The US Congress had recently approved Presidential powers to intervene militarily in areas likely to fall to Communism. Communism had been spreading throughout Syria, already governed by a conspicuously Left-wing administration, and the United States was concerned that the country may lean towards an alliance with the Soviet Union. This would not be a problem if it wasn't for the fact that the US was heavily dependent on oil pipelines that passed through Syria. The possibility for the USSR to influence whether or not the USA could access oil was anathema to Eisenhower. All of a sudden the British position on Suez (needing access to a Canal, important to the economy, which had recently been nationalised) which the Americans had so condemned was completely acceptable in Syria. The Americans looked set to go to war unless Macmillan could talk them down. He sent his Principal Private Secretary, Frederick Bishop, to Washington to point out to the Americans the glaring hypocrisy of their position.

Once they had been convinced to back down Macmillan paid a visit to Washington in October to make another attempt at restoring the old relationship. This time the visit went much better than Bermuda had gone. Not only was Eisenhower more amiable on this occasion, but the Prime Minister successfully convinced the President to repudiate the McMahon Act (an Act of Congress which prevented the United States from sharing nuclear technological developments with other countries) and open up a joint defence initiative in which both countries would pool resources to counter the Soviet threat. No doubt the President had been satisfactorily shaken in the weeks prior to the meeting by the launch of the world's first man-made satellite – *Sputnik* – by the Soviet Union. The fear that the USSR was winning the technological race put Eisenhower in the perfect position for Macmillan to push for the repeal of McMahon.[7] Macmillan could return to the UK a success and end the year a lot more optimistic than he had been at the beginning of it.

In politics optimism is invariably short lived. Macmillan's Christmas of peace in 1957 was no exception as, by the first week of January 1958, he would suffer from difficulties within his own Cabinet. The seeds of trouble had first been sown in the autumn when Thorneycroft had tried to reduce inflation by raising interest rates to target the money supply. This went against the commonly-accepted Keynesian principles that unemployment was a greater evil than inflation. Unemployment could be countered by increased government expenditure and therefore control of the money supply was to be avoided. By the turn of the year Thorneycroft had been arguing for reductions in government expenditure against the wishes of the Cabinet. Macmillan had organised a Cabinet meeting for 3 January to settle the matter. Thorneycroft did not get his way and on a further meeting with the Prime Minister on 5 January he was told in no uncertain terms that he must now toe the line. The following day Macmillan received a letter of resignation from Thorneycroft. The resignation of a minister as senior as the Chancellor of the Exchequer on a matter of principle could be fatal to a government. Once again Macmillan would be fighting to stay afloat rather than sailing comfortably along.

His response was to act as though the event was of no real significance, which succeeded in creating the illusion that this disaster was not, in fact, a disaster. He had appointed a new Chancellor by dinner time (Derick Heathcote Amory) and on the 9th left the country for a tour of the Commonwealth as if to reinforce the notion that there was no crisis to manage at home. Once he returned in mid-February the storm, if ever one had occurred, had well and truly blown over. Although there were significant developments in the world (Cyprus was still causing trouble, the repeal of the McMahon Act was passing through the US Congress, Charles de Gaulle was close to overthrowing the Fourth Republic in France) Macmillan found little to challenge him during 1958. The Treaty of Rome had been signed by six European nations in 1957 with the aim of creating a free trade Area between them. At this time Eden and also Macmillan had aspired for a plan to bring in another seven nations, Britain included, into a free trade zone (so called 'Plan G').[8] However, de Gaulle was insistent that if Britain wished to see this aspiration realised he would need a commitment from the Prime Minister for assistance to develop France's nuclear weapons programme, which Macmillan had promised Eisenhower would not happen (the McMahon Act was to be repealed so that Britain and the US could share a defence strategy, not so that Britain could share US secrets with the rest of the world). This was not seen as a particularly sizeable problem, though.

July witnessed a *coup d'état* in Iraq leading to the overthrow of the crown Prince and August saw negotiations between Brits, Turks and Greeks over the future of Cyprus. In both of these incidents Macmillan played a leading role (sending paratroopers to Jordan in order to ensure that the violence did not overspill the borders of Iraq, and personally attending Athens to discuss options with Turkish and Greek delegations) but within a short time both had been settled, or as settled as they could be for the time being, and the Prime Minister could enjoy his recess.

Once Parliament reconvened in October, Macmillan was once again at a low on what was becoming a rollercoaster of emotions during his premiership. De Gaulle terminated British hopes of joining a free trade zone owing to Macmillan's unwillingness to co-operate over nuclear secrets. The Treaty of Rome came into effect on 1 January 1959 and Britain was accordingly excluded. At this point in time British trade with Commonwealth nations was four times as great as that with Europe, so it is difficult to appreciate why British Prime Ministers over the following decades spent so much time trying to pursue stronger trade links with the continent rather than freeing up trade elsewhere. However, Macmillan was despondent at the result and, despite continuing negotiations on-and-off with de Gaulle over the rest of his time in office, probably never again really held out hope of a settlement.

The Cold War was now at its height and international developments dominated Macmillan's agenda far more than domestic politics did, just as it had with at least his four immediate Prime Ministerial predecessors. At the end of 1958 Khrushchev had announced that he intended to hand the access zone connecting West Germany to the Allied-controlled West Berlin, currently managed by the Soviet Union, over to East Germany. This shocked Eisenhower, Konrad Adenauer, the West German Chancellor, and Macmillan as East Germans in control of the only route that the Allies had in or out of their side of Berlin meant that surely the entire city would fall, by force, to Communism. West Berlin was the West's only foothold in East Germany. Eisenhower and de Gaulle, though affronted, seemed unwilling to act, so Macmillan arranged a personal visit to Moscow to negotiate with Khrushchev.

He left the UK on 21 February and was welcomed cordially by his Russian counterpart. However, Khrushchev made life as difficult as possible for the Prime Minister. Whether he knew that Eisenhower and Adenauer had been opposed to Macmillan attending the USSR cannot be determined but either way he attempted to drive a wedge between the Allies at every opportunity throughout the trip. On 24 February Khrushchev made a public speech criticising the American President and the West German Chancellor, while using friendly language in reference to the British Prime Minister.[9] This was highly embarrassing, designed to insult all three Western leaders in one way or another. Macmillan, in a meeting with Khrushchev on 26 February, condemned his actions. Khrushchev responded by telling Macmillan that he would not accompany him, as had been planned, to Kiev, owing to a toothache. This was a further insult that Macmillan arguably should have taken as his reason to leave, but he didn't. He stayed in the Soviet Union for ten days in total and, once he had returned to Moscow from Kiev he found that Khrushchev had made a miraculous recovery and even proposed a summit meeting of the heads of all involved countries to discuss the future of Germany. Macmillan felt a sense of triumph upon returning to London. He then went to visit all the other Western leaders individually in their home countries to discuss this possibility. Evidently they were less enthusiastic than he had been.

De Gaulle in Paris felt that a summit had little merit. Adenauer in Bonn thought that Macmillan had been too soft but would follow France's lead in deciding how to act next. Eisenhower in Washington was unenthusiastic about the idea, eventually agreeing to a meeting of foreign ministers, rather than heads of state, mainly due to Macmillan's persistence than any genuine conviction that it could amount to anything. Consequently having achieved very little (no agreement on anything of substance with Khrushchev, no support from de Gaulle for his plan, anger from Adenauer and reluctant, almost humouring acquiescence from Eisenhower) Macmillan looked forward to returning home a hero, believing that he must look like an international diplomat not unlike Churchill. This, he hoped, could only benefit his approval ratings four years into a five year maximum parliamentary term.

When the Foreign Ministers' Conference met in Geneva in mid-May there was, predictably, little progress. Lloyd was out of his depth and the American representative, Christian Herter, had only been in his role for a month. As a result neither was able to forward the Western agenda. Luckily for the Prime Minister, he had not put all of his electoral eggs in the international basket. In April Heathcote Amory had announced an incredibly popular budget, slashing taxes across the board. Parliament broke up for the summer recess in August and by the beginning of September the Prime Minister had announced that he had asked the Queen for a dissolution.[10]

Macmillan was shameless in the timing of his request as in the last week of August he had managed to convince an extremely reluctant Eisenhower to stop in Britain on the way back from a world tour. Knowing that an election was due Eisenhower had initially rejected invitations from Macmillan on the basis that he didn't want to be seen to be supporting the Prime Minister in a contest that did not involve him. However, Macmillan applied pressure, emotional blackmail and even the threat of deteriorating relations between the two countries to secure a stopover from the President. Prime Minister and President then toured the country together in full view of the media and, regardless of either of their protestations, it looked as though Eisenhower was throwing Macmillan his support. When an election was called just over a week after Eisenhower's departure, the memory of the visit was still very much in the public mind.

Somehow Macmillan had transformed a 13-point deficit at the beginning of 1959 into electoral victory on 8 October (helped in no small part by in-fighting between Gaitskell and Bevan on the Labour side). The Conservatives returned 365 MPs compared with Labour's 258 (the Liberals still clinging to their six seats).[11] The incoming government had much the same face as the one that Macmillan had led into the election, although Heath was moved to the Department for Labour.

With the election out of the way Macmillan went about trying to achieve what he had started at the beginning of the year: a leaders' summit involving himself, Eisenhower, de Gaulle and Khrushchev. He travelled to Paris on 18 December to speak with the Western leaders whereupon it was agreed that a series of summits, one in each capital, would be preferable to just one. Macmillan was delighted and, ensuring that an invitation was extended to Khrushchev as soon as possible, travelled back to London in high spirits just in time for Christmas.

The beginning of the new year saw much of the same routines as before the election: trying to procure nuclear weapons from the Unites States and trying to get de Gaulle to agree to an expansion of the European Economic Community, all the while plans moved forward for the series of summit meetings, the first of which – Paris – was schedule for 16 May.

However, a major setback was delivered from the Western side by May. For a long while Britain and the US had been spying on Soviet missile silos using Utility-2 (U-2) aircraft which had the capability of flying at such a high altitude that they could evade anti-aircraft defences. Once the summit series had been agreed Britain desisted in this activity as Macmillan didn't want to be caught out breaching Khrushchev's (hard won) trust. The Americans initially did the same but could not contain themselves for long. By the spring of 1960 they had resumed their espionage missions and, almost as if scripted, the USSR shot one down on 1 May. Khrushchev still wanted to salvage the summit series but was boxed into a corner by the US State Department who initially denied having sent a spy plane, then admitted to it publicly. Khrushchev could not accept this breach of trust without suffering reprisals from within his own government, who were already concerned that he was becoming too friendly with the West, unless the Unites States issued an apology and a formal promise that it would never happen again.

On the first day of the Paris summit Khrushchev kept to the same resolute line and went further in stating that Eisenhower would not be welcome at the Moscow round. There then followed an angry discussion between all four leaders before de Gaulle called an end to the proceedings for the day. Macmillan met with Eisenhower afterwards and tried, in vain, to convince him to apologise.[12] The next day the conference formally broke down. As long as Eisenhower and

Khrushchev were both in charge of their respective countries talks between East and West would never resume.

Upon arriving back home Macmillan decided that in order to deflect attention from the fact that the summit talks which he had cajoled the other world leaders into had broken down without any steps forward agreed upon, he would reshuffle his Cabinet. Heathcote Amory was removed altogether to be replaced by Selwyn Lloyd as Chancellor of the Exchequer. Lloyd was replaced at the Foreign Office by the Earl of Home.[13] Heath was made Lord Privy Seal and, startlingly, Thorneycroft made a return as Minister for Aviation (as well as Enoch Powell, who had resigned with Thorneycroft in 1958, returning to the Cabinet as Minister for Health). The main controversy, though, was the appointment of Home. Every Cabinet ever constructed had contained ministers from the House of Lords but recently all the Great Offices of State (Prime Minister, Chancellor of the Exchequer, Foreign Secretary, Home Secretary) had been held by MPs. Many Members of the Lower House were uncomfortable with reverting to a Lord holding such a senior position. Indeed the outcry against Home's appointment should have acted as a warning signal for the reaction that the Earl would receive when taking yet another step upwards three years later.

Parliament broke up for the summer recess and in September Macmillan flew to New York for a meeting of the United Nations, but only because he had learned in advance that Khrushchev was there and he therefore sensed an opportunity. The few discussions that he managed to obtain with the Soviet leader in private came to nothing but both men were very aware that a general election in the United States was less than two months away, four months after which, on 20 January 1961, a new President would be sworn in. Eisenhower couldn't stand again thanks to the 22nd Amendment passed during Truman's Presidency.

In that November Presidential election the Democrat John F. Kennedy beat the Republican candidate, Vice-President Richard Nixon. Macmillan saw the change in leadership not just as an opportunity to restart his plans for international summits (which, in the end, he decided to hold off from proposing until he had gotten to know the new President better) but also to suggest, as if it was the first time he had thought of it, allowing France access to nuclear weapons. His logic was that if he secured this prize for de Gaulle, the French President might just return the favour by allowing an expansion of the EEC to include Britain.

However, following two meetings between Macmillan and Kennedy in March and April the President made it clear that allowing the French into the nuclear club was not an option.[14] Macmillan's EEC dreams seemed destined to be thwarted at every turn. Worse than this, barely had Macmillan left Washington than the President ordered an operation that was to set off a chain reaction which would change the world forever. For a long while the United States had been drawing up plans to remove the Cuban leader, Fidel Castro, from his post. They were uncomfortable with such a Left-wing administration having control of a country just 90 miles from American shores. On 17 April 1961 around fourteen hundred Cuban refugees, who had fled Castro and escaped to Florida, were transported to the Bay of Pigs in Cuba.[15] The plan was simple enough: The United States would not invade Cuba, would not bear arms against Cuba or interfere directly there, but would allow the Cuban people to do it. By shipping these dissidents back to Cuba they were just taking people home but the plan was that they would revolt and, surely, the whole country would follow them within hours and overthrow Castro. What they didn't count upon was the presence of 20,000 Cuban soldiers confronting the invading force and forcing them to surrender with almost no resistance.[16] The clear involvement of the United States, as well as their failure, was documented around the world, much to the embarrassment of the new President. The consequences would be dire. In the meantime, though, Macmillan had domestic problems to keep him occupied.

He had not made any particular mistakes at home during the first years of the 1960s but by the end of 1961 the Tories were lagging behind Labour in the opinion polls.[17] After ten years of power the public were evidently becoming restless. On top of the fact that the government looked tired there was stagnation in the economy and unrest amongst MPs and even Cabinet ministers who felt that they needed to combat the image of fatigue by *doing*. Throughout the winter of 1961-62 Macmillan was constantly concerned with the possibility of a Cabinet revolt or, equally as bad, a Cabinet split. To emphasise the point the Conservatives lost several by-elections, including in constituencies that were believed to be safe.[18]

As the government staggered through the year into the spring the Prime Minister became obsessed with the idea of his favourite recurring remedy whenever he found himself in political trouble – a Cabinet reshuffle. While pondering this throughout May and June he came up with a plan to rescue the economy. This included the establishment of a National Incomes Council, which led to fears that he was drifting towards central planning, a socialist ideal, rather than allowing the market to determine wages. He delivered his proposals to Cabinet on 22 June. Lloyd, who, as Chancellor of the Exchequer, had the most reason to be interested in the plan, spoke out against it as unworkable. Now Macmillan had found his scapegoat. The Party looked tired, the economy stagnant, and the Chancellor was nothing more than a naysayer.

Over the following weeks Macmillan planned his reshuffle, informing only a few close confidantes of his intentions. He intended to meet with Lloyd on 12 July to break the news to him. However, on the 11th Rab Butler, aware of the plan because Macmillan had confided in him, leaked it to the press. Lloyd found the truth splashed all over the papers on 12 July, just hours before he met with the Prime Minister to hear it first-hand. The Chancellor took the news badly and suggested to at least one other minister that they should resign in protest at his treatment. Macmillan, concerned that resignations may appear *en masse*, which would be damaging for him politically, decided to effect an immediate and complete reshuffle, purging the Cabinet of anybody suspected of having disloyal inclinations. In all around one third of the Cabinet was replaced. Reginald Maudling became Chancellor of the Exchequer and Rab Butler was removed from the Home Office to be replaced by Henry Brooke. Any onlooker could tell that Macmillan had lost his nerve and panicked. Consequently his approval rating dropped by 11 points in just nine days.[19]

With a new face to it the ageing government was in place just in time for the summer recess, immediately followed by the biggest direct consequence of the Bay of Pigs fiasco and one of the most dangerous crises that the world has ever witnessed. The Americans were aware that the Soviet Union had been storing Medium Range Ballistic Missiles in Cuba for a full three weeks before they disclosed it to the British. It was 22 October when Macmillan was briefed and he duly informed the Cabinet the following day. The United States proposed to blockade Cuba in order to force the withdrawal of the missiles. Nobody was in any doubt about what this meant: one wrong move could lead to war, which would effectively lead to the absolute destruction of both sides.

The blockade went into effect on 24 October and the military in the United States went onto full alert. No further Soviet ships were able to pass through to Cuba and, after a tense stand-off, those that approached turned away rather than engage. However, there were still missiles present and Khrushchev did not appear to be of a mind to negotiate their removal. Kennedy had to consider that his only option was to invade Cuba, which could provoke full-scale war.

On the night of 26 October in Washington/morning of 27 October in Moscow and London, Khrushchev sent a message to Kennedy stating that if the United States promised never to invade Cuba then there would be no reason for the USSR to keep missiles there. While the President was considering his response another demand came through: the USSR would remove the missiles if the US promised not to invade Cuba and also removed their own warheads from Turkey, which were a threat to the Soviet Union. Concerned that if he agreed it may look to his European allies as though he was abandoning them, there was only one course of action open to the President: not to reject this last demand, but to ignore it. Kennedy replied to Khrushchev's first message and made a pledge not to invade Cuba in return for the removal of the missiles. On 28 October the Kremlin agreed and the crisis was over.

As the year 1962 drew to a close Macmillan reflected on it as having been a bad year.[20] His government still looked tired and weak, his reshuffle had only given the impression that he had been rattled. The Cuban Missile Crisis had made very public the real dangers of nuclear arms, for which Labour were in favour of abolition. Within the first couple of weeks of 1963 things got worse. It was public knowledge that Macmillan favoured British entry into the EEC and, although he had been unsuccessful so far in securing entry, he could gloss over this failure as long as he could claim that discussions were ongoing.

This came to an abrupt end on 13 January when de Gaulle announced in a press conference that Britain did not belong in Europe and so would not be permitted into the group. Then on 18 January Hugh Gaitskell died, meaning, as tragic as it was, amnesty for Macmillan from parliamentary attacks while the Labour Party went about finding a new leader. In February Harold Wilson was selected.

Wilson was far more prepared to play politics than Gaitskell had been. For him principles could come and go as long as they resulted in electoral success. Consequently he would cause the Conservatives a lot more trouble than Gaitskell would have done. Macmillan's real problem, though, was that Conservatives were far too capable of making trouble for themselves. To add to his plethora of problems in the spring of 1963 the government suddenly became enveloped in a scandal which, although damaging in itself, when added to everything else almost made life unmanageable.

The Secretary for War, John Profumo, had embarked on a month-long affair with a female named Christine Keeler. For the prudish British public of the early 1960s, not yet liberalised by the sexual revolution that was shortly to come, this was bad enough. But this wasn't the full story. Initially Profumo denied the affair, even to the House of Commons, but was, within a couple of months, forced to confess the truth by the weight of circumstantial evidence against him and resign. For the public in any modern democracy, who hold their leaders to exceptionally high standards, this was bad enough. But this wasn't the full story. Christine Keeler had certainly been in contact with, and possibly also having an affair with, a Russian military attaché who was, it transpired, also a KGB spy.

Now a government minister was involved in a sex scandal, lying and compromising UK security at the height of the Cold War. The Tories were damaged. The strain was too much for Macmillan. Through the summer he continued to feel exhausted and frail and he considered for the first time that he might not be able to lead the Party into a general election, which was due by the autumn of 1964 at the latest.

He therefore started to plan how to retire and how to install a successor. He felt that Butler would be bad for the Party and so wanted to ensure that senior Conservatives were united behind somebody else before he made his intentions public. At this point in time Viscount Hailsham was his favoured candidate.[21]

Significantly, the Earl of Home was one of few people that the Prime Minister confided in during the late summer, and he seemed in favour of a Hailsham leadership. The plan was for Macmillan to leave in January. At the end of September he disclosed his plan to the Queen but by the first week of October he had become severely ill, to the point where it was clear that he could not go on. His timetable would have to be moved forward.

On 9 October Macmillan was in hospital with urinary problems, the day before the Conservative Party Conference was due to commence in Blackpool. The only course of action that he could see was to draft a statement announcing that he was stepping down, get someone to read it out in Blackpool and allow whoever wished to put their names forward as candidates to thrash it out over the following week or so. The person tasked with reading the statement, fatefully, was Home, who duly did this on Friday 10 October in Blackpool as promised.[22] Next to this bombshell the other Conference speeches fell flat. Neither Hailsham nor Butler impressed the gathered Party faithful. Home surprised everyone by announcing that he was a candidate and suddenly, compared with such unimpressive rivals, he looked like a frontrunner.

A few days later Macmillan took soundings from his Cabinet colleagues which made it clear that the only two candidates with any chance of success were Home and Butler. At this point the Prime Minister decided to act. Butler was not an acceptable option but the problem was that even if he renounced his peerage, Home would be an egregious choice in the eyes of many senior Conservatives, raised in an age of democracy. No peer had been Prime Minister since Salisbury's resignation in 1902, so surely one would not be accepted now?

On 17 October the Queen visited Macmillan in hospital and this was the moment that he directed the future course of Conservative Party history. He told Elizabeth that he intended to resign immediately and then asked if she would like to hear his advice. When she assented he went into a history lesson. Harking back to the days of another great Queen – Victoria – Macmillan recalled how, rather than appointing a Prime Minister directly, she would often summon someone and ask them whether it would be possible for them to form a government. Thought must have been drawn to Derby, who was asked to form a government on so many occasions that he must have lost count. But he never gave an immediate answer, always going away to consult his supporters before returning to accept, or, more frequently, decline. The Queen should send for Home and ask him to *try*.

For now, though, whatever happened, Macmillan's leadership tenure was at an end. His time as Prime Minister saw Britain for the first time not a major power on the world stage. In the greatest trial of the age – the Cuban Missile Crisis – all Britain could do was stand helplessly by while the real power blocs of the world decided their fate. He was unable to convince even de Gaulle to let him have his way over Britain joining the EEC. His plans for a series of summits blew up spectacularly. In this sense his international diplomacy was not successful. That said he was, by the end of his tenure, on friendly terms with all the world leaders which, considering the frosty relationships he inherited from Eden, can be seen as an achievement in itself.

Domestically he was afflicted by scandals, a stagnated economy, declining approval ratings and a scarcity of ideas to deal with issues such as unemployment. However, after thirteen years in power as a Party this is somewhat understandable. His successes included winning the 1959 general election and by a much greater margin than had been anticipated.

There was not a single year that Macmillan held office which did not end with him reflecting that it had been a bad one. However, he had successfully ridden every storm and, had he resigned twelve months before he did, he would probably have been remembered as a success rather than as Prime Minister during the Profumo affair.

This alone, though, should not determine Macmillan's legacy. He achieved nothing of major significance – no historic event that can be attributed to him. But history needs stability and, therefore, it needs people who can deliver it. Macmillan's phrase that Britons had 'never had it so good' was probably true in 1957. He gave them the stability and security to enjoy it. He kept Britain out of war and rebuilt a shattered national reputation. In order to achieve the euphoria of VE Day, inextricably linked to Churchill, the country had to endure six years of travails. Macmillan did not have a VE Day, but neither is he associated with a difficult war. He is remembered as a

steady operator who allowed the British people to rediscover
themselves in an uncertain post-war world.

Sir Alec Douglas-Home
(1963 − 1965)

You proposed the government's health – rather for us an unusual experience – but I should like to say at once that we are very well. We had, you see, a holiday by the sea at Blackpool...

Sir Alec Douglas-Home, 11 November 1963

How come, you and I to be so concern'd...for the interest of Mob, who will sing Ballads upon us under the gallows, when we are hanging for their sakes?

Daniel Defoe's *Tory*, 1692

UPON HEARING THE NEWS that the Queen was to send for the Earl of Home, supporters of Butler started their revolt. Enoch Powell, the junior Minister for Health; Iain Macleod, Chairman of the Conservative Party; even Reginald Maudling, the Chancellor of the Exchequer, *inter alios*, began to collude in finding ways to prevent the move. They saw it as an insult to the hundreds of Conservatives in the House of Commons who were effectively deemed not good enough. They also saw it as an affront to the custom which had been adopted ever since King George V had chosen Stanley Baldwin over Lord Curzon, apparently influenced, quite rightly, by the effects of the 1911 Parliament Act, that a Member of the House of Commons should be the Prime Minister.

On 18 October Home duly met with the Queen and was asked to attempt to form an administration but did not kiss hands. He returned to 10 Downing Street, which had for the past week temporarily been used by Butler to manage the affairs of the government, and started the process of sounding out his colleagues.[1] Maudling was initially noncommittal but Home advised him that to hold out for Butler was foolish as his being successful was not a possibility. Powell and Macleod outright refused to serve. This was a blow but it was not decisive. The real test was Butler himself. When he attended Downing Street he had already made up his mind to act honourably. The Queen had chosen Home, he would not cause a fuss. Six years earlier he had been thwarted in his leadership ambitions by the Old Boys' Club, harshly undemocratic, but he had not made a song and dance about it and, arguably, was now suffering the consequences. Because the Old Boys' Club had been allowed to get away with it in 1957, they were there once again to scupper his hopes in 1963.

The following day Butler agreed to become Foreign Secretary under Home, Maudling falling behind him and agreeing to stay on as Chancellor of the Exchequer. Home made his way over to the palace immediately to kiss hands as Prime Minister. Parliament was due to meet on 24 October but Home had it postponed until after he was able to stand in a by-election and take up a seat in the House of Commons. Harold Wilson felt that this was a deplorable act, forcing Parliament to meet around Home's personal timetable. From the point at which he accepted the premiership things moved very quickly. On 21 October Home put his name forward for candidacy for the Kinross and West Perthshire by-election, for which the local association had already shoe-horned in a local favourite but were now told that they were overruled. On the 22nd he held his first Cabinet.[2] On the 23rd he renounced his peerage, from this point forth being known as Sir Alec Douglas-Home. A couple of days later he was up in Perthshire campaigning for his election and, by the time the results filtered in on the morning of Friday 8 November, Douglas-Home found that he had been returned as a Member of Parliament, with nearly three times the number of votes of his nearest rival[3] (a Liberal) to lead the Conservative majority there. The State Opening of Parliament then took place on 12 November.

Ten days later, on 22 November 1963, news broke that the American President Kennedy had been shot dead by an assassin in Dallas, Texas. That evening all three Party leaders, Douglas-Home for the Conservatives, Wilson for Labour and Jo Grimond for the Liberals, made televised broadcasts to the nation. This was the first occasion that the new Prime Minister had addressed the country and he rose to the occasion, reflecting perfectly the mood of shock and trauma felt throughout. He then prepared for a trip to Washington for the funeral and his first meeting with a US President, Kennedy's successor, Lyndon B. Johnson. The trip lasted just a couple of days but once it was completed Douglas-Home was able to look forward to a Christmas break away from politics. The only real matter to consider was when an election should be held, which had to be done by the autumn of 1964. In the event the Prime Minister leant towards letting the Parliament run to its maximum limit but deferred making an ultimate decision until the new year, instead taking a relaxing Christmas.

In February 1964 Douglas-Home paid a visit to Washington where he was reprimanded by President Johnson for continuing trade with Cuba in spite of an embargo placed on the island by the United States following the missile crisis. The Prime Minister courteously warned Johnson not to interfere with British trade and, although the relationship between the two men probably suffered as a consequence, the matter was buried there.

By April the Prime Minister had settled on an October election and duly informed the nation of this so as to end speculation. Fortunately for him through the spring and summer the Conservatives started to improve their position in the opinion polls, albeit from a particularly low base.[4] Parliament rose for its summer recess in July and would not return before the general election, which in the event took place on 15 October. Parliament was therefore officially dissolved in mid-September and the battle for Downing Street began. The contest was between a Conservative Party that had been in government for thirteen years but with a relatively new leader that they had selected following the previous one being forced to retire through ill-health, and a Labour Party that had been in opposition for thirteen years but with a relatively new leader that they had selected following the previous one being forced out by death.

The campaign was impassioned and fiercely contested on both sides to the point that, in spite of Labour having had a large lead in the opinion polls just a few short months earlier, by the time of the election it was too close to call for certain, albeit the Conservatives were still polling marginally behind. It was close right down until well into the following day, 16 October, when the results were finalised: Labour 317 seats, Conservatives 304 seats, Liberals nine.[5] After thirteen years in power the Conservatives were returned to the opposition benches.

Speculation became rife about the future of Douglas-Home as leader of the Conservative Party. Having lost an election was it sensible for him to continue? It is unclear how he perceived his future at this point in time but he must have known that a snap general election was a possibility, given the closeness of the recent election result and therefore decided to stay on for the time being.

By the end of the month he had reconstructed his front bench team (Maudling, previously Chancellor of the Exchequer, was made Shadow Foreign Secretary. Ted Heath was made Shadow Chancellor). For the following nine months the new team parried the government as best they could. With roughly equal number of government and opposition in the House of Commons life was not easy for Wilson in his first year in office. On 26 June 1965 the Prime Minister announced that there would be no general election that year, meaning that Douglas-Home was free to step down if he wished to.[6] After consulting with his family he made his decision and, on 20 July, he announced to the parliamentary party that he was stepping down.

In order to quell any concerns about how leaders were chosen in future, following the discontent felt at the manner in which he himself had succeeded the premiership, not to mention Macmillan and Eden, Home had, earlier in the year, reformed the policy of the Conservative Party to elect its leader by a secret ballot of parliamentary party members. In future the Old Boys' Club would have to win over the rank-and-file MPs if they wanted their candidate to get the top job.   Maudling and Heath both put their names forward and the vote on 27 July was between them. Douglas-Home did not campaign either way but he voted for Heath.[7] Whatever the result, Alec Douglas-Home was no longer leader of the Conservative Party.

His tenure had been short and it is often argued that his only mission had been to steer them through an election which Macmillan had been physically unable to do. Therefore, given the result, he was a failure. However, when reflecting on the events of 1964 Douglas-Home did something that few politicians can ever claim to have done. He turned a fifteen point electoral deficit into a hair's-breadth contest in the space of only a few months. He is, quite understandably, seen as a stop-gap in the flow of twentieth century Conservative leaders but he did much more than this. He took an ailing Party and gave life to the next generation who would go on to lead the Conservatives for the twenty-five years after he had stepped down. He reformed the selection of leadership candidates (albeit this was so as not to allow a repeat of his own promotion). However, aside from this, owing to the brevity of his tenure, he achieved very little in terms of policies or reforms. His legacy is limited to his promoting Heath (as well as being the last Lord to become Prime Minister).

Edward Heath
(1965 — 1975)

Let there be in power a government who will pursue policies which are essential...for this country to take its rightful place in the wider Europe

Edward Heath, 25 February 1970

I am for the King's relying on one Party as much as you are (tho not yours)

Daniel Defoe's *Tory*, 1692

ON THE BALLOT OF 27 JULY, Heath took 150 votes to Maudling's 133 (Powell, who also threw his hat into the ring, took only nine)[1] which meant that the contest was close enough that there could have been a second round of voting. However, Maudling immediately withdrew, thereby handing Heath the leadership. What should have been seen from the outset (and possibly was by some) was that the politics of the following ten years would be driven not by a contest of ideas or values but by a personal animosity between Heath and Harold Wilson. Both career politicians and prepared to use anything to their advantage, they would each become frustrated and angry when the other did the same. The writing was on the wall within days of the Conservative leadership ballot. 2 August was to be Heath's first Commons debate as Party leader. Realising that the small margin that Labour held in the Lower Chamber combined with an even further narrowing of the gap in the opinion polls meant that he might have a chance to defeat the government, he decided to propose a motion of censure against them. The Conservatives were in optimistic spirits going into the debate but Heath managed to flatten them very quickly with a dull performance in attack of the government. Wilson, on the other hand, whipped his Party up into a frenzy during his speeches. By the end of it the government's slender majority held and Heath was beaten in his first challenge, just in time for Parliament to rise for the summer recess.

Due to the fact that Wilson was expected to call an election sooner rather than later, Heath was not comfortable making many changes to his Shadow Cabinet, other than to bring Douglas-Home in as Shadow Foreign Secretary. Over the rest of 1965 the Conservatives slipped further behind Labour in the polls, with Heath's personal approval rating being lower still as he failed to connect with the public. By the start of 1966 Wilson set the election date for 31 March.[2] Opinion polls aside the public were still not ready for another Tory government following thirteen years of power and probably felt that Labour had not been given a fair chance yet. It was an astute decision by the Prime Minister to set the election at that point and it worked in his favour: Labour, 363 seats; Conservatives, 253; Liberals 12.[3] The government had increased its lead on the Conservatives nearly ten times over.

Following the election there was no serious question of Heath stepping down. Although he was not particularly popular in the country it was generally accepted that the Tories could not have won in 1966 regardless of who the leader was. Losing the election, though, may have been a rather fortunate turn of events for Heath politically, as he could in no way be associated with the economic difficulties which followed. In May 1966 the government faced a Seamen's strike and then, when the Chancellor of the Exchequer, James Callaghan, introduced that year's budget in the same month he was heavily criticised for reneging on the government's election pledge not to increase taxes. Taking the lead in the assaults against the government on this front were the Shadow Chancellor, Iain Macleod, and the new junior Treasury spokesperson, Margaret Thatcher.[4] The opposition got a good press but the government's problems were to continue as, throughout the summer, inflation began to spiral uncontrollably.[5]

Strong unions were pushing up wages for their members, which in turn led both to inflation of sterling and higher unemployment as workers became too costly. In order to deal with the unemployment side the government cut interest rates, thereby encouraging borrowing: effectively increasing the money supply to encourage businesses to spend more, including on wages.[6] However, this only had a short term effect on unemployment while contributing to the upwards inflationary pressures in the medium and longer term.

The problem for the Conservatives was that while they attacked the government (successfully, as the public could hardly blame anybody else) for their inability to resolve unemployment or bring inflation under control, they were unable to formulate any feasible alternative policies. Increasing the money supply caused inflation, restricting it caused unemployment. It would be another fifteen years before a Prime Minister considered combining restrictions on the power of the unions – in order to prevent them from causing unemployment – with control of the money supply to dampen inflation. By then, though, the economy had suffered almost irreparable damage.

The years from 1966-70 were largely a matter of sitting and waiting for the Conservatives. Few doubted that they would be returned to office as long as they did not do anything to harm their own chances because Labour's economic management was making life hard for people. In November 1967 inflation had become such a problem that Wilson took the decision to devalue sterling, which was a necessary step but Heath still publicly attacked him for cheapening the pound in the pocket of the people.[7]

However, sitting and waiting came easier to some than it did others. In April 1968 Callaghan (now at the Home Office rather than the Treasury and so halfway towards becoming the only person in history to have held all four Great Offices of State) introduced a Race Relations Bill into Parliament. The intention of the Bill was to end discrimination in employment and housing on the basis of race.[8] The Shadow Cabinet collectively agreed to support ending discrimination but to attach a wrecking amendment to the Bill nonetheless. Heath was concerned at this point with balancing his desire to defeat Wilson on the one hand with a need not to appear racist on the other. Then, at the end of April, Enoch Powell delivered a talk in Birmingham, which is now known as his 'Rivers of Blood' speech.[9] The topic of the speech was immigration but from the point of view of most of the Shadow Cabinet the content was nefarious. He spoke of black men holding a whip over white men and, in short, public order breaking down if Britain accepted immigrants from Commonwealth nations. Heath sacked Powell from the front bench the following day and the two men never spoke again.[10]

Heath allowed Wilson to keep managing the economy in his own manner and, with little assistance from the opposition, Labour's approval ratings slipped throughout 1968-9. As the Conservatives gradually climbed further and further ahead in the polls Heath became obsessed with preparing for government. He was determined that his team should be ready to implement changes immediately upon taking office. The problem, as would become apparent, was that a strategy of sitting and waiting for years on end did not give Shadow Ministers opportunities to experiment with new ideas. This meant that however convinced Heath was that his colleagues should be ready to take over, he hadn't done enough to prepare them.

This first became apparent to him at the end of January 1970 when he had arranged a weekend at Selsdon Park, South London, dedicated to meetings of senior Conservatives to discuss how their various departments would operate from day one in government. The idea was to take MPs away from Westminster, with its various distractions, while keeping them all in the same place.[11] When the press discovered that prominent opposition MPs were all spending a weekend together away from Westminster they naturally wanted to know why. At the end of the weekend someone had to brief the press as to what had been discussed but, realising that there had been a terrifying lack of innovation in almost every department, all Heath could do was to sanction a statement claiming that all discussion had been centred around law and order.[12] By a fluke this actually gave the Tories a further boost in the polls as the economic situation had led people to fear a breakdown of public order.

Therefore Heath had inadvertently given himself a temporary advance in the polls but there was no escaping his complete lack of policy. This followed through until the election that June, in which the Conservative manifesto claimed that 'The main causes of rising prices are Labour's policies...'[13] – hardly an inspiring vision for the future. In the months that followed Selsdon the Conservative lead was whittled down until, by May, some polls had Labour back in the lead.[14] Consequently on 18 May Wilson asked the Queen to dissolve Parliament for a June election. Throughout the campaign the polls stubbornly remained indicating a Labour win but on polling day, 18 June, the result defied all predictions. Heath was returned as Prime Minister, not with a large majority, but with one clear enough to govern (Conservatives 330 seats; Labour, 287; Liberals, six).[15]

Finally Heath could focus on forming a ministry, which was simply a matter of transferring his front bench team from their Shadow portfolios into the respective ministerial departments: Douglas-Home became Foreign Secretary; Iain Macleod, Chancellor of the Exchequer; and Reginald Maudling became Home Secretary. Margaret Thatcher, who had spent two years as Shadow Education Secretary was duly appointed as Education Secretary. However, within a few weeks the front bench was shaken by the news that, on 20 July, Iain Macleod had suffered a heart attack and died.[16] He was replaced by Anthony Barber who was not largely believed to be of the same political calibre.

Now came the implementation of policy. Two areas above all others dominated Heath's agenda when he initially entered office: continuing Macmillan's unfinished crusade to gain access to the EEC for Britain and reforming industrial relations. Regarding Europe, Charles de Gaulle had resigned as President of France in 1969 meaning that there was one barrier to EEC entry fewer than there had been during Macmillan's premiership. Heath was convinced that the new French President, Georges Pompidou, could be convinced of the merits of British inclusion and that when he came around the other member nations would follow suit.

Regarding industrial relations, inflation was spiralling out of control and industrial action was undoubtedly to blame. 95 per cent of walk-outs in Britain at the time were spontaneous and the cause was that, whereas in other countries freely negotiated collective agreements were binding on both sides, in Britain they were not. Consequently regardless of any agreement made, unions could instruct their members to demand more pay and walk out at any time if it was refused. The result was that pay was increasing by around 15 per cent per year, while prices were increasing by 7 per cent, yet there was no significant increase in productivity.[17] Britain was fast becoming one of the least competitive nations in the world.

These were the two battles that Heath decided to fight head-on during the early days of his premiership. After the summer recess he met with TUC leaders in October 1970 and in the same month went to Brussels to negotiate EEC entry. The costs of both policies would be high. The trades unions would not voluntarily urge pay restraint on their members, meaning that legislation would be required to force their hand. In Europe EEC members were not obliging in allowing an exemption to the external tariffs for New Zealand (whence Britain sourced a substantial amount of lamb) or about reducing the Common Agricultural Policy, which heavily subsidised (mainly French) farmers, to the detriment of other nations who were forced to contribute financially.

On 27 October Barber introduced a mini-budget into the House of Commons in order to change the spending plan introduced by the Labour government in the spring, to cover the period until the next budget was due in 1971. The result was sweeping spending cuts by the government (including, famously, removing free milk from schools, which led to the Education Secretary being taunted as 'Margaret Thatcher, milk snatcher). The budget was a statement of intent: the government was going to bring spending under control and rebuild the economy.

Then, in December, the government introduced its Industrial Relations Bill, designed to curb the power of the unions and make collective agreements binding, so that neither side (but more applicable to workers) could renege on it and walk out when it suited. Heath spoke in the House in support of the measures on the second reading on 17 December. As if to mark the need for reform, on 7 December power station employees began to work-to-rule demanding a 30 per cent pay rise; in January 1971 post office workers went on strike demanding 20 per cent; and then in March workers for Ford motor vehicles walked out, eventually achieving a 33 per cent pay rise.[18] This last issue was private, rather than public sector, but was largely seen as being fuelled by the incredible pay rises that public sector workers seemed able to achieve simply by walking out. In the end Labour were unable to overcome the Conservative majority and the Bill became law in August 1971.

In the meantime the Prime Minister was having rather more success than he had hoped for regarding Europe. It is true that the cost of entry was high, but Heath was prepared to pay almost any price, viewing British entry to the EEC as his political *pièce de résistance*. Discussions had to take place via back channels because there were many senior French politicians who were still opposed to British entry and would have attempted to stymie talks. Consequently all discussions were kept strictly between Heath, Douglas-Home and Pompidou, who had explicitly, although off-the-record, confirmed his support. After nearly a year of talks a summit was to be held between Heath and Pompidou in Paris from 20-21 May 1971 openly to discuss British entry. After hours of negotiation in which the French President made it clear that Britain had to focus on Europe, rather than the United States as it had done for thirty years, if entry was to be permitted, and Heath argued vehemently that he was serious about a commitment to the continent, talks ended with a press conference in which both men confirmed that Britain would be accepted by the six current member states.

Heath travelled back to Britain and prepared to introduce a Bill to Parliament approving in principle Britain's accession. The United Kingdom and the European Communities White Paper was put before the Commons in July. In October, when parliament reconvened following the summer recess, Heath allowed a free vote of Conservative members on the Bill. There was opposition to it but, thanks to assistance from a significant number of Labour rebels who defied a three line whip, the Bill passed.[19]

By the time that the 1971 parliamentary session drew to an end Heath, never unconvinced of his own self-importance anyway, was particularly happy with the course that his premiership was taking. However, any sense of triumphalism that he experienced at this point would quickly come to pass due to problems in his other priority area, industrial relations. The National Union of Mineworkers (NUM) had spent much of 1970-71 trying to frustrate government attempts to reform union law. They had rallied opposition to the Industrial Relations Bill, they had rejected offers of pay increases and productivity bonuses and they had tried unsuccessfully to organise a strike in 1970 when the motion was narrowly voted against by the union-body. By their actions it seemed that their objective was to end the tenure of the Conservative government, rather than to secure better conditions for their members. At the end of 1971 they changed their constitution so that a majority of 55 per cent of votes, rather than two-thirds, was required for strike action to become official.[20] Then in December they voted 59 per cent in favour of a strike. The problem was that the ability of miners effectively to shut the country down by turning the electricity off meant that the government felt bound to appease them. Looking into the matter that December, in anticipation of a

January strike, Heath found that coal was stockpiled enough to see the country through several weeks of strikes without upsetting the electricity supply. Nobody believed that miners would walk out without pay for that long. On 9 January 1972 the strike duly began, Heath in confident mood that he could see it through.

At the end of the month the Prime Minister flew to Brussels to sign the Treaty accepting the negotiated terms of Britain's joining the EEC. In the years since then he referred to it as the proudest moment of his life. However, no sooner had he arrived back in the country than he discovered that the government had been completely outplayed by the NUM. Arthur Scargill, a militant senior member of the union, had organised 'flying pickets' to travel the country preventing coal getting to where it was needed. Heath had taken the advice that there were plenty of coal stock piles in good faith, which there were, but had never thought to check whether they were in a place that they could be used (for example already at the power stations). Stock pile facilities were picketed to prevent the movement of coal out and power stations were picketed to prevent transport in. It was a disaster. On 9 February a State of Emergency was called and the following day the Cabinet learned that what stock piles they could access would last no more than a week or so.[21] Most of the provisions of the Industrial Relations Act were not due to take effect as law until the end of the month, most of the picketing had been lawful at that point. In some instances a few hundred police officers were overwhelmed by thousands of picketers that they could do nothing to prevent from acting as they pleased. This set the stage for the next phase of battle in the life of the Tory Party. From fighting the Whigs to the Liberals to the Labour Party, now it was the turn of the trades unions. On this occasion, violence and intimidation was winning the day. It would be over a decade before democracy was able to overcome this growing threat.

Heath had no choice but to cave. He appointed a Court of Inquiry who almost immediately recommended a greater than 20 per cent increase in salary for the miners but, astonishingly, the NUM rejected the offer and demanded more. Heath invited the NUM leadership to Downing Street to settle matters and got a compromise thrashed out by the end of

February. However, it was not a settlement so much as a temporary ceasefire. The NUM had learned that they could force the people to bend to their will and they would use these tactics again.

February was a busy month for Heath. Following his return from Brussels he had tried to push the Act ratifying British entry into the EEC through Parliament, as well as dealing with the miners' strike. Although in the previous October he had won a comfortable victory on the *principle* of British accession, with many Labour MPs defying a three line whip, on this occasion the result would be far less clear. Labour whips worked in force to convince their MPs to vote as a Party, not as individuals. The government whips worked just as furiously, but there were still Conservative rebels, Enoch Powell among them. In the vote on the second reading on 17 February the government carried the Bill by 309 votes to 301.[22]

The opposition continued to try to frustrate the Bill through committee stage but eventually, in July 1972, it passed into law. It had been a strenuous few months for Heath and although he could claim to have achieved a great deal – the passing of the Industrial Relations Act, taking Britain into Europe and ending the miners' strike – he was rapidly building a comprehensive catalogue of enemies. Anti-Europeans were furious that he had risked British sovereignty by taking the country into the EEC; trades unionists hated him firstly for being a Tory and secondly for being exactly what they expected a Tory to be (challenging their constitutions, their powers, their rights, their privileges); anti-unionists felt that he had been unprepared for a showdown with the miners, particularly when it came to the use of stockpiles, and that when the time came he had shown weakness by bowing to their demands. By the early summer of 1972 Heath was Prime Minister and leader of the Conservative Party, with no rivals lurking in the shadows that he could see. However, as a person he was, and had been all his life, so absolutely convinced that he was special that, even when the storm clouds gathered, he would not have believed that they were coming for him.

Just before Parliament prorogued the Cabinet discussed options to end the ongoing war with the unions. Heath foresaw three issues which he found unacceptable. Firstly, the unions were trying to bring down a democratically elected government. Secondly, they were acting in their own interests at the expense of the public. Thirdly, their demands for unreasonable wages drove up prices and caused unemployment. One way or another the situation needed resolving. The problem was that the government had tried legislation with the Industrial Relations Act, which only incensed the union leaders and there was fear that the next step would be widespread public disorder. Another possibility was negotiation but the leadership of the TUC, for example, had been consulted in the past and shown themselves to be unreasonable in compromising. However, in order to keep public opinion onside Heath invited the TUC leadership to Downing Street for talks in July. Predictably nothing was achieved but at least goodwill had been demonstrated on both sides.

Heath now decided to take economic matters into his own hands. On 3 November the government introduced a statutory ninety day freeze on both prices and incomes in order to get inflation under control. The Labour Party was incensed that wages were being frozen and Conservatives were alarmed at such a drastic level of state-interference. The measures were therefore heavily criticised in Parliament but Heath pressed on, extending the freeze from January 1973 for a further ninety days.[23] For the rest of the year Heath desperately tried to keep wages under control but must have felt like Sisyphus pushing the boulder up the hill, with ever increasing demands being placed on him from various quarters. In July 1973 it was the turn of the old scourge, the NUM.

At their national conference at the beginning of the month the leadership of the NUM demanded a 35 per cent pay increase which would be unacceptable to Heath even if they hadn't had extremely generous rises over each of the preceding years. In this instance the head of the NUM, Joe Gormley, was not pushing for such an excessive rise, but the militants such as Scargill were going to squeeze whatever they could get from the government. Gormley met with Heath on 16 July at Downing Street and between them they came up with a plan to pay the miners an unsociable hours allowance. That way Heath could claim that direct wages were not going up and that his wage freeze was being honoured but the miners would still get their money. The problem for the government was that, if accepted, it would not help the matter of inflation. If this had concerned him he needn't have worried: the NUM body rejected the proposals.

In October the National Coal Board (NCB) offered miners a 13 per cent pay rise, which was again rejected and the miners began working-to-rule. It looked like another strike was looming and the Cabinet became nervous that they would lose yet another confrontation with this organisation. They attempted to ready themselves for the forthcoming battle: a loss would be humiliating and would undoubtedly give the impression that the government could never win a contest with the miners, possibly with any major union. Ultimately it was events thousands of miles away that decided the outcome just as the conflict was beginning. October 1973 witnessed the Yom Kippur War, also known as the Arab-Israeli war whereby a coalition of Arab states led by Egypt and Syria attacked Israel. The government strategy in the event of a miners' strike had been to replace coal with imported oil from the Middle East to see the country through. Owing to the war the oil may not be forthcoming but, even if it was, prices increased by 70 per cent within days of the outbreak of the conflict.[24]

With the miners on slowdown, even without all-out strike action, Britain's supplies dwindled and electricity shortages became a genuine concern. In December, with imports of oil no longer an option, Heath announced that beginning in January industry would be limited to a three-day week in order to conserve electricity. Throughout the following weeks the NUM, the TUC and Heath talked on several occasions but the Prime Minister was passed negotiating. Whatever suggestions were made by the union leaders Heath refused. In a sense he was only being as obstinate as they had been with him for years. However, his conduct did not reflect well and, rather than being able to say that he had made a deal and they had refused to stick to it (if they didn't) he was forced to face the public in the position that he hadn't even tried. It was becoming increasingly clear that a general election would have to be called soon, as the government would struggle to see through another eighteen months constantly fighting with industry without a fresh mandate from the public. Consequently it was these negotiations upon which the public would be judging the government's policy of industrial relations.

On 4 February the NUM held a ballot proposing strike action which passed comfortably.[25] Upon hearing this news

Heath went straight to the palace to ask for a dissolution. The election date was set for 28 February and the Conservatives campaigned with the slogan 'Who Governs Britain?', the implication being that the voters were being asked to decide between the unions and a democratic government. The public clearly didn't see it that way and when the results came in Labour ended up with more seats, although only just (Labour, 301; Conservatives, 297; Liberals, 14).[26] This election, seen as one that the NUM had forced the government into and subsequently seen it defeated, created a widespread belief that the miners could make or break governments. This belief, which pervaded both Whitehall and the union itself, would lead to bitter conflicts in the coming years.

Heath opted against resigning straight away, instead attempting to form a coalition with the Liberals. It was the Monday after the election, 4 March, before Heath conceded defeat and resigned as Prime Minister.[27] Wilson would be returning to Downing Street.

Immediately after the election Conservative MPs as well as the media began to question whether Heath should stay on as leader. Ultimately, though, the fact that the numbers in the Commons were so closely aligned meant that another election would probably be called imminently, meaning that a change in leadership was not desirable.

The Tories could have prompted an immediate dissolution by forcing a vote of no confidence in the new government but senior advisers were aware that this would play badly with the public, who generally felt put out by elections. Not giving Wilson a chance to cause his own downfall would only mean that he would gain more seats following a forced dissolution. Consequently Heath played a game of challenging the government when necessary but not being overly forceful about it.

This was almost physically painful for Heath. For the majority of his political career and indeed for every second of his years as the head of the Conservatives Wilson had been his enemy. Politically they were opposed and personally there was no love lost. Wilson didn't like Heath but Heath positively hated Wilson. Heath could be extremely bitter at times, probably fuelled by his conviction that he was so important to the country that any challenge against him was tantamount to

treason. Now he had to watch the man he loathed doing the job
he coveted, taunting him from the despatch box on the floor of
the House of Commons, often being – Heath felt – simply
wrong on policy or dishonest about his actions. Yet he could
not criticise him too heavily or push him too far for fear of
Wilson claiming that the government could not continue and
calling a dissolution. So 1974 dragged on with Wilson working
in almost impossible circumstances but Heath unwilling or
unable to deliver a *coup de grâce.*

In September Wilson finally announced a dissolution
for an election on 10 October. The result, as predicted, was
worse than the February election had been for the Tories. They
won 277 seats to Labour's 319. [28] Wilson now had his majority.
Heath, on the other hand, had now lost three elections in nine
years but still saw no reason to step aside. Edward du Cann,
Chairman of the 1922 Committee, contacted Heath shortly after
the election to warn him that the Conservative backbenchers
had lost confidence in him and he must go.[29] He did not heed
this advice. However, in November, as a sop to the '22, Heath
fatefully pledged to introduce a new system for electing the
Conservative Party leader and he set up a panel led by Alec
Douglas-Home and including du Cann to investigate options.
In December the panel reported that there should be an annual
election for the leader as long as a challenger could find a
proposer and seconder.

Within days of this verdict Margaret Thatcher
announced that she was challenging Heath. On 6 January Airey
Neave, a backbench MP with nothing in common with
Thatcher other than a shared desire to remove the incumbent
leader, took over management of her campaign.[30] Up until
Thatcher announced her candidacy the assumption had been
that a challenger would take the form of either Keith Joseph or
du Cann himself. Joseph threw his support behind Thatcher,
which prompted her to stand, whereas Neave and du Cann were
close. Consequently when du Cann opted not to stand, all his
supporters followed Neave in joining Thatcher's campaign.

Going into polling day on 4 February Heath was
confident of success. He was stunned by the news that Thatcher
had beaten him by 130 votes to 119.[31] She had not won the
required 15 per cent majority of votes to prevent a second ballot
but the message was clear enough: the Party had no confidence
in Heath. He immediately announced that he would not be

contesting a second ballot. He was no longer leader of the Conservative Party.

Heath had been leader for nearly ten years. Conventional wisdom is that his time at the top, and particularly his time as Prime Minister, was an unmitigated disaster defined by a lack of direction, lack of policy and lack of achievement. This is not strictly true. The one major goal that Heath had set his heart on before taking office was achieving British entry into the EEC and, regardless of the (very mixed) opinions of future generations of Conservatives as to the merits of this particular policy, there is no doubt as to his success in attaining it. That said, his other major preoccupation was the economy and industrial relations. His relationship with the unions was a disaster as he neither appeased them nor succeeded in confronting them, rather walking a dangerous middle line of antagonising them before backing down at the last instance. He never got control of inflation, which was exacerbated by the wage inflation driven by his failed policy towards the unions while not being helped by his constant interfering in the economy by, among other things, imposing price and wage freezes.

Politically, Heath lost three out of four elections that he contested as leader of the Conservative Party. No other leader has had such a poor electoral record and, when considering his performance from this aspect, it is difficult to see why he expected that the Party would accept him staying on as leader from 1975.

Heath's legacy, therefore, was not electoral success, achieving Party unity, providing stability in the economy or giving the Conservatives a sense of Party pride. His legacy is instead confined to British entry into what is now the European Union (EU). The problem for him in this sense is that Europe has become the new defining issue for the Party today, splitting the Conservatives between Europhiles and Eurosceptics. The issue is potentially the most divisive one since Robert Peel's decision to repeal the Corn Laws led to the breaking of the Peelites from the Conservatives in the 1840s. More divisive even than the issue of Home Rule for Ireland in the early twentieth century. Depending on which way the Conservatives go on this issue in the future, and indeed whether Britain accepts its position in the EU or chooses to withdraw, Heath's legacy will either be as a visionary who started something that determined the future or as a naïve leader who gave up Britain's sovereignty to Europe, only for someone else to correct the mistake later.

Margaret Thatcher
(1975 — 1990)

For those waiting with baited breath for that favourite media catchphrase, the 'u-turn', I have only one thing to say: You turn if you want to. The lady's not for turning.

Margaret Thatcher, 10 October 1980

If this Devil of a Tory be so black as you paint him, I wonder how he comes by so fair a character?

Daniel Defoe's *Tory*, 1692

ONCE HEATH WITHDREW from the leadership contest, several other aspirants, who saw Margaret Thatcher's role as that of a stalking horse, threw their hats into the ring for the second ballot. Willie Whitelaw became the favourite as soon as he declared his candidacy. Geoffrey Howe, Jim Prior and John Peyton also put themselves forward. When the second ballot was held on 11 February, one week after the first, Thatcher received 146 votes with Whitelaw receiving 79. She had won a clear victory and was now the first female leader in the history of the Conservative Party.

Within a couple of days Thatcher had visited Heath to discuss with him how to move forward. He refused to serve in her Shadow Cabinet, which gave the new leader almost a free hand to appoint whomever she liked. Willie Whitelaw was made Deputy Leader of the Conservative Party. Keith Joseph, who had so influenced Thatcher's economic policies over the past few years and would continue to do so in future, was given a brief to research and examine policy. Reginald Maudling was appointed as Shadow Foreign Secretary and Geoffrey Howe became Shadow Chancellor of the Exchequer.

Thatcher now needed to take the opportunity to stamp her authority over the Conservative Party. Those who were still loyal to Heath, those who didn't believe that a woman belonged at the top of a profession dominated by men and those who thought her too inexperienced would all need to be made to toe the line. However, it was tentative first steps for the new leader. She and Keith Joseph had already been heavily influenced by monetarist ideas for managing the economy, including the ever-escalating rate of inflation (which reached a summit of 26.9 per cent in August 1975)[1] and non-interference in industry. However, in the first test of her new principles Thatcher failed to stick to her guns. In April Wilson's government announced a £1.4 billion package to rescue British Leyland from collapse.[2] In spite of the effect this would have on the already-unhealthy national deficit, on inflation, and how it was contrary to her non-interventionist values, Thatcher failed to denounce the government for it, possibly influenced by political (the need to win parliamentary seats in the Leyland heartland of the West Midlands) rather than economic factors. Taxing successful businesses in order to keep unsuccessful ones afloat, however, was not acceptable to the increasingly vocal Tory Right. Sooner or later Thatcher would have to make a stand on economic policy. Fortunately for her for the time being her position was bolstered by the poor economy for which Wilson was being blamed. By the autumn the Conservatives were 23 points ahead in the opinion polls.[3]

Into 1976 and Thatcher made the token gesture of reshuffling her Shadow Cabinet (moving Willie Whitelaw to the Home Office Brief) as if to acknowledge that her first year of opposition had not been as aggressive as it could have been and soon afterwards she caught another break. All the success she had enjoyed thus far in the opinion polls had undoubtedly been due to the government's handling of the economy rather than her personal abilities. New to the front bench, Thatcher had spent much of 1975 completely outperformed by Harold Wilson on the floor of the House of Commons. In March 1976, probably becoming aware of the early effects of a dementia that would blight his later life, Wilson announced that he was resigning as Prime Minister. Labour elected as his successor Jim Callaghan, who was a much less slippery opponent.

Relations between Thatcher and Callaghan got off to a rocky start but in doing so they inadvertently united the hitherto fragmented Conservatives behind their leader rather than picking fights with each other. The saga began in the spring of 1976 with a government Bill aimed at nationalising aircraft and shipbuilding industries. All political parties have historically whipped support amongst their members for or against government legislation in order that they may win a division in either House of Parliament. However, there had also been a longstanding custom, recently abolished, of 'pairing' whereby an individual on one side who was unable or reluctant to take part in a vote would find someone in a similar position from the other side and, subject to agreement and registering the plan with the Chief Whips on both sides, agree that both would abstain from voting. This way neither side was in a better or worse position than they would have been had both members voted. Pairing relied upon Chief Whips from both the government and the opposition playing an honest game.

For the debate around Labour's plans for nationalisation of aircraft and shipbuilding in the spring of 1976 several Conservative and Labour MPs were accordingly paired. When it came to the crunch moment there were two divisions. For the first, government and opposition were tied so the speaker voted to defeat the government. Immediately afterwards, realising that they were going to be beaten twice, Labour brought a paired MP into the House to vote and the government subsequently won the second division by that one vote. The Conservatives saw this as an affront to a long established procedure and, on 9 June, Thatcher moved a motion of no confidence in the government. She was defeated, but had tested the water. It was a course of action that she felt she may use again should circumstances move further in her favour.

A series of Conservative by-election victories throughout 1976 quickly whittled away the government's overall majority and, by the summer, Labour had fewer MPs than all other parties combined. If these smaller parties could be made to vote together then the government may well be brought down. Then in the autumn came the issue of devolution in Scotland and Wales, first given a voice in Westminster by Heath several years earlier, much to the dismay of the heavily unionist Tories that he was leading at the time. However, it was Wilson who first drew up the necessary legislation and Callaghan who attempted to pass it.

There were no end of difficulties with devolution. Firstly there was the concern that devolution may one day lead to independence, particularly in Scotland (as a way to combat this threat one proposal was that a proportional representation, rather than a first-past-the-post, voting system should be adopted. That way, it was believed, the emerging Scottish

Nationalist Party could never win an outright majority). On the other hand some felt that devolution would sufficiently appease Scottish nationalists so as to deter them from demanding more. This latter argument did not sway the majority of the Shadow Cabinet, who opted in favour of opposing the Bill with a three line whip. Many of those in the minority resigned from the front bench including Malcolm Rifkind and the Shadow Scottish Secretary Alick Buchanan-Smith.

The Bill succeeded in passing its second reading but in committee stage over 350 amendments were attached, most of which were designed to delay its passage. The government attempted to pass a guillotine motion (limiting the amount of time that could be spent debating the Bill and its various amendments) but it was defeated and so, in February 1977, the Devolution Bill was withdrawn. In March the Conservatives once again tabled a motion of no confidence in the Government but a combination of the Liberals supporting Labour and a poor speech from Thatcher in the Commons upon introducing the motion led to its defeat. In spite of this the Conservatives knew that with Labour's majority having disappeared it would only be a matter of time before they were defeated and forced to resign. Consequently the Shadow Cabinet began to work on a substantive manifesto, rather than just the policy of opposition for the sake of it that drives most parties in their early years out of office. For Thatcher this meant striking a balance between those sympathetic to more Keynesian economic principles, such as Jim Prior and Ian Gilmour, and those who were being increasingly influenced by monetarist methods such as herself, Keith Joseph and Geoffrey Howe.

The balance wasn't always easy and indeed even led on occasion to public inconsistencies. For example towards the end of 1976 a number of workers at a photograph printing firm called Grunwick had walked out and therefore been dismissed by management. A trade union known as APEX had subsequently signed up the dismissed workers and demanded to negotiate on their behalf, which Grunwick would not do. By the summer of 1977 flying pickets from all sorts of other unions across the country had descended on Grunwick's premises in London to try to force them to back down. Jim Prior publicly declared that the government should try to conciliate both sides. Keith Joseph had publicly condemned the picketers. Disciplining both sides to adhere to a collectively agreed policy in future would not be easy. During 1978, in anticipation of an autumn election, the Party started to produce some vague pledges for a Conservative government, including tax cuts and reductions in welfare spending. By the summer opinion polls had Labour within a couple of points of the Conservatives, which only fuelled expectations that Callaghan would call for a dissolution.

However, the Prime Minister announced in the September that there would be no early election (the Parliament could run until October 1979 at the latest) apparently expecting that Labour's incline in the polls could continue through to the new year and put him on a better footing than he was currently. What he had not reckoned on was the most difficult industrial crisis in living memory. What is now known as The Winter of Discontent was about to begin.

The government had been employing a policy of voluntary pay restraints with industry in order to ty to dampen inflation. Under this policy workers in all sectors were expected to accept a 5 per cent per annum pay increase and nothing more. On 12 December 1978 National Health Service and Local Authority unions rejected the 5 per cent rise and prepared to strike in January 1979.

On 3 January the Transport and General Workers' Union (TGWU) called lorry drivers out on strike in demand of a 25 per cent rise. So hospitals wouldn't receive patients and goods could not be transported. Grave diggers in Liverpool went out on strike – a relatively minor affair compared with the national walk outs in other industries but when the public had televised images broadcast into their homes of bodies piling up unburied it added a sense of horror to the worry that they already felt. This relatively localised dispute, therefore, had a far more powerful effect on public opinion than any of the larger strikes.

To make matters worse Callaghan left the country for an international summit in Guadeloupe that January, giving the impression that he was aloof from all that was going on. Upon his return, having landed in the airport he was accosted by the press demanding to know why he had been absent at such a critical time. His reply was that people elsewhere in the world did not believe that there was growing chaos in the UK, which prompted The Sun to splash across its front page a picture of

Callaghan next to the paraphrase 'Crisis? What Crisis?'[4] It was a public relations disaster for the Prime Minister.

Debating the matter in the Commons upon the reopening of Parliament Thatcher offered Callaghan Conservative support if the government introduced legislation to reform trade unions including outlawing secondary picketing and introducing secret ballots when voting for strike action. The Prime Minister turned this down, suggesting that conciliation with the unions to encourage further voluntary pay restraints[5] such as the 5 per cent that had been awarded for previous years.

When, in March, new devolution Bills for Scotland and Wales were introduced by the government, the Shadow Cabinet considered tabling their third no confidence motion against the government. It was agreed and in the last week of March Thatcher introduced the motion. The division that took place on 28 March saw the government defeated by 311 votes to 310.[6] The government resigned and Parliament was dissolved. The sense of triumph for the Tories would be short-lived. Two days later Airey Neave, the Shadow Northern Ireland Secretary and close friend of Thatcher since his management of her leadership campaign in 1975, was killed by a bomb planted under his car by Irish nationalists. An air of grief would hang over the forthcoming election campaign.

The election date was set for Thursday 3 May and the result was a comfortable Conservative majority with 339 seats over Labour's 269 (the Liberals took 11).[7] Thatcher kissed hands as Prime Minister in the afternoon of 5 May. The Cabinet was formed within 24 hours: Geoffrey Howe became Chancellor of the Exchequer; Keith Joseph took over at Industry; Willie Whitelaw was appointed Home Secretary; and Peter Carrington became Foreign Secretary.[8]

In the Queen's Speech that May the government announced an intense programme to curb the influence of the state, extend privatisation and even to give council tenants the right to buy their homes. The new government had to introduce its first budget in June and therefore much of the first month in office was dedicated to drawing that up. At a time of recession, which Britain had been thrust into several months earlier, the conventional wisdom was that an increase in direct taxation should be combined with an increase in government spending in order to stimulate growth. If Thatcher was going to introduce the principles that she was by now convinced should govern economic thinking, and which were entirely contrary to this conventional wisdom, now was the time. Howe therefore proposed to reduce income taxes (the top rate was presently set at 83 per cent)[9] on the top and basic rates in order to reduce unemployment by making working more affordable. This would be funded by cuts in public spending and an increase in VAT. It was an enormous shift in economic management from everything that had been assumed for half a century.

On 21 June Thatcher travelled to Strasbourg for her first European Council meeting. Here, too, she saw the need for financial reform. At this time Britain made a disproportionate contribution to the European budget and received very little back. 70 per cent of budget spending went to supporting agriculture and came from contributions from member states known as the Common Agricultural Policy (CAP). A substantial portion of this spending went to subsidising farmers in France, British farmers requiring little support.[10] Thatcher went to Strasbourg and demanded a £1 billion rebate from the CAP for Britain, a discussion for which the French President Giscard reluctantly added to the agenda for their next Council meeting, scheduled for the end of November in Dublin. When that meeting came about the Prime Minister pressed her claim for a rebate and by the time the Council broke up she had been offered £350 million back, which she was not prepared to countenance.[11]

Back home the Prime Minister found that public opinion was in favour of her stance towards the European Community, not least because public spending in general had been cut so the CAP contribution seemed unjustifiable. She had further meetings with European leaders over the coming months before another Council summit in Luxembourg on 27 April. At this meeting Britain was offered a limit on its contribution of £325 million, meaning an effective rebate double the size offered the previous autumn, but only for one year. The argument would have to start all over again in 1981. Again Thatcher refused.

Other European leaders, shocked at the Prime Minister's intransigence, quickly organised further talks for May 1980 to settle the matter. Peter Carrington was despatched to Brussels to represent Britain. After a day of negotiations Carrington reported back that Britain would receive a rebate equal to over £600 million per annum, guaranteed for three years, rather than one. Thatcher felt that it was still too low but decided against pushing her luck.

Meanwhile the economic situation at home was still poor. Inflation continued to run high, albeit much lower than its apogee of 1975, unemployment was high and the unions still had a stranglehold over wages. It was this last factor that the government set its mind to during 1980 as a means of reducing the other problems. While the country was plunged into recession and firms were met with increasing costs with reduced demand, they were still forced to pay ever-increasing salaries because the alternative was mass strikes and picketing of their premises. In the early spring the government introduced an Employment Bill aimed at controlling three areas of industrial disputes. The first was picketing: presently, and as happened with Grunwick, among others, unions could organise pickets in support of other unions, known as secondary picketing. This meant that workers that had absolutely nothing to do with the trade dispute at hand could turn up and form a blockade outside the premises of the business concerned. The government wanted this limiting to those involved in the dispute.

The second area for reform was the 'closed shop'. At this time it was possible for unions to have such a hold over a business as to be able to force management not to hire someone, or indeed to dismiss someone, on the basis that they were not a member of their union. The consequences if management refused would be a picket line outside the premises. The government believed that people should have a free choice as to whether or not they join a union, or any organisation for that matter, and therefore the closed shop should be banned.

Thirdly there was the matter of secret ballots, which needed to be introduced for industrial action in the same way that they had been introduced for general elections for a century. The possibility for people to be intimidated into voting one way or another by having to declare to all present their intentions was not fair to them or to the other people who were affected by industrial action. The legislation moved comfortably through both Houses of Parliament.

By 1981 the government was lagging in the polls. The reforms that had been made to taxes and trade union legislation had made the Left bitterly angry without yet having the desired effect of pulling the economy out of recession. During 1980 and

1981 the government had faced strikes by British Steel and a crisis over the future of the car manufacturer, British Leyland. Across the country nationalised industries were showing their discontent and it was widely feared among Conservatives that the unions may decide to bring down the government, just as the NUM had brought Heath's government down in 1974. Ultimately, like so many Prime Ministers before her, it was events abroad, rather than at home, which rescued Thatcher's popularity.

On 19 March 1982 some Argentinians had landed in South Georgia, an island 800 miles south-east of the Falkland Islands, and raised the Argentine flag. Ostensibly these Argentinians claimed to be scrap metal dealers whereas actually they were more than likely agents acting on instructions from the military junta that had seized power in Buenos Aires the previous winter (summer in the southern hemisphere). The Argentine government claimed to have had no knowledge of the incident. Then on 31 March the Prime Minister received intelligence reports that an Argentine naval fleet had been despatched and would land in the Falklands on Friday 2 April. Almost immediately the Chief of the Naval staff was ordered to prepare a fleet to head for the South Atlantic in order to recapture the islands if they were taken. The problem was that it would take two days to prepare the ships to leave and then weeks to make the 8,000 mile journey south, all the while the Argentine President General Galtieri would be fortifying his position on the islands.

The task force of naval ships left Britain on the Monday 5 April and on the same day Peter Carrington resigned as Foreign Secretary, believing that the country needed a scapegoat for the fall of the islands.[12] He was replaced by Francis Pym. The following day Thatcher messaged US President Regan asking for him to place economic sanctions on Argentina in order to force them to withdraw peacefully but the President refused to get involved. For the rest of April the British task force made its way steadily south while Thatcher and Pym took their case to the UN hoping for a resolution which would never come.

At the end of April the task force neared the islands and set up a 200 mile exclusion zone around them: any ships or aircraft coming inside that perimeter would be attacked.

Consequently the Argentine fleet circled the islands just outside this exclusion zone. On 2 May Thatcher received intelligence that *HMS Conqueror*, a Royal Naval submarine, had been shadowing the Argentine battle-cruise *General Belgrano* and believed it to be involved in one side of a pincer movement which would shortly strike the task force from two sides of the exclusion zone. The Prime Minister subsequently gave the order to attack the *Belgrano*, an act which she would come under heavy criticism for over the coming years. The sinking of the *Belgrano* was, if nothing else, a decisive moment in the conflict. What followed was the British recapture of the islands, culminating in a ceasefire on 14 June.

Back in Britain it seemed that Margaret Thatcher had restored national pride and buried the international inferiority complex that the nation had carried since Suez nearly thirty years earlier. Her approval ratings soared. Neil Kinnock later remarked that she was blessed by her enemies. Politically General Galtieri had been a good enemy to have.

Opinion moved towards the Conservatives for other reasons, too. First of all in 1980 Michael Foot had replaced Callaghan as leader of the Labour Party. If Callaghan had been a slave to the Left then Foot was one of the slave drivers. Whereas Callaghan had sympathised with union interests, Foot forwarded them wherever possible and was known positively to advocate mass nationalisation of all industry. To those fearful of a return to the 1970s, Foot was the wrong person to lead an opposition. Secondly, and strongly linked to the first point, some Labour members themselves had become concerned by the Party's lurch to the Left. This had caused some of them to leave in 1981, establish a separate political party and seek re-election under the new brand. The Social Democratic Party (SDP) was not just formed from faceless, aggrieved backbenchers, but by such significant figures as Roy Jenkins, who had served as both Chancellor of the Exchequer and Home Secretary in previous governments.

Thirdly from the beginning of 1982 Britain had shaken off the recession that it had suffered for the previous couple of years. Inflation had come down to an acceptable level and standards of living were improving. The government could take credit for all of this and, added to the 'Falklands Factor', the Party surged ahead in the polls. Thatcher shamelessly took advantage by calling an election for June 1983. The result was better than any optimist could have hoped for. The

Conservatives increased their majority, winning 397 seats to Labour's 209. The SDP had, for the purposes of the election, entered into an alliance with the Liberals (thus sowing the seeds of a merger between the parties to become what is now the Liberal Democrats) and much was made of the possibility of them emerging as a new force in British politics. In the event the Alliance took only 23 seats (although, incredibly, they received almost as many votes as Labour: 7.9 million compared with 8.5 million).[13]

The 1983 general election, more so than that of 1979, saw an overwhelming defeat for what Thatcher would one day call 'democratic socialism'. However, there were still countless extremists, particularly in the trade union movement, who felt that if they were defeated electorally then they would have to resort to *undemocratic* socialism. That is that democracy should be met with force. Most notably the militant unionist Arthur Scargill, who as an influential member of the NUM had organised the flying pickets during the miners' disputes ten years earlier against the judgement of his superiors, was now General Secretary of that same union. He now had far more authority to challenge the government than he had had when Heath had been Prime Minister.

From the time of Scargill's election as leader of the NUM in 1981 Thatcher had ordered the Energy Secretary, Nigel Lawson, to start discreetly building up supplies of coal but also to ensure that these supplies were at power stations, rather than pit heads. Her logic was that when Scargill ordered his members to walk out, the government would not suffer from the same difficulties that Heath's had; namely an inability to get the coal from the pit heads to the power stations for usage.

In June 1983, after the general election, Thatcher reshuffled her Cabinet replacing her Foreign Secretary, Francis Pym, with whom she agreed on little, with Geoffrey Howe; promoting Nigel Lawson to Howe's old position of Chancellor of the Exchequer; and bringing Peter Walker in to Lawson's old position as Energy Secretary at what would prove to be a crucial time. Willie Whitelaw remained Deputy Prime Minster but retired from the Home Office to be replace by Leon Brittan. Brittan, like Walker, was about to receive a baptism of fire.

In the summer the National Coal Board offered miners a 5.2 per cent pay rise and at the same time declared that several unprofitable pits would have to be closed.[14] In October the NUM responded by banning overtime in protest both at what they saw as an ungenerous pay increase and at the closure of pits. Their stance was that as long as coal existed the pits should remain open. However, an overtime ban was as far as they could go, as over the past three years Scargill had organised no fewer than three ballots proposing strike action, none of which had achieved the necessary 55 per cent of votes to allow for a national strike.

On 1 March 1984 the NCB announced the closure of Cortonwood colliery in Yorkshire. The local NUM decided the strike against this action, which they could do at a local level without the need to consult the national executive. Here Scargill found his loophole for a strike. Although a ballot had to be held with 55 per cent of members voting in favour in order to have a national walk out, if each local area decided to strike independently, the national executive could support them and this would have the effect of a national strike without it officially being so. In the second week of March Yorkshire and, separately, Scottish NUM workers walked out on strike and the NUM planned to send them to picket elsewhere in the country in order to intimidate working miners into joining them. At the beginning of the first day of action around half the mines in the UK had closed but by the end of the day, thanks to flying pickets forcing working miners to turn home, this number had increased to around five in eight. Shortly Nottinghamshire, Derbyshire and Lancashire miners were all holding ballots proposing strike actions over local conditions. None of the ballots, however, could go ahead fairly as flying pickets descended from the striking areas to intimidate members into voting the way the NUM wanted. Brittan assured the Prime Minister than the legislation passed before the election gave the police plenty of powers to deal with secondary picketing and other forms of intimidation, the problem was that the sheer numbers that turned out overwhelmed local constabularies.

Flying pickets from Yorkshire were in force in Nottinghamshire on 14 March for their ballot but, in spite of this, the Nottinghamshire workers voted overwhelmingly against action and, in doing so, may well have helped to save the government as coal stocks would go that much further. The NUM kept tight control over those pits that it could prevent people from working in, assuming that the government would eventually be broken just as they had in 1974. However, Scargill misjudged not just the amount of coal already at power stations but also both the amount that was successfully being transported from functioning pits and the nation's ability to generate electricity by burning (admittedly expensive) oil, which began at the end of March.

As the strike wore on into the spring the picketers became increasingly violent. On the news the public were broadcast images of striking miners clashing with police or else intimidating their working colleagues. It didn't end at the entrances to pits though: the families – wives and children – of working miners were targeted for intimidation. So the strike went on through the summer and into the autumn by which time the government started to become nervous that coal supplies may run out before the end of winter. If this happened it would guarantee the miners a victory as power cuts during January and February would be a disaster for the country. It was against this backdrop that the Conservative Party Conference was held in Brighton during the second week of October.

For the most part nothing spectacular occurred at that Conference. Thatcher and much of the Cabinet stayed at the Grand Hotel. Then, at 2.54 a.m. on the morning of Friday 12 October a bomb exploded inside the hotel. It had been planted by members of the IRA with the intention of killing the Prime Minister. She survived but others were not so fortunate: five people were killed and many others injured including Norman Tebbit, who was a staunch ally of Thatcher, and his wife Margaret who was left permanently paralysed. Thatcher's allies must have considered how many of them would be targeted by the IRA in the years to come, given that, following the death of Airey Neave, targeting the Prime Minister and those close to her seemed now to be somewhat of a theme. The Prime Minister delivered her speech to Conference later that day as arranged, determined not to let terrorists see that they had affected her.

By the end of October the Cabinet returned to business as usual. And business at this point meant defeating the NUM. Miners were struggling with not having earned money for seven months (although the NUM was paying striking miners who were prepared also to join their picket lines) and the NCB capitalised on this by announcing that any miner who returned to work by 19 November would be entitled to a Christmas bonus. Slowly they started to return. In the meantime, though, working miners were savagely beaten, sometimes even in their own homes, by those desperate to keep the strike going.[15]

However, the rate of return to work for previously-striking miners was such that the government need no longer worry about depletion of coal stocks. The only question going into the new year was when the strike would end completely. It was 27 February 1985 before it was reported that more than half of miners were at work. Four days later the NUM voted to support a return to work. The strike was finally over, twelve months after it had begun.

For the most part the rest of 1985 passed off without incident, at least until the summer recess. Neil Kinnock, the leader of the Labour Party who had replaced Foot following the 1983 election, had been put in an impossible position during the miners' strike. He could not support the NUM and keep public opinion onside but he could not condemn them without losing his Party. Consequently he struggled to make a dent on the Tory lead in the polls. In the summer Thatcher made some minor changes to the Cabinet including demoting Leon Brittan to the Department of Trade & Industry to be replaced by Douglas Hurd as Home Secretary. It would not be Brittan's last disappointment during the course of that Parliament.

One of the first issues that Brittan had to deal with in his new post was difficulties faced by a small West Country helicopter manufacturer called Westland, which was in financial difficulties and looked set to go into receivership within a couple of months if a financial rescue package could not be secured. Michael Heseltine, as Defence Secretary, had been monitoring the situation at Westland for much of the year due to the company producing the country's military helicopters. The fact that a military supplier was about to go into receivership clearly affected both the Departments of Defence and Trade & Industry.

In October Brittan and Heseltine met to discuss Westland. In the days leading up to the meeting Sikorsky, an American firm, had proposed to purchase a minority stake (just under one third) of Westland, thereby injecting enough cash into the business to save it. Westland's board was in favour but Heseltine felt that the decision was not a corporate one that should be made by the board, rather a political one that should be made by the Ministry of Defence. He felt that Sikorsky would reduce the quality of products coming out of Westland, which directly affected the British military, and therefore their bid should be blocked. In Heseltine's opinion a European purchaser should be found. However, Brittan and Thatcher were in favour of leaving Westland's board to decide their own future, which meant allowing the Sikorsky purchase to go ahead. When he didn't get his way in his meeting with Brittan (and at the end of November Sikorsky made a formal bid for the shareholding) Heseltine took the unilateral decision of calling a meeting of National Armaments Directors (those in charge of procurement for the Defence Departments) for the UK, France, Italy and Germany. During the summit all representatives signed an agreement that none would purchase any helicopters from companies not entirely European-owned.

In meetings of senior Cabinet ministers in December Heseltine was overruled – it was up to the board and shareholders of Westland to manage their own affairs – and he was made to look unprofessional in the process. However, he could not let the matter lie. At a Cabinet meeting on 12 December Heseltine raised the issue, which Thatcher immediately told him to drop because it was not on the agenda, had already been decided and nobody had papers to hand.[16] Heseltine then started to brief the press about the divisions in Cabinet over Westland as well as lobbying Conservative backbenchers against the Prime Minister and the Trade & Industry Secretary. The issue had now escalated from a disagreement in Cabinet (which is common in every government) to a public challenge of the Prime Minister's authority. Thatcher accordingly scheduled a discussion on Westland for 9 January so that the Cabinet could make a final and collective decision. When it went against Heseltine he stormed out of the meeting, left Number 10 and immediately told the press that he had resigned. This was a fallout that would come back to haunt the Prime Minister.

In the days that followed a letter sent from the Solicitor-General to Heseltine claiming that he had made material inaccuracies during some of the public claims he had made over the threat of the Sikorsky bid was leaked to the press, completely discrediting Heseltine. However, the leak was clearly a breach of the Official Secrets Act and somebody needed to take the fall if the government was to survive. So Leon Brittan's ministerial career came to an end. Meanwhile

Thatcher kept going. In early 1986 she aroused controversy by allowing the United States to use British military bases to launch air strikes against Colonel Gaddafi in Libya as retribution for a recent Libyan terrorist attack against the US. The fact that she had taken the decision without discussing it in Cabinet offended her ministerial colleagues. The fact that she had been so quick to say yes to President Reagan, when he had not supported Britain over the Falkland Islands, offended many within her own backbenches. It was these actions that lingered in the minds of the public going into 1987, when a general election was expected to be held. A dissolution was duly called in May for an election in June and the Conservatives again won quite comfortably. Thatcher became the first Tory since Lord Liverpool in the 1820s to have won three consecutive elections. The ease with which she had won yet another election (Conservatives, 376 seats; Labour, 229; Alliance, 22) meant that Labour would have to do some soul-searching. The transition that the opposition underwent following the 1987 election took a long time to implement but would have revolutionary effects.

In the meantime, though, Thatcher remained in Number 10, probably starting to believe her own invincibility. But while she rejoiced in her historic triumph, genuinely thinking that there was no end in sight for her premiership, forces were already starting to work against her within her own Party.

It was in this new Parliament, with an increased sense of confidence, that Thatcher introduced the most politically disastrous of all her initiatives. For years local councils had been funded by rates paid by around half of adult residents along with subsidies from central government. Many local councils adopted a spendthrift approach without any fear of reprisals from the electorate because the majority of people were unaffected by their lavish spending. It was against this attitude of councillors that Thatcher introduced the Local Authority Bill which introduced a 'community charge' – a tax payable by all adults to their local council. The logic was that local authorities would be held to account by their residents over how much they were spending because the tax would go up and down according to how they set their own budgets. Therefore there should be an incentive for councils to curb their budgets. Economically there may well have been an argument for the charge. Politically it was suicide. Several Conservative backbench MPs recognised this, causing the government concern over whether the Bill would pass. Eventually it received Royal Assent in July 1988, ready to come into effect on 1 April 1990.

Meanwhile another situation was developing, this time within the Cabinet itself, which would eventually combine with the Community Charge and other factors to make a perfect storm against Thatcher. After the 1987 election Nigel Lawson, the Chancellor of the Exchequer, put to the Prime Minister proposals for the UK joining the European Exchange Rate Mechanism (ERM). The idea behind this scheme was that subscribing European nations would tie their currencies to one another in order to keep the exchange rates fixed (or within a certain margin). The consequences, it was believed, would be greater certainty about the value of money for businesses that traded overseas. However, the problem was that each nation gave up sovereignty of its own economic policy and its ability to, for example, set interest rates. If external factors affected the economy of one member then this could have harmful consequences for other members whose currencies would similarly be affected yet less responsive. Another foreseen consequence of the ERM was that it was widely regarded as a forerunner for Economic and Monetary Union (EMU) in which member states would eventually subscribe to a single European currency, rather than their domestic ones.

All this considered the Prime Minister was opposed to entry into the ERM and made that clear to the Chancellor. Lawson, undeterred, amended interest rates according to changes in German interest rates for the rest of the year, in order that the pound could shadow the deutschmark. In this way he felt that he would have evidence of success to present to the Cabinet in 1988. In December 1987, upon learning of what Lawson had been doing at the Treasury, Thatcher challenged him but was unable to get him to bring it to an end. At this point he was keeping the value of the pound low but then putting up interest rates in order to prevent the inflationary pressure that this caused. There was a risk that abandoning the policy at this point could cause high inflation or else recession. By the summer of 1988 it became clear that not just the Chancellor but also the Foreign Secretary, Geoffrey Howe, was angling for British entry to the ERM. With her two most senior Cabinet

colleagues united against her on this policy the Prime Minister
would struggle to resist.

Discussions between this Cabinet triumvirate
continued throughout the year but Thatcher was always
dismissive of the policy. By mid-1989 inflation was rising,
which Thatcher saw as further evidence that control of fiscal
policy should not be put in the hands of a supra-national
institution, but Lawson and Howe were importunate. On 24
June 1989, as the Prime Minister prepared for a summit in
Madrid, she received notification that Howe and Lawson both
wished to meet with her the following morning. The pair
attended Number 10 the following day and told the Prime
Minister that if she didn't set a date for British entry to the ERM
they would resign. Put in what seemed to be an impossible
position she conceded to consider entry 'when the time is right'.
In spite of her not setting a date neither man resigned.

Both Howe and Lawson felt that they had won a
victory over her and so Thatcher's response was to remind them
who was in charge. In July 1989 she reshuffled her Cabinet,
demoting Howe to Leader of the House of Commons to be
replaced by the much younger and less experienced John
Major. There is no doubt that this was a shock to the outgoing
Foreign Secretary. Lawson was to remain but having seen what
happened to Howe he made up his mind that he would not be
staying for long. In the end he found his excuse to leave that
autumn. In October the *Financial Times* published an article by
one of Thatcher's economic advisers, Alan Walters, in which
he referred to the ERM as 'half-baked'.[17] Lawson decided to
take personal offence and confronted Thatcher with the
ultimatum that Walters must resign or else he would. She
refused and later that day he resigned, to be replaced, with an
alarming sense of *déjà vu*, by John Major. Douglas Hurd
succeeded Major as Foreign Secretary just in time to see the
Berlin Wall torn down in the November. The West had won the
Cold War but in spite of her successes abroad, Thatcher was
increasingly tormented by the troubles at home.

The government staggered into the new year as,
Cabinet splits aside, the Conservatives were languishing in the
polls, not least because the Community Charge (popularly
dubbed the 'poll tax') was due to take effect in April. On 31
March, the day before the introduction of the charge, a protest
against it in Trafalgar Square descended into rioting. Public
opinion was clearly set against the government.

To make matters worse for the Prime Minister only a few months into his new job, John Major, much to Thatcher's alarm, started to argue that for the sake of Party unity Britain should enter the ERM. The Prime Minister was blindsided by this statement but after much discussion she found that the Chancellor was quite adamant. Realising that she by now lacked the political capital to see her through a rift with yet another senior colleague she bowed to Major's wish and Britain duly entered the ERM in October 1990.

That same month Thatcher made her famous 'No, No, No' speech to the Commons (No to the European Parliament being the democratic body of the community; No to the Commission being the executive; No to the Council of Ministers becoming a Senate). Her fear was that Europe was heading towards federalisation and she would not accept it. She had always been famous for standing up to other European leaders but the Conservative Party at this time (and, as it transpired, ever since) was hopelessly divided over where Britain's destiny lay. Was it in Europe, in the Commonwealth, with closer ties to America or alone in the world?

The 'No, No, No' speech was a step too far for Geoffrey Howe. As Foreign Secretary he had been heavily influenced by other European Foreign Ministers, hence his support for the ERM. He had then been humiliated by his 'out of the blue' demotion from the Foreign Office in 1989 and evidently since then Thatcher had regularly treated him badly in Cabinet meetings. One such occasion occurred on 31 October, by which point Howe had probably already made up his mind that he no longer belonged in Thatcher's government. She 'took him to task, probably too sharply'[18] about his drawing up of the government's legislative programme. The following day he resigned.

Within the next few days Michael Heseltine made public declarations of the need for the government to change course. This was widely interpreted as meaning that the government needed to change its leader. Thatcher's Westland chickens were coming home to roost.

The mortal blow to her leadership was struck on Tuesday 13 November when, immediately after Prime Minister's Questions, Howe gave a speech to a packed House of Commons explaining why he had resigned. It was

devastating. Whereas convention dictated that outgoing
ministers find an excuse to resign – a point of principle or
morality over a particular issue – Howe, with Lawson
strategically positioned to his immediate left for all the cameras
to capture, stated that the government could not function under
Thatcher. From any ex-minister this could be harmful. From
the one man who had been by Thatcher's side in every Cabinet
since 1979 it was fatal. He said during his speech that being a
Foreign Secretary trying to negotiate Britain's future in Europe
with Thatcher as Prime Minister was 'rather like sending your
opening batsmen to the crease only for them to find, the
moment the first balls are bowled, that their bats have been
broken before the game by the team captain'. This line
produced vociferous laughter, cheers and applause from the
opposition benches, but more was to come. He concluded by
opening the field for a challenger, should one be forthcoming:
'The time has come for others to consider their own response to
the tragic conflict of loyalties with which I have myself
wrestled for perhaps too long.'

Anybody watching or listening knew what he meant:
Heseltine.

The following day Michael Heseltine announced that
he was challenging the Prime Minister for the leadership of the
Conservative Party.[19] His campaign was soon in full swing,
while Thatcher seemed to think that she shouldn't canvass the
votes of her parliamentary colleagues either out of
complacency or pride. Instead on 18 November she went to
Paris for a European conference to discuss the future of the
continent following the fall of the Soviet Union. The first ballot
was held in her absence on Tuesday 20 November and when the
results came in that evening they were not as good as expected:
Thatcher, 204; Heseltine, 152; Abstentions, 16. This meant that
the Prime Minister won a clear majority but did not win the
surplus of 15 per cent of eligible votes required to prevent a
second ballot. Upon hearing the news Thatcher ran out to the
press gathered outside her hotel and announced that she would
contest a second ballot. Little did she know that back in Britain
a substantial number of senior Tory MPs had gathered to
discuss the future. Their conclusion had been that she was done
for.

On the following day, Wednesday 21 November, the
Prime Minister returned home at midday, took strategy
meetings throughout the afternoon, then contacted Douglas

Hurd and John Major in the evening to request that they propose and second her nomination for the second ballot. They both agreed. She then summoned the Cabinet to her room in the House of Commons with the intention of getting them to commit to backing her. Rather than seeing them all together, she summoned them in one at a time, meaning that the process took over two hours.[20] This was the point at which it must have dawned on the Prime Minister that her Cabinet had been discussing a unified approach in advance, because individually and apparently independently they all gave exactly the same response. Should she wish to stand for the second ballot of course they, individually, would support her. But they did not think that she could win. It was all over.

At 9 a.m. the following day a Cabinet meeting was held in Downing Street at which Thatcher informed ministers that she would be resigning. Within hours Douglas Hurd and John Major had entered the contest to prevent Heseltine from becoming Prime Minister. On Tuesday 27 November the second ballot was held in which the Conservative Party nominated John Major as its next leader. Thatcher stood down the following day.

Margaret Thatcher had revolutionised the Conservative Party during her fifteen years as its leader. She had changed it from a defeatist Party, content to hold off the rise of the Left for as long as possible but never striking back, to a Party that reversed the effects of socialism and whose new doctrines became the accepted norm in Britain. Monetarist economic policies are far more commonplace in government today than Keynesian ones; when the European Single Currency was finally introduced Britain declined to join; following her first election victory in 1979 Labour had to abandon Clause IV altogether in order to become electable once again.

The grocer's daughter who rose to become Prime Minister in a Party that had traditionally been seen as an Old Boys' Club made the Conservatives adopt her own meritocratic values. These values were translated in her policies, which held the underlying principle that anybody can get ahead if they are prepared to work for it. When she took over as Prime Minister Britain was economically without a doubt the 'sick man of Europe', with unprecedented inflation, an embarrassing balance of payments deficit and flying pickets disrupting people's lives. By the time she left office Britain had the fourth strongest economy on the planet.

She not only made the Conservatives electable, she gave them a sense of purpose and a sense of pride. They now *knew* that they were electable, they knew that their policies were popular and they now had some intrinsically conservative principles. But then what are conservative principles? The Party, historically, has had none. Its purpose was, throughout history, to protect what was and stop the changes proposed by other political parties that may make the country something that it was not. Thatcher never seemed to accept this. Her legacy to the Conservative Party, then, was to give it a set of principles. From now on it would be seen as the libertarian Party, viewing with suspicion any action designed to increase the influence of the state. It would promote free markets and criticise any attempt to interfere there. Then, in order to answer the question posed by Disraeli in *Coningsby* – 'What will you conserve?' – the Party would promote traditional family values and respect for law & order.

Moving forward, how a Party that had survived for two hundred years with no constitution would fare in a world where they had specific and identifiable values was impossible to say. With all the certainty that Thatcher had brought, the future was now decidedly uncertain.

John Major
(1990 — 1997)

Every leader is leader only with the support of his Party. That is true
of me as well. That is why I am no longer prepared to tolerate the
present situation. In short it is time to put up or shut up.

John Major, 22 July 1995

Why are you angry at us for being in Places? Were we not sought,
courted, intreated to accept Employments?

Daniel Defoe's *Tory*, 1692

AT 10.30 A.M., forty five minutes after Thatcher had attended
the palace to resign, Major attended to be offered the chance to
form a government.[1] This he confidently stated that he could do
but when it came to it Cabinet-making was difficult. After
much deliberation Heseltine was offered, and accepted, the role
of Environment Secretary. Major had agonised over whether or
not to bring Heseltine into the Cabinet – desperate for his
support but terrified of alienating the Thatcherites by appearing
too close to 'the snake'. In the event the appointment was a
shrewd one – a position important enough to tempt Heseltine in
but not senior enough to make Thatcher feel affronted.[2]

Another difficulty was who should be Chancellor of
the Exchequer. The only men who had spent any time at all in
the position of Chancellor or Shadow Chancellor, aside from
Major himself, were Geoffrey Howe and Nigel Lawson.
However, for political reasons (again not offending Thatcher)
and concerns about the Prime Minister being overshadowed
(not to mention the fact that they would never accept) these men
were not options. In the end the job fell to Norman Lamont who
had been Chief Secretary to the Treasury while Major had been
Chancellor. The easiest appointment by far was keeping
Douglas Hurd at the Foreign Office.

The new Prime Minister was almost immediately
embroiled in international difficulties, specifically in the Gulf.
In August 1990 Iraq had invaded Kuwait which had
subsequently caused the UN to deliver an ultimatum to Iraq:

withdraw by 15 January 1991 or face military action.[3] It was clear to the most casual of observers both that Iraq's leader, Saddam Hussein, would not accept the terms imposed and that Britain would have to play a part in the military action that followed. So Major's immediate concern was to prepare for war.

Throughout December diplomatic talks continued but they were to no avail. Just before Christmas Major flew to Washington to discuss with US President Bush strategy for a joint Anglo-American venture into the Gulf and in early January 1991 he visited Saudi Arabia, widely believed to be Saddam Hussein's next target. When 15 January came and went the US-led forces entered the conflict with aerial bombings of Iraqi ports and transport links including bridges to Kuwait in order to isolate their forces there before the land invasion commenced.[4]

Once the land forces did begin their assault, towards the end of February, the end came fairly swiftly. By the end of the month all Iraqi forces had been pulled out of Kuwait and Saddam had agreed a ceasefire. Some, Margaret Thatcher included, called for the UN troops to march to Baghdad to remove Saddam from power. However, the operation had been put together to liberate Kuwait and once this was achieved the coalition forces could not justify carrying on.[5] However, there was a little more work to be done. Once the war had been won the Kurds of northern Iraq rose up against Saddam and were easily beaten back, but Saddam did not stop there. He wanted retribution for the international humiliation he had just received at the hands of the West and the Kurds had given him the chance to exact that retribution. His troops moved north and the Kurds living there either fled or died. Watching this go on through March Major quickly tried to build a new coalition in the UNSC to provide relief for the Kurds. His plan was to put troops on the ground that would protect several pockets in the north where refugee Kurds could flee to in order to escape Saddam's forces. European nations quickly fell behind him and, after some intense lobbying,[6] so did President Bush.

Once the initial conflict in Iraq had ended on 28 February, and with only two weeks left until the Major's government's first budget was due, Lamont, Major and Heseltine met to discuss how to rid themselves of the politically fatal poll tax. Heseltine had been charged with finding a solution, which he was only too happy to do given that any change in policy would be seen as a snub to Thatcher, while Lamont's department would ultimately have to fund any implemented cuts. Once the budget was announced on 17 March the results were a clear refusal to accept Thatcher's insistence that the poll tax had been fine as it was. The average bill would be cut by £140, funded by the Treasury at a cost of £4.5 billion. This would be paid for by an increase in VAT from 15 per cent to 17.5 per cent. Further, in order to stop irresponsible councils from raising the rate in future years there was to be an enforced cap on council expenditure. Politically, this budget kept the Tories alive, at least for the time being.

Major had been given a lifeline that allowed him to survive through to the end of the parliamentary session but this would prove to be the calm before the political storm which would engulf his premiership. Events began towards the end of that year.

The Prime Minister was due to attend an EC summit in Maastricht, the Netherlands, in December. The summit would be aimed at drafting a charter to define the levels of economic and political union between the member states, ultimately evolving the grouping of nations from a European Community into the European Union. In the spring, at a Community meeting in Luxembourg, various proposals had been put forward for things such as Economic and Monetary Union. This was bad enough for Major's backbench Right-wingers. However, as Maastricht crept closer the Dutch started to press for Federalism to be drawn into the Treaty that was to be agreed there, meaning European control of foreign policy, among other things.

Conservatives, worried that Major was not tough enough to stand up to other European leaders, or else that he may even be a closet Europhile, started to become concerned. Before he was at Maastricht negotiating Britain's future he was already being challenged about what was happening. On 20 November he held a Commons debate on the matter in which he batted questions by outlining his own position for a fair while before Thatcher rose and demanded that a referendum be held before accepting a single currency.[7] The following day Number 10, under instruction from Major who was by now feeling the pressure, suggested to the press that a referendum would be a possibility in future. Later that same day the Cabinet persuaded the Prime Minister not to be pushed around by his predecessor and they released a statement saying that a referendum was an option. Major was all over the place.

The Maastricht summit was to be held on 9-10 December and Major, Hurd and Lamont made up the British representation. On the first day Major stated in no uncertain terms that the UK could not accept an imposed ERM but that he was happy for other nations to go ahead if he got an opt-out. It was late on the Tuesday before Lamont secured agreement from other leaders to append an opt-out guarantee to the Treaty that was drawn up. This was a small success but the summit was about much more than ERM. There was also discussion of a Social Chapter being added to the Treaty in which signatory states would share a common social policy. Thatcher had rejected a similar proposal in 1989. Major would look weak if he did not achieve the same position. When he managed to convince the Dutch Prime Minister to allow Britain an exclusion from the Social Chapter as well, Major felt he had achieved everything that he had set out to and so returned to Britain in triumphalist mood. Little did he know that his problems were only just beginning.

The Maastricht Treaty (officially the Treaty of European Union) was signed on 7 February 1992 but would need ratifying by the Commons before it came into effect in 1993. However, the Prime Minister opted to delay the necessary debate until after a general election so that any in-fighting within the Conservative Party over the Treaty would not hamper his election chances. Major opted to set the election for April, so as to capitalise on his newfound reputation as a tough negotiator in Europe. The alternative was to allow the Parliament to run the extra two months to June, which would be the five year limit. It was not a time for optimism, even without the headache of fighting his own Party over ratification of Maastricht. The opinion polls indicated that the Conservatives would get 39 per cent of the vote. Labour were ahead on 41 per cent. Any gambler would be putting money on Neil Kinnock to become Prime Minister after the election on 9 April.

The distortion of the polls was probably caused by people at this point in time being embarrassed to admit that they were going to vote Tory, even to a pollster that they were never going to meet in person. Arguments have also been made that Neil Kinnock shouting 'We're all right!' to an excited rally made him appear complacent, which turned voters off. Another theory is that Major campaigning on a soap box made him appear more personable, which swung the vote in his favour.[8] Whatever the reason the polls, right up until election day, got the result completely wrong. In the event the Conservatives won an absolute (albeit reduced) majority with 336 seats to Labour's 271.[9] The old Alliance parties of the Liberals and Social Democrats had formally merged in 1988 to form a new third party called the Liberal Democrats, who duly returned 20 MPs after the election.

The Prime Minister now had a mandate of his own. His first act was to reshuffle the Cabinet, free from the constraints of having to keep his predecessor onside because now this was *his* Parliament. He therefore moved Heseltine to the Department of Trade & Industry, which pleased both men. Another significant move was Ken Clarke becoming Home Secretary. Hurd remained as Foreign Secretary and Lawson as Chancellor. The months from April until August were the most peaceful Major would ever experience as Prime Minister. The only real difficulties he faced were economic and seemed to be of minor significance at the time. However, these small grey clouds would develop into a storm by the end of the summer and one which would destroy Major's credibility forever.

Major had been the Chancellor that had convinced Thatcher to take sterling into the ERM back in October 1990. At that point the conditions were that sterling, as well as various other European currencies, would shadow the deutschmark. This gave a guarantee over exchange rates because as one rose or fell the others would follow. Sterling entered at a value of DM2.95 and had to remain within the bracket of DM2.778 – DM3.12.[10] The problem with economic ties (such as this) without a political union is that if one country changes policy and another cannot the whole thing can have devastating economic effects. A further problem with the ERM was the nature of the mechanism. Because all currencies had to follow the deutschmark, Germany could do whatever was best for Germany, while all other nations had to follow their lead, even if it was to their own detriment. Throughout 1991-92 the pound had become weak due to high levels of inflation eroding its value. Meanwhile German interest rates increased gradually over that time. This caused a surge in the value of the deutschmark as foreign investors traded their own currency for deutschmarks in order to get a decent return of interest. By the summer of 1992 the pound was close to the lower limit of its ERM commitment. This was something for Major to be aware of during his post-election honeymoon period but not something that he was particularly worried about.

By the time September came around it had become clear that this minor problem was becoming quite a substantial one. Sterling was about to fall through the lower limit and, given that there was no way that a British government could plausibly affect the policy of a German bank whose entire *raison d'être* was to support the German economy, the obvious course of action was to remove the UK from the ERM. However, Major and Lamont would not accept such suggestions, knowing that having pushed so hard to get Britain in, there would be a political fallout to withdrawal.[11] Consequently all talks between Prime Minister and Chancellor were centred around how to improve the economy within the existing framework.

Throughout September Major and Lamont tried to apply pressure on the German *Bundesbank* to reduce its interest rates, to no avail. On 13 September the Italian Prime Minister announced that it was unsustainable to keep the Lira at its current value relative to the deutschmark so the Italian government was going to devalue its currency. The pressure for Britain to do so intensified but Major was determined to keep sterling in the ERM at existing rates.

On the morning of Wednesday 16 September the Prime Minister awoke to news that sterling had fallen below the lower ERM limit overnight. This had forced the Bank of England to intervene and buy the currency from investors at the 'intervention rate' – just above the ERM lower limit. Foreign exchange speculators in America and Asia had made easy money overnight buying sterling low then selling it back to the Bank of England at the intervention rate.[12] The Bank lost billions of pounds in just a few hours trying to keep the currency artificially high. Apparently comments from the head of the *Bundesbank* the previous day that sterling should have been devalued with the Lira had made investors lose confidence.[13]

It is difficult to understand why Major was so determined to support sterling's position, rather than just allowing it to withdraw from the ERM and float as it had done previously. He would argue that he genuinely believed that the

ERM was a mechanism which could control inflation. Others would claim that, having been the Chancellor who took Britain in, maintaining the position was a matter of hubris. Either way, he could not be convinced to change course. Sterling must remain within the mechanism and that meant that one way or another the government must prop up the value of the pound.

With it still flailing below its bottom limit there were now two options available. The first was to raise interest rates but this would lead to higher unemployment, difficulty for people with mortgages and maybe even a recession. The second option was for the Treasury to buy more sterling at a higher rate than market value, as the Bank of England had done overnight. This second option had been tried and failed. At 10.30 a.m. the government announced a rise in interest rates from 10 per cent to 12 per cent. By 11 a.m. the rise had come into effect but within minutes it was clear that it had not positively altered sterling's position. On the contrary market speculators, sensing the panic, had started offloading sterling, forcing the value down, in the belief that they could buy it back more cheaply if the government devalued.

At 12.45 p.m. Major, Hurd, Heseltine, Lamont and Ken Clarke met with officials from the Treasury and the Bank of England. Lamont and the Treasury officials stated that enough was enough and Britain should withdraw from the ERM. Billions could be lost supporting an unsustainable position. Hurd, Clarke and Heseltine argued that they should go on supporting the currency. Major agreed with them.

At 2.15 p.m. the Treasury announced a rise in interest rates to 15 per cent to take effect the following day. By the time the markets closed it was clear that this announcement had had no effect either. The battle was lost. Sterling had crashed out of the ERM in spite of Major's determination to keep it in. The only difference between being forced out now and going voluntarily 24 hours earlier was that billions of pounds of Treasury reserves had been spent trying to prop the value up and the government had lost its economic credibility by changing interest rates twice in one day. The debacle became known as Black Wednesday.

At 7 p.m. Lamont announced that the planned interest rate rise to 15 per cent would not go ahead after all. Notwithstanding this travesty Major was insistent that Britain should re-join the ERM 'as soon as conditions allow'. John Smith, leader of the Labour Party since Kinnock's post-election resignation, demanded a recall of Parliament to discuss the issue the following week.

There was little Major could do to defend himself. Smith was a tough opponent anyway – witty and powerful in speech. With all the errors that the government had made in economic management over the preceding weeks he was able to make mincemeat of the Prime Minister in the debates. Major secured the support of the House in the subsequent division but, having only just won a general election, this was to be expected.

The Prime Minister's troubles continued to mount as the Maastricht Treaty still needed ratification. In the early summer Neil Kinnock had forced Major to concede a 'Paving Debate' before reintroduction of the Treaty. Effectively this was a debate about the consequences of other nations (namely Denmark) rejecting the Treaty. The debate was scheduled for 4 November and the Labour Party, as well as Thatcherites within the Conservative Party, now brandishing the term 'Euro-sceptic', worked hard to whip up opposition to the government. In the event Major carried the day but only by three votes.[14] So it went to committee stage in early 1993. However, all opponents of the Bill and opponents of the Conservative Party (the two not necessarily being the same thing) used whatever devices were in their power to delay the passing of the legislation. On 8 March 1993 a Labour amendment to require new MEPs to be elected councillors, which would force the Bill to go to report stage, passed with the help of Conservative Euro-sceptic rebels. Report stage is another process that most legislation never has to go through, which involves the whole House assessing the merits of various amendments and is extremely time consuming.

In spite of this the Bill made its way through committee stage in April and passed its third reading on 20 May, with a catch. During committee stage the government had been forced to accept an amendment by Labour that there must be a future vote on the inclusion of the Social Chapter in the Bill before it could take effect. Major had triumphantly secured an opt-out for Britain from the Social Chapter because he was determined not to see its inclusion. However, he didn't believe that a vote on its inclusion would pass and so he could accept this amendment. The Prime Minister believed that the passage of the Maastricht Treaty through the Commons was the end of the matter and so, with the issue now safely behind him, he decided to reshuffle his Cabinet. Norman Lamont was told that he was to be moved from the Treasury but, realising that he was basically taking the fall for Black Wednesday, he resigned from the government altogether, rather than take a junior position. His post was filled by Ken Clarke, whose previous position of Home Secretary was taken over by Michael Howard.

The European Communities (Amendment) Act received Royal Assent on 20 July 1993 but before it could come into effect there had to be the debate about the inclusion of the Social Chapter, which was scheduled for 22 July. On the same date the government had scheduled a vote to record that they had secured an opt-out for the Social Chapter, effectively it was a counter-motion to Labour's amendment and it gave them something to whip their Euro-sceptic colleagues over. In the days leading up to the debate Major became aware that around twenty-five Conservative rebels were planning to vote against the government. Labour and the Liberal Democrats were both voting in favour of the Social Chapter. The Conservative rebels were principally opposed to this but they would join the opposition as a way to punish a Tory leader that they wanted humiliating.

At 10 p.m. on the night of 22 July, the House of Commons divided to vote on Labour's amendment. The result was a tie: 317 votes to 317. The speaker broke the deadlock by voting to maintain the status quo.[15] Then came the second vote, Major's positive vote to record his achievements, which the government then lost by 324 votes to 316. The Prime Minister immediately stood and announced that he was calling a vote of confidence in the government the following morning. When that debate came about Major was once again upstaged by Smith but once again he was able to carry a majority. For this division the rebels came back to the fold. They had humiliated their leader but they weren't yet ready to destroy him.[16] Major had won the Battle of Maastricht but at what cost? The Conservatives no longer looked like a unified Party.

What did happen was that the Euro-sceptics made it clear to anybody who would listen that there was a substantial portion of Major's Cabinet (namely Peter Lilley, Michael Portillo and John Redwood) who had threatened to resign if the Social Chapter had been included in the legislation that passed through Parliament. These three (as well as Michael Howard) were notoriously right wing and made up the most Euro-sceptic contingent of the Cabinet. The day after the debate an exhausted John Major concluded a TV interview with ITN about the whole saga and, believing that all recording equipment had been switched off afterwards, entered into a relaxed conversation with the interviewer. In it Major said of three unnamed Cabinet ministers:

> I could bring in other people but where do you think most of the poison is coming from? From the dispossessed and the never-possessed. You can think of ex-ministers who are going around causing all sorts of trouble. We don't want another three more of the bastards out there.

His microphone was still switched on and the recording immediately leaked. According to Portillo, Howard telephoned him straight away and said 'The Prime Minister has called us bastards', implying that he believed that he was one of the three. The fact that he had referred to three members of his Cabinet, whoever they may be, as 'bastards' led to an uncomfortable summer for the Prime Minister, with the press intriguing about Cabinet rifts. It was in desperate mood, then, that Major decided to try to recapture the Tory Right, who seemed to be drifting inexorably away from him. At the Conservative Party Conference in October he laid out in his speech a new plan for the future, which he called 'Back to Basics'. In setting out this plan he seemed to hit all the right buttons for a traditional Tory. He talked about the need to reintroduce a sense of morality to Britain. Criminals would be punished harder; schools would be better funded; parents, teachers, mentors and religious leaders would be given the support they needed to make people decent citizens. Clearly, the Conservatives were to be viewed as the Party of morality. He received tumultuous applause.[16] However, although the 'Back to Basics' speech was clearly a sop to the Tory Right (and an effective one at that), the Prime Minister and his advisers clearly had not thought out the consequences. Within weeks the media had seized on this new campaign against immorality…by putting the Conservative Party under the microscope.

It started on Boxing Day when newspapers ran a story that Tim Yeo, a fairly junior Conservative minister who was also married, had fathered a child by his mistress. When Major decided to stand by Yeo both the Tory Right and the media had a field day, seizing on the 'Back to Basics' theme and asking who was really leading this moral crusade. In the first week of January 1994, Yeo resigned.

Later in the week Lord Caithness, a minister within the Department of Transport, resigned from the government following the suicide of his wife. The press reported that she shot herself after discovering that he was leaving her for another woman. The morality issues were not going to go away. Later in the week news broke that a backbench MP named David Ashby had shared a hotel room with another man, again in spite of being married. The story, although possibly distorted, intensified the impression of a sleazy political party.

The next week was no better. Thursday 13 January saw stories that Conservative councillors had rigged votes to win an election. On Friday 14th news broke that Teresa Gorman MP had made £1 million by buying council houses under the right-to-buy scheme open to tenants and then selling them on. On Saturday 15th it was alleged that Wandsworth council – a Conservative-controlled council – had deliberately redrawn ward boundaries to give their Party an electoral advantage.

John Smith was in his element – this was a good Party to be opposing. Yet there was a sense that Major had brought this on himself. By declaring war on immorality he had encouraged the media closely to scrutinise the affairs of his Party. Somehow he staggered through to the spring, in which he was given a political reprieve when, on 12 May, it was reported that Smith had died. It had come as a surprise because he was still relatively young. Whoever was to replace him would probably want to make a mark on the Labour Party before forcing a general election. In the end Labour elected the Shadow Home Secretary, Tony Blair, as its leader. He had spent the last year shadowing – very effectively – Michael Howard. His position, on the Right of the Labour Party, meant that he had the potential to cause Major a lot of trouble as moderate voters abandoned an apparently sleazy, and certainly disunited Tory Party.

This disunity would now intensify for the following twelve months. In the autumn the government introduced to the Commons a European Communities (Finance) Bill, which was to agree Britain's contribution to the European Union up until the end of the century. At a European summit in Edinburgh the previous year Major had agreed to increased Britain's net contributions and this now needed ratifying in Parliament. Unwilling to see a repeat of the in-fighting caused by the last European Bill that he had introduced Major told the House that the passage of this legislation would be seen as a matter of confidence in the government. Ken Clarke then briefed the press that this had been agreed by the Cabinet. However, Portillo, Redwood and Lilley were annoyed because they had actually had no prior knowledge that the legislation would be treated in this manner.[18] The 'bastards' were still bastards to Major.

The government worked hard to whip support for the Bill, imposing a three line whip and making it clear to the parliamentary party that anybody who didn't vote in favour would lose the whip. As a result the Bill passed with a huge majority but eight Tories abstained and were consequently removed of the whip. A ninth, Richard Body, resigned it in protest. It was a PR nightmare for the Prime Minister.

Throughout early 1995 the whipless rebels, now free to act as they pleased, were a constant source of irritation for Major. They attacked his policies over Europe time and again, trying to create opposition to him from within the Party. The government was unable to function. By late spring the Prime Minister was at his wit's end and decided that he had to act. Constant talk of a leadership contest was undermining his authority and, when one did not come, he had no chance to reassert it. Consequently, by the June, Major decided to take matters into his own hands and force a leadership contest.

On Tuesday 22 June 1995 Major held a morning Cabinet, went to the House of Commons to answer Prime Minister's Questions then, at 4.15 p.m., he met with the executive officers of the 1922 Committee to tell them that he was about to resign the Party leadership and contend the subsequent election.[19] Whatever the outcome he expected the Party to fall in line behind the victor.

The Prime Minister then returned to Number 10 and, at 5 p.m. told the assembled press that:

...For the last three years I've been opposed by a small minority in our Party. During those three years there have been repeated threats of a leadership election. In each year they turned out to be phoney threats...I have this afternoon tendered my resignation as leader of the Conservative Party to Sir Marcus Fox, the Chairman of the 1922 Committee and requested him to set the machinery in motion for the election of a successor...I shall be a candidate in that election...

Over the weekend John Redwood and Michael Portillo had no contact with the Prime Minister and, on Monday 26 June, Redwood announced his candidacy. Portillo kept out of it, not joining either campaign team, apparently keeping his options open in the event of a second ballot.

On 4 July the ballot was held. Major got 218 votes to Redwood's 89, an outright victory not requiring a second ballot.[20] It was a clear win but with 89 MPs effectively saying that they no longer wanted him to be their leader (and with abstentions and spoiled ballots the figure may well have exceeded 100) he was to have difficulty uniting the Party.

Major now focused on a Cabinet reshuffle, feeling that he now had an excuse to suck out some of the 'poison'. In any event he would need a replacement for Redwood, as well as for Douglas Hurd who had decided to retire. Clarke and Howard remained at the Exchequer and Home Office respectively. Heseltine became Deputy Prime Minister. Malcolm Rifkind replaced Hurd as Foreign Secretary and William Hague replaced Redwood as Secretary of State for Wales.

Having taken control of the leadership issue Major did not have any further explicit trouble from the Maastricht rebels, the Euro-sceptics or the Bastards but the Conservative Party was damaged. As it limped towards the 1997 general election it was further hindered by the fact that Blair had moved Labour from the Left into the political centre ground. On top of this Blair had grown in confidence week by week and consistently bettered Major at the despatch box in the Commons. Labour now looked like a united Party for the first time in decades.

By 1 May 1997 – the date of the general election – the economy had been managed into a decent state yet again but even this wasn't enough to save the Tories from their self-inflicted destruction. Major allowed the Parliament to extend to the full five-year maximum before dissolving. When it did, Labour received its greatest ever victory: 419 seats to the Conservatives' 165. The Liberal Democrats had made an incredible improvement to take 46 seats. On 2 May, the morning after the election, Major resigned as leader of the Conservative Party, allowing for yet another leadership contest.

John Major had led the Conservative Party for just under seven years and was Prime Minister for that entire time. His rise to the top had been meteoric – too fast, some might say. He had been a junior minister in mid-1989, then was moved first to the Foreign Office, then to the Treasury and then into Number 10 in a little over a year. He was unfortunate in that he succeeded a leader that had been forced out of office by a significant minority but who still retained the loyalty of a substantial portion of the Party. This loyal following longed for a return of the 'Queen Across the Water', much like their seventeenth century predecessors may have yearned for the return of King James when he was exiled in France. Consequently Major would always have a fractious and difficult Party to manage.

On the other hand Thatcher had also inherited a Party in which many people had felt a strong affiliation for the leader that she ousted. Whereas her mentality had been that the Party would fall in line when she was proved right, Major was hindered by the negative effects of policies with which he was inextricably linked. British participation in the ERM led to Black Wednesday. At a time when he was being criticised from all quarters for not being as tough as Thatcher had been with other European leaders he agreed to increase Britain's EU budget contribution. The launch of 'Back to Basics' caused the media, predictably, to look in the Prime Minister's own back yard. Labour were not ready to govern in 1992 and so the Conservatives won the election *faute de mieux*. If the opposition had have offered something more, it is hard to see that Major could have held them off. By 1997 the public were sick of the Tories but it wasn't just the sleaze or a boredom with more of the same. The Party had turned on itself and once it started it could not stop. Had Major not made some of the policy mistakes that he had (ERM, EU finance, 'Back to Basics') then a lot of this fighting could have been avoided. By 1997 Labour were a new Party and probably would have won the election regardless of what the government did. However, the margin by which they won was a reflection of Major's leadership and the contempt that one wing of the Conservative Party now held for the other wing.

Labour may have won the election but the Conservatives were the ones who lost by a landslide. The issue of Europe is not one that would go away and it would be a long time before the Conservative Party would get a taste of power once again.

Wilderness Years
(1997- 2010)

LABOUR DID WELL to win the general election in 1997 but the reality was that the Conservatives did more to lose it than their opponents did to win it. So what went wrong? Well the answer is that there was an unlikely coincidence of a number of factors which led to the obliteration of the Party as a genuine parliamentary force. For an explanation of the first we need to hark back to the destruction of another ancient political Party. At the end of the nineteenth- and start of the twentieth centuries the Liberal Party had become dismayed at their inability to enact any significant legislative changes regardless of how strong their numbers were in the House of Commons. Reforming the House of Lords became almost like a crusade for the Liberal faithful over many decades (see chapter on Balfour for more detail). Finally, in 1911, they achieved their most coveted of prizes with the Parliament Act and their followers cherished the victory as their finest hour. The Party was never elected to government again. Having achieved their principal objective the electorate had no use for them and they were swiftly discarded in favour of the rising Labour Party.

During the post-war years the Conservative Party saw its mission as being to halt the advance of socialism which, as we have seen, they had limited success with in the years before 1979. Once Thatcher was elected to power and enacted her purge against the unions and nationalised industry Britain emerged as a more liberal (with a lower case 'l') society than it had been at any point since before 1945. Now that they had captured their own white whale, what would they stand for? Socialism had been defeated in Britain and all-but eradicated internationally. Consequently the electorate did not need a Party whose *raison d'être* was to stand against this ideology.

This, though, was not the whole story. The Tories also made themselves unelectable with the (very public) way that they fought with each other. No Party in the history of British politics has been electable when divided and the in-fighting that pervaded every facet of the Conservatives from 1990 onwards was poison. There are invariably disagreements between individuals in any large group but most can keep their issues private. Following Thatcher's downfall those who were still loyal to her did their utmost to undermine Major.

The issue of Europe provided a focal point for their cause. The Maastricht rebels would not just vote against the government but would canvass against it and even leak information to the press to further their own cause. Whether years in office had made them feel invincible or whether they just didn't care about losing elections is unclear but once these tactics were employed there was no electoral hope for the Conservatives.

So they were swept aside in the 1997 general election but still many believed it would be a blip in which they would regroup and come back. Contrary to this, the election result preceded the longest continuous period out of office that the Party had endured since 1832,[1] before it even adopted the name 'Conservative'.

In the decades that have followed Major's accession to the premiership the Party has still been unable to put the issue of Europe to bed. There have been divisive issues previously in the Party's history. In the early twentieth century Bonar Law had to accept that Unionists and Home Rulers would never be reconciled The end to the tensions within the Conservatives in this instance only occurred once Ireland had gone and there was nothing left for the Unionists to fight for. In the mid-nineteenth century, Peel had to accept that Free Traders and Protectionists would never live in harmony. He accepted that if his views were to go forward the Party would have to collapse. Lord Liverpool, at the start of the nineteenth century, placed a ban on discussions of Catholic emancipation within Cabinet as this was the only way to force ministers to get along.

In the years since Major's removal from office the Conservatives initially argued over Europe time and again until, after three successive election defeats, they realised that the public did not want to hear it. They have since learnt to adopt the Lord Liverpool strategy. Allowing the Party to collapse as Peel did is a step too far, so they don't discuss it. Possibly like Bonar Law they hope that something will happen to make it go away but it is a well-known fact that when selecting new candidates for Parliament, Conservative Campaign Headquarters will never ask the question 'where do you stand on Maastricht?' There is no point. The Party cannot have an official line without alienating half of its supporters.

After Major's downfall the Party went on to select three successive leaders from its Euro-sceptic wing. This fact alone suggests that the Party had chosen its direction. But that is not the whole story. In each of the first two selections the runner-up was the most famous pro-European in the Party. In the third, no other candidate stood. No matter how many times they changed their leadership or rebranded their image, the Tories remained unelectable.

The damage that the Party did to themselves during these years was such that even some faithful and active supporters jumped ship. The Referendum Party was formed by the Euro-sceptic James Goldsmith to fight the 1997 election on the issue of giving the country a referendum to determine entry into the single currency. The UK Independence Party was formed in the early 1990s out of anti-federalists who had previously supported the Conservatives.

So the Tories had lost the support of the public following their success in defeating socialism and they had become unelectable due to in-fighting. There was also a third reason why they couldn't seem to bring themselves back into the hearts of the public. This was simply that they were not trusted. The economy had been fixed from the terrible nadir of the 1970s but Black Wednesday had removed their right to be known as the Party of safe economic management. Blair's stint as Home Secretary and his pledge to be 'Tough on Crime and Tough on the Causes of Crime' – a catchy slogan – stole the Conservatives' ground as the Party of traditional values that would not be a soft touch on criminals. They had no answer to Labour's pledges to fix public services. They did not know where they stood on Europe (even if one disagreed with Labour on this point at least they provided clarity and a vision for where Britain belonged within the EU). They could not agree on whether to oppose or support the introduction of a minimum wage. All in all they appeared uncaring or, as Teresa May, then Conservative Party Chairman, put it in 2002, 'The Nasty Party'.

The problem for them was that people saw them arguing about British sovereignty being eroded by the European Union, while the Labour Party was making the arguments to improve the lot of the people at home. The impression was that while the Tories claimed to be filled with a burning patriotism, they just did not care about the struggles of everyday people. It invoked memories of Kipling's Absent-Minded Beggar:

> When you've shouted 'Rule Britannia',
> When you've sung 'God Save the Queen,'
> When you've finished killing Kruger with
> your mouth,
> Will you kindly drop a shilling in my little
> tambourine?

It took them a decade to regroup and start to put together policies that looked like they were worthy of government. This improvement in their organisation coincided with the greatest economic downturn in a century presided over by the Labour government. However, in spite of all this the Conservatives were still unable to win an overall majority in Parliament.

That is to get ahead of ourselves. The story of the process of rebuilding the parliamentary party began in the days after 2 May 1997, when John Major stepped down as leader.

William Hague
(1997 – 2001)

Tory values...stretch back to the days when Wilberforce freed the slaves, and Pitt led a war against tyranny and Burke wrote his great tracts and Shaftesbury stood and watched the pauper's funeral and dedicated his life to the poor.

William Hague, 4 March 2001

Great Numbers prove nothing...Fools and Knaves have in all Ages out-numbered the Wise and Honest

Daniel Defoe's *Whig*, 1692

MAJOR'S RESIGNATION meant that senior former ministers had to consider whether they wished to stand for the Party leadership. The problem was that the Conservatives had been so utterly devastated at the election that many obvious candidates had been removed from Parliament. The Foreign Secretary, Malcolm Rifkind, lost his seat on 1 May as did Michael Portillo, the 'Darling of the Right'. Many, including William Hague, had assumed that the Conservatives would lose the election, Major would resign and they would be supporting a Portillo leadership bid. In the event this was not an option that could be followed through.

Ken Clarke put himself forward from the pro-European wing. Peter Lilley, John Redwood and Michael Howard entered from the Euro-sceptic Right. A little while later William Hague also entered the fray. Realising that the Euro-sceptic vote would be split four ways, Hague focused his campaign on his youth as an asset which could lead the Party in making a 'fresh start'. The first ballot on 10 June saw Clarke with 49 votes, Hague with 41 and Redwood with 27.[1] Howard and Lilley were knocked out and threw their support behind Hague. In the second ballot on 17 June, the results were similar. Clarke came first, Hague second, Redwood third, but none with enough votes to win outright. Clarke, realising that he was in trouble if either of the Euro-sceptics dropped out of the race, made a pact with Redwood that they would be a leadership team uniting both Conservative factions. For Clarke the idea was that he could use Redwood to placate the Euro-sceptics who would otherwise never vote for him. For Redwood it gave him a chance at some form of influence after Howard and Lilley effectively destroyed his chances of winning by backing Hague. It didn't work. Margaret Thatcher, alarmed at the thought of Clarke as leader, came out in support of Hague. The balance was tipped. Hague won the third ballot and Clarke dropped out.

So, on 19 June 1997, William Hague arrived at the top as leader of the Conservative Party, succeeding a line of individuals who had almost all gone on to become Prime Minister.

The new leader immediately set out to modernise the Conservatives, making them appear in tune with young people, open to change and willing to listen. He had limited success, not least because many of his parliamentary colleagues were in denial about how unpopular they actually were. There was a wide held belief that the election had been a mistake and that the electorate would eventually come to its senses. As a result 'New Labour' enjoyed an extended honeymoon with the Tories unable to challenge them in any substantial manner.

Fighting over Europe had destroyed Major's premiership. Hague had challenged for the leadership on a platform of Euro-scepticism, saying, for example, that he 'would oppose further political integration in Europe'. Now he was leader, though, he had to find a way to unite the Party. He offered Ken Clarke a Shadow Cabinet post early on but this was declined. Undeterred, in the spirit of Party unity Hague attempted to balance pro-Europeans with Euro-sceptics inside his Shadow Cabinet. Ken Clarke's refusal aside, the new leader was able to keep both sides of the divide in senior positions. The problem was that contrary to uniting the Party, the clear divide existing among Shadow Cabinet colleagues who were supposed to be exercising collective responsibility led to divisions.

As part of his modernising theme Hague, along with several advisors, attended Flambards theme park in Cornwall on 4 August. The idea of the venture was to shake off the image of Tories as old and out of touch. Hague attempted to demonstrate that Conservatives could have fun and they were, on the whole, normal people. However, the whole exercise had an air of falseness about it. The team were all recorded wearing baseball caps with 'HAGUE' emblazoned across the front, which suggested that it was a stunt for the press, rather than a genuine recreational trip. Other such ideas involved the leader and his fiancée, Ffion, attending the Notting Hill carnival on 25 August but, again, the public could not believe that Conservatives could go out and enjoy themselves in such a trendy way. It seemed that no matter how hard he tried (or perhaps *because* of how hard he tried) he could not reform the image of the Party. Meanwhile Labour's approval ratings soared under the leadership of Tony Blair. On 31 August Diana, Princess of Wales died in a car crash in Paris. Blair's performances in front of the press – dubbing her the 'People's Princess – made him appear in touch with the *zeitgeist*, a stark contrast to a Conservative Party that could seemingly talk about nothing but Europe.

Hague knew that he had to convince obstinate Tory MPs of the need for reform. Consequently he gave the Conservative grassroots half a day at the Party Conference that autumn to tell the leadership exactly what they thought of them. Local association members heavily criticised the parliamentary party for the in-fighting which had preceded the general election. When Sir Archie Hamilton, Chairman of the 1922 Committee, tried to defend MPs he was jeered.[2] As a concession to the rank and file the '22 agreed to a new format for electing the Party leader. In the new process the winner would not be elected by MPs. Instead MPs would select two candidates who could then be put to the wider Party membership for a final decision. At this point it may have hit home to the parliamentary party just how strong the feelings of the electorate were.

Just after the conference the Shadow Cabinet, possibly shaken by the strength of feeling in the grassroots, came out with a defined policy to oppose any attempt by the government to take Britain into a single European currency. However, they did append the caveat that this policy applied only 'for the foreseeable future' as a sop to the pro-Europeans in their number.

As a result of the many problems within the Conservatives, in 1998, while Blair was focused on military intervention in Kosovo, Hague concentrated on reshaping his Party. Their campaign capabilities were improved (eighteen years in government had left Central Office hopelessly outdated) with more internet terminals, phone lines and immediate access to media publications allowing more efficient reaction. During the same period Hague authorised Peter Lilley, at this point Deputy Leader of the Party, to investigate policy strategy for the future. In his investigation Lilley found that the public accepted that the Conservatives were better at handling the economy than their opponents but there was a strong belief that they wished to cut public services, maybe even to privatise the NHS. Lilley encouraged Shadow Cabinet ministers to speak with public sector workers to get a feel for what was happening in Britain. Subsequently, in April 1999, he gave a speech in which he appeared to suggest that the Conservatives should 'abandon Thatcherism'. His view was that in order to move forwards a break with the past was necessary, however, many of his colleagues were unable to accept this idea, still clinging to their glory days. The speech caused a split in the Shadow Cabinet and, in June, Lilley was removed from it. Life at the top, Hague was finding, is not easy.

The next development in policy came in June 1999, when in the European elections the Conservatives fared particularly well. They returned 36 MEPs in spite of their consistently poor approval ratings. Hague took this as a sign that the country was drawn to Euro-scepticism, which only the Conservative Party offered at this time. This was to fuel his conviction to keep fighting the government along the lines of Europe, rather than domestic issues. However, the reality was that the public generally didn't care about Europe as much as the Conservative Party did. When Hague campaigned on these issues it did not resonate with the voters as well as Labour's cries of further NHS funding did.

The success of the Party in the European elections may well have saved Hague's leadership. Given all his other difficulties a poor showing in these elections could well have resulted in a backbench coup. As it was he was able to stagger through 1999. When Alan Clark, the colourful (if sometimes indiscreet) MP for Kensington and Chelsea, died in September 1999, it forced a by-election which was won by none other than Michael Portillo, returning to the Commons for the Conservatives. This would prove crucial to the developing story of the Party. In February 2000 Hague brought Portillo into the Shadow Cabinet to replace Francis Maude as Shadow Chancellor (Maude being moved to Foreign Affairs). However, Maude and Portillo would soon form a personal alliance that would clash with Hague in many areas of policy.

Portillo did not take his time in making an impact. Almost as soon as he took up his new position he reversed the Party's policies over the minimum wage and Bank of England independence (previously they had opposed the government over both but would now be supporting them). Almost inconceivably, this did not make a difference to the Conservatives' popularity. They could oppose the government on such important issues, then turn around and support them and were still unable to make a dent in Labour's lead in the polls. Senior Conservatives must have been asking themselves the question 'What on earth *can* we do?'

Even when the government blundered they remained more popular than the Tories. This became apparent in September 2000 when an increase in fuel duties led to farmers and transport workers blockading petrol stations and oil refineries in protest. The government's authority was questioned but even in these circumstances the Conservatives couldn't capitalise, finding themselves in the impossible position of having to decide between supporting the government in an unpopular policy and supporting the protestors in an unlawful campaign.

As the fuel crisis came to an end later in the month the Conservatives managed to force themselves into another difficult position. At the Party Conference in October their Shadow Home Secretary, Ann Widdecombe, proposed that Fixed Penalty Notices should be issued to people found in possession of cannabis. The idea was to appear tough on crime once again but all the suggested policy did, much like 'Back to Basics' several years earlier, was encourage the media to turn the spotlight onto senior Conservatives. They started digging into the past lives of many Tories and were able to report that some of the Shadow Cabinet had smoked cannabis. The policy idea subsequently collapsed.

Meanwhile there were tensions at the top of the Tory leadership. Hague was struggling with Portillo and Maude, who disagreed with almost everything he was doing. Hague, in turn, became frustrated at Portillo's inability to conquer Chancellor Gordon Brown in debates or to suggest popular policies. As their relationships with Hague deteriorated,

Portillo and Maude started to believe that they were being briefed against in the press. All of them have since declared that this period was among some of the most miserable of their careers.[3]

By the time of the general election in June 2001 the Party was clearly not in a position to govern. The campaign was focused around a narrow, Euro-sceptic theme, with 'Save the £' being central to it. Although Euro-sceptics were delighted with the position of the Party, the majority of the country could not relate to what was being said. Their concerns were about the economy and the state of public services, which the Tories completely failed to address. The result was another landslide victory for Labour. In fact the Conservatives only gained a single seat from their 1997 defeat (Labour, 413 seats; Conservatives, 166 seats; Liberal Democrats, 52 seats).[4] The following day Hague resigned as Party leader.

During his four years as leader he was unable to give the Conservatives a sense of direction or unite the warring factions over Europe. Consequently he did not win the election in 2001. That said, there is no serious historian that believes that the Conservatives could have won that election, regardless of what they did in the four years after their routing in 1997.

What Hague did, which was significant, was threefold. Firstly, he kept the Tories from completely destroying themselves, which was a genuine possibility. Not presiding over the destruction of a Party is hardly aiming for the stars but the Tories had not seen a defeat on the scale of 1997 since Lord Grey's Great Reform Bill had allowed him to reduce Wellington's Party to around 150 seats in 1832. On that occasion the only way that the Tories found their way back into power was to disband the old Party and start again as Conservatives. The possibility of the Conservatives now destroying themselves like their forebears had done was a real one and Hague prevented this.

His second achievement was that he developed a Party infrastructure that allowed them, in future, to contend as a 21st Century opposition Party, which they could not have done had their headquarters remained in the sorry state that he inherited in 1997. Blair had made the Labour Party a PR machine which, under the management of Alistair Campbell, could spin negative stories to make Labour look good. The 1997

Conservative operation never really stood a chance and, had it continued as it was, the Party may never have recovered.

Thirdly, Hague succeeded in keeping Britain out of the single European currency, which a Clarke leadership would have supported and, therefore, may have resulted in British entry. Years later, when it became clear that the project was unworkable without political union (for the same reasons that forced Britain to crash out of the ERM in 1992) the Conservatives were able to present themselves as a Party of foresight. This was down to the determination of William Hague.

Success can be measured in different ways. Winning an election and bringing the Conservatives back to power in 2001, short of a miracle, was not a realistic possibility. What Hague did was give the Party a future. That said, he was remembered at the time as the first leader for a century (and the first ever leader of the entire Party) not to become Prime Minister. Fortunately for him it would not be long before he was joined by another in that respect.

Iain Duncan Smith
(2001 – 2003)

I love my country. For me, this is the greatest country on earth, and the tolerance, the decency and the strength of the British people are worth fighting for. That is why I am here.

Iain Duncan Smith, 10 October 2002

You have no Government, no Discipline in your Party, no Firmness to one another or to any Point

Daniel Defoe's *Tory*, 1692

ONCE HAGUE STOOD DOWN, the Party did not take the time to soul-search or discuss its clear identity crisis. Instead it was straight into another leadership election. This time the candidates were Michael Portillo, Iain Duncan Smith, Michael Ancram, David Davis and Ken Clarke (again). Portillo was the favourite from the outset and most expected a contest between him and Clarke.[1] After the first ballot, though, Portillo took 49 votes but it was Duncan Smith who came second with 39. Clarke managed to poll third with 36, Ancram and Davis being eliminated.

In the second round the results were: Clarke, 59; Duncan Smith, 54; Portillo, 53. Portillo was thus knocked out and, owing to the changes implemented by Hague, the final two would be presented to the wider Party for a decision. Over the summer Clarke and Duncan Smith toured the country campaigning for votes. In another display of intent, when it came to a choice between a well-known pro-European with vast ministerial experience and a relatively unknown Euro-sceptic who had never had a job in government, the Party chose the Euro-sceptic by a convincing margin.[2] Duncan Smith was now the leader of the opposition.

The result was announced on 13 September 2001 (delayed by twenty-four hours from the formal date set because of the events of 11 September that year). However, the world's media was, quite understandably, focused on events across the Atlantic and the consequences of two commercial aircraft that had flown into the Twin Towers in New York. Nobody was interested in Duncan Smith or the Tories. Tony Blair now showed himself as an international statesman, forging a compact relationship with US President George W. Bush. Meanwhile Duncan Smith could not get a camera to face in his direction.

When it came to shaping his Shadow Cabinet he decided that he was not going to accept the divisions that had plagued Hague, not to mention Major. Consequently he surrounded himself with right-wingers like himself. Michael Howard became Shadow Chancellor and Michael Ancram Shadow Foreign Secretary. There was to be no doubt as to which direction the Party would be taking. The new leader wanted to start reforming Conservative domestic policy in order to prove to the electorate that the Party did care about public services and the NHS – policies that had previously been neglected – but the message did not get through. The political world was too heavily focused on post-9/11 foreign affairs. As the United States and the United Kingdom sent troops into Afghanistan, commencing the so-called 'War on Terror' in December 2001, Duncan Smith could find no audience willing to listen to him talk about how the Tories had changed. His position was to support the government in its foreign policy, meaning that he was leader of an opposition with nothing to oppose.

Throughout 2002 Duncan Smith had a difficult time. He constantly clashed with Howard, who wanted to offer tax cuts to the electorate, while the leader preferred to pledge to maintain public expenditure. He was unable to touch Blair at Prime Minister's Questions due to the Prime Minister being an adept debater whilst Duncan Smith struggled to communicate. As the parliamentary session wore on Duncan Smith came under increasing criticism for his ineffective oratory. Whatever else they said about Hague (and they said a lot), the Tory backbenchers could never complain about how he handled himself at the despatch box, proving himself more than a match for the Prime Minister every week.

Consequently, during Conference season, Duncan Smith decided to address the criticisms head on. He took to the stage and delivered his speech, including the now-famous line 'never underestimate the determination of a quiet man'. In doing so he set himself up for ridicule in the press and by MPs on the government benches during every appearance he made in the Commons from that point onwards.

When Parliament reconvened after the Conference season the government introduced into the Commons its Adoption and Children Bill, which aimed to allow both unmarried and gay couples to adopt. To the horror of many liberal-minded Tories, Duncan Smith planned not only to oppose the legislation but to impose a three line whip on the vote. When several MPs broke ranks and voted with the government Duncan Smith began to become concerned that his leadership was being undermined. On 5 November he, apparently spontaneously, addressed a gathering of the press and made a statement in which he said that he was being undermined by some within his Party and that the Conservatives must 'unite or die'. Memories of 'put up or shut up' were invoked. He would never command the authority of the Party again. Duncan Smith had been a Maastricht rebel ten years earlier, so for many now causing him problems there was a sense of poetic justice about his travails.

In the spring of 2003 the government began to prepare to go to war to remove Saddam Hussein from power in Iraq. Saddam had consistently refused to allow UN weapons inspectors into his country to confirm that he was not in possession of 'weapons of mass destruction'. The conflict that had begun with Major and Bush senior a decade earlier would be finished by Blair and Bush junior. Duncan Smith provided the government his unqualified support. On 18 March the Conservatives joined Labour in the 'aye' lobby to back the government in the decision over whether to go to war. Had the Conservatives opposed Labour, given the large number of Labour MPs who rebelled[3] and the Liberal Democrats who voted against, Blair would have been defeated. Had this happened the entire course of UK foreign policy from that point onwards would have been altered.

That was not to be. Duncan Smith's support for the government, effectively denying the bloodthirsty backbenchers their opportunity to witness a leader attack and wound the Prime Minister, was yet another cause of discontent. Throughout the summer mutterings of dissatisfaction within the Party could be heard all over Westminster. By the autumn it looked as though Duncan Smith's days were numbered.

It was against this backdrop that he attended the Party Conference in Blackpool at the beginning of October in defiant mood. He and his speechwriters prepared a speech that would show that he was prepared to come out fighting and hopefully stir the excitement and the passions of a restless Party. When Duncan Smith delivered his speech, in the middle of a stage with no lectern in order to give the impression of authority, he decried Blair as a liar. Then, at the climax, he delivered his killer line: 'The quiet man is here to stay and he's turning up the volume!'

Had he roared this phrase out at the audience he may have succeeded in winning over the delegates. However, he merely muttered the line in the same, monotonous tone that he used to deliver the rest of the speech. It was cringe-worthy. Duncan Smith had done nothing at Blackpool to reassert himself and now the discontented masses would come for him.

Under Conservative Party rules, if 15 per cent of the parliamentary party write to the Chairman of the 1922 Committee stating their dissatisfaction with the leadership, then a no confidence vote is forced. In 2003 15 per cent of the parliamentary party meant 25 MPs.[4] By 28 October the magic number had been reached. Duncan Smith refused to resign, proposing that a no confidence vote go ahead, which he felt confident that he could win. The following day the ballot took place and Duncan Smith was defeated by 90 votes to 75.[5] It was over and he would have to stand down.

Having led the Tories for two years he achieved very little. The Conservative Party was led from a more right-of-centre position than it ever had been before, at a time when Labour occupied the centre ground. Consequently no recovery from the previous two disastrous general elections looked apparent.

He had once claimed that people should not 'underestimate the determination of a quiet man'. He claimed to be determined but, when compared to some idolised twentieth century Tory Prime Ministers, there is little to suggest that he really was. Churchill had been attacked from all sides of Parliament throughout the 1930s for what were seen as his eccentric views on Nazism. He had the resilience, the determination to carry his convictions and was proved correct. Thatcher was opposed by powerful forces in the form of the trades unions when attempting to reform Britain in the 1980s but she had the determination to see those reforms through. Duncan

Smith could not even carry his Party for two years, let alone carry the country through an election. Churchill and Thatcher both won over their dissenters with the force of their determination. On this front, Duncan Smith failed.

He was an ineffective communicator, debater and, worse, he was unlucky. At a time when he had come up with a positive strategy to convince voters that the Conservatives had a genuinely acceptable domestic policy – the sort of policies that may have won them some ground in 2001 – the political landscape had shifted to foreign affairs and events over which the opposition had no influence.

Going back to the two previous Tory leaders just used as examples, Churchill had spent years in the political wilderness before appearing something like a prophet at the outbreak of the Second World War. Had that not happened, had appeasement worked, he could never have become Prime Minister and Chamberlain would have been a celebrated hero. But that was largely down to luck. Thatcher's approval ratings were abysmal for much of her first term in office but when Galtieri decided to invade the Falklands and she took them back she became idolised. That was lucky. To be successful in politics everybody needs luck. For all his faults – a lack of charisma, ineffectiveness in debates and speeches – it was a want of luck that was Duncan Smith's greatest.

Michael Howard
(2003 − 2005)

My grandmother was one of those killed in the concentration camps.
If it hadn't been for Winston Churchill and if it hadn't been for
Britain, I would have been one of them too. That's why when I say I
owe everything I am to this country, I really do mean it.

Michael Howard, 5 October 2004

We plainly and honestly told him our Principle…our Honour in this
point made him rely upon our Honour in others

Daniel Defoe's *Tory*, 1692

THE FALL OF DUNCAN SMITH meant that the
Conservatives had done away with their third leader in a little
over six years. They now faced the prospect of a sixth
leadership contest in fourteen years. This meant that an average
of once every two years the Party decided that a leader should
be challenged, which presented the country with the impression
that they would never be satisfied. There was no stability in the
Conservatives at this point.

For the first time in many years, senior Conservatives
seem to have realised the truth that the public had known for
years. The in-fighting for which the grassroots had been so
critical for so long was damaging their standing in the country
and, consequently, their electoral prospects. Another
leadership contest, therefore, was too damaging to
contemplate. It would cause divisions, it would distract them
from opposition and, more to the point, the emerging leader
would necessarily have been voted against by a substantial
number of both the parliamentary party and the grassroots. No,
this time it had to be different.

With an election roughly two years away (maybe more,
probably less) the Party had to unite behind a leader and give
that person their full confidence. The problem was that Party
rules necessitated an election for a new leader. The Old Boys'
Club that had promoted Heath, Douglas-Home, Macmillan and

Eden was a thing of the past. Democracy was the future. But democracy meant death.

In the days leading up to Duncan Smith's downfall, Howard's friends, namely Oliver Letwin and Liam Fox, urged him to challenge for the leadership. Howard had refused but, once Duncan Smith was defeated in the no confidence motion, he considered going for it. Senior Party officials realised that, regardless of who their ideal choice would be, they needed to throw their support behind one individual, rather than allow an open contest. The main threat to the plan was David Davis, who was widely known to have leadership ambitions. However, when his long-term ally Graham Brady told him that he couldn't defeat Howard, Davis announced that he would not be standing.[1] Shortly afterwards Fox and Letwin, among others, started to announce publicly their support for Howard to step into the leadership immediately, in order to deter any potential challengers. Howard declared his candidacy the day after Duncan Smith's resignation and a week later nobody else had challenged for it. He was now leader by default.

Party morale immediately improved. Not only did Howard 'lead from the centre' and 'refuse to accept anything but loyalty' as he had alluded in his nomination speech, but the Conservatives found that in him they had a leader who was able to take Blair on at Prime Minister's Questions. This had been lacking during the Duncan Smith years.

Over Christmas 2003, the political world was waiting for the Hutton Inquiry to report on the events leading up to the death of Dr David Kelly. Kelly was a scientists and was viewed as an expert on biological warfare. Earlier in the year he had had a non-attributable discussion with a BBC journalist in which he stated that he believed to be false the government's claim that Iraq had the capability to launch an attack on the West within 45 minutes of an order being given. His name was subsequently leaked to other media outlets as the source, some believed by the government.

On 14 January 2004, Howard challenged the Prime Minister over his involvement in the episode. He won enthusiasm from the Tory backbenches for refusing to give Blair an inch. Possibly Howard was inspired by his treatment at the hands of Jeremy Paxman in 1997. On that occasion he had appeared on *Newsnight* having put himself forward as a

candidate for the leadership. In the interview he had with
Paxman, Howard was asked the same 'yes or no' question
twelve times, giving a politician's answer on each occasion and
destroying his own leadership prospects in the process. On
challenging Blair over the David Kelly saga, Howard forced
the Prime Minister to answer the same uncomfortable question
time and time again:

> I'm asking the Prime Minister about what he
> said in this House seven days ago and what he
> said in a television studio three days ago. Let
> me put to the Prime Minister this very, very
> simple and straightforward question. When on
> 22 July he denied authorising the naming of
> David Kelly, is that a statement he stands by or
> is that one of the 'bits out here and there' that
> he wants us all to ignore?

The Prime Minister gave an answer to the effect of 'let's wait
for the report'. This was a particularly difficult area because
Howard's suggestion was that if the Prime Minister had not
been honest then he had not just lied to the House of Commons
but he had pushed a man to suicide. Blair must have hoped that
the line of questioning would move on to other things. It usually
does because the leader of the opposition is entitled only to ask
six questions in a session. However, Howard pressed on:

> The Prime Minister hasn't answered the
> question. It's a very, very simple question and
> the answer, Mr. Speaker, is either 'yes' or 'no'.
> I'll give him another opportunity. On 22 July
> he was asked 'Why did you authorise the
> naming of David Kelly?' and he replied
> 'That's completely untrue.' Does he stand by
> that statement, 'yes' or 'no'?

Again the Prime Minister replied that the House should wait for
the Hutton Report. Howard kept pressing, amid cheers on the
Conservative benches:

> Does the Prime Minister have the faintest idea
> of how much damage he is doing to what is left
> of his reputation by his refusal to answer this

> very simple question? He hasn't answered the
> question and the whole country knows it. I will
> give him one last chance and I will carry on
> asking this question until we get a straight
> answer. On 22 July he was asked 'Why did you
> authorise the naming of David Kelly?' and he
> replied 'That is completely untrue.' Does he
> stand by that statement, 'yes' or 'no'?

The Prime Minister claimed that he had already answered and
that the House should await the result of the inquiry. He then
stated he believed that Howard was effectively calling him a
liar. Howard came back a fourth time:

> If the Prime Minister takes that view of the
> charges I have been making, why on earth
> hasn't he answered today the very simple,
> straightforward question I have been putting
> to him? Isn't it the case, Mr. Speaker, that this
> afternoon the whole country has seen just how
> desperately dodgy the Prime Minister's
> position has become?[2]

The Tories were delighted. They finally had someone who was
prepared to challenge the government, rather than support
them. Even when Duncan Smith had disagreed with Blair, he
had not had the skills to discomfit him. However, Howard's
assertiveness towards Labour would also land him in
difficulties, particularly when tackling them over Iraq. After all
he, as a Conservative, had supported the invasion, following
Iain Duncan Smith's lead.

Throughout 2004 he attacked Blair saying that he
believed that the country had been led to war under false
pretences. He argued that claims that Iraq had possessed
weapons of mass destruction and a '45 minute' capability were
completely unfounded. He claimed that Blair had misled the
House, in fact taking Britain to war after promising President
Bush that he would do so. This change in policy would have
been difficult to pull off in the best of circumstances but
Howard made it more so. He declared that he still agreed with
the war in principle because of the terror of Saddam Hussein

and the instability that would have been caused had Britain not entered. Blair was able to claim that Howard was both for and against the war, completely wrong-footing him. The strong boost to Conservative morale was, therefore, soon halted.

By the end of the year it was clear that an election was looming. The Parliament could run to mid-2006 but nobody expected that. There was not, in reality, enough time to overturn Labour's majority, for which a swing of 10.5 per cent from the 2001 figures was necessary.[3] Howard now saw it as his job simply to make in-roads. 1997 had been the nadir. 2001 had seen stabilisation but no progress. In 2005, victory was almost impossible but progress was a realistic target. If they couldn't do it at the height of anti-government feelings due to Iraq then they never would.

The election was duly called for 5 May 2005 and it was another strong Labour victory, albeit both the Conservatives and the Liberal Democrats improved their standing. It was a depressing day for the Tories, realising that they had now lost three consecutive elections. If the Parliament ran anything near its full length then they would be out of office for a longer single period than any since before William Pitt took office in 1783.

However, there was room for hope. They had made gains in this last election, and not insignificant ones. Labour had won 356 seats. The Conservatives took 197. The Liberal Democrats won 62.[4] This was an increase of 31 seats for the Tories but given that Labour had lost 56 their relative difference was substantially cut.

The day after the election, Friday 6 May, Howard announced that he would be standing down as leader, but not immediately. At the end of the forthcoming Parliament he would be 69, which he felt was too old to fight an election campaign (by current standards, not the standards of Palmerston and Gladstone, or even Churchill, all of whom were octogenarian Prime Ministers). However, he would be staying on for the time being for the dual purpose of allowing the Party to settle (a mistake he felt that both Hague and Major made was resigning immediately after losing their elections and therefore not giving the Party time to think about where it wanted to go) and reforming the leadership election rules.

Howard felt that the current rules were unfavourable. The parliamentary party voted for candidates and the two leaders then went to the wider Party membership for a decision.

However, as the selection of Duncan Smith had demonstrated, this method meant that a leader could be elected without the support of a majority of MPs, which was unworkable.

In the meantime, Howard was aware that David Davis had not lost his ambitions for a leadership challenge following his decision not to stand in 2003. Howard didn't believe that Davis was the right person to take the Party forward but his problem was that the only people who could really stand up to him were either an even worse option, Ken Clarke, or completely lacking in both experience and visibility. The new generation of Conservative MPs who had entered Parliament since 2001 fell into this category, lacking both experience and visibility. Consequently Howard used his time as a lame duck leader to reshuffle his Shadow Cabinet, moving those who may be able to lead in future to more active and senior roles in order that they may attract a following now. Davis remained as Shadow Home Secretary but all around him he found that rivals for the crown were promoted. Liam Fox became Shadow Foreign Secretary. George Osborne was promoted to Shadow Chancellor of the Exchequer. David Cameron became Shadow Education Secretary.

The focus of the Conservative Party had moved away from its leader towards those who would lead in future. Having discussed which one of them would step forward to challenge Davis, Cameron and Osborne announced in mid-June that they would be candidate and campaign manager respectively. Liam Fox and Ken Clarke (again) put themselves forwards.

Once the contenders had revealed themselves, Howard let it be known that he would be resigning after the Party Conference, scheduled for the first week of October. Consequently Conference that year was seen as a sales platform for the candidates. Davis was the clear frontrunner and attended every event he could at Conference. However, by the end of the week there was a clear contrast between a 60 year old Davis and a 38 year old Cameron. During his Conference speech Cameron spoke without notes, not giving much substance to what he said but the manner in which he delivered it impressed everyone. Davis gave lectures to fringe events. One of these was humorously reported by ITV news with a camera facing towards the audience and their Political Editor,

Tom Bradby, commenting 'How many do you count asleep, exactly?'

Clarke also used the opportunity to pitch himself, delivering a speech from a lectern: 'We are searching for a leader who will be seen by the public as a Prime Minister-in-waiting. Well, oh boy, have you kept me waiting!'

Howard sent his letter of resignation to Michael Spicer, Chairman of the 1922 Committee, on 7 October and the first ballots were held later in the month. From this point forward, he relinquished all authority.

Michael Howard's tenure as leader of the Tories was brief. In fact, only Canning and Goderich had shorter periods at the top than him but at least they have the distinction of also having been Prime Minister. However, notwithstanding its brevity, Howard's time as leader played a significant role in the story of modern Conservatism, if not modern conservatism. It has been argued that the Party did not achieve the success it should have done in the 2005 general election, given the difficulties that the Labour government had brought upon itself with Iraq. Those who argue this viewpoint condemn Howard as a failure. However, that is to miss the point somewhat.

At the end of 2003 the Conservative Party was in danger of doing what it had done several times since 1990 – tearing itself apart over discontent with the leader. Whereas in 1990 and 1995 the Party had been in government with a comfortable majority in the House of Commons when leaders were toppled, this did not apply in 2003. In 1997 and 2001 the leaders of the Party had gone voluntarily but this was not the case in 2003. In other words, just before Howard took over, the Conservative Party was heading for a devastating coincidence of removing a leader by force and being only a small Party in the Commons. The threat of a Liberal Democrat resurgence, which could force the Tories into the demeaning role of a third party, was real.

Howard did not win the election and he did not make significant enough gains to give the Party a genuine belief that they could force the hand of the government during the next Parliament. What he did, though, was to unite a fractious Party, stabilise a volatile situation, give the demoralised backbenchers something to cheer about and put the Party on the course to victory. On the one hand 2005 represented a third election defeat, but in only eighteen months could Howard really have changed that? On the other hand it represented the first time since 1983 that the Conservatives had increased their number of seats from one election to the next, apart from an increase of one in 2001.

Michael Howard, then, cannot be said to share the same sort of influence that is attributed to Pitt, Peel, Disraeli, Churchill or Thatcher. But he can credibly claim to have saved a Party from annihilation and given it the chance to fight another day.

David Cameron
(2005-)

I don't claim to be a great leader but I'm your public servant, standing here, wanting to make our country so much better for your children and mine. I love this country and I will do my duty by it.

David Cameron, 1 October 2014

[The Tories] never refused to accept any Whig, that would comply

Daniel Defoe's *Tory*, 1692

AFTER THE PERFORMANCES at the Party Conference in Blackpool, Davis remained the front runner for no other reason than that he was known and he wasn't Ken Clarke. But Cameron's standing had improved. Bookmakers across the land slashed their odds on him winning. At the first ballot on 18 October both Davis and Cameron were clearly ahead of the pack with 62 and 56 votes respectively. Fox received 42 and Clarke was eliminated with only 38.[1]

The second ballot was held two days later and Cameron on this occasion took 90 votes. Davis, embarrassingly, actually got fewer votes even though there were fewer candidates to choose from with Clarke gone. With only 57 votes he beat Fox by only six. It was now Cameron and Davis going through to the ballot of the wider Party membership. The following six weeks saw something that the Conservative Party had never before known: a positive leadership election that got people talking excitedly about the future, rather than divisively about the difference between the candidates.

On 6 December Cameron was declared the winner. For the first time, the Party had not chosen the more right-wing candidate and for Cameron it was a coup. He had less parliamentary experience than any leader since William Pitt. During 2006, the Conservatives started to look like a serious Party of opposition for the first time in years. Cameron battled honourably against Blair at the despatch box in the Commons, a more liberal policy line was adopted and at the local elections in the spring they came top. All in all the Cameron revolution seemed to be going well. He was helped in all this by a growing schism in the Labour Party between the 'Blairites' (those supporting the Prime Minister through thick and thin) and the 'Brownites' (those wishing to see Blair step aside in favour of the Chancellor, Gordon Brown as had apparently been agreed between the two men back in 1994).

Things came to a head between the Prime Minister and the Chancellor during the summer and, by early autumn, Blair had announced that he would be gone within a year. The Tories were delighted. Blair had led Labour to three election victories, arguably owing to his 'infuriating smoothness', as William Hague would put it eight years later. This was not a quality that the socially awkward Brown was blessed with. The future looked bright.

In May 2007, Blair announced that he would step down on 27 June. He then used his last six weeks in office to give a 'long goodbye', or a 'lap of honour'.[2] Brown was now the man for Cameron to prove himself against. The most pressing consideration for the Party was what to do in the event of Brown calling for an immediate general election. The Conservatives were confident that the new Prime Minister would be an easier opponent than Blair in the long term. However, Labour had received a temporary boost in the polls with Blair having gone, the spectre of Iraq having departed with him. If an election were to be called, there was a good chance that Labour would win. The difficulty for Cameron was that to oppose the possibility would make his Party look afraid. Consequently he laid down the gauntlet and challenged Brown to 'stop dithering' and call a snap general election, in the hope that he could bluff the Prime Minister out of doing it.[3] When Brown opted against, probably concerned that history would remember him as the shortest-lived Prime Minister since Goderich, Cameron could claim that he had 'bottled it', compounding the Prime Minister's reputation as indecisive.

The Conservatives were riding high going into 2008. Then a run on the building society Northern Rock, based on the fact that it was unable to pay loans for money borrowed from other banks, led to the government nationalising the institution in the February. This was seen as of little significance at the time. However, the reason that Northern Rock had been unable to pay its debts was because its traditional way of making money (selling its mortgages to international firms) had dried up. This, in turn, was because of many financial institutions realising that they were over-exposed to bad debts. In other words, the apparently isolated Northern Rock incident precipitated what would prove to be the biggest financial crisis since the Great Depression of the 1930s.

In August 2008 the US government provided billions of dollars in funding to support the mortgage giants Fannie Mae and Freddie Mac. In September Lehmann Brothers, one of Americas largest investment banks, filed for bankruptcy. Due to the inextricable nature of money markets, British institutions soon followed suit. Within days Halifax Bank of Scotland was on the point of collapse, prompting the government to draw up a deal for Lloyds TSB to take them over.[4] Then in mid-October, the government announced that they were nationalising part of the new Lloyds TSB/HBoS group as well as RBS with a £37 billion rescue package to prevent them all from going under.

With the economy falling into tatters, Brown's approval ratings improved as the British public decided to trust a man who had spent ten years as Chancellor, rather than support Cameron and Osborne, who had never spent a day in a government position. The Conservatives, unwilling to capitalise at this point on the people's economic hardships, had no option but to sit and wait.

Then, in February 2009, Cameron's eldest child, Ivan, died. He had been born with a rare condition called Ohtahara Syndrome, meaning that he had not been expected to live long and suffered regularly from epileptic fits. Cameron was obviously devastated and politics took a back seat for the most part of the spring. He returned to front line politics at a crucial time. In April and May the *Telegraph* newspaper started printing stories about expenses claims made by MPs, many of which were extravagant at best, outright ludicrous at worst. It started by exposing expenses made by the Labour front bench before turning its attention to the Tories. Once Shadow Cabinet ministers were exposed, Cameron returned to seize the initiative. In mid-May he made a statement naming his own colleagues, including himself, and how much that they had agreed to pay back. He apologised for claims made 'even if they were within the rules', because doing so was wrong. Meanwhile the Prime Minister had not made any public statement. Suddenly Cameron came across as a sincere reformer, whereas Brown looked either stuck in the past or, once again, a ditherer.

The effect of the 'expenses scandal' was that the Prime Minister, now languishing in the polls, was not going to call an election until the last possible moment. This meant that the Conservatives could wait until the Party Conference in October to put together a financial plan for the future, including spending cuts to help pull the country out of the financial crisis. One final development would come about before the new year, though. Throughout 2009 *Sky News*, the television broadcaster, had been campaigning to hold televised debates between leaders of the main political parties before a general election. The idea had been taken up enthusiastically by Cameron and the leader of the Liberal Democrats, Nick Clegg (who both saw the advantage of putting themselves on the same platform as the Prime Minister). By December *Sky* had managed to convince Brown to go along with it and, by the end of the month, there was a consensus that three debates should be held during the month before the election. The next general election, as a result, would be more similar to a US Presidential election, than a UK parliamentary one.

Parliament was dissolved in April for an election on 6 May. Opinion polls at this point suggested that the Conservatives would come away with the most seats but that it would probably not be enough for an overall majority. The first leader's debate was around domestic issues and was held on 15 April. Most opinion polls showed that Clegg won (with Cameron second and Brown last)[5] as he portrayed the other two individuals as unable to lead because they spent time bickering with each other rather than taking action.

In the second debate, held on 22 April and based on international affairs, Brown and Cameron did much better, with polls roughly split between Clegg and Cameron as the winner and Brown just behind. The final debate was then based on economic matters, held on 29 April and in this one there was a consensus in all polls that Cameron had won, with Clegg second and Brown coming last once again.

On the day of the election, however, the results were exactly as had been forecast a month earlier. The Conservatives came top with 306. Labour second with 258. The Lib Dems third with 57.[6] In other words the Conservatives had won but they did not have an overall majority. If the Prime Minister is the person who can command a majority of MPs, then the next Prime Minister would be the individual who could convince the Liberal Democrats to throw their support behind him.

Early on the morning of Friday 7 May, Cameron and Brown got to work on convincing Nick Clegg's Liberal Democrats that they should enter into a coalition with their respective parties. With 650 MPs in the Commons, in theory 326 is required for an overall majority of one. Labour and the Liberal Democrats together totalled 315 but Brown calculated the following: with the Speaker and his two deputies plus the five Sinn Fein MPs (who refused to take their seats on principle) removed from the calculation, a majority only required 322. This meant that on any given matter, if the Chamber was absolutely full, he only needed the support of 7 MPs from other Parties (there were 28 elected to the Commons from other groupings such as the Northern Ireland Parties, Scottish and Welsh Nationalists, independents and a Green MP)[6] to carry the confidence of the House. It was a thin argument for clinging on to power but it was all he had.

In the morning Clegg made a statement to the press saying that as the Conservatives had won the most seats, they had the right to be consulted first on forming a coalition. Brown, clearly flustered by this, made a statement from Downing Street a few hours later. In it he stated that he was not stepping aside because he had 'a constitutional duty to seek to resolve the situation'. He claimed that he was 'willing to see any of the party leaders'. Then he laid his cards out on the table and offered to introduce proportional representation at elections.[7] He knew that this was the Holy Grail for Liberal Democrats who, in spite of often coming close to second place in terms of number of votes at elections, never got anywhere near a similar proportion of Commons seats.

Later in the day, Cameron made a speech stating that he was open to compromise with the Liberal Democrats. However, after Brown's speech, Clegg was able to force the Conservatives to concede a referendum on proportional representation, confident that Labour would give him that. The Tories and Lib Dems met on that Friday evening, with Labour and the Lib Dems meeting the following day. However, with newspaper headlines such as the *Sun*'s 'Squatter, 59, Holed Up in No 10' being published that day, the Lib Dems could not have felt that propping up the Prime Minister was a good idea. That same article went on to say that the squatter, Brown, was 'denying entry to the rightful tenant'. The mood of the nation was against him. It would not be until 11 May before he finally conceded defeat with the Conservatives and the Liberal Democrats entering into a coalition government together.

The result, though, raised a great deal of concern among Conservatives. If they could not win an election outright against a leader as unpopular as Brown, in the middle of an economic crisis, could they ever win an election again? This was a question for another time but it would surely linger in the minds of many Tories.

For now David Cameron and Nick Clegg were content with walking out into the rear garden of Downing Street to announce to the gathered press their delight at having formed a coalition government together.

The new government's main aim would be to try to bring Britain back on the road to economic recovery, a large part of which involved paying down an unprecedented peacetime deficit. However, there were other matters to be dealt with. In order to bring the Liberal Democrats on board, the Tories had had to promise certain constitutional reforms. Firstly, the most important thing for the Lib Dems was the possibility of bringing about a reform to the electoral system so that they, as a third party, could gain more seats in Parliament. The coalition agreement stated that they would allow a referendum on this issue so that the people could decide. Secondly, the Liberal Democrats wanted, instead of a House of Lords made up of life peers, bishops and some hereditary peers, an elected Upper Chamber. Thirdly, there were to be five Lib Dems in the Cabinet.

Another agreement was that there should be fixed term Parliaments, so that there is greater certainty and the incumbent Party no longer has the advantage of calling elections at their own choosing. The Conservatives, for their part, wanted a promise for an independent Boundary Commission to consider redrawing the constituency boundaries for three reasons. Firstly they wished to reduce the number of MPs so as to save taxpayers' money on salaries. Secondly they wanted to even up the number of constituents that an MP served. Finally was that the average number of constituents in Labour-controlled constituencies was around 4,000 less than in Conservative ones, meaning that if both parties had a similar share of the vote, Labour would return more MPs. So the Tories wanted to make the system fairer. All of the above was put into the coalition agreement.

In forming the new Cabinet Clegg was brought in as Deputy Prime Minister but, to the irritation of some Liberal Democrats, with no departmental brief of his own. Osborne, Cameron's most loyal ally since long before his leadership bid, became Chancellor of the Exchequer. Theresa May entered as Home Secretary and William Hague became Foreign Secretary. In July the new government announced that a referendum would be held on 5 May 2011 on whether or not to introduce an Alternative Vote (AV) method of polling at elections. Under this method voters would be asked to rank candidates in preferential order, rather than to select just one. For the Liberal Democrats this meant that, because they were rarely anybody's last choice, they had a better chance of having candidates elected.

Late in that same month the government introduced its Fixed Term Parliaments Bill, in order to implement yet another phase of the coalition agreement. Due to both coalition parties supporting the measure, it passed through Parliament comfortably, gaining Royal Assent in late 2011.

For the time being this was as far as constitutional reforms went. An elected Upper Chamber and boundary changes would be postponed until the dust had settled on the AV vote. The government got through the summer recess and seemed to be on its way to seeing out 2010 without much incident. Then, on 18 December, protests occurred in Tunisia against police corruption. Little notice was taken of this at the time. However, in a little over a month protests had broken out in other countries all across the Arab region including Algeria, Jordan, Egypt and Yemen. Suddenly what appeared at first glance to have been a protest against policing practices now seemed to be a general outcry from the people of the Arab world for a fairer society. Events moved rapidly from then on. On 14 January 2011, the Tunisian President fled in the wake of increasingly violent protests. Hosni Mubarak, who had been President of Egypt for thirty years, was removed from power following nearly three weeks of demonstrations in Cairo.

When similar demonstrations began in Libya, the Libyan leader, Muammar Gaddafi, ordered the army to open fire on protestors in Benghazi. In order to protect the Libyan people from human rights abuses, NATO began to enforce a no-fly zone over the country, to prevent aerial bombardment. Air strikes began soon afterwards on specific Libyan military targets. In August 2011 Gaddafi fled office, ending 42 years of rule and in doing so becoming the third leader to fall victim of the 'Arab Spring'. He was eventually killed at the end of October.

If the Arab Spring represented the great foreign policy issue of the day, domestically the new government was also presented with innumerate challenges. In May 2011 the referendum on the Alternative Vote was held. For the coalition government this was the first issue over which the two parties campaigned on different sides. The Lib Dems were desperate to see a 'Yes' vote for changing to AV, the Conservatives (and Labour) eager to maintain the status quo. In the event around two thirds of people voted against.

Then on 4 August the shooting by police in Tottenham of Mark Duggan, a suspected armed robber who subsequently died of his injuries, led initially to rioting in the immediate area. However, over the next few days the rioting soon swept across the country. Under the guise of protest, these riots were simply the actions of a criminal minority taking the excuse to attack the state. As I wrote at the time 'once [people] have overcome the fear that the State will be able to punish them for their recalcitrance, many people will try to further their own ends by any means possible'.[10] The incident exposed weaknesses within the police as night after night the law abiding masses watched news coverage of police using running lines to charge at protestors but then falling short of using force. On 9 August Cameron made a statement in which he called for more robust police action to be taken. Although the violence eventually subsided, there was a genuine concern across the country that order had broken down irrevocably. Once the riots had died down magistrates and judges started to hand out extremely stern sentences to those involved, in order to reflect the horror of the nation. However, if putting to bed the public order problems of the nation was a hurdle overcome, the coalition was about to trip on the political hurdle that was to follow.

Enacting the next part of the coalition agreement was due to be attempted in 2012. In the June Nick Clegg proudly introduced to Parliament a House of Lords Reform Bill.

Another prize for the Liberal Democrats, who felt that an
unelected Upper Chamber was an affront to democracy and
that the size (and growing size) of the House of Lords made it
unsustainable. The Bill would aim to correct these perceived
irregularities. Some of the changes included reducing the
number of Lords (currently a little under 900) to 450 Members,
80 per cent of whom would be elected, while 20 per cent should
be appointed.

      Clegg introduced the Bill for first reading on 27 June.
On 9 July it returned for second reading and, simultaneously,
the House was asked to debate a Programme Motion, which
would curb the amount of time that could be spent debating the
Bill. However, it soon became clear that opposition from
Labour MPs and many Conservatives would kill the
Programme Motion and it was withdrawn. When the division
occurred for the Bill itself, it passed by 462 votes to 124.
However, 91 of the 'Noes' were from Conservative MPs,
defying a three line whip. Given the removal of the Programme
Motion along with the number of Conservative MPs opposed
to the Bill, Clegg became convinced that his opponents would
filibuster the legislation in the subsequent debates. He
subsequently withdrew the legislation but warned the
Conservatives that there would be consequences. It would not
be long until those consequences were felt.

      One of the other deals of the coalition, the
Conservative desire redraw constituency boundaries to make
elections fairer, was due to be debated in the new year. Clegg
soon made it clear that in retaliation for the Conservative
rebellion over Lords Reform, he was withdrawing Lib Dem
support for redrawing constituency boundaries in time for the
2015 election. In other words, even though the Boundary
Commission would eventually be redrawing the boundaries,
the Deputy Prime Minister wanted to hurt the Conservatives at
the next election so would not support a Bill to speed up the
process. In the division in January 2013 Cameron was defeated.
Coalition relations had hit an all-time low. It was the beginning
of what would prove to be a particularly difficult year for the
government.

      Concerned about the rise of the United Kingdom
Independence Party (UKIP) and that at least three of his
predecessors as Conservative Party leader had fallen over the
issue of Europe, Cameron pledged that he would hold an In/Out
referendum on Britain's continuing membership of the EU.

However, it would only be held in 2017 after he had had the chance to renegotiate the terms of British membership. Those who favoured his position argued that there was no point in holding a referendum immediately. If Cameron planned to change the terms of membership in future the result of a referendum in the present could be made redundant. However, sceptics felt that he was simply stalling for time, ensuring that the issue of Europe did not come to haunt him before a general election. This issue would fuel heated conversations within the Conservative Party, from the Cabinet Office, to the backbenches, to local associations up and down the country until the time of writing. However, for the time being the matter would take a back seat to a development in the Arab Spring.

In August the Civil War in Syria, which had begun as an uprising against President Bashar al-Assad in 2011, took a sinister twist. On 21 August it was reported that al-Assad had used chemical weapons against his own people just outside Damascus, killing hundreds. Cameron called an emergency meeting of Parliament on 29 August in which he proposed taking military action against al-Assad if the UN could prove that chemical weapons had been used. His motion was defeated by 285 votes to 272.[11] This was an embarrassing defeat for Cameron who clearly believed that given the horrors taking place in Syria he would be given a mandate by Parliament to act. The executive is under no obligation to consult Parliament on matters of foreign policy but the fact that he did was seen as a sign that Cameron believed MPs would support him, which further means that he misjudged the situation. Labour leader Ed Miliband led opposition to the proposals and, owing to a number of Tory MPs rebelling (probably a hangover from criticisms levelled at MPs following the vote to go into Iraq) he was able to defeat the government. This was the final defeat of a year that seemed to be littered with difficulties for the coalition.

If 2013 was a difficult year, it was nothing compared to what faced Cameron in the late summer and early autumn of 2014. A combination of foreign affairs, domestic turbulence and political difficulties combined to make a perfect storm for the Prime Minister, challenging his leadership on the eve of the general election. The first began in August when a Sunni jihadist group calling themselves the Islamic State of Iraq and

Syria released a video. 'ISIS' had risen up to fight the Iraqi army, mercilessly killing any Shia Muslims and non-Muslims in their wake. This particular video, released on 19 August, appeared to show a British-born Muslim beheading an American journalist by the name of James Foley, who had gone missing in Syria in 2012. The video claimed that a second American journalist – Steven Sotloff – would soon follow the same fate it the US did not cease airstrikes against ISIS. On 2 September, a video was released depicting the same British-born Muslim beheading Sotloff. Then, on 13 September, another video was released in a similar format, this time showing the beheading of a British aid worker named David Haines, apparently as a warning 'to the allies of America'. The nation was outraged but Cameron, who had wanted to take military action in the Middle East the previous year, ultimately being thwarted by Miliband, felt that action may be politically impossible. The video depicting the beheading of David Haines threatened that another British aid worker – Alan Henning – would be next.

        This was the foreign affairs nightmare that faced David Cameron and it happened against the backdrop of the most serious threat to the constitution of the United Kingdom for nearly a century. At the beginning of the Parliament, Cameron had promised the Scottish National Party that they could have a referendum on independence, similar to the referendum that the UK would have on membership of the EU. On 18 September 2014, the Scottish people would be asked the question 'Should Scotland be an independent country?' Throughout the preceding years 'Yes' and 'No' campaigners had become increasingly vocal. For the most part the 'Yes' campaign were not given much of a chance. However, in the weeks leading up to the referendum some polls started to suggest that the two sides were neck-and-neck. Suddenly panic set in within the Westminster parties and the realisation dawned on Cameron that he may well be remembered as the Prime Minister who lost Scotland.

        Throughout the summer the 'No' campaign had been lecturing the Scottish people on how much better they would be, economically, as part of a United Kingdom, while the 'Yes' campaign tried to play to sense of Scottish national pride. The fact that no effort was made to play up to British national pride was a source of heavy criticism for the 'No' campaign at the time.[12]

Before either of these issues (ISIS or the Scottish referendum) were resolved, Cameron had one more challenge to face, this time a political one. On 28 August, Douglas Carswell, a Conservative MP for Clacton, announced that he had resigned from the Party and was joining UKIP. This was an incredible blow to the Tories, who were trying to downplay the importance of UKIP but who faced the genuine possibility of being defeated by Labour in the next election because of potential Conservative voters instead voting for UKIP.

September was a stressful month for the Prime Minister. He spent much of the week before the 18th campaigning in Scotland, trying to convince voters to stay in the Union. He promised to devolve more power to Scotland, including the right for the Scottish Parliament to receive all tax revenues raised in Scotland. In the end, the result was around 55 per cent in favour of staying: closer than unionists would have liked, but better than a defeat.

On 26 September, Cameron recalled Parliament in the middle of Conference season to debate making air strikes against ISIS. This time Labour supported the government, who won by 524 votes to 43. Soldiers would not be returning to Iraq but RAF Tornados would attack key ISIS targets in order to help the Iraqi army recover lost ground. It would be the third time in as many decades that Britain had become involved militarily in Iraq.

On 27 September, Mark Reckless, another backbench Conservative MP, took to the stage at the UKIP Party Conference. He had been introduced by a grinning leader of UKIP, Nigel Farage, and announced to tumultuous applause that 'Today I am leaving the Conservative Party and joining UKIP'. It was yet another shattering blow for the Tories.

During their own Conference the following week in Birmingham, senior Conservatives tried to boost the morale of the rank-and-file in the light of these defections. Cameron gave a speech in which he pointed to the future and the need for him to be allowed to create a Conservative majority in Parliament. However, with constituency boundaries working against them, with the Euro-sceptic wing of the Party being charmed by UKIP and with the Party being so inextricably linked with unpopular austerity measures, however necessary they were, he faces an uphill challenge. His political fight was best captured by the mood of the nation waking up on 4 October. Alan Henning, the second British aid worker threatened by ISIS, was beheaded in a video released on the 3rd. The following morning the public woke up to ask themselves 'What can be done?' It seems that there is no answer. Air strikes are not enough to win the war but British boots on the ground is not a politically viable option. Likewise for Cameron, UKIP march onwards and upwards, but what can he do? Pandering to the Euro-sceptic Right forced the Party to stare into the abyss for thirteen years. However he chooses to fight the upcoming election, it will be a tough fight.

The following week saw the Clacton by-election caused by Carswell's defection to UKIP. Carswell was returned as UKIP's first ever MP. This was bad enough but the scale of the victory was devastating for the Conservatives. He won over 21,000 votes to their 8,700. With another by-election just around the corner in Rochester and Strood following Mark Reckless' switch of Party allegiance, the present really does represent a torrid time for the Conservative Party.

When Cameron accepted what many may perceive to have been a poisoned chalice of the premiership in 2010, there were few who saw the alternatives as preferable. With the advantage of hindsight, though, many would now consider that *for the Conservative Party* the two alternative courses of action would have been more beneficial than Cameron accepting office on the terms that he did. Firstly there was the option of forming a minority government. This would have meant no concessions to another political party but, also, the prospect of the government being defeated in the Commons time and again. No measures to tackle the financial crisis, difficult but necessary decisions such as public sector cuts, could have been taken because the opposition would have been too great. This scenario would have necessitated another general election, for which the outcome is impossible to calculate. However, it must be considered that the public, wanting an end to a prolonged recession, would tire of opposition to the government and vote to give the Conservatives a chance at a majority.

The second alternative for Cameron in 2010 would have been to have rejected office and forced a Lib-Lab coalition. Due to the political ideologies of these two parties the policy of such a government would have been to borrow more to try to encourage the country to grow its way out of debt. It would have taken longer for the flaws in this policy to become apparent but by the end of the Parliament, again, the Conservatives would undoubtedly have a genuine shot at a majority election victory.

However, the Tories, throughout the years covered in this book, have generally been about putting the country before the Party. Indeed, all too often they are prepared to tear themselves apart on a point of principle. A coalition government, however bad it was for the Conservatives in terms of their popularity and in terms of their being forced into distasteful compromises, was right to tackle the biggest problem facing the country; namely the economic downturn.

In taking office in 2010 Cameron may well have had the words of Thomas Young ringing in his ears. When Viscount Melbourne, who was undecided about whether to accept the King's invitation to form a government in 1834, Young, his good friend, told him:

> Why, damn it, such a position never was occupied by any Greek or Roman, and, if it only lasts two months, it is well worth while to have been Prime Minister of England.[13]

In May 2010 Cameron had to consider the good of the country and the very real possibility that the chance to form a government may never again present itself to him. His tenure in office may well continue past 2015 or it may stop dead at the next election. Either way, on a personal level, it will surely have been worth it.

Epilogue
The Future

BRITAIN TODAY is not the same as the Britain of 1783. Consequently the governing classes – the Tories among them – have had to evolve over time better to reflect the nation that they serve. William Pitt, the first Tory Prime Minister, would probably be astonished to see just how entrenched party politics has become over the centuries since his death. He governed at a time of faction. When he first entered the House of Commons there were distinct groups that followed their separate leaders; Lord North, Lord Portland, Charles James Fox among others. He tried to build himself a bigger faction than the others had in order to prevent himself being defeated. It necessarily followed that to be Prime Minister one needed at least half of Parliament on their side, and therefore the emergence of two distinct political parties was inevitable. That said, it is unlikely that Pitt would recognise the powerful grip that modern central establishments in all the political parties hold over their members and their local associations. This is a consequence that he probably never envisaged.

On the other hand the Tories have seen plenty of continuity in their time. From Pitt to Cameron they have been about protecting what they perceive as being good about Britain whilst being open to the need for reform. 'Protecting what is good' has often meant fighting against Whigs, Radicals, Nationalists, Liberals or Labour who they perceive as wanting completely to revolutionise historic traditions. This, in turn, has allowed the Tories to be open to charges of being too reactionary, backward-looking, or even unwilling to adapt to the times. However, it is precisely their ability to adapt that has led to their success. Where other parties have come and gone, the Tories, in one guise or another, have survived as a Party of government since the Glorious Revolution and it looks as though there is no end in sight for them.

Further to this, while many claim that they are fundamentally opposed to change, some of the greatest constitutional alterations that this country has ever witnessed happened under Tory management. Slavery was abolished by Grenville's Ministry of All The Talents with a Tory Majority in the Commons, Grenville himself being Pitt's cousin and one of his followers. Catholic emancipation was achieved by the Ultra Tory Duke of Wellington after decades of strife following the Act of Union between Great Britain and Ireland. Repeal of the Corn Laws was passed by Sir Robert Peel, which allowed Britain to become the world's first nation to embrace free trade, an ideal that the Conservatives still champion today. Salisbury passed legislation providing state-funded primary schools for children. The Representation of the People Act 1918 – giving women the right to vote for the first time – was passed by Lloyd George's war government, which was in essence a Tory government with a Liberal Prime Minister. The Representation of the People Act 1928 was passed by Baldwin's Conservatives and reduced the voting age for women to bring it in line with that of men. So there is little substance to the argument that the Party is not open to reform. Further to this the Party boasts the first Prime Minister of Jewish heritage (Disraeli) and the first female Prime Minister (Thatcher).

Going forward and the challenges the Conservatives face are substantial. The Party still has not buried the issue of Europe, the spectre of which has lingered on the shoulder of every leader since Heath. Consequently there is a genuine threat from UKIP, who look set to harm the Conservatives electorally unless the matter can be resolved one way or the other. Perhaps the danger that UKIP pose to the Conservatives can be overestimated. After all, they survived the issue of Catholic emancipation, which destroyed Pitt's first premiership and haunted every leader from Liverpool, through Canning and Goderich until Wellington lanced the boil by legislating in favour of it. They survived repeal of the Corn Laws, even though it meant that, following its passage in 1846, the Party would only spend two years in government over the next two decades. They survived the problem of Home Rule for Ireland, which was inevitable in hindsight but resisted by the Unionists who were desperate to cling on with every sinew. Finally, they survived the Thatcher revolution, which threatened the doctrines endorsed by every wartime Tory leader from Eden to Heath and was, consequently, an affront to the old-guard of the Tory Party. So maybe we give UKIP too much credit. Then again, maybe not.

There is a sense that this is different. There is a sense that UKIP could genuinely transform the political scene. A century ago the Liberal Party was in power having won a convincing election in 1911. They had evolved from the Whigs, who had themselves been involved in the governing of Britain since the fall of King James II. However, the rise of the Labour Party removed the Liberals as a major political force, apparently indefinitely. What Labour did was to galvanise the Left wing of British politics, meaning that as long as the Tories held the centre-Right, or even just the Right, the Liberals would be squeezed out. This led to the contest of ideologies that dominated the twentieth-century as socialism under Labour went head-to-head with liberalism under the Conservatives, rather than under the Party whose name suggested more of an affiliation with the ideology.

In the twenty-first century there is a genuine possibility that UKIP could do to the Tories what Labour did to the Liberals one hundred years ago. They could out-flank the Conservatives on the Right then watch as the Tories are squeezed between themselves and Labour, ultimately into extinction. Then another *ancien regime* will disappear. Whatever the outcome of this contest between UKIP and the Conservatives, a century from now historians will look back and determine that this was the greatest defining issue that the Tories faced since the repeal of the Corn Laws. Either the Conservatives will still be standing, thus proving yet again their historic ability to adapt, or they will die, thus proving that this one issue was as important as people are starting to believe – the one issue to bring down the Conservative and Unionist Party of Great Britain, the oldest and most successful political party in the world.

The incredible irony is that it was a Tory, Lord Liverpool, who first proposed the idea of a European Council to fend off the possibility of another Napoleon. It was a Conservative, Winston Churchill, who suggested dual nationality for all British and French citizens in order to strengthen ties and prevent another Hitler. It was successive Conservative governments under Macmillan, Douglas-Home and Heath that strived for, and eventually achieved, British membership of the European Economic Community. And it was a Conservative, John Major, who signed the Treaty of European Union at Maastricht, taking Britain into an EU that had confirmed political union, rather than the looser ties of the EEC. Finding closer ties with Europe is one of the consistent themes throughout Tory history, right up until the last quarter of the twentieth century. How perplexing, then, that this is the issue that has caused the Party more difficulty than any other.

Can a victory be achieved in 2015? Can the Conservatives make the twenty-first century as successful in terms of electoral victories as the twentieth century was? The recent referendum on Scottish independence provides some insight into the answers for these questions. Leading the 'No' campaign was the former (Labour) Chancellor of the Exchequer, Alistair Darling. Brought out in the last month of the campaign to galvanise 'No' voters was the former (extremely unpopular) Labour Prime Minister, Gordon Brown. Apart from a desperate bid in the last week, Cameron stayed away. The reason for this is because nobody wanted the Tories associated with the 'No' campaign. However unpopular Brown had been across the UK, he was still more popular than the Tories in Scotland, where at the last election the Party won just a single seat. In their 1997 landslide defeat, the Conservatives won no seats in Scotland and no seats in Wales (candidates aren't even fielded in Northern Ireland). The real story of the recent Conservative Party is their transformation from one of the two big parties in the UK, to the single biggest Party of England but one that is all but extinct in the rest of the country. If they are again to return to their position as the Party for whom 'the country calls aloud', the Party 'remembered with expressions of goodwill in the abodes of those whose lot it is to labour', or the Party of '*Imperium et Libertas*', they will have to find a way of engaging with voters everywhere. This will be easier said than done.

> They stand now on the threshold of public life. They are in the leash, but in a moment they will be slipped. What will be their fate? Will they maintain in august assemblies and high places the great truths which, in study and in solitude, they have embraced? Or will their courage exhaust itself in the struggle, their enthusiasm evaporate before hollow-hearted ridicule, their generous impulses yield with a vulgar catastrophe to the tawdry temptations of a low ambition? Will their skilled intelligence subside into being the adroit tool of a corrupt

party? Will Vanity confound their fortunes, or
Jealousy wither their sympathies? Or will they
remain brave, single, and true; refuse to bow
before shadows and worship phrases; sensible
of the greatness of their position, recognise the
greatness of their duties; denounce to a
perplexed and disheartened world the frigid
theories of a generalising age that have
destroyed the individuality of man, and restore
the happiness of their country by believing in
their own energies, and daring to be great?

Disraeli, *Coningsby*, 1844

Bibliography

Print Books

Adams, R.J.Q., *Bonar Law*, John Murray (Publishers) Ltd, London, 1999

Aldous, R., *The Lion and the Unicorn*, Pimlico, London, 2007

Ayling, S., *The Elder Pitt*, Collins, London, 1976

Boulton, A., *Memoirs of the Blair Administration: Tony's Ten Years*, Simon & Schuster, London, 2008

Burke, E., *Works,* 3 November, vol. 1, (1854-56 [1774])

Carlton, D., *Anthony Eden*, Penguin Books, London, 1981

Chambers, J., *Palmerston*, John Murray (Publishers), London, 2004

Chesterton, G.K., *A Short History of England*, William Clowes and Sons, London, 1917

Derry, J.W., *William Pitt*, B.T. Batsford, London, 1962

Dutton, D., *Neville Chamberlain (Reputations)*, Arnold, London, 2001

Egremont, M., *Balfour: A Life of Arthur James Balfour*, Phoenix, London, 1998

Gash, N., *Lord Liverpool: The Life and Political Career of Robert Banks Jenkinson Second Earl of Liverpool 1770-1828*, George Weidenfeld & Nicolson Ltd, London, 1984

Gash, N., *Peel*, Longman Group Ltd, London, 1976

GoodHart, P., *The 1922: The Story of the 1922 Committee*, Macmillan, London, 1973

Hague, W., *William Pitt the Younger,* HarperCollins Publishers, London, 2004

Hawkins, A., *The Forgotten Prime Minister: The 14th Earl of Derby, Ascent, 1799-1851*, Oxford University Press, 2007

Hawkins, A., *The Forgotten Prime Minister: The 14th Earl of Derby, Achievement, 1851-1869,* Oxford University Press, 2007

Heath, E., *The Course of My Life*, Hodder & Stoughton, London, 1998

Heywood, A., *Politics Third Edition,* Palgrave Macmillan, Basingstoke, 2007

Hibbert, C., *Disraeli, A Personal History*, HarperCollins, London, 2004

Hinde, W., *George Canning*, William Collins Sons & Co, London, 1973

Horne, A., *Macmillan 1957-1986*, Macmillan, London, 1989

Hurd, D., *Robert Peel: A Biography*, Weidenfeld and Nicolson, London, 2007

James, R.R., *Anthony Eden*, Weidenfeld and Nicolson, London, 1986

Jenkins, R., *Baldwin*, William Collins, London, 1987

Jenkins, R., *Churchill*, Pan Books, London, 2002

Jenkins, R., *Gladstone*, Pan Books, London, 2002

Jones, W.D., *'Prosperity' Robinson, The Life of Viscount Goderich 1782-1859*, Macmillan & Co., London, 1967

Longford, E., *Wellington Pillar of State*, Weidenfeld & Nicolson, London, 1972 (1985)

Major, J., *John Major: The Autobiography*, HarperCollins Publishers, London, 1999

Pearson, H., *Dizzy: A Life of Benjamin Disraeli*, 'Classic Biography', Penguin Books, London, 2001

Rieu, E.V., *Homer, The Iliad*, Penguin Books, Book IX, 1954

Roberts, A., *Salisbury Victorian Titan*, Phoenix, London, 2000

Seldon, A., *Major: A Political Life*, paperback edition, Phoenix, London, 1998

Snowdon, P., *Back From the Brink*, HarperCollins Publishers, London, 2010

Taylor, R., *Lord Salisbury*, Penguin Books, London, 1975

Thatcher, M., *The Downing Street Years*, paperback edition, HarperCollins Publishers, London, 1995

Thatcher, M., *The Path to Power*, paperback edition, Harper Press, London, 2011

Thompson, N., *Wellington after Waterloo*, Routledge and Kegan Paul, London, 1986

Thorpe, D.R., *Alec Douglas-Home*, Sinclair-Stevenson, London, 1996

Toye, R., *Lloyd George & Churchill: Rivals for Greatness*, Macmillan, London, 2007

Weintraub, S., *Disraeli: A Biography*, Hamish Hamilton, London, 1993

Wheatcroft, G., *The Strange Death of Tory England*, Penguin Books, London, 2005

Williams, C., *Harold Macmillan*, Weidenfeld & Nicolson, London, 2009

Wordsworth, A., *Collected Political Musings; The Coalition Years*, Springlands Press, 2014

Young, G.M., *Stanley Baldwin*, Rupert Hart-Davis, London, 1952

Ziegler, P., *Edward Heath*, paperback edition, Harper Press, London, 2011

Ziegler, P., *King William IV*, William Collins and Sons, Glasgow, 1971
Ziegler, P., *Melbourne*, William Collins Son & Co, Glasgow, 1976

E-Books

Adonis, A., *5 Days in May, The Coalition and Beyond*, Biteback Publishing, Kindle Edition, 2013
Defoe, D., 1692, *A Dialogue Betwixt Whig and Tory. Wherein the Principles and Practices of Each Party are Fairly and Impartially Stated*, Kindle Edition
Disraeli, B., Coningsby, [1844] Kindle Edition, 2014
Hanrahan, D.C., *The Assasination of the Prime Minister: John Bellingham and the Murder of Spencer Perceval*, The History Press, Kindle Edition, 2013
Hurd, D. & Young, E., *Disraeli, or The Two Lives*, Weidenfeld & Nicolson, London, Kindle Edition, 2013
The Perfect Library, *Works of Sir Robert Peel*, Kindle Edition, 2013
Queen of Great Britain Victoria, *The Letters of Queen Victoria: A Selection of Her Majesty's Correspondence Between the Years 1837 and 1861 vol.i 1837-1843*, (First Published 1908) Kindle Edition, 2011
Correspondence Between the Years 1837 and 1861 vol.ii 1843-1854, (First Published 1908) Kindle Edition, 2011
Correspondence Between the Years 1837 and 1861 vol.iii 1854-1861, (First Published 1908) Kindle Edition, 2011
Ziegler, P., *Addington: A Life of Henry Addington, First Viscount Sidmouth*, Kindle Edition, Collins

News Articles

Gibbon, G., *Cameron Wants Snap Election,* Channel 4 News, 30/09/2007,
http://www.channel4.com/news/articles/politics/domestic_politics/cameron+wants+snap+election/862457.html
Curtis, P., *Reality Check: Is The Electoral System Biased In Favour Of Labour?*, 13/09/2011,
http://www.theguardian.com/politics/reality-check-with-polly-curtis/2011/sep/13/reality-check-bourndary-reform

Notes

Introduction

1. Wheatcroft, *The Strange Death of Tory England*, p.21
2. Defoe, *A Dialogue Betwixt Whig and Tory. Wherein the Principles and Practices of Each Party are Fairly and Impartially Stated*

William Pitt the Younger

1. Hague, *William Pitt the Younger*, pp.7-11
2. Ayling, *The Elder Pitt*, p.326
3. Ibid, p.414
4. Hague, *William Pitt the Younger*, p.62
5. Derry, *William Pitt*, p.24
6. Ibid
7. Hague, *William Pitt the Younger*, p.109
8. Ibid, p.137
9. Ibid, p.145
10. Derry, *William Pitt*, p.39
11. Hague, *William Pitt the Younger*, p.154
12. Ibid, p.160
13. Ibid, p.169
14. Ibid, p.173
15. Derry, *William Pitt*, p.47
16. Ibid, p.50
17. Hague, *William Pitt the Younger*, p.226
18. Derry, *William Pitt*, p.63
19. Hague, *William Pitt the Younger*, p.253
20. Ibid, p.266
21. Ibid, p.281
22. Derry, *William Pitt*, p.86
23. Hague, *William Pitt the Younger*, p.289
24. Ibid, p.299
25. Derry, *William Pitt*, p.92
26. Hague, *William Pitt the Younger*, p.352
27. Ibid, p.381
28. Derry, *William Pitt*, p.106
29. Ibid
30. Hinde, *George Canning*, p.54
31. Hague, *William Pitt the Younger*, p.418

31. Hinde, *George Canning*, pp.68-9
33. Hague, *William Pitt the Younger*, p.468
34. Hinde, *George Canning*, p.97
35. Hague, *William Pitt the Younger*, p.481

Henry Addington

1. Hague, *William Pitt the Younger*, p.492
2. Hinde, *George Canning*, p.95
3. Ziegler, *Addington*, location 1856
4. Hague, *William Pitt the Younger*, p.476
5. Ziegler, *Addington*, location 2346
6. Ibid, location 2506
7. Hague, *William Pitt the Younger*, p.514
8. Ziegler, *Addington*, location 2820
9. Hinde, *George Canning*, p.109
10. Hague, *William Pitt the Younger*, p.506
11. Ziegler, *Addington*, location 3186
12. Ibid, location 3320
13. Ibid, location 3366
14. Ibid, location 3483
15. Ibid, location 3632
16. De Tocqueville, quoted in Heywood, *Politics Third Edition*, p.271

William Pitt the Younger (2)

1. Ziegler, *Addington*, location 4028
2. Hague, *William Pitt the Younger*, p.537
3. Ibid
4. Ibid, p.539
5. Ziegler, *Addington*, location 4120
6. Hague, *William Pitt the Younger*, p.541
7. Ibid, p.546
8. Hinde, *George Canning*, p.132
9. Ziegler, *Addington*, location 4234
10. Hague, *William Pitt the Younger*, p.551
11. Ziegler, *Addington*, location 4254
12. Hinde, *George Canning*, p.137
13. Hague, *William Pitt the Younger*, p.569
14. Ibid, p.578
15. Rieu, Homer, *The Iliad*, Book IX, p.172

Spencer Perceval

1. Hanrahan, *The Assassination of the Prime Minister,* location 653
2. Hague, *William Pitt the Younger,* p.582
3. Ziegler, *Addington,* location 4464
4. Ibid, location 4491
5. Ibid, location 4537
6. Hanrahan, *The Assassination of the Prime Minister,* location 500
7. Hinde, *George Canning,* p.143
8. Hanrahan, *The Assassination of the Prime Minister,* location 816
9. Ziegler, *Addington,* location 4665
10. Hanrahan, *The Assassination of the Prime Minister,* location 829
11. Ibid, 850
12. Ibid, 872
13. Hinde, *George Canning,* p.176
14. Ibid, p.237
15. Hanrahan, *The Assassination of the Prime Minister,* location 1053
16. Ibid, location 87

Robert Jenkinson, 2nd Earl of Liverpool

1. Ziegler, *Addington,* location 5475
2. Gash, *Lord Liverpool*
3. Ziegler, *Addington,* location 5484
4. Hinde, *George Canning,* p.251
5. Ibid, p.253
6. Ibid, p.252
7. Gash, *Lord Liverpool,* p.106
8. Hinde, *George Canning,* p.270
9. Gash, *Lord Liverpool,* p.111
10. Ibid, p.114
11. Ibid, p.117
12. Ibid
13. Ibid, p.124
14. Ziegler, *Addington,* location 6291
15. Gash, *Lord Liverpool,* p.135
16. Ziegler, *Addington,* location 6704
17. Hurd, *Robert Peel: A Biography,* p.56
18. Gash, *Lord Liverpool,* p.151

19. Ibid, p.159
20. Hinde, *George Canning,* p.304
21. Gash, *Lord Liverpool,* p.174
22. Ibid, p.177
23. Gash, *Peel,* p.62
24. Gash, *Lord Liverpool,* p.187
25. Hinde, *George Canning,* p.318
26. Thompson, *Wellington After Waterloo,* p.44
27. Hinde, *George Canning,* p.390
28. Thompson, *Wellington After Waterloo,* p.45
29. Hansard, 1825, *HC Deb 23 March 1825 vol 12 cc 1143-51,* referenced March 2014, www.hansard.millbanksystems.com
30. Gash, *Peel,* p.84
31. Ibid
32. Gash, *Lord Liverpool,* p.239

George Canning

1. Hinde, *George Canning,* p.437
2. Thompson, *Wellington After Waterloo,* p.58
3. Hinde, *George Canning,* p.438
4. Gash, *Peel,* p.88
5. Longford, *Wellington Pillar of State,* p.179
6. Hinde, *George Canning,* p.443
7. Ibid, p.446
8. Ibid, p.452

Frederick Robinson, 1st Viscount Goderich

1. Jones, *'Prosperity' Robinson,* p.153
2. Ibid, p.173
3. Longford, *Wellington Pillar of State,* p.189
4. Jones, *'Prosperity' Robinson,* p.189
5. Thompson, *Wellington After Waterloo,* p.69
6. Ibid
7. Jones, *'Prosperity' Robinson,* p.204

Arthur Wellesley, 1st Duke of Wellington

1. Thompson, *Wellington After Waterloo,* p.74
2. Ibid, p.76
3. Ibid

4. Longford, *Wellington Pillar of State*, p.205
5. Ibid, p.206
6. Ibid, p.207
7. Hurd, *Robert Peel: A Biography*, p.109
8. Ibid, p.112
9. Gash, *Peel*, p.115
10. Ibid, p.119
11. Thompson, *Wellington After Waterloo*, p.92
12. Hurd, *Robert Peel: A Biography*, p.127
13. Ziegler, *King William IV*, p.162
14. Gash, *Peel*, p.134
15. Thompson, *Wellington after Waterloo*, p.104
16. Ibid, p.107
17. Longford, *Wellington Pillar of State*, p.292
18. Thompson, *Wellington after Waterloo*, p.108
19. Gash, *Peel*, p.145
20. Hurd, *Robert Peel: A Biography*, p.149
21. Gash, *Peel*, p.147
22. Longford, *Wellington Pillar of State*, p.338
23. Hurd, *Robert Peel: A Biography*, p.158
24. Ibid
25. Ibid, p.162
26. Thompson, *Wellington after Waterloo*, p.135
27. Gash, *Peel*, p.161
28. Ziegler, *King William IV*, p.254
29. Ibid, p.255
30. Ibid, p.256

From Tories to Conservatives

1. Hurd, R*obert Peel: A Biography*, p.146
2. Hawkins, *The Forgotten Prime Minister: The 14th Earl of Derby, Ascent, 1799-1851*, p.144
3. Peel, *Works*, location 222-236
4. Burke, *Works*, pp.446-8
5. Disraeli, *Coningsby*, location 1366
6. Ibid, location 1412

Sir Robert Peel

1. Gash, *Peel*, p.165
2. Hurd, *Robert Peel: A Biography*, p.180
3. Ibid, p.182
4. Longford, *Wellington Pillar of State*, p.385

5. Hawkins, *The Forgotten Prime Minister (Ascent)*, p.182
6. Ibid, p.192
7. Hurd, *Robert Peel: A Biography*, p.202
8. Gash, *Peel*, p.184
9. Hurd, *Robert Peel: A Biography*, p.207
10. Ibid, p.210
11. *The Letters of Queen Victoria*, location 3454
12. Hurd, *Robert Peel: A Biography*, p.218
13. Thatcher, *The Downing Street Years*, p.3
14. *The Letters of Queen Victoria*, location 6462
15. Hurd, *Robert Peel: A Biography*, p.245
16. Jones, *'Prosperity' Robinson*, p.245
17. Gash, *Peel*, p.219
18. Ibid, p.228
19. Hurd, *Robert Peel: A Biography*, p.300
20. Gash, *Peel*, p.228
21. Ibid, p.234
22. Hurd, *Robert Peel: A Biography*, p.309
23. Ibid, p.330
24. Ibid, p.311
25. Gash, *Peel* p.245
26. Longford, *Wellington Pillar of State*, p.440
27. Ibid, p.441
28. Thompson, *Wellington After Waterloo*, p.224
29. Jenkins, *Gladstone*, p.84
30. Hurd & Young, *Disraeli, or the Two Lives*, location 1877
31. Ibid, location 1914
32. Hurd, *Robert Peel: A Biography*, p.361
33. Longford, *Wellington Pillar of State*, p.447
34. Gash, *Peel*, p.278
35. Hurd, *Robert Peel: A Biography*, p.368
36. Ibid, p.384

Edward Smith-Stanley, 14th Earl of Derby

1. Hawkins, *The Forgotten Prime Minister, 'Ascent'*, p.314
2. Gash, *Peel*, p.284
3. Ibid
4. Ibid
5. Hawkins, *The Forgotten Prime Minister, 'Ascent'*, p.315
6. Ibid, p.316
7. Ibid, p.321

8. Chambers, *Palmerston*, p.262

9. Hibbert, *Disraeli: A Personal History*, p.363

10. Weintraub, *Disraeli: A Biography*, p.32

11. Hurd & Young, *Disraeli, or the Two Lives*, location 2092

12. Hawkins, *The Forgotten Prime Minister, 'Ascent'*, p.339

13. Ibid, p.351

14. Hibbert, *Disraeli: A Personal History*, p.191

15. Hawkins, *The Forgotten Prime Minister, 'Ascent'*, p.366

16. Chambers, *Palmerston*, p.316

17. Ibid, p.318

18. Gash, *Peel*, p.306

19. Hawkins, *The Forgotten Prime Minister, 'Ascent'*, p.393

20. Ibid, p.400

21. Jenkins, *Gladstone*, p.111

22. Chambers, *Palmerston*, p.337

23. Hibbert, *Disraeli: A Personal History*, p.203

24. Hawkins, *The Forgotten Prime Minister, 'Achievement'*, pp.19-20

25. Jenkins, *Gladstone*, p.139

26. Hawkins, *The Forgotten Prime Minister, 'Achievement'*, p.45

27. Ibid, p.42

28. Ibid, p.47

29. Jenkins, *Gladstone*, pp.141-3

30. Hawkins, *The Forgotten Prime Minister, 'Achievement'*, p.69

31. Chambers, *Palmerston*, p.369

32. Hawkins, *The Forgotten Prime Minister, 'Achievement'*, p.94

33. Chambers, *Palmerston*, p.370

34. Hawkins, *The Forgotten Prime Minister, 'Achievement'*, p.106

35. Chambers, *Palmerston*, p.373

36. Ibid, p.399

37. Ibid, p.401

38. Hawkins, *The Forgotten Prime Minister, 'Achievement'*, p.117

39. Ibid, p.137

40. Chambers, *Palmerston*, p.439

41. Jenkins, *Gladstone*, p.186

42. Ibid, p.187
43. Hawkins, *The Forgotten Prime Minister,*
'Achievement', pp.171-2
44. Hurd & Young, *Disraeli, or the Two Lives*, location
2100
45. Hawkins, *The Forgotten Prime Minister,*
'Achievement', p.181
46. Ibid, p.204
47. Chambers, *Palmerston*, p.452
48. Jenkins, *Gladstone*, pp.204-5
49. Chambers, *Palmerston*, p.465
50. Jenkins, *Gladstone*, p.235
51. Hawkins, *The Forgotten Prime Minister,*
'Achievement', p.278
52. Ibid, p.280
53. Jenkins, *Gladstone*, p.230
54. Hawkins, *The Forgotten Prime Minister,*
'Achievement', p.296
55. Ibid, p.297
56. Ibid, p.vii
57. Ibid, p.314
58. Hibbert, *Disraeli: A Personal History*, p.258
59. Hawkins, *The Forgotten Prime Minister,*
'Achievement', p.334
60. Jenkins, *Gladstone*, p.270
61. Hurd & Young, *Disraeli, or the Two Lives*, location
3085
62. Hawkins, *The Forgotten Prime Minister,*
'Achievement', pp.351-2

Benjamin Disraeli, 1st Earl of Beaconsfield

1. Pearson, *Dizzy: A Life of Benjamin Disraeli*, p.173
2. Aldous, *The Lion and the Unicorn*, p.189
3. Ibid, pp.9-11
4. Jenkins, *Gladstone*, p.324
5. Weintraub, *Disraeli*, p.467
6. Aldous, *The Lion and the Unicorn*, p.200
7. Weintraub, *Disraeli*, pp.473-4
8. Ibid, p.467
9. Pearson, *Dizzy: A Life of Benjamin Disraeli*, p.184
10. Roberts, *Salisbury Victorian Titan*, p.124
11. Pearson, *Dizzy: A Life of Benjamin Disraeli*, p.191

12. Aldous, *The Lion and the Unicorn*, p.219
13. Jenkins, *Gladstone*, p.365
14. Ibid, pp.332-4
15. Weintraub, *Disraeli*, p.509
16. Pearson, *Dizzy: A Life of Benjamin Disraeli*, p.183
17. Aldous, *The Lion and the Unicorn*, p.233
18. Jenkins, *Gladstone*, p.366
19. Aldous, *The Lion and the Unicorn*, p.238
20. Weintraub, *Disraeli*, p.515
21. Ibid, p.517
22. Pearson, *Dizzy: A Life of Benjamin Disraeli*, p.199
23. Jenkins, *Gladstone*, p.377
24. Aldous, *The Lion and the Unicorn*, p.244
25. Weintraub, *Disraeli*, p.519
26. Jenkins, *Gladstone*, p.385
27. Aldous, *The Lion and the Unicorn*, pp.241-2
28. Hurd & Young, *Disraeli, or the Two Lives*, location 3614
29. Ibid
30. Roberts, *Salisbury Victorian Titan*, p.135
31. Weintraub, *Disraeli*, p.534
32. Jenkins, *Gladstone*, p.387
33. Aldous, *The Lion and the Unicorn*, p.265
34. Pearson, *Dizzy: A Life of Benjamin Disraeli*, p.220
35. Aldous, *The Lion and the Unicorn*, p.262
36. Weintraub, *Disraeli*, p.548
37. Aldous, *The Lion and the Unicorn*, p.264
38. Weintraub, *Disraeli*, p.553
39. Pearson, *Dizzy: A Life of Benjamin Disraeli*, p.236
40. Aldous, *The Lion and the Unicorn*, p.268
41. Ibid
42. Jenkins, *Gladstone*, p.400
43. Weintraub, *Disraeli*, p.564
44. Pearson, *Dizzy: A Life of Benjamin Disraeli*, p.241
45. Roberts, *Salisbury Victorian Titan*, p.167
46. Pearson, *Dizzy: A Life of Benjamin Disraeli*, p.242
47. Aldous, *The Lion and the Unicorn*, p.283
48. Pearson, *Dizzy: A Life of Benjamin Disraeli*, p.250
49. Ibid, p.257
50. Weintraub, *Disraeli*, p.609
51. Pearson, *Dizzy: A Life of Benjamin Disraeli*, p.261
52. Ibid, p.259
53. Aldous, *The Lion and the Unicorn*, p.300
54. Ibid, p.290

55. Weintraub, *Disraeli*, p.624
56. Jenkins, *Gladstone*, pp.436-7

Sir Stafford Northcote & Robert Gascoyne-Cecil, 3rd Marquess of Salisbury

1. Egremont, *Balfour*, p.55
2. Roberts, *Salisbury Victorian Titan*, p.254
3. Jenkins, *Gladstone*, p.476
4. Roberts, *Salisbury Victorian Titan*, p.268
5. Ibid, p.273
6. Jenkins, *Gladstone*, p.505
7. Ibid, pp.500-16
8. Roberts, *Salisbury Victorian Titan*, p.291
9. Ibid, p.295
10. Jenkins, *Gladstone*, p.494
11. Taylor, *Lord Salisbury*, p.88
12. Roberts, *Salisbury Victorian Titan*, p.303
13. Taylor, *Lord Salisbury*, p.88
14. Jenkins, *Gladstone*, pp.496-7
15. Ibid, p.515
16. Roberts, *Salisbury Victorian Titan*, p.324

Robert Gascoyne-Cecil, 3rd Marquess of Salisbury

1. Roberts, *Salisbury Victorian Titan*, p.326
2. Taylor, *Lord Salisbury*, p.92
3. Ibid, p.96
4. Ibid
5. Roberts, *Salisbury Victorian Titan*, p.355
6. Jenkins, *Gladstone*, p.520
7. Ibid, pp.526-31
8. Roberts, *Salisbury Victorian Titan*, p.370
9. Ibid, p.382
10. Ibid, p.387
11. Taylor, *Lord Salisbury*, p.107
12. Roberts, *Salisbury Victorian Titan*, p.397
13. Ibid, pp.399-401
14. Jenkins, *Gladstone*, p.563
15. Roberts, *Salisbury Victorian Titan*, p.428
16. Ibid, p.552
17. Jenkins, *Gladstone*, p.584
18. Ibid, p.606

19. Roberts, *Salisbury Victorian Titan*, p.598
20. Taylor, *Lord Salisbury*, p.154
21. Roberts, *Salisbury Victorian Titan*, p.704
22. Ibid, p.721
23. Ibid, p.729
24. Ibid, p.778
25. Egremont, *Balfour*, p.147

Arthur Balfour

1. Egremont, *Balfour*, p.152
2. Ibid, p.164
3. Ibid, p.177
4. Taylor, *Lord Salisbury*, p.185
5. Toye, *Lloyd George & Churchill*, p.27
6. Egremont, *Balfour*, p.164
7. Ibid, p.196
8. Toye, *Lloyd George & Churchill*, p.41
9. Egremont, *Balfour*, p.206
10. Ibid, p.214
11. Toye, *Lloyd George & Churchill*, p.63
12. Ibid, p.64
13. Egremont, *Balfour*, p.230
14. Ibid
15. Ibid, p.237

Andrew Bonar Law

1. Adams, R.J.Q., *Bonar Law*, p.57
2. Egremont, *Balfour*, p.241
3. Adams, R.J.Q., *Bonar Law*, p.74
4. Ibid, p.82
5. Ibid, p.90
6. Toye, *Lloyd George & Churchill*, p.114
7. Adams, R.J.Q., *Bonar Law*, p.152
8. Ibid, p.175
9. Jenkins, *Churchill*, p.276
10. Adams, R.J.Q., *Bonar Law*, p.208
11. Ibid, p.221
12. Toye, *Lloyd George & Churchill*, p.170
13. Adams, R.J.Q., *Bonar Law*, pp.255-61
14. Ibid, p.280
15. Jenkins, *Churchill*, p.338
16. Adams, R.J.Q., *Bonar Law*, p.280

17. Ibid, p.296
18. Ibid, p.309
19. Jenkins, *Baldwin*, p.52
20. Young, *Stanley Baldwin*, pp.41-2
21. Adams, R.J.Q., *Bonar Law*, p.355

The 1922 Committee

1. Goodhart, *The 1922*, p.15
2. Gash, *Peel*, p.14
3. Weintraub, *Disraeli*, p.161
4. Weintraub, *Disraeli*, p.176

Stanley Baldwin

1. Jenkins, *Baldwin*, p.58
2. Ibid, p.69
3. Young, *Stanley Baldwin*, p.65
4. Jenkins, *Baldwin*, p.77
5. Toye, *Lloyd George & Churchill*, p.252
6. Jenkins, *Churchill*, p.393
7. Jenkins, *Baldwin*, p.91
8. Young, *Stanley Baldwin*, p.99
9. Jenkins, *Baldwin*, p.102
10. Ibid, p.105
11. Young, *Stanley Baldwin*, p.138
12. Ibid, p.142
13. Ibid, p.149
14. Jenkins, *Baldwin*, pp.109-10
15. Ibid, p.116
16. Ibid, p.131
17. Young, *Stanley Baldwin*, p.176
18. Ibid, p.177
19. Jenkins, *Baldwin*, p.146
20. Young, *Stanley Baldwin*, p.239

Neville Chamberlain

1. Dutton, *Neville Chamberlain*, p.41
2. Jenkins, *Churchill*, p.514
3. Dutton, *Neville Chamberlain*, p.27
4. James, *Anthony Eden*, p.175
5. Ibid, p.177

6. Ibid, p.188
7. Jenkins, *Churchill*, p.524
8. Dutton, *Neville Chamberlain*, p.22
9. Jenkins, *Churchill*, pp.524-5
10. James, *Anthony Eden*, p.211
11. Jenkins, *Churchill*, pp.536-7
12. Dutton, *Neville Chamberlain*, p.25
13. Ibid, p.48 & p.126
14. James, *Anthony Eden*, p.221
15. Jenkins, *Churchill*, p.575
16. Ibid, p.582
17. Dutton, *Neville Chamberlain*, p.216

Winston Churchill

1. Jenkins, *Churchill*, p.642
2. Ibid, p.654
3. James, *Anthony Eden*, pp.256-7
4. Carlton, *Anthony Eden*, p.191
5. Jenkins, *Churchill*, p.677
6. Ibid, p.681
7. Ibid, p.687
8. Ibid, p.697
9. Ibid, p.748
10. Ibid, p.778
11. James, *Anthony Eden*, p.290
12. Ibid, p.294
13. Ibid, p.309
14. Williams, *Harold Macmillan*, pp.180-2
15. James, *Anthony Eden*, p. 318
16. Jenkins, *Churchill*, p.829
17. Williams, *Harold Macmillan*, p.199
18. Jenkins, *Churchill*, p.828
19. Ibid, p.838
20. Ibid, p.841
21. Ibid, p.860
22. James, *Anthony Eden*, p.369
23. Jenkins, *Churchill*, p.874

Post-War Conservative Failures

1. Disraeli, *Coningsby*, location 941
2. Ibid, location 1420
3. Thatcher, *The Downing Street Years*, p.7

4. Boulton, *Memories of the Blair Administration*, p.9

Anthony Eden

1. Carlton, *Anthony Eden*, p.370
2. Ibid, p.372
3. James, *Anthony Eden*, p.409
4. Carlton, *Anthony Eden*, p.375
5. James, *Anthony Eden*, p.447
6. Carlton, *Anthony Eden*, p.433
7. Ibid, pp.438-9
8. Ibid, p.449
9. James, *Anthony Eden*, p.575
10. Carlton, *Anthony Eden*, p.463

Harold Macmillan

1. Wheatcroft, *The Strange Death of Tory England,* p.5
2. Williams, *Harold Macmillan*, p.274
3. Horne, *Macmillan 1957-1986*, p.4
4. Williams, *Harold Macmillan*, p.280
5. Ibid, p.286
6. Ibid, p.288
7. Horne, *Macmillan 1957-1986*, p.55
8. Ibid, p.30
9. Williams, *Harold Macmillan*, p.332
10. Horne, *Macmillan 1957-1986*, p.145
11. Wheatcroft, *The Strange Death of Tory England,* p.44
12. Williams, *Harold Macmillan*, p.368
13. Thorpe, *Alec Douglas-Home*, pp.210-11
14. Williams, *Harold Macmillan*, pp.385-6
15. Horne, *Macmillan 1957-1986*, p.299
16. Williams, *Harold Macmillan*, p.387
17. Horne, *Macmillan 1957-1986*, p.333
18. Ibid, p.335
19. Ibid, p.350
20. Williams, *Harold Macmillan*, p.429
21. Ibid, p.444
22. Ibid, p.448

Sir Alec Douglas-Home

1. Thorpe, *Alec Douglas-Home*, p.314
2. Ibid, p.324
3. Ibid, p.334
4. Ibid, p.359
5. Wheatcroft, *The Strange Death of Tory England*, p.17
6. Heath, *The Course of My Life*, p.267
7. Thorpe, *Alec Douglas-Home*, p.390

Edward Heath

1. Ziegler, *Edward Heath*, p.159
2. Ibid, p.173
3. Wheatcroft, *The Strange Death of Tory England*, p.76
4. Thatcher, *The Path to Power*, p.139
5. Wheatcroft, *The Strange Death of Tory England*, p.77
6. Thatcher, *The Path to Power*, p.141
7. Ziegler, *Edward Heath*, p.189
8. Heath, *The Course of My Life*, p.291
9. Ibid, p.292
10. Ibid, p.293
11. Ziegler, *Edward Heath*, pp.214-5
12. Ibid, p.216
13. Thatcher, *The Path to Power*, p.160
14. Ziegler, *Edward Heath*, p.217
15. Wheatcroft, *The Strange Death of Tory England*, p.82
16. Thatcher, *The Path to Power*, pp.198-9
17. Heath, *The Course of My Life*, pp.325-6
18. Ibid, pp.336-7
19. Ziegler, *Edward Heath*, p.288
20. Thatcher, *The Path to Power*, p.215
21. Ibid, p.217
22. Heath, *The Course of My Life*, p.384
23. Thatcher, *The Path to Power*, pp.224-5
24. Ziegler, *Edward Heath*, p.416
25. Ibid, p.423
26. Ibid, p.436
27. Thatcher, *The Path to Power*, p.239
28. Heath, *The Course of My Life*, p.525
29. Heath, *The Course of My Life*, pp.528-9
30. Ziegler, *Edward Heath*, p.485
31. Thatcher, *The Path to Power*, p.272
32. Ziegler, *Edward Heath*, p.487

Margaret Thatcher

1. Thatcher, *The Path to Power*, p.299
2. Ibid, p.300
3. Ibid, p.305
4. Wheatcroft, *The Strange Death of Tory England,* p.96
5. Thatcher, *The Path to Power*, p.428
6. Ibid, p.433
7. Wheatcroft, *The Strange Death of Tory England,* p.98
8. Thatcher, *The Downing Street Years*, pp.26-7
9. Wheatcroft, *The Strange Death of Tory England,* p.101
10. Thatcher, *The Downing Street Years*, p.62
11. Ibid, p.81
12. Ibid, p.186
13. Wheatcroft, *The Strange Death of Tory England,* p.115
14. Thatcher, *The Downing Street Years*, p.342
15. Ibid, p.371
16. Ibid, p.430
17. Ibid, p.715
18. Ibid, p.834
19. Wheatcroft, *The Strange Death of Tory England,* p.177
20. Thatcher, *The Downing Street Years*, p.851

John Major

1. Seldon, *Major*, p.131
2. Ibid, p.135
3. Major, *The Autobiography*, p.223
4. Ibid, p.234
5. Ibid, p.240
6. Seldon, *Major*, p.162
7. Ibid, p.244
8. Ibid, pp.280-1
9. Wheatcroft, *The Strange Death of Tory England,* p.194
10. Major, *The Autobiography*, p.313
11. Seldon, *Major*, p.310
12. Major, *The Autobiography*, p.329
13. Seldon, *Major*, p.314
14. Major, *The Autobiography*, p.368
15. Ibid, p.383
16. Seldon, *Major*, p.388
17. Ibid, p.403

18. Major, *The Autobiography*, p.601
19. Ibid, p.627
20. Ibid, p.645

Wilderness Years

1. Snowdon, *Back From the Brink*, p.xi

William Hague

1. Snowdon, *Back From the Brink*, p.45
2. Ibid, p.50
3. Ibid, pp.70-1
4. Wheatcroft, *The Strange Death of Tory England*, p.249

Iain Duncan Smith

1. Snowdon, *Back From the Brink*, p.82
2. Wheatcroft, *The Strange Death of Tory England*, p.254
3. Ibid, p.258
4. Snowdon, *Back From the Brink*, p.118
5. Wheatcroft, *The Strange Death of Tory England*, p.265

Michael Howard

1. Snowdon, *Back From the Brink*, p.127
2. Hansard, 14 Jan 2004, col. 809-11
3. Snowdon, *Back From the Brink*, p.157
4. Wheatcroft, *The Strange Death of Tory England*, p.281

David Cameron

1. Snowdon, *Back From the Brink*, p.206
2. Boulton, *Memories of the Blair Administration*, p.xiii
3. Gibbon, *Cameron Wants Snap Election*, 30 September 2007
4. Snowdon, *Back From the Brink*, p.311
5. See polls from YouGov & ComRes/ITV http://uk.reuters.com/article/2010/04/15/uk-britain-election-debate-polls-idUKTRE63E60120100415
6. Adonis, *5 Days in May*, location 336

7. Ibid, location 345
8. Brown statement of 7 May 2010, courtesy of Labour Party Website, http://www2.labour.org.uk/statement-by-gordon-brown
9. Curtis, *Reality Check: Is The Electoral System Biased In Favour of Labour?*, 13 September 2011, http://www.theguardian.com/politics/reality-check-with-polly-curtis/2011/sep/13/reality-check-bourndary-reform
10. Wordsworth, *Collected Political Musings*, p.41
11. Hansard, 29 Aug 2013, col. 1547
12. See my blog from August and September 2014 www.adamwordsworth.blog.com
13. Ziegler, *Melbourne*, p.170

Epilogue

End quotation: Disraeli, *Coningsby*, Final Paragraph (location 6415)

Index

To contact the author please get in touch with Springlands Press using the contact details below.

Enquiries
Springlands Press Ltd,
10 Broad Birches,
Ellesmere Port,
Cheshire,
CH65 3AB

Or alternatively fill out an enquiry form via our website:
www.springlandspublishing.co.uk

Made in the USA
Charleston, SC
24 November 2014